MW00624429

A Survey of
Chemical
and Biological
Warfare

A Survey of
Chemical
and Biological
Warfare

John Cookson
and
Judith Nottingham

New York and London

Copyright © 1969 by John Cookson and Judith Nottingham
All Rights Reserved

Library of Congress Catalog Card Number: 79-128595

First Printing

ISBN 978-0-85345-223-2

MANUFACTURED IN THE UNITED STATES OF AMERICA

CONTENTS

INTRODUCTION

This book has its origin in a document published by a group of students at Newcastle University and written by the two authors. In its present form it is the product of three years' work and research.

It was our intention initially to present information on a subject previously somewhat neglected, in the hope of stimulating some rational discussion. This is not intended as a scientific treatise but rather as a layman's guide. We have tried to assume the minimum of previous knowledge.

We recognise that some of the sources we have drawn upon are not totally unbiased. We have not attempted to judge at second hand the veracity of this information, but have instead commented upon its credibility in the light of the known facts. Where we have used secondary sources, we have tried to check them, but this has not always been possible. Some of the information is contradictory. We have tried to indicate where this is so and, when possible, suggested reasons.

We must emphasise that we have no political allegiance to any party. In examination of some of the more controversial issues we hope our conclusions will be accepted as being due more to rational appraisal than party political bias.

The book is divided into two parts. The first deals with documentation to show the extent of the use of these weapons and research into their development. It also provides a description of the attitudes and the politics involved. Comment and description of the agents and weapons systems is restricted mainly to the second half. We hope this may provide an easier introduction to the subject. A more general assessment of all the data provided here is reserved for the conclusion.

The study of cbw is unsatisfying in many respects, and particularly in that there are no easy solutions to the problems raised. This book does not offer answers, but tries to stimulate what we believe to be the right questions. Any other approach would not be in keeping with the large gaps in our present knowledge of cbw.

J.C.
J.N.

Note to the US Edition

Since the publication of the British edition of this book it has been shown that the letter reproduced on pp. 310–11 and reported in the *Sunday Times* (see p. 67 below) purporting to be written by Gordon Goldstein is a forgery. Although the relevant sections of the book must now be read with this in mind, some points should be noted. The suggestion that there are bases in Thailand is by no means implausible. The storage of cw munitions on bases in Germany and on Okinawa has been admitted by the us. Preparations for the deployment of bw munitions, possibly at the same bases, are quite likely to have been made. us aircraft fly missions from Okinawa to Vietnam, and this has caused some embarrassment to the Japanese government.

Part 1

Information

This part is intended to provide a fairly full documentation of past and current use of CBW weapons in warfare. Allegations of use are also dealt with as, in some cases, especially with biological weapons, it is impossible to find any really concrete proof after the event. Research and expenditure are also considered in some detail and a detailed description of all the various institutions involved is provided.

For obvious reasons, information on many aspects of this subject is not very readily available. In some cases considerable difficulty was experienced in obtaining it. Wherever possible, sources have been given so that the reader can make his own assessment of the data concerned.

Comment has been kept to a minimum, but in the few cases where comment has been made, should the reader disagree, it is hoped this will not detract from the value of the information itself.

1

CHEMICAL AND BIOLOGICAL WARFARE

1. CHEMICAL WARFARE

The use of chemicals in war has a very long history. The effectiveness of poisoned arrows has long been recognised, and as early as 400 BC the Spartans employed the gas sulphur dioxide (obtained by burning sulphur with pitch) during sieges of Athenian cities.

Contemporary chemical warfare began in 1914 during World War I with the French use of tear-gas grenades against the Germans, who retaliated with tear-gas artillery shells. On 22 April 1915 the Germans launched a chlorine gas attack against British and French troops at Ypres resulting in 5000 deaths and general demoralisation. British retaliation, also with chlorine, came six months later at Loos. There followed a considerable escalation both in the use of and protection against gases of various types.

The second major development was the use by the Germans of mustard gas and phosgene at Verdun in 1917. These events led directly to the 1925 Geneva Protocols, which outlawed the use of poison gases and other chemical and biological weapons.

After the war there was quite extensive cooperation between Germany and the USSR in the development of poison gases, marked by the formation of the German–Soviet joint stock company 'Bersol', in 1923, for the manufacture of gases at Trotsk in Samara province. At about the same time Japan entered the field, and from 1929 to 1945 a factory on the island of Okuno-jima in Hiroshima Prefecture was producing, amongst others, mustard gas and phosgene.

The only incidents involving the actual use of gases between the wars were in 1936, when the Italians employed a type of mustard gas against the Abyssinians, and several occasions between 1937 and 1943, when Japan attacked China. These constituted the first authenticated contraventions of the Geneva Protocols.

By 1944 Germany had succeeded in developing the nerve gases tabun and sarin, on the basis of research which had been conducted into insecticides in the 1930s. These gases were stockpiled by the Germans but were never used. By the end of the war Britain was producing sarin, and had also developed a more powerful nerve agent, soman. Britain was prepared in other ways as well:

> ... towards the end of World War I, the US Chemical Warfare Service began an investigation of ricin, the toxic compound contained in castor beans, which reached a reasonable state of development in the British W Bomb of World War II, reckoned to be seven times as effective as the comparable phosgene bomb.
>
> [Julian Perry Robinson, *Science Journal*, April 1967]

When the war ended, some of the German stocks were taken over by the allies. They were mostly sunk in the sea, but it is known that the USSR took over a large tabun plant.

Since then, in spite of large-scale stockpiling, there have been only two authenticated cases of the use of CW, in the Yemen and in Vietnam.

(a) The Yemen

The first allegations of poison gas being used in the Yemen began to appear in 1963. On 16 June of that year the *Sunday Telegraph* reported:

> German chemists in Egypt are working on gas and germ warfare projects, according to reliable sources in Teheran and in other Middle Eastern capitals.
>
> These Germans are said to be operating in strict secrecy under the direct orders of President Nasser's Cabinet. It appears they are experimenting with gas and bacteriological weapons that can be delivered either by bombs from aircraft or in rocket warheads.
>
> The Saudi Arabian Government and Yemeni Royalists are preparing full reports on several recent cases when Egyptian Air Force planes were said to have dropped gas bombs on pro-royalist Yemeni tribesmen. These reports will be sent to the United Nations and the International Red Cross.

Other articles appeared from time to time over the next three years, and at the end of 1966 they became more frequent and more specific. In an article in *The Times* on 12 November 1966, Wilfred Thesiger mentioned almost in passing:

> ... The Egyptians have used mustard gas and a blinding gas extensively and I saw a number of people who had been permanently blinded by them....

The Times on 9 January 1967 reported:

> Twelve Ilyushin heavy bombers attacked Katar near Sada, with poison gas, killing more than 125 persons, sources reported at

Royalist headquarters here today. It was believed that 600 gas bombs had been shipped from China to Arrahiba air base as direct aid to the republican regime. Some 120 people were in hospital in a critical condition, including, it was said, more than 50 blinded soldiers.

On 2 February *The Times* carried a long article by Nicholas Herbert reporting an attack on the village of Kitaf in the early hours of the morning of 5 January which, according to other reports (*Statist*, 3 February), had resulted in some 150 deaths and 200 casualties.

Egypt said today that she would accept a United Nations investigation of allegations that she had used poison gas in the war against the Yemen Royalists.... Mr. Wilson's statement in the Commons yesterday that he had evidence strongly suggesting that poison gas might have been used produced an immediate response from Muhammad Fayek, Egypt's Minister of National Guidance, who said it put the allegations in another light. Egypt had formerly ignored them, but he would now like to state categorically that the UAR did not and had not used poison gas. The Yemen Republic had agreed to give a UN investigating commission every assistance in making its study.

No one, I suspect, would be better pleased to see a properly constituted UN mission making an investigation than the 20 Western correspondents who visited the Yemen royalist village of Kitaf recently and reported the lay view that something like poison gas had been used....

Chemical analysis of the white powdery substance found in the shallow bomb craters, of tissues from the dead animals and perhaps of thorn trees, which seem to have been affected, would surely prove the answer. There are bomb fragments in plenty in the area, there are human corpses and a dozen alleged victims in hospital at Taif in Saudi Arabia, and Mr. Bushrod Howard, the Royalists' American publicity man, claims to have several deep-frozen animal carcasses ready for examination.

On 22 March Jamil M. Barody, the UN representative for Saudi Arabia, wrote to U Thant, accusing the UAR of bombing Kitaf on 5 January, and also of using a lethal gas causing between 100 and 200 deaths. Enclosed with the letter was a copy of the medical reports on the casualties of this attack. From tests conducted on twelve of the casualties who had been removed to the military hospital in Taif, in Saudi Arabia, the Saudi Ministry of Health doctors concluded:

it is evident that the symptoms appearing in the victims and the death of the animals were probably the result of the absorption or contact with organic phosphoric compounds. . . .[1]

On 28 July a report appeared in the *New York Times* by Mr André Rochat which was the text of a statement issued by the ICRC[2] to the Yemen, the Mutawakalite Kingdom, Saudi Arabia and the UAR. It had not been intended for publication.

On May 11 1967, the ICRC delegation in Jidda received appeals for assistance from the two villages of Gadafa and Gahar in the Wadi Herran, in the south western Jayf. According to these appeals a proportion of the inhabitants of these villages had been poisoned by gas dropped from raiding airplanes. Some hours later this news was confirmed by representatives of the Yemen royalists and the Saudi Arabian authorities who requested the ICRC delegation to go immediately to the assistance of the victims. The head of the delegation decided to proceed immediately to the scene accompanied by another delegate, two doctors and a male nurse, members of the ICRC medical team and a Yemeni escort. The two lorry convoy loaded with food and medical supplies left Amara on May 13th after having given due notice of its line of march and time-table to the Egyptian authorities. Unfortunately, following an air attack on the ICRC convoy, it was not until the night of May 15–16 that the mission reached Gahar. This village is situated atop a hill some 500 feet in height. All the houses are clustered closely around, giving the appearance of a small fortress.

According to the inhabitants, 75 people were gassed during a raid in the early hours of May 10 1967. The account given by the survivors is as follows:

The bombers circled the village for some time, then dropped three bombs on the hillside east of and below the village, two or three hundred yards away to the windward (wind direction from east to west). No houses were damaged. The explosions were relatively mild. The bomb craters were about 8 feet in diameter and 20 inches deep, smaller than the usual craters. Twenty minutes after dropping the three gas bombs, the planes dropped 4 or 5 high explosive bombs on the village and the western flank of the hill. Only one of these bombs caused any damage. This was sustained by a house in the centre of the village. Many animals, including almost 200 cattle, sheep, goats and donkeys and numerous

---

[1] This will be dealt with more fully in Part II.
[2] International Committee of the Red Cross.

birds, were also killed. The villagers who were not contaminated buried the dead animals in a large pit west of the village while the 75 humans killed were buried in 4 large communal graves.

The ICRC delegates for their part observed the following: They inspected the village for several hours, checking, whenever possible, the accuracy of the information mentioned above. The doctors examined the 4 surviving gas cases. Their medical report is attached hereto. The head of the Commission had one of the communal graves opened. There were 15 corpses in it. An immediate autopsy by Dr. Brutschin and Dr. Janin left no doubt that death was due to pulmonary edema. The 75 gas casualties were either within range of the gas when it was released, or were in its path as it was blown by the wind. Some of the victims were found dead in their homes as if they had died in their sleep. Other inhabitants working in the fields or watching over livestock were eastward of the area where the gas bombs fell, some of them very near to the spot, and none of them were affected. The four survivors who were in the contaminated area are all in pain from their eyes and almost blind. All have pains in the chest and none has any wound. The doctors cannot testify to an air raid with gas bombs of which they are not personal witnesses. On the other hand, they stress that all the evidence leads to the conclusion that edema was caused by the breathing of poison gas. The delegates were later informed that on May 17 and 18 the villages of Gabas, Nofal, Gadr and for the second time Gadafa, were raided with gas bombs, and as a result 243 persons were killed.

The text of what was allegedly the medical report from the ICRC Mission was published in *US News and World Report* on 3 July. It was signed by ICRC Doctor-Delegate Raymond Janin and ICRC Doctor-Delegate Willy Brutschin, and stated in part:

The following statements were made by the inhabitants who witnessed the incident:

(1) 75 persons died of poison gas shortly after the raid. They showed the following symptoms: shortness of breath, coughing, pink foam at the mouth, general edema especially on the face; no physical injuries.

(2) The undersigned doctors examined the four surviving victims and observed the following:

Subjective symptoms: burning eyes and trachea, internal thorax pain, extreme fatigue, anorexia.

Objective symptoms: dry cough, negative ausculation in two patients, signs of bronchitis in the other two, conjunctivitis, facial edema, no traumatic lesions, tympanum intact.

(3) The undersigned doctors examined a corpse 4 days after death and 12 hours after burial.

Immediately the common grave was opened, and, well before the corpses which were only wrapped in shrouds without coffins, were visible, there was a sweet penetrating smell not unlike garlic. The bodies showed no traumatic lesions. The skin was pink. Advanced and general edema all over the body.

Examination of lungs: reddish-brown throughout enlargement consistence and fragility greatly increased, crepitation considerably reduced.

The undersigned doctors draw the following logical conclusions from their findings:

I. None of the victims examined, whether survivors or corpses exhumed from the common grave, showed any traumatic lesions.

II. The statements made by witnesses who escaped from the raid unharmed in respect of the circumstances in which 75 inhabitants were killed, are consistent with the ICRC medical mission's own findings by examination of the four survivors and the corpse exhumed from one of the graves.

III. The cause of death in the case of the corpse examined was pulmonary edema. The overall consistency of the ICRC medical missions findings shows that in all probability this edema was caused by inhalation of toxic gas.

This report was submitted to the University of Berne's Institute of Forensic Medicine for assessment. The conclusions drawn by Professor Lauppi, Director of the Institute, were as follows:

The conclusions according to which the death of the deceased persons as a result of bombing is ascribed to a toxic gas seems to us to be perfectly justified. This conclusion is supported by the total absence of traumatic lesions caused by the effects of pressure explosion.

Amongst the various poison gases which can produce the effects observed, phosphonic esters—nervine gas—would not in our opinion be involved in view of the local irritations observed. . . .

On the other hand the employment of halogenous derivatives—phosgene, mustard gas, lewisite, chloride or cyanogen bromide, or Clark I and II etc.,—would appear to us the most likely . . . all the symptoms observed are explainable by the hypothesis of the use of mustard gas, lewisite or similar substances. The odor resembling garlic smelled on opening the common grave would indicate rather the employment of mustard gas.

Any such use of gas by the UAR constitutes a direct contravention of the 1925 Geneva Protocol which was signed and ratified by Egypt before World War II.

One of the most distressing aspects of the situation in the Yemen was the remarkable reluctance on the part of any official authority to recognise even the existence, let alone the dimensions of the problem. This is well illustrated by the fact that the UAR did not find it necessary to make any official denials of any sort until January 1967, although the first reports had been received some three years earlier.

A number of questions asked in the House of Commons give an indication of both the concern felt by the British government in this matter and the effectiveness of the United Nations in dealing with it.

In answer to a question asked in the House of Commons on 31 July 1963, the then Lord Privy Seal, Mr Heath, stated:

> The UN Secretary General announced on 12th July that he had given instructions on the 7th July to the United Nations Yemen Observation Mission to investigate a Saudi Arabian complaint received the same day that gas had been used. The United Nations does not recognise the Imam's government and would not therefore make any formal approach to it, but I understand the Imam has said he would welcome an investigation. . . . So far as the material sent to Her Majesty's Government is concerned, investigation has so far shown no evidence of the use of any gas other than a form of tear gas.
>
> [*Hansard*, 31 July 1963]

The mission was subsequently withdrawn.

10 May 1965

> MR BIGGS-DAVISON asked the Secretary of State for Foreign Affairs whether Her Majesty's Government will invite the signatories of the 1923 Geneva Protocol to the Geneva Convention on the use of noxious gases to a conference in London in order to secure the full implementation of the Protocol in view of the use of gas by Egyptian forces in the Yemen contrary to international conventions.
>
> MR PADLEY: 'No. I do not believe this would serve any useful purpose.'

21 June 1965

MR BIGGS-DAVISON asked the Secretary of State for Foreign Affairs whether he will represent to U Thant that once the UK and other member states of the UN recognise the Imam's government he should reconsider his decision made on the grounds of non-recognition not to proceed with the investigation of allegations of Egyptian use of poison gas in the Yemen.

MR GEORGE THOMSON: 'I am not aware that the Secretary General of the UN has ever decided not to investigate such allegations for the reason given. There would however be practical difficulties now that the UN Observation Mission has been withdrawn from the Yemen.'

1 June 1967

SIR T. BEAMISH asked the Secretary of State for Foreign Affairs whether he will now take the initiative at the UN to propose an investigation of the evidence that poison gas has been used by the UAR in the Yemen.

MR GEORGE THOMSON: 'Her Majesty's Government has no representation in the Republic of the Yemen and therefore is not in a position to have direct evidence of these allegations. In the circumstances it would not be appropriate for Her Majesty's Government to take the initiative suggested at the UN.'

8 June 1967

MR DODDS PARKER asked the Secretary of State for Foreign Affairs what action he is now taking to bring the Egyptian use of gas in the Yemen, as attested by the International Red Cross, before the United Nations.

MR GEORGE THOMSON: 'I have seen the statement by the International Red Cross on its delegates' reports of the use of poison gas in the Yemen. The International Red Cross has asked all the Authorities concerned in the Yemen conflict to "take the solemn engagement not to resort in any circumstances whatsoever to the use of asphyxiating gases or any other similar toxic substances". Our efforts at the United Nations are in present circumstances concentrated on contributing to a peaceful settlement of the Arab/Israel conflict and I do not think it would serve any useful purpose at this stage if Her Majesty's Government were to seek to bring the Egyptian use of gas before the United Nations.'

This reply was referred to, and no further statements made, in answer to the several subsequent questions, including the following, asked on

12 June 1967

> MR BIGGS-DAVIDSON asked ... if he will make a statement on the new reports now received by Her Majesty's Government about the use of poison gas by Egyptian forces in the Yemen.
>
> SIR KNOX CUNNINGHAM asked ... whether Her Majesty's Government will now take steps to bring a motion before the Security Council of the UN condemning the use of poison gas by Egyptian forces in the Yemen, calling on Egypt to stop its use and failing compliance by Egypt, providing for the imposition of sanctions.

In this situation a great responsibility was thrust upon the ICRC, which although deeply involved showed an almost pathological fear of becoming in any way politically committed. It is perhaps fair to say that informed public opinion would have been more effective than the unofficial diplomacy practised by the ICRC at this time.

An official statement issued by the International Red Cross on 31 January 1967 read as follows:

> The International Committee of the Red Cross in Geneva is extremely concerned about the air-raids against the civilian population and the alleged use of poisonous gases recently in the Yemen and the neighbouring regions. In view of the suffering caused thereby, the ICRC earnestly appeals to all authorities involved in this conflict for respect in all circumstances of the universally recognised humanitarian rules of international morality and law. The ICRC depends on the understanding and support of all the powers involved in order to enable its doctors and delegates in the Yemen to continue under the best conditions possible to carry out their work of impartial assistance to the victims of this conflict. The ICRC takes this opportunity to affirm that in the interest of the persons in need of its assistance, it has adopted as a general rule to give no publicity to the observations made by its delegates in the exercise of their functions. Nevertheless these observations are used to back up the appropriate negotiations which it unfailingly undertakes whenever necessary.

And in Nicholas Herbert's article in *The Times* on 2 February:

> ... The absence of technical advice was complete as the Red Cross representatives in the area refused to make any statements, but

there was no other explanation for what we saw, and none has since been advanced. The evidence however is in Kitaf.

... According to the Emir of Kitaf, the Red Cross arrived on the scene on the fourth day after the raid, inspected the town and saw the effects. They are reported to have removed parts of the lungs of some dead animals, but reports from Geneva say the results of analysis of them will not be made public.

The Times, 8 February 1967:

The International Committee of the Red Cross and the International Commission of Jurists have been asked to investigate charges that Egyptian aircraft have dropped poison gas in Yemen. ... Neither the Red Cross nor the Jurists had any comment.... They both regard the poison gas allegations as a matter for the United Nations.

The official press release (No. 829b) dated 2 June, after the attack on Gahar, does go a little further, but still makes an interesting comparison with the delegates' report itself (quoted in full above) which was never intended for publication. The statement read as follows:

The International Committee of the Red Cross has again received from its delegates in the Yemen reports of bombing by toxic gas. A medical team led by the head of the ICRC mission in the Yemen went on May 15th and 16th to a village in the northern part of the country to attempt to give aid to the victims of bombing having taken place some days previously and as a result of which, according to survivors, many inhabitants had died of asphyxiation. Delayed by an air raid of which their convoy was victim, the ICRC doctors on arrival at the site immediately gave treatment to some of the wounded and collected various indications pointing to the use of gas. Extremely disturbed and concerned by these methods of warfare, which are absolutely forbidden by codified international and customary law, the International Committee at once communicated its delegates' reports to all authorities concerned in the Yemen conflict requesting them to take the solemn engagement not to resort in any circumstances whatsoever to the use of asphyxiating gases or any other similar toxic substances.

(b) Vietnam

A consideration of chemical warfare in Vietnam is more complicated for several reasons. There are two distinct aspects to the situation neither of which in itself is straightforward. Firstly, the gases officially admitted to be in use in Vietnam are said officially to be riot control agents, and it has been argued that they do not qualify as poison or war gases. Secondly, the use of defoliants and herbicides in warfare is unprecedented and not specifically mentioned in any international law.

Gases

The following documentation shows a gradual escalation in the use of gases, and the development of novel ways of employing them. It also includes reports of agents which appear to be gases other than the three officially admitted to by the American authorities, or which are less innocuous than it is claimed.

The United States apparently began equipping the South Vietnamese Army with two of its three standard riot control gases in 1962 under the existing Military Assistance Program.... The third riot control agent DM ... apparently did not reach Vietnam until 1964.... In missions carried out in strictest secrecy, the munitions were used on December 23 in Xuyen province, on December 25 in Tay Ninh province near Saigon, and on January 28 1965 in Phu Yen province.

[Seymour Hersh, *New York Review of Books*, 9 May 1968]

In March 1965 an Associated Press photographer, Horst Faas, revealed that the us had used and was using gas for military purposes in Vietnam. Confirmation came from a us spokesman in Saigon who told the Associated Press that 'U.S. and Vietnamese Forces are now using non-lethal gases in certain tactical situations [*New York Post*, 22 March 1965].

The following statement was then issued by the Defense Department:

In tactical situations in which the Vietcong intermingle with or take refuge among non-combatants rather than use artillery or aerial bombardments, Vietnamese troops have used a type of tear-gas. It is a non-lethal gas which disables temporarily, making the enemy incapable of fighting. Its use in such situations is no different from the use of disabling gases in riot control.

The State Department added:

Tear gas in standard form as well as tear gas inducing nausea has been supplied by the United States and used by Vietnamese Forces in a few instances.   [*New York Times*, 23 March 1965]

A White House statement on 23 March said that President Johnson had not been consulted about the use of nausea-inducing gases in the South Vietnamese War, and according to George Reedy, the President's Press Secretary, 'That's not the sort of thing that comes up for that kind of approval. For many years this kind of authority has been delegated to Area Commanders.'

The gases, which had first been supplied in 1962, were described by Mr McNamara as follows:

> DM (Diphenylaminochloroarsine), a pepper-like irritant that causes sneezing, coughing, headaches, tightness in the chest, nausea and vomiting for half an hour to two hours.
>
> CS (Chlorobenzalmalononitrile), a recently developed tear-inducing agent that irritates eyes, nose and respiratory tract and causing chest pains, choking and vomiting. Its effects last five to ten minutes.
>
> CN (Chloroacetophenone), a tear-inducing irritant that also causes irritation of the skin. Its effects last about three minutes.
>
> [*New York Times*, 24 March 1965]

The following day, Secretary of State Dean Rusk, gave a press conference in order to explain and defend American policy. He stated:

> We are not embarking upon gas warfare in Vietnam.
>
> There has been no policy decision to engage in gas warfare in Vietnam.
>
> We are not talking about agents or weapons that are associated with gas warfare, the military arsenals of many countries. We are not talking about gas that is prohibited by the Geneva Convention of 1925, or any other understanding about the use of gas. . . .
>
> The decision was made to employ tear gas to try to deal with that situation as a riot-control type of problem in order to avoid the problem of whether to use artillery or aerial bombs that would inflict great damage upon innocent people. . . .
>
> Now, these are the essential policy aspects of the problem. We do not expect that gas will be used in ordinary military operations. . . .
>
> We were not specifically asked in Washington on the day before any one of these incidents whether we approved the use of this particular weapon. . . . In the three incidents which have been reported, the gas wasn't very effective. When the wind blew it away it was dissipated. It didn't achieve the purpose. . . .
>
> No new directives have been issued. The anticipation is, of

course, that these weapons be used only in those situations involving riot-control or situations analogous to riot-control.

Senator Fulbright, chairman of the Senate Foreign Relations Committee, took this argument even further by saying he felt the use of
gas was 'the most humane way to deal with the disorder' [*New
York Times*, 25 March 1965]. Reaction, both national and international, to this disclosure was immediate and of such force that
the use of gas was suspended.

However, this initial explosion of publicity and protest soon died
down, and during the next eighteen months the American public
was treated to accounts of the renewed use of gases. On 7 September
1965, Col. L. N. Utter, commander of the 2nd Battalion 7th Marine
Regiment, was placed under investigation for violating standing
orders by using forty-eight canisters of CN gas in a military offensive.
He was sent home, but cleared of the charge a month later. It is
possible that the whole incident was engineered simply to test public
opinion. This time the outcry was negligible.

The North Vietnamese branch of the International Red Cross
have alleged that CN used by Col. Utter resulted in thirty-five deaths.
Confirmation for this comes from other sources:

> ... during the raid carried out on 5th September, 1965, against the
> village of Vinh Quang (Binh Dinh province), a battalion of
> Marines commanded by Lieutenant-Colonel Leon Utter dropped
> 48 containers of toxic gas on civilians hiding in the air raid pro-
> tection trenches, killing 35 and wounding 19 (26 women and 28
> children).
>
> [Swiss National Committee for Aid to Vietnam]

On 9 October 1965, the *Liberation Press Agency*, according to *Vietnam Courier* (21 October 1965), reported that 'tear gas' had killed
thirty-five inhabitants in Vinh Quang Hamlet (Binh Dinh province)
on 5 September 1965 and injured nineteen others, including eight
women, three teenagers, eighteen old people and twenty-five
children:

> They killed 4 persons taking shelter in a trench and a whole
> family of 7 persons. Among the injured, 3 had their eye balls
> destroyed, the rest had blistered faces, scorched skin, burnt hair,
> erupted skin, or suffered from dizziness.

The *New York Times* reported on 6 October 1965 that General
William C. Westmoreland, the US military commander in Vietnam,

had—again—'received permission to use tear gas in military operations when it will save lives' and that 'tear gas would be used almost as a matter of daily military routine.'

On 8 October General Westmoreland officially authorised the use of gas once more. This constituted 'the first authorisation that had been given since the world-wide outcry last March' [*New York Herald Tribune*, 9 October 1965].

Charles Mohr reported in the *New York Times* (9–10 October 1965) about a paratrooper probe into the 'Iron Triangle' near Saigon:

> Some of the troops engaged today carried grenades resembling baseballs and containing a tear gas designated as 'CN' and 'CS'.
>
> Held in reserve at the brigade artillery position were three small gasoline motordriven commercial fumigating machines, dubbed 'Mighty Mites' by their American manufacturer, which can blow gas at a velocity of 185 miles an hour and which may be able to flush out the larger Vietcong tunnel systems.
>
> The first shipment of 'Mighty Mites', which weigh 25 pounds, reached Vietnam on September 13, and, if successful, will probably be issued to all major troop units here.

Under the headline 'United States might step up use of non-lethal gases in Vietnam fighting', the *Wall Street Journal* of 5 January 1966 went on to say:

> The United States contemplates expanding gas warfare in South Vietnam using chemicals just as non-lethal as the tear gas currently being employed and certainly more effective. The proposal to dig more deeply into Uncle Sam's bag of exotic weapons is now before the five-man Joint Chiefs of Staff. They are expected to favour and forward the idea to President Johnson within the next few weeks. The decision will be up to him.

The article mentioned the strong feelings against gas warfare but continued:

> Yet proponents are convinced that using certain nonpoisonous chemicals might save lives and speed the end of the war. If the public were calmly and thoroughly appraised, they argue, the reaction would be overwhelmingly favorable.
>
> So far, however, no such information is available. No one is willing to say precisely what chemical agents are being proposed except to remark that their persistency may range from a minimum of 2 hours to as much as 24 hours. But an unclassified mili-

tary manual gives details of two types of potential new chemical agents.

One, called CNS, is a compound of chloroform and chloropicrin and is said to smell 'like flypaper'. Even in small doses it may cause considerable crying, nausea, colic and diarrhoea that may persist for weeks. Dispensed from bombs, spray tanks, mortar shells, or grenades, CNS dissipates rather rapidly in fresh air, so friendly forces can move in right behind an attack.

Another new agent known as BZ, has been stockpiled extensively by the Army. Powdered, it is normally disseminated by burning grenades or bombs. The heat vaporises the compound into particles so small they are wafted on the slightest breeze. Even in low concentrations it is able to render a man useless for military duties for 1–10 days. Principally it causes him to lose muscle co-ordination temporarily, frequently he slumps to the ground and dozes off; when awake he may suffer from fever, headaches, disorientation, and even hallucinations. After the effects have worn off, however, experts say he will show no permanent injury and won't even recall having been drugged.

According to *Le Monde* (5 January 1966)

US specialists in chemical warfare are studying the actual use of new methods with tear gases which the commanders have authorised in certain sectors against the Liberation Front. The most recent method consists of drops from low-flying aircraft of clusters of grenades to cover an area almost the size of a football pitch with an irritant gas in aerosol form. This same dispatch talks about cylindrical grenades thrown by hand or fired from rifles. The effect of the gas is 'to cause violent mucous membrane irritation causing salivation. The victims get a burning sensation in the lungs and at the sweat gland areas of the skin. But above all the gas produces an insurmountable desire to run'—says a US officer. . . .

On 13 January 1966 the *Brisbane Courier Mail* reported that an Australian corporal, Robert William Bowtell, 24, who was wearing a gas mask, 'died of asphyxiation' when he was trapped in a tunnel into which tear-gas had been thrown during 'Operation Crimp'.

Two other Australian soldiers were overcome by the gas when they attempted to rescue Bowtell. . . . Four Australian engineers were overcome by carbon monoxide poisoning during the same operation. Army dogs brought in to help in the tunnel were also overcome.

Additional information is provided by a list of gas attacks in *Vietnam Courier*, 19 May 1966, among them the incident described above:

> From January 8th to 15th, strong gas was sprayed into shelters of the inhabitants of Bau Trai and Hua Ngia (Cholon province) by 8000 US, Australian and New Zealand troops. The gas was so thick that it remained for several days and killed some 100 people, mostly old folk and children. One Australian was killed and six other raiders were seriously affected.

The *New York Times* (15 January), commenting on this operation, said:

> The assault force failed to find the enemy ... but it captured tons of rice, munitions and other supplies and destroyed or *neutralised a huge network of underground tunnels or bunkers* [our emphasis].

Describing a marine patrol which he accompanied, AP journalist Peter Arnott reported:

> Trung Lap 13th January 1966. It was a long and bloody kilometre we covered on Wednesday. Gas filtered down from the trees and burned our skin. The wounded writhed in the sun looking like monsters with their grotesque gas-masks. Then came helicopters dropping gas on Liberation Front positions. When the commander saw the strike coming towards us the order was 'gas-masks on'. [exact date of report not known]

Le Monde on 14 January 1966 reported the following incident:

> The commander called to the medics, 'Keep the wounded covered, get them dressed; the gas will burn them.' In any case the gas was catching bare arms and the exposed neck area, leaving men with the same pain as when burned.

In a dispatch from Washington, the *New York Times* for 22 February 1966 reported:

> Defense Department officials explained today that the new tactics of a helicopter borne gas attack was designed to flush Vietcong troops out of the bunkers and tunnels before the attack of B52 bombers. . . . The purpose of the gas attacks was to force the Vietcong troops to the surface where they would be vulnerable to the fragmentation effects of the bomb bursts.

The following day the *New York Times* reported:

> Before the bombers struck the area 12 miles southwest of Bongson,

hundreds of tear gas grenades were dropped from helicopters. The first soldiers to enter the area wore gas masks.

In March 1966 Pierre Darcourt in *L'Express* reported that '3000 grenades containing the gas BZ' had been used by the 1st Cavalry Airmobile in Bongson. He continued:

> BZ is a lethargy-inducing gas which causes one to lose one's memory . . . of the Vietcong battalion (350–500 men) treated with the gas only 100 guerillas escaped. The US specialists are at the same time studying the effect of 'Mighty Mite', an air pump which sends out a jet of gas at about 200 m.p.h. and penetrates tunnels and hideouts.

On the same day the *World Trade Journal* reported:

> Most of the rural habitations have underground shelters which serve as refuges from typhoons and wars. Today when the American troops enter into the villages of South Vietnam, they make it a habit to throw gas grenades into these shelters. Obviously, there are some innocent victims. . . .

On 22 March 1966 a statement was issued by the Foreign Ministry in Hanoi which read as follows:

> To step up the use of toxic chemicals and poison gas the United States imperialists have brought from Japan to South Vietnam the so-called Mobile Research Institute of the United States Bacteriological and Chemical Warfare Corps No. 406. With the assistance of West German militarists, they have built a number of centres of production of so-called combat gas. They also intend to bring in units of the West German Army to help them produce and use various types of poison gases.
>
> [*The Times*, 23 March 1966]

In May 1966 a US military spokesman informed the Saigon press corps that a 'large-scale tear gas drop' had been performed near the Cambodian border. According to the *New York Times* for 11 May 1966:

> He said men of the First Infantry Division, protected by gas masks, searched the area about 70 miles northwest of Saigon hours after three helicopters had dropped 7,200 pounds of a tear gas-producing powder. The drop was one of the largest of the war.
> For the first time the powder was dropped in 80-pound drums fitted with explosive charges designed to detonate 25 seconds after leaving the aircraft. With the helicopters flying at 3000 feet, the

drums were supposed to burst open just after they crashed through the treetops.

Major William G. Dismore, division chemical officer, said that the drop was an experiment and that even though no enemy soldiers had been killed or captured, he considered it a success.

'Had the enemy been in there we could pretty well have knocked out his will to fight before we went in there,' he said. 'The whole purpose for using riot-control agents is to reduce casualties.'

Major Dismore said the division would probably use the gas again in the same way when it felt it faced a sizable troop concentration.

After the initial dense clouds are formed by the exploding canisters, crystals fall on the foliage and remain active for up to a week, Major Dismore said. When agitated, as by a soldier's foot, they give off gas.

After the drop last Thursday, the initial cloud rolled across the country, forcing the men in a headquarters four miles away to pull on their masks.

There were unconfirmed reports of a similar drop in which five army transport planes were used, but the spokesman said he had no information of a gas's being used since May 5.

Further comment on this incident came from an earlier report in the *New York Times* (9 May 1966):

A North Vietnamese broadcast after tear gas was used in September said 'U.S. Marines impudently used toxic gas, killing or seriously affecting many civilians.' United States spokesman, however, said the material was 'just old-fashioned tear gas that affects the eyes and makes people cry'.

At that time defense spokesmen said the policy concerning the use of tear gas or other non-lethal gas was set by Gen. William C. Westmoreland, commander of the United States forces, and not by the Pentagon.

Science on 20 January 1967 referring to the use of 'riot control agents' being the responsibility of local commanders, said:

The Pentagon told 'Science' that it no longer knows how many times and for what purposes they have been employed.

On 17 August 1967 a UPI despatch from Da Nang said:

Marine helicopter gunships dropped thousands of gallons of combination tear-nausea gas on a suspected Communist position last Thursday, the first use of gas this way in Vietnam.

A UPI despatch of 19 August 1967 said:

> US forces previously have used tear gas and nausea gas to drive Vietcong guerillas out of tunnels and bunkers, but today's action marked the first extensive use of gas above ground for several months.

The official report of the South Vietnam (NLF) Ad Hoc Committee lists the following incidents:

28 January 1965 Phu-Lac (province of Phu-Yen): 100 dead among civilians.

9 March 1965 in Tan Uyen (province of Bien-Heh): several dead.

13 May 1965 in Vinh Chau (province of Long An): thirty dead— among 146 poisoned inhabitants.

5 September 1965, during a search combined operations in the hamlet of Vinh Qyang, village of Pguoc-Son, district of Tuy Phuoc, province of Binh Dinh, 100 inhabitants were intoxicated, thirty-five dead, seven blind. Most of them were women, children and old people.

8 September 1965 in Ba Lang An (province of Quang Ngai): seventy-eight dead, almost all women, children and old people.

8 October 1965 in Ben Cat (province of Binh Duong): three dead.

2 January 1966; use of the Mighty Mite machine in shelters in Bau Trai (province of Long An): several hundred people were poisoned, several dead. The same day other dead in Duc Hoa (province of Che Lon).

From 8 to 15 January 1966 occurred numerous attacks with gases in Hua Nghia (province of Long An). We remember this is the very place where Bowtell's death took place.

From the 9 to 14 January 1966 in Cu Chi (province of Gia Binh): use of the Mighty Mite machine—more than 100 dead.

10 January 1966 in Kim Tai, district of An Nhon (province of Binh Dinh): 40 women, children and old people died. In this place US and South Korean soldiers are reported to have gathered the village population, then forced them into shelters, and then thrown the gas grenades.

1 February 1966: fourteen children died in Ky Anh, district of Tam Ky, province of Quang Nam.

26 and 28 February in eleven hamlets of the district of Binh Khe (province of Binh Dinh): 288 dead.

Finally, at the end of 1967, Professor Pfeiffer, of the Department of Zoology at Montana University, received a letter from Dr Alje Vennema, Director of the Canadian Medical Services in Vietnam, who was at that time working at the Tuberculosis Hospital at Quang Ngai. The letter, dated 23 November, was subsequently published, contrary to Dr Vennema's wishes. It read in part:

> During the last three years I have examined and treated a number of patients, men, women and children, who had been exposed to a type of war gas, the name of which I do not know. The type of gas used makes one quite sick when one touches the patient or inhales the breath from their lungs. After contact with them for more than three minutes one has to leave the room in order not to get ill.
>
> The patient usually gave a history of having been hiding in a cave or tunnel or bunker or shelter into which a canister of gas was thrown in order to force them to leave their hiding place. Those patients that have come to my attention were very ill with signs and symptoms of gas poisoning similar to those that I have seen in veterans from the first world war treated at Queen Mary Veterans Hospital in Montreal. The only difference between the cases was that those Vietnamese patients were more acutely ill and when getting over their acute stage presented a similar picture to that of the war veterans.
>
> Patients are feverish, semi-comatose, severely short of breath, vomit, are restless and irritable. Most of their physical signs are in the respiratory and circulatory systems. Both lungs exhibit rales throughout, severe bronchial spasm; heart rate is usually very high, and all the patients had pulmonary edema. In most cases active treatment for pulmonary edema and complicating pneumonia was helpful and they survived. Those that survived developed chronic bronchitic type of picture complicated by infections.
>
> The mortality rate in adults is about 10%, while the mortality rate in children is about 90%. I have only kept accurate records of the number of such cases that I have seen since last June. Since then I have seen 7 cases of which ... there was 1 child of 6 years of age who died, 1 of 15 who survived, 1 lady of 40 who died and 4 other adults who survived.

There are so far only three instances in which it is alleged that the Vietcong have used gas. The first was in November 1966.

American forces pushing deep into the jungle north of Saigon in pursuit of a Vietcong division have found large quantities of supplies including Chinese-made tear-gas grenades. A US infantry patrol reported last night that the Vietcong had used tear gas against them. A US military spokesman said today that 1,200 gas grenades were found in a dump 65 miles northwest of Saigon.

[*The Times*, 12 November 1966]

Two months later:

... In another sector 20 fleeing members of the Vietcong were reported by the US Command to have used 'what appeared to be riot control gas' against pursuing American troops. This is the second time that the Americans have accused the Vietcong of retaliating with gas, but apparently it had no serious effect and there were no American casualties. Two of the Vietcong were reported to have been killed, which suggests that the gas helped the rest get away.

[*The Times*, 18 January 1967]

A more recent allegation was on 9 July 1968 when the BBC announced that a gas had been used against the Americans which had caused them 'to vomit blood'.

Public opinion

The position of the United States with respect to international law is complicated and will be dealt with below. It may, however, be useful at this point to mention the part played by public opinion in this matter.

The first American use of gas was internationally condemned. The press in Europe and Asia, to say nothing of American newspapers, criticised loudly. The *New York Times* editorial said:

in Vietnam gas was supplied and sanctioned by white men against Asians. This is something that no Asian, Communist or not, will forget. No other country has employed such a weapon in recent warfare.

When the news broke the British Foreign Secretary, Michael Stewart, was in Washington. He received a strong telegram of protest from six Labour backbenchers, and a critical motion was tabled in the Commons.

The USSR took the issue to the UN on the grounds that America was:

grossly violating the accepted rules of international law and of the elementary principles of humanity and morality. The US Government is of course aware that the use of asphyxiating, poisonous and other gases has long since been prohibited and vigorously condemned by the peoples of the world.

A note was also handed to the US embassy in Moscow.

The US information Service protested to the White House that the use of gas in Vietnam had resulted in serious loss of prestige. As a consequence of all this, gas was not used again for some six months.

The US Administration had evidently learnt a valuable lesson, for in September, when gas was again used, 'it was accompanied by a careful public relations programme' (Seymour Hersh, *New York Review of Books*, 9 May 1968). The 'investigation' on Col. Utter has been described as 'a carefully planned trial balloon designed to make tear gas operational once again in Vietnam without public outcry' (Hersh). In this it apparently succeeded.

Very carefully worded and restrained reports of an operation in which gas was used appeared in the press on 8 October. The extent of the success is well illustrated by the editorial which appeared in the magazine *Navy*:

> the reaction in the press this time has been heavily favorable indicating that there is now a much better understanding at least among American editors of the humaneness of gas . . .

The defoliants

Reports on the use of defoliants and herbicides in Vietnam have been confusing and contradictory in many respects. For this reason documentation will be divided into subsections as follows:

Development of use.
The agents.
The effects of the agents used.
The consequences of drift and miscalculation.
The extent and costs of the defoliation and herbicide programme.
Protests.

Development of use

Seymour Hersh explains:

> The American defoliation program ostensibly aimed at jungle growth had begun modestly enough in late 1961. In November, 6 C-123 transport planes normally used for carrying troops were flown to South Vietnam from Clark Field in the Philippines and

outfitted with special tanks and high pressure nozzles. Each was capable of carrying 10,000 pounds of defoliant, enough to spray more than 300 acres. Only 60 flights were flown that November and December and 102 flights were made in all of 1962, when the program was still considered experimental.... The program is known as Operation Ranch Hand. The group's slogan is 'Only We Can Prevent Forests'... Major Ralph Dresser, head of Ranch Hand... noted that in an emergency the planes' high-pressure spray nozzles can eject the 1000 gallon cargo in just 30 seconds. Emergencies apparently happen quite often....

[*New York Review of Books*, 25 April 1968]

Newsweek reported on 27 November 1961:

Elsewhere special warfare men were showing Vietnamese fliers how to spray Communist-held areas with a chemical that turns the rice fields yellow, killing any crops being grown in rebel strongholds.

On 16 March 1963 a UPI correspondent, Charles E. Smith, wrote:

chemical defoliants and herbicides are used in certain places in the central highlands where the Vietcong terrorists grow crops. In such cases the aim is to eliminate sources of food.

The following report appeared in the *Minneapolis Tribune* on 14 April 1963 by Jack Wilson:

crop spraying has been limited to areas dominated by the Vietcong in the central highlands area dominated by the Montagnard tribesmen. Defense Department officials who receive regular reports on food spraying campaign feel that the Vietnam Government is conducting it with proper regard for its touchy aspects.

At this stage there was still considerable caution, especially on the part of the State Department, which protested to the Pentagon about:

...a Pentagon-approved plan to test the chemicals in other South-east Asian nations. In a manner that was to become habitual, the Pentagon went ahead with a series of highly classified tests.... One such programme was known as 'Oconus Defoliation Test' and involved the aerial application of chemical anticrop agents in Thailand, in 1964 and 1965.

[Hersh, ibid]

A classified test summary reported later:

Aerial spray treatments were applied at a rate of $\frac{1}{2}$ to 3 gallons per acre on two test sites representing tropical dry evergreen forest and secondary forest and shrub vegetation.

In March 1965 the first long detailed reports began to appear.

The weed killers such as are used in many American gardens are employed to strip jungle areas of foliage to expose Vietcong insurgents and to deprive them of possible ambush sites. They are also used to damage farm crops in areas where Vietcong control has long been established. United States forces while participating in most of the defoliating operations have not taken part in crop-damaging operations. Defoliation operations have been carried out in South Vietnam since 1961.... U.S. Air Force crews have flown two-engine C123 cargo planes with internal tanks that feed spray devices under the wings. The technique is similar to commercial crop dusting. Similarly the Army has occasionally put HU-1B helicopters at the disposal of South Vietnamese forces....

[New York Times, 28 March 1965]

The uncertainty at policy level is well illustrated by the answer given by Lt-Gen William W. Dick, the then chief of the army research programme, to a query from Representative Daniel J. Flood as to why defoliation was necessary.

Why this was decided to be essential I do not know ... it is certainly not the answer to all the problems in Vietnam ... I have seen reports that it has not solved all the problems in a given area where it has taken the foliage off.... We still have requirements from the commanders in Vietnam for defoliating agents. They continue to ask for supplies of it. They continue to use it. I can only assume that they find it has an ability to perform a job they want done.

[House Defense Subcommittee appropriations hearing, 1965]

An article by Charles Mohr later that year finally reported US participation in anti-crop operations:

US Air Force planes spraying chemicals have undertaken a drive to destroy rice crops in some areas under Vietcong control. The program uses the same chemicals as the defoliation program.... It is not poisonous and officials say that any food that survives its deadening touch will not be toxic or unpalatable. Crop destruction or herbicide is a politically delicate subject. Civilian officials have not publicised it and the Air Force officers have said they are forbidden to discuss it.... Officials say that no herbicide missions have been flown or will be flown in heavily populated areas.... The Air Force transport planes that carry on both defoliation and herbicide are spending more than half their time on herbicide. . . . Experience has shown that when the chemical is applied in the growing season before rice and other food plants are ripe it will destroy 60–90% of the crop. . . . The political control of the crop destruction program begins with the South Vietnamese. A province chief must approve and at least technically must request any spray mission. His request is passed to Saigon's Joint General Staff which passes it on to the US Military Assistance Command. After approval by the American command each project must receive approval by a high officer of the US Embassy. In areas where such missions are likely to create refugees, plans must be made to receive them.

[*New York Times*, 21 December 1965]

The agents

The first official statements admitted to only two agents. The *New York Times* reported on 28 March 1965:

Military officials say that just as tear and nausea gases are commonplace police weapons, the weed-killers are ordinary chemical compounds. The compounds known as 2,4-D, 2,5-T are variations of dichlorophenoxyacetic acid and trichlorophenoxyacetic acid and are available on the commercial market. . . . Depending upon the mixture and concentration however these chemical compounds may be used to destroy many kinds of plant life. Military officials emphasize that they are not harmful to people, animals, soil or water.

The medical diary of a North Vietnamese Doctor, Dr Nguyen (which was given to Ralph Schoenman as evidence to go before Lord Russell's War Crimes Tribunal), alleged the use of other compounds.

They have used various kinds of poisons which I have analysed. . . . I understand that the U.S. authorities state that these chemicals are intended to clear trees and grass. The truth is that these chemicals combine in heavy toxic concentrations which affect fatally both human and animal life. Among the chemicals I have analysed are:

DNP (Dinitrophenol)
DNOC (Dinitricorto)
2:4D (Acid Disclophenocyncetic)
2. 4:5T (Acid 2.4.5 Triclophenocyacetic) [inaccuracy in original text]

The list was somewhat extended by Red Cross and South Vietnam Liberation Front analyses, which, according to a French doctor, Charles Fourniau, had discovered since April 1963:

Arsenic anhydride or trioxide.
Arsenites of sodium and calcium.
Arsenates of sodium, calcium, lead and manganese.
2–4 dinitrophenol.
Dinitro-orthocresol.
Calcium cyanamide.

[*Combat pour la paix*, December 1966/January 1967]

The province of Tayninh ... has been heavily attacked by defoliants. I saw large surfaces of rice fields and of jungle which had previously received amounts of DNOC. ... I saw heavy damage caused by DNOC in the plantations including banana trees, papayas, desiccated leaves, swollen cracked and fissured stems and stunted fruits unfit for eating.

[Dr M. F. Kahn]

On 29 October at the National Foreign Policy Conference in Washington, Deputy Secretary of Defense Cyrus Vance was questioned about the use of aerosol-sprayed cyanide and arsenic compounds over rice fields in South Vietnam. His reply was as follows:

We are making limited use of them in the South Vietnam but not yet in the North.

[*Daily Pennsylvanian*, 1 November 1965
(Pennsylvania State University Student Paper)]

An AP report in March 1967 said that the agents in use in Vietnam are:

Agent Orange, a 50 : 50 mixture of two commonly used defoliants, 2,4 D and 2,4,5 T. The mixture is used against heavy jungle and crops.
Agent Blue, a neutralised cacodylic acid sprayed over tall elephant grass and heavier crop concentrations.
Agent White, also known as Tordon 101, a weaker mixture of unknown chemicals used in areas of sizeable population.

This was to some extent substantiated a few months later.

A Pentagon defoliant adviser has said here that the programme designed to deprive the enemy of hiding-places will have no long-term effect. He is Dr Charles Minarik, director of the plant science laboratory at Fort Detrick, Maryland. In an address to the northeast weed control conference here he dismissed assertions by Dr

Barry Commoner of Washington University, St Louis, that an area about a third of the size of Montana had been sprayed with cacodylic acid, an arsenical compound, and that another herbicide in use had been shown to cause cancer in mice.

'We have engaged in a massive environmental intrusion without being aware of the biological consequences,' Dr. Commoner told the recent meeting of the American Association for the Advancement of Science. Dr. Minarik said that maleic hydrazide, the alleged carcinogen, had not been used and that cacodylic acid, like most other herbicides in the programme, was broken down quickly by bacteria in the soil. Cattle which ingested it with their fodder excreted it in their urine and unlike DDT and other insecticides it did not appear in their milk. He admitted that one chemical in use contained picloram which did not break down quickly. It had been employed sparingly to meet the problem of destroying trees up to 150 ft high, which presented a major problem.

Dr. Minarik said that the programme had no more serious effect than weedspraying along transport routes in the United States. Animal life retreated from defoliated areas into the adjacent forest with little effect on the region as a whole.

[*The Times*, 6 January 1968]

Confirmation came from the Pentagon summary of a report of a study undertaken by the Midwest Research Institute for the Defense Department. According to the summary published in February 1968, the three herbicides used in Vietnam are:

1. A 50:50 mixture of n-butyl esters of 2,4D and 2,4,5T, used for jungle defoliation.

2. A combination of picloram and 2,4D in a low-volatile amine formulation for woody plant control and for use when accurate spraying is essential.

3. Cacodylic acid, a contact herbicide for grass control and destruction of rice crops.

On 8 September 1967, Defense Secretary MacNamara announced an anti-infiltration barrier between North and South Vietnam. The AP reported next day:

The soil poisoners are required because military commanders have found that thriving vegetation starts growing back almost as quickly as bulldozers clear a strip.

Two agents specifically mentioned which might be used were chlorophenyl-dimethylurea, and dichlorophenyl-dimethylurea.

The Effects of the Agents Used

An interview with a woman in Bien Hoa province (Vietnam) in 1964 resulted in the following description of a defoliant attack:

> ...I was on my way to market when a plane came down quite low with what looked like whitish smoke coming out of its tail.... When the 'smoke' drifted over me, I thought at first I was going to choke. My chest started to burn. All the way to market I had difficulty breathing. I had to keep stopping to sit down. After a while my nose started bleeding. When I got to the market I found other women suffered the same thing. Two of them were bleeding from the mouth as well.... When I got back to the village I found that one of my neighbours...was paralysed.... By evening she was able to move about alright, but had severe pains in the chest and difficulty in breathing.
>
> [Wilfred Burchett, *The Furtive War*]

Huot Sambath, the Minister for Foreign Affairs for Cambodia, stated in 1964 that between 13th June and 23rd July six Cambodian villages in Rattankirir province, near the Vietnamese border, had been sprayed with defoliant—'a deadly yellow powder'. This resulted in 76 deaths, mostly children.

[Malcolm Browne, *The New Face of War*]

Dr Nguyen, whose medical diary was used as evidence at the Russell War Crimes Tribunal, described a chemical attack as follows:

> In the beginning of November 1964 four sky raider bombers bombed and strafed the area where I lived in Lam Dong province. Then came one helicopter and two Dakotas. The smell of chemical was unbearable. After five minutes leaves of sweet potatoes, rice plants and trees became completely desiccated. Domestic animals would not eat and almost all died...only 15 minutes later Dakota planes returned and sprayed chemicals a second time...no one was able to eat that day, everyone was unable to sleep, the effects on the nervous system were very unusual ...the next day all our poultry were dead, the fish in streams and lakes were floating in the water, discoloured, the buffalo were dead. The grass was poisoned. All crops were without leaves and burned and the unburned vegetation was rotting.
>
> All the women who were pregnant and all pregnant animals had miscarried on the spot.... Ten days later, a squadron of

U.S. aircraft came and spread chemicals a third time . . . for weeks
and months I was unable to move. I vomited all the time. My
throat, mouth, stomach and bowels were inflamed. 15 days later
I could not read. One month later I could not see. In 3 months I
could eat only soup. The effects on my nervous system made it
impossible to gain unconsciousness. . . . Everytime they spray
chemicals they threaten us with loudspeakers, broadcasting from
aeroplanes, telling people to go to areas controlled by Saigon or
they will suffer death.

And on chemicals in general:

These toxic chemicals poison water, food, vegetation and animal
and human life. . . . I have personally examined 41 people killed
who died as a result of drinking this poisoned water; they died
in great pain. I have examined children who were critically ill as
a result of having swum in a stream which had been poisoned in
this way. Three of the children were blinded.

The following description of three-day chemical attack near Da
Nang from 25 to 27 February 1966 was given by Pham Duc Nam
and quoted in the report of the study made by the Japan Science
Council, published in 1967.

Affected areas covered 120 kilometers east–west and 150 kilometers
north–south. Five minutes was all that was needed to wither
tapioca, sweet potato . . . and banana plants. Livestock suffered
heavy injuries. Unlike men, who could keep clear of chemical
stricken things as food, animals had to eat just anything. Most
of the fish were found lying dead on the surface of mountain
streams and brooks. The 3 days of chemical attack poisoned scores
of people, took lives of about 10 and inflicted a natus disease
(with symptoms like a severe rash) upon 18,000 inhabitants.

The Japanese study alleges that more than 13,000 livestock have
died as a result of defoliant and herbicide attacks, and nearly 1000
peasants. One village was apparently attacked more than thirty
times in this way [Study by Japan Science Council, 1967].

On 22 March 1966 the Minister of Foreign Affairs for North Vietnam issued the following statement concerning the effects of the
chemical defoliants being used:

In the affected regions 50% of the cattle have lost the power to
move and have become sterile—the animal population has been
completely decimated. There have been thousands killed and
hundreds of thousands of people affected.

The Commission of Inquiry into war crimes in Vietnam, set up by the Government of Hanoi, reported in October 1966:

> The aim is clear when U.S. troops and allies cannot control an area. They must destroy all crops and thus force the population to give up through hunger. Entire regions like the Ben Tre province have been hit by chemical products which not only kill vegetation but also cause serious poisoning to the inhabitants. Each time after the U.S. aircraft have gone by it is the same story of destruction—yellowing rice, bananas and other fruit shrivelled up. Poultry and fish dead. Women, children and old men and the sick taken by colic, diarrhoea, vomiting and often terrible burns. The weakest die from this poison.

The Consequences of Drift and Miscalculation

An article on Saigon in the January edition of the *National Geographic Magazine* in 1965 contained the following passage:

> Mr. Nhon spoke of the island's remarkable flora [Pho island near Saigon]... and the famous grapefruit trees whose seeds were brought from the north many years ago. Mr. Nhon owned 2000 trees, as a rule each produced some 100 grapefruit twice a year. Mr. Nhon was the Grapefruit King of Saigon. 'No more,' he said. 'Look, not one tree has more than 50, and 20% of my trees are dead.'
>
> Last year, he explained, chemicals were sprayed along the highway to kill vegetation and make it more difficult for the VC to set ambushes. 'A bit of those chemicals floated this way,' said Nhon. 'Grapefruit are expensive in Saigon this year.'

On 14 April 1965 an attaché of the United States Operation Mission agricultural team in the Bien Hoa area north-east of Saigon issued the following private report to his superiors:

> I have repeatedly complained of the reckless use of defoliants in the Bien Hoa area. Last season drift over a considerable area of water spinach caused mis-shapen unmarketable stems. The stems were fed to pigs and several pigs were reported to have died... other plants were damaged. The peasants report it is damaging the health of the children....

As a result of this a team of officials and military advisers was sent to inspect the area. They reported on 4 May:

> The agricultural team said that 500 complaints or requests for damage had been filed with hamlet chiefs for transmission to

province chiefs.... I suspect this number is an inaccurate exaggeration and of those claims submitted many were for damage not associated with defoliants.

On 13 December 1965, a defoliation operation was carried out near Thoi An Dong village in Phong Phu district of the fertile Can Tho areas of the Mekong Delta. A United States Operations Mission field report states:

As a result, maturing water melons, rice, vegetables and fruits ... were all damaged, thus inflicting serious losses to the farmers. ... Thoi An Dong village of Phong Phu district is located in a rather secure area but, ... was unbelievably categorised as an area supplying food to the Vietcong. ...

After one of his visits to Vietnam, at the end of 1965, Bernard B. Fall wrote:

In Asia vegetation is always lush, but now when you fly over parts of Vietnam you can see the dead brown surface of the areas that were sprayed on purpose, and the places defoliated by accident. Ben Cat, a huge plantation near Saigon, was almost completely destroyed by accident; 3000 acres were transformed into the tropical equivalent of a winter forest ... a Catholic refugee village, Honai, along Highway 1 in South Vietnam ... was sprayed by mistake. All its fruit trees died. United States Air Force planes were defoliating the jungle along Highway 1, but the wind shifted and blew the killer spray towards the villages instead. In a supreme irony, the jungle now stands in the background, lush and thick, while the villages are barren.
When I was there. the villagers were chopping down the trees. The only resource they had left was the remains of their dead fruit trees to be sold in Saigon for firewood.

[*Ramparts*, December 1965]

Another USOM report dated January 1966 stated:

The damages caused by the spraying of defoliant on crop plantings ... ranged from 40–100% ... rendering the farmers unable to harvest their crops for profitable marketing during the lunar New Year Season as otherwise expected.... The total area defoliated is believed to be much greater than those villages mentioned as the assumption is that quite a few farmers have not filed complaints at the local Government offices.

The reason given for the failure was the red tape, bureaucracy and corruption entailed in the process.

A Saigon dispatch from Eric Pace to the *New York Times*, 27 July 1966, stated:

> American military officials have called the chemical poisons 'weed killer, the same as you buy in the hardware store at home'. So potent is the poison, experts said, that if borne by a wind it can kill things 15 miles from where it is sprayed.

And Professor Arthur Galston wrote in the *New Scientist* on 13 June 1968:

> Since herbicides are usually dispensed by equipment producing fine sprays, it is obvious that great care must be taken to prevent the inadvertent drifting of spray onto nearby susceptible plants. Such accidents have become common in ordinary peacetime agriculture. When as in Vietnam the spray operations are accomplished by low-flying aircraft, the dangers of drift are much magnified. In one Vietnam accident, 2,4D inadvertently defoliated an entire Michelin rubber plantation at a cost to the US taxpayer of 87 dollars per tree.

The Extent and Cost of Defoliation and Herbicide

The following selection of statistics on the extent of defoliation and anti-crop operations shows the escalation over the last three years.

> The program which began last spring has touched only a small fraction—50,000 to 75,000 acres, of more than 8 million acres of cultivated land in South Vietnam. This is the intention of the policy makers.
>
> [*New York Times*, 21 December 1965]

According to an official statement issued on 13 March 1966 by the Central Committee of the NLF and the Ministry for Foreign Affairs of North Vietnam, large-scale devastation by defoliation started in 1965 and 1·8 million acres were affected during 1965. The statement claims that during December 1965 alone, 50,000 acres of growing crops were treated, resulting in losses of 30%.

In March 1966 the State Department announced that about 20,000 acres of South Vietnam's land under cultivation had been destroyed. In July 1966 the *New York Times* dispatch stated:

> The spraying begun in 1962 has blighted about 130,000 acres of rice and other foods.

Two months later:

> Pleased with the effectiveness of chemical defoliation and crop-

destruction missions, the United States is taking steps to triple its present capability in both techniques.

So far this year Operation Ranch Hand, using an average of six C-123 spray planes, has squirted 1,324,430 gallons of non-toxic herbicide over 550,872 acres of jungle hideouts, trails and croplands in enemy-dominated areas of South Vietnam.

[New York Times, 11 September 1966]

On 24 October 1966 a Pentagon spokesman confirmed that the US had recently extended the spraying operation to include western areas of South Vietnam's portion of the six-mile-wide demilitarised zone separating the country from North Vietnam:

More than 640,000 acres of jungle and cropland have been coated with what the Pentagon described as non-toxic chemicals since January, 1965.

The figure does not include the last three months, and a spokesman emphasized that the 640,000 is cumulative. Some thick jungle regions have been sprayed more than once.

[New York Herald Tribune, 25 October 1966]

The American magazine Science obtained information from the Pentagon that:

more than 500,000 acres of jungle and brush and more than 150,000 acres of crop-land have been treated with herbicides. . . .

[20 January 1967]

According to Seymour Hersh:

1967 Japanese study of US anticrop and defoliation methods prepared by Yoichi Fukushima, head of the Agronomy Section of the Japan Science Council . . . claimed that US anticrop attacks have ruined more than 3.8 million acres of arable land in South Vietnam.

[New York Review of Books, May 1968]

In February 1968:

The Defence Department defoliation study stated that 965,000 acres were treated with herbicide in 1967 but because of re-application 'the total defoliated area was less significant'.

The 1967 figures already indicate a sharp increase. In the first 9 months 834,606 acres in Vietnam were drenched with defoliants and 121,400 acres treated with crop killing agents. This is more than during the whole of 1966.

[Guardian, 25 June 1968]

The following selection of reports on costs of the defoliation programme have been arranged more or less in chronological order.
According to Seymour Hersh:

> The Air Force's C-123s are designed to distribute their 1000
> gallon, 10,000 pound loads in 4 minutes over about 300 acres, a
> rate of roughly more than 3 gallons/acre, the maximum dosage
> recommended by Army Manuals.

The *New York Herald Tribune* of 25 October 1966 stated that:

> defoliating operations require about 3 gallons per acre at a cost
> of $5 a gallon.

An AP dispatch from Washington revealed that

> The cost of the U.S. effort to wipe out Vietnam's jungle and
> crops, which hide and feed the Communists, is approaching
> $100 million.
>
> In 1966, American planes spewed out defoliants and herbicides
> worth an estimated $10 million over hundreds of acres of dense
> jungle as well as over Viet Cong-held riceland.
>
> This year's Air Force budget provides $39.5 million for about
> five million gallons of vegetation-poisoning chemicals.
>
> And in the next fiscal year beginning July 1, the Air Force
> says it is asking Congress for $49.5 million more to expand the
> spring programme.

An article in *Scientist and Citizen* by Professor Galston (August/
September 1967) quoted some further estimates:

> It was announced on July 11th that contracts for 57,690,000
> dollars worth of chemicals for defoliation and crop destruction
> have been awarded by the Defense Supply Agency. The quantity
> of chemicals being purchased was not announced, but even
> allowing for some price increase, the amount in dollars suggests a
> purchase of between six and seven million gallons. (The Air
> Force budget for fiscal year that ended June 30th 1967 provided
> $39,500,000 for about 5 million gallons...)

The contracts were awarded to eight chemical companies, namely
Dow; Diamond Alkali; Uniroyal; Thompson Chemical; Monsanto;
Ansul; and Thompson Hayward.

The following article appeared in *Newsweek*, 26 February 1968:

> No spraying this year explains one of the largest forest manage-
> ment companies in the US. '2,4D and 2,4,5T have gone to war.'
> At least 50 million pounds of these two leading herbicides in fact

were used in South Vietnam last year alone. By spraying along the Ho Chi Minh Trail over the dense forests of the DMZ or into the mangrove sanctuaries of the Mekong Delta, the US Air Force sought to deprive the Vietcong of more than a million acres of jungle cover and precious cropland in 1967. But the Vietcong may not be the only losers.

The *Guardian* on 25 June 1968 reported that:

The US Air Force will spend $70·8 million on crop killing and defoliating chemicals in Vietnam from July 1st for a year which means about 10 million gallons of chemical spray—a 50% increase on the 1967/8 amount.

This escalation can also be seen from the production side. On 22 April 1967, *Business Week* announced that:

The heavy military purchases of commercial defoliants have vastly outstripped existing production capacity in the US and a shortage of the chemicals is anticipated ... some industry sources believe the military demand for 2,4,5T to be four times production capacity. The *Pesticide Review*, October 66, estimated the 1965 production of 2,4D and 2,4,5T to have been nearly 77 million pounds.

Newsweek, on 26 February 1968, reported:

With the entire US production of 2,4,5T pre-empted now for use in Vietnam many scientists are beginning to worry that defoliation may be doing irreparable violence to the natural balance of the land itself.

The entire US production of 2,4,5T for 1967 and 1968 is about 14 million pounds, according to Tariff Commission reports. Many attempts have been made to draw conclusions from the various statistics that have been published of which the following two are fair examples:

The going rate for a 1000 gallon cargo of crop killing chemicals is $5000. In 1967 the Pentagon announced the purchase of nearly $60m worth of defoliants and herbicides, enough for 12,000 plane rides over the countryside, each of which would theoretically blanket 300 acres of cropland. If each mission was successful, 3·6 million acres, nearly half the arable land of South Vietnam, would be covered.

There can be no doubt that the DOD is in the short run going beyond mere genocide to biocide. It commandeered the entire

US production of 2,4,5T for 1967 and 1968. If one combines this with other chemicals the DOD concedes it is using, there is a sufficient amount to kill 97% of the above ground vegetation on over 10 million acres of land. . . .

[Letter from Thomas Perry to *Science*, 10 May 1968]

For this reason the following tables have been drawn up in order to try to clarify matters.

US *Estimates of area covered* (*acres*)

Description	Jungle cover	Crop land	Total	Date of estimate
Treated		50–75,000		Up to Dec. 1965
Destroyed		20,000		Up to March 1966
'Blighted'		130,000		Up to July 1966
Treated			550,872	Jan.–Sept. 1966
Treated (cumulative)			640,000	Jan.–Oct. 1966
Treated	500,000	150,000	650,000	Up to Jan. 1967
Treated	834,606	121,400	955,006	Jan.–Sept. 1967
Treated	1,334,606	271,400	1,605,006	Up to Sept. 1967

Other estimates of area (*Vietnamese and Japanese*)

Description	Jungle cover	Crop land	Total	Date of estimate
Treated			1·8 m.	1965
Treated		50,000		December, 1965
Destroyed		15,000		December, 1965
Destroyed		3·8 m.		Up to Mid-1967

Estimates of cost and deductions

Fiscal year	1966	1966/7	1967/8	Total (1966/8)	1968/9
Budget ($)	10 m.	39·5 m.	59·0 m.	98·5 m.	70·8 m.
1. Assume $5/gal. Then quantity (gal.) =	2 m.	7·9 m.	11·9 m.	19·8 m.	14·2 m.
At 3 gal./acre, possible acreage =	650,000	2·6 m.	3·9 m.	6·5 m.	4·7 m.
2. Assume $8/gal. Then quantity (gal.) =	1·25 m.	5 m.	7·4 m.	12·4 m.	8·85 m.
At 3 gal./acre, possible acreage =	415,000	1·6 m.	2·5 m.	4·1 m.	3 m.

There are several reasons why any attempt to draw conclusions from these figures must be regarded with suspicion.

(1) There are two separate estimates for the cost of defoliant per gallon: one on the basis of the *New York Herald Tribune* report, and one on the basis of 1966/67 budget, and the quantity said to have been purchased with that amount. On the first estimate, Mr Hersh's calculations are reasonable and the official figures of acreage covered appear gross under-estimates. On the second estimate the official figures are comparatively consistent.

(2) There are a number of unknowns in this.

(*a*) How many acres are re-treated?

(*b*) How do the prices of the different agents used differ? If either figure given is an average, it is probably meaningless. If it is merely the price of the agents most widely used, then it is even more meaningless. As far as costs are concerned, no distinction has even been made between defoliant and herbicide.

(3) The areas of cropland relative to jungle sprayed may be inaccurate, as it is not known whether they incorporate acres of cropland sprayed by accident.

Perhaps an indication of the extent of the damage currently being done by the use of chemicals in Vietnam can be gleaned from a Department of Agriculture estimate that as a result of the defoliation and herbicide operations, Vietnam, which exported 49 million metric tons of rice in 1964, may have to receive up to 800,000 metric tons of US supplied rice in 1968.

Protests

In March 1965 the non-political Federation of American Scientists condemned the use of chemical and biological warfare agents in Vietnam. It said in a statement:

> The use of United States-produced chemical and biological weapons in Asia will be interpreted widely as 'field-testing' of these weapons among foreign people and will hurt our efforts immeasurably in good will and moral respect all over the world.
>
> We find it morally repugnant that the United States should find itself party to the use of weapons of indiscriminate effect, with principle effectiveness against civilian populations.
>
> The justification of such weapons in warfare as 'humane' will,

in the long run, hurt the security of the United States, even if military effectiveness in a specific situation can be demonstrated.

In recent weeks we have been treated to a succession of stories which have included the employment of napalm against villages, the use of crop-destroying agents, so-called defoliating chemicals, and now the use of gas against civilians.

Whether a chemical which induces extreme nausea and acts as a cathartic inflicts lasting effects on its victims of all ages and in varying states of health, we cannot possibly know.

In January 1966 the use of anti-crop agents was condemned in a statement by twenty-nine scientists and physicians from Harvard, Massachusetts Institute of Technology, and several nearby institutions.

We emphatically condemn the use of chemical agents for the destruction of crops by United States Forces in Vietnam as recently reported in the *New York Times* of Tuesday 21st December 1965. Even if it can be shown that the chemicals are not toxic to man, such tactics are barbarous because they are indiscriminate; they represent an attack on the entire population of the region where the crops are destroyed, combatants and non-combatants alike. In the crisis of World War II, in which the direct threat to our country was far greater than any arising in Vietnam today, our Government firmly resisted any proposals to employ chemicals or biological warfare against our enemies. The fact that we are now resorting to such methods shows a shocking deterioration of our moral standards. These attacks are also abhorrent to the general standard of civilised mankind, and their use will earn us hatred throughout Asia and elsewhere.

Such attacks serve moreover as a precedent for the use of similar but even more dangerous chemical agents against our allies and ourselves. Chemical warfare is cheap; small countries can practise it effectively against us and will probably do so if we lead the way. In the long run the use of such weapons by the United States is thus a threat, not an asset, to our national security.

We urge the President to proclaim publicly that the use of such chemical weapons by our armed forces is forbidden, and to oppose their use by the South Vietnamese or any of our allies.

The signatories of the statement were as follows:

Harvard: John Edsall, Bernard Davis, Keith R. Porter, George Gaylord Simpson, Matthew S. Meselson, George Wald, Stephen

Kuffler, Mahlon B. Hoagland, Eugene P. Kennedy, David H. Hubel, Warren Gold, Sanford Gifford, Peter Reich, Robert Goldwyn, Jack Clark and Bernard Lown.

Massachusetts General Hospital: Victor W. Sidel, Stanley Cobb and Herbert M. Kalckar.

M.I.T.: Alexander Rich, Patrick D. Wall and Charles D. Coryell.

Brandeis: Nathan O. Kapland and William P. Jencks.

Amherst: Henry T. Yost.

Dartmouth: Peter H. von Hippel.

Tufts: Charles E. Magraw.

Also, Albert Szent-Gyorgi, Director for Muscle Research, Woods-hole and Hudson Hoagland, Director of the Worcester Institute of Experimental Biology.

In answer to this protest, Major-General Davison wrote a letter which read in part:

> Great care has been taken to select areas in which most harm would be done to the Vietcong and least harm to the local population. In some instances the local inhabitants, who have been forced to grow food for the Vietcong, have requested that the herbicides be used. The Government of Vietnam has taken precautions to care for non-combatants whose food supplies have been affected . . . this is not chemical or biological warfare, nor is it a precedent for such. It is in actuality a relatively mild method of putting pressure on a ruthless enemy. . . .

On 15 April 1966 the following letter appeared in *Science*:

> I am addressing myself in this letter to the practical and the ethical implications of our destruction of rice crops and grain stores, by chemicals and by fire, in South Vietnam. . . . The aim of the program is to starve the Viet Cong by destroying those fields that provide the rice for their rest—and field—rations. This aim is, in essence, similar to that which every food blockade (such as the one imposed against the Central Powers in World War I) has attempted. As a nutritionist who has seen famines on three continents, one of them Asia, and as a historian of public health with an interest in famines, I can say flatly that there has never been a famine or a food shortage—whether created by lack of water (droughts, often followed by dust storms and loss of seeds, being the most frequent), by plant disease (such as fungous blights), by large-scale natural disturbances affecting both crops and farmers (such as floods and earthquakes), by disruption of

farming operations due to wars and civil disorders or by blockade or other war measures directly aimed at the food supply—which has not first and over-whelmingly affected the small children.

In fact, it is very clear that death from starvation occurs first of all in young children and in the elderly with adults and adolescents surviving better (pregnant women often abort; lactating mothers cease to have milk and the babies die). Children under five, who in many parts of the world—including Vietnam—are often on the verge of kwashiorkor (a protein-deficiency syndrome which often hits children after weaning and until they are old enough to eat 'adult' food) and of marasmus (a combination of deficiency of calories and of protein), are the most vulnerable. In addition, a general consequence of famine is a state of social disruption (including panic). People who are starving at home tend to leave, if they can, and march toward the area where it is rumoured that food is available. This increases the prevailing chaos. Families are separated and children are lost—and in all likelihood die. Adolescents are particularly threatened by tuberculosis; however, finding themselves on their own, they often band together in foraging gangs, which avoid starvation but create additional disruption. The prolonged and successful practice of banditry makes it difficult to rehabilitate members of these gangs.

I have already said that adults, and particularly adult men, survive usually much better than the rest of the population. Bands of armed men do not starve and—particularly if not indigenous to the population and therefore unhampered by direct family ties with their victims—find themselves entirely justified in seizing what little food is available so as to be able to continue to fight. Destruction of food thus never seems to hamper enemy military operations but always victimises large numbers of children. During World War I, the blockade had no effect on the nutrition and fighting performance of the German and Austrian armies, but—for the first time since the 18th century—starvation, vitamin-A deficiency, and protein deficiency destroyed the health, the sight, and even the lives of thousands of children in Western Europe.

We obviously do not want to take war measures that are primarily if not exclusively, directed at children, the elderly and pregnant and lactating women. To state it in other words, my point is not that innocent bystanders will be hurt by such measures, but that only the bystanders will be hurt. Our primary aim —to disable the Viet Cong—will not be achieved and our prolonged secondary aim—to win over the civilian population—is made a hollow mockery.

[Jean Mayer, School of Public Health, Harvard University]

In the following September a letter was sent to President Johnson by the American Society of Plant Physiologists:

The undersigned Plant Physiologists wish to make known to you their serious misgivings concerning the alleged use of chemical herbicides for the destruction of food crops and for defoliation operations in Vietnam. . . . We would assert in the first place that even the most specific herbicides known do not affect only a single type of plant. Thus a chemical designed to defoliate trees might also be expected to have some side effects on other plants, including food crops. Secondly, the persistence of some of these chemicals in soil is such that productive agriculture may be prevented for some years into the future, possibly even after peace has been restored. Thirdly, the toxicology of some herbicides is such that one cannot assert that there are no deleterious effects on human and domestic animal population. . . . The first and major victims of any food shortage or famine caused by whatever agent, are inevitably children, especially those under five. This results mainly from their special nutritional needs and vulnerability to stress.

Finally, it must be noted that the use of chemical herbicides, no matter how represented, is a resort to a kind of operation classed as biological warfare, and heightens the possibility of increasing the level of barbarity in an already terrible war.

Also in September, the following petition was presented to President Johnson:

Dear Mr. President,

We, the American Scientists whose names appear below, wish to warn against any weakening of the world-wide prohibitions and restraints on the use of chemical and biological (CB) weapons.

CB Weapons have the potential of inflicting, especially on civilians, enormous devastation and death which may be unpredictable in scope and intensity; they could become far cheaper and easier to produce than nuclear weapons, thereby placing great mass destructive power within reach of nations not now possessing it; they lend themselves to use by leadership that may be desperate, irresponsible, or unscrupulous. The barriers to the use of these weapons must not be allowed to break down.

During the Second World War, the United States maintained a firm and clearly stated policy of not initiating the use of CB weapons. However, in the last few years the U.S. position has become less clear. Since the 1950s Defense Department expenditure on CB weapons has risen several fold—and there has been no categorical reaffirmation of the World War II policy.

Most recently, U.S. forces have begun the large-scale use of anti-crop and 'non-lethal' anti-personnel chemical weapons in Vietnam. We believe that this sets a dangerous precedent, with long-term hazards far outweighing any probable short term military advantage. The employment of any one CB weapon weakens the barriers to the use of others. No lasting distinction seems feasible between incapacitating and lethal weapons or between chemical and biological warfare. The great variety of possible agents forms a continuous spectrum from the temporarily incapacitating to the highly lethal. If the restraints on the use of one kind of CB weapon are broken down, the use of others will be encouraged.

Therefore, Mr. President, we urge that you:

Institute a White House study of overall Government policy regarding CB weapons and the possibility of arms control measures with a view to maintaining and reinforcing the worldwide restraints against CB warfare.

Order an end to the employment of anti-personnel and anti-crop chemical weapons in Vietnam.

Re-establish and categorically declare the intention of the United States to refrain from initiating the use of chemical and biological weapons.

The signatories:

Felix Bloch, Physics, Stanford University; Nobel Laureate 1952.
Konrad E. Bloch, Chemistry, Harvard University; Nobel Laureate 1964.
James F. Crow, Medical Genetics, University of Wisconsin.
William Docring, Sterling Chemicals Laboratory, Yale University.
Paul Doty, Chemistry, Harvard University.
Freeman J. Dyson, Institute for Advanced Study.
John T. Edsall, The Biological Laboratories, Harvard University.
Bernard Field, Physics, Massachusetts Institute of Technology.
Irwin G. Gunsalus, Chemistry and Chemical Engineering, University of Illinois.

Robert Hofstadter, Physics, Stanford University; Nobel Laureate 1961.

Arthur Kornberg, Biochemistry, Stanford University, Medical School; Nobel Laureate 1959.

Fritz Lipmann, Rockefeller University; Nobel Laureate 1953.

Robert B. Livingstone, School of Medicine, University of California at San Diego.

Matthew Meselson, The Biological Laboratories, Harvard University.

Severo Ochoa, New York University School of Medicine; Nobel Laureate 1959.

Ray D. Owen, Division of Biological Sciences, California Institute of Technology.

Keith R. Porter, The Biological Laboratories, Harvard University.

Charles Price, Chemistry, University of Pennsylvania.

Eugene Rabinowitch, Botany, University of Illinois.

E. L. Tatum, Rockefeller University; Nobel Laureate 1958.

George Wald, The Biological Laboratories, Harvard University.

Paul Dudley White, Boston, Massachusetts.

Before this was presented it collected signatures of 50,000 scientists.

Resolutions expressing concern over or opposition to CBW have also been passed by the American Anthropological Society, The American Society for the Advancement of Science, and the Physicians for Social Responsibility. In addition, numerous individuals have written pamphlets and articles in an attempt to inform the Administration of their disapproval and present the facts to the public.

With respect to defoliants in particular, the American Association for the Advancement of Science began applying pressure in 1966 for a consideration of the long-term effects of the use of herbicides and defoliants in Vietnam. A response from the Defense Department came in the form of a letter signed by John S. Foster, Jr, Director of Defense Research and Engineering. This letter, dated 29 September 1967, read in part:

As you know, we have considered the possibility that the use of herbicides and defoliants might cause short or long-term ecological impacts in the areas concerned. The questions of whether such impacts exist, and, if they do, whether they are detrimental or advantageous, have not yet been answered definitively, even though these chemicals have been used commercially in large quantities for many years. Qualified scientists, both inside and outside our government, and in the governments of other nations, have judged that seriously adverse consequences will not occur. Unless we had confidence in these judgments, we would not continue to employ these materials.

The AAAS considered sending an investigating team to Vietnam but came up against financial and practical difficulties. As a compromise, the Defense Department conducted an investigation of its own, under contract no. DAHC 15-68-C-0119 from the Advance Research Projects Agency. This contract went to the Midwest Research Institute, which undertook a review of all the available literature on the subject of the effects of defoliation and herbicide. The summary report, 'Assessment of Ecological Effects of Extensive or Repeated Use of Herbicides', was released by the Pentagon in February 1968 and listed six conclusions:

(1) Destruction of vegetation is the greatest ecological consequence of using herbicides. . . . Secondary growth or replacement vegetation invades rapidly under the tropical conditions of Vietnam, and partially killed or defoliated trees exhibit rapid recovery.

(2) Long term effects on wildlife may be beneficial or detrimental. In many temperate zones, herbicidal treatment of forest has improved the wildlife habitat and favoured animal production through increases in wildlife food plants. Destruction or modification of the habitat may greatly influence fauna that are rare or in danger of extinction.

(3) Herbicides now in use in Vietnam will not persist at a phytotoxic (poisonous to plants) level in the soil for long periods.

(4) The possibility of lethal toxicity to humans, domestic animals or wildlife by the use of herbicides is highly unlikely. Direct toxicity to people and animals on the ground is nonexistent.

(5) . . . herbicides seldom persist in animal or insect tissue. Transfer of herbicides to the next animal in the chain . . . is negligible. Most herbicides including those used in Vietnam are readily excreted and do not accumulate in the animal body.

(6) . . . Direct toxic effects on fish and aquatic organisms are negligible. Destruction of specific plants used for fish foods will lead to changes in the food chain of the aquatic exosystem. Application of herbicides to remove floating weeds will provide important benefits because their presence depletes the oxygen content of the water.

The summary is less specific about defoliants:

> reliable judgement could not be made with respect to the effect
> of defoliants on water quality, on mammals and birds in danger
> of extinction, on climate and the hydrological cycle or on soil
> erosion.

The full report was then passed to the National Academy of Sciences
for further assessment. Both this assessment and the report itself
then went to the AAAS for comment. The issue of *Science* (the AAAS
journal) for 19 July 1968 carried a statement by the Board of
Directors of the Association, which included the following:

> Our review of these documents leaves us with the conviction that
> many questions concerning the long-range ecological influences of
> chemical herbicides remain unanswered. The extent of long-term
> deleterious effects of the forest defoliation in Vietnam is one of
> these unanswered questions. We do agree that the use of arsenicals
> on crops may have serious hazards, and we are concerned with the
> ultimate route taken by arsenical compounds in plants, soil, and
> animals. Therefore, on the basis of the information available to
> us, we do not share the confidence expressed by the Department
> of Defense (in the letter of 29 September 1967 quoted above) that
> seriously adverse consequences will not occur as a result of the use
> of herbicidal chemicals in Vietnam, insofar as arsenical com-
> pounds are concerned.
>
> In the course of our study, we became aware of the serious
> concern expressed by scientists in Vietnam over long-term en-
> vironmental consequences of the military use of herbicides.
> Extensive claims of environmental poisoning through use of these
> agents have been made. Because of uncertainties in available
> evidence on the long-term effects of such materials, such charges
> cannot now be answered unequivocally.
>
> Because large-scale employment of herbicides has taken place in
> Vietnam, and because questions of the long-term welfare of all the
> people of Vietnam are of great importance to the United States
> and other countries, we urge that steps be promptly undertaken
> to initiate detailed, long-term, on-the-spot studies of the regions of
> Vietnam affected by the use of herbicides. If rehabilitation of
> lands adversely affected by these agents is required, ecological
> studies initiated now will be of substantial value in defining the
> required programs. If defoliation has produced or can produce
> beneficial influences on the food-producing capacity of the affected
> regions, these possibilities should be evaluated fully so that they

can be most effectively exploited for the benefit of the Vietnamese people.

Accordingly, we urge that a field study be undertaken under the auspices and direction of the United Nations, with the participation of Vietnamese scientists and scientists from other countries, and with cooperation, support, and protection provided by the contending forces in the area. This study, which could well be supplemented by experimental work elsewhere, should provide a detailed environmental analysis of the long-range effects of the agents used and of the steps necessary to assure optimum future productivity of the environment for the welfare of its inhabitants.

Further, we urge that the maximum possible amount of relevant data be released from military security, so that the scientists conducting the study may know the areas affected, the agents used, the dates applied, and the dosages employed.

We express especial concern about the use of arsenical herbicides in Vietnam, and urge that their use be suspended, if it has not already been stopped, until the ultimate fate of the degraded arsenical compounds can be more reliably determined.

We recognize the difficulties involved in the proposed field study; however, it is our hope that the feasibility of such a study may be increased as a result of the current peace talks in Paris.

Finally, we hope the recommended study can be initiated promptly and we proffer the good offices of the Association in helping to plan it and to publicize its findings.

This report was signed by the following people:

Don K. Price, *Retiring President and Chairman, Board of Directors*
Walter Orr Roberts, *President*
H. Bentley Glass, *President-Elect*
Paul E. Klopsteg, *Treasurer*
Barry Commoner, Hudson Hoagland, Gerald Holton, Mina S. Rees, Leonard M. Rieser, H. B. Steinbach, Kenneth V. Thimann, Dael Wolfle

Two supplementary statements were published by other members:

The confidence of the Department of Defense that seriously adverse consequences will not occur as a result of the dissemination of herbicides by military operations in Vietnam is unwarranted, we believe, not only with respect to arsenical materials, but also with respect to 2,4-D and 2,4,5-T. According to the Midwest Research Institute report, the latter are being sprayed in Vietnam at dosage levels about ten times greater than the levels used in domestic applications. Therefore the estimates regarding possible long-term effects that are derived from domestic experience are not applicable in Vietnam. Since, to our knowledge, there are no relevant observations in Vietnam itself, it is not possible at this time to make a reasonably accurate prediction of the long-term effects of dissemination of 2,4-D and 2,4,5-T. However, there are specific reasons to anticipate certain important hazards from the use of these herbicides in Vietnam. According to the MRI report (pages 198–200), 2,4-D inhibits the formation of nitrogen-fixing nodules in leguminous plants; plants of this type are particularly important in tropical vegetation. In addition, according to the MRI report (pages 201–203), 2,4-D and related herbicides induce serious chromosomal abnormalities in various higher plants by interfering with the mitotic apparatus that governs the behaviour of chromosomes during cell division. Evidence advanced by the MRI report that these herbicides do not cause mutations in bacteria is irrelevant since bacteria lack the chromosomal apparatus which is affected by the herbicides. Hence, intensive use of 2,4-D and 2,4,5-T in Vietnam may cause widespread chromosomal damage among plants, with effects—on the genetic characteristics of the affected plants and therefore on their ecological behaviour—that cannot be foreseen at this time. For these reasons, we believe that the scientific grounds for the use of herbicide chemical weapons in Vietnam—that is, Department of Defense confidence in the judgment that they will cause no long-term effects—are not valid. Accordingly, in keeping with the precept stated in the Department's letter of 29 September 1967, the herbicide program should be stopped. Apart from the morality of the war itself, which is not at issue here, continued use of a weapon with effects that are so poorly understood raises serious moral and political questions for the U.S. government and for the American people. These ought to be carefully considered in the present national debate on the morality and political wisdom of the war in Vietnam.

Barry Commoner, Gerald Holton, H. Burr Steinbach

And a different view:

We consider that the use of 2,4-D and 2,4,5-T for defoliation of forest cover probably represents a military device for saving lives

that has an unprecedented degree of harmlessness to the environment. We consider that the material in the Midwest Research
Institute report in general supports this view.

Walter Orr Roberts, Kenneth V. Thimann

This whole process took almost two years, and seems to have left us
in the same state of uncertainty as before. No official investigation
has yet been undertaken, use of these substances is still escalating,
and concern in scientific circles still growing.

The British Government's Attitude

The British government's attitude to the use of chemicals in Vietnam is one of purposeful ignorance. When the news of the use of
gas in Vietnam first broke in March 1965, Michael Stewart (Foreign
Secretary) was in Washington. He received a strong telegram of
protest from six Labour back benchers:

> Urge you convey United States Government horror indignation
> aroused Parliament and country at use by United States forces in
> Vietnam of gas and napalm and at threat by United States Ambas-
> sador at Saigon of unlimited extension of war. Signed on behalf
> of large number M.P.s Philip Noel-Baker, Arthur Blenkinsop,
> Tom Driberg, John Mendelson, Michael Foot, Sydney Silverman.

At the same time a motion was tabled in parliament:

> That this house deplores the use of napalm and gas by United
> States forces in Vietnam; and, in view of the statement by the
> United States Ambassador in Saigon that there is no limit to the
> potential increase of the war in Vietnam, calls on her Majesty's
> Government to dissociate Great Britain from these actions and
> views, in order to be able more effectively to mediate in this
> conflict.

(It collected 104 signatures before it was withdrawn.)

On Michael Stewart's return there was a foreign affairs debate
in the House of Commons (1 April 1965) at which Mr Stewart said:

> I think at this point I ought to say something about methods
> of warfare. If this debate had occurred a few days earlier I should
> have been expected to deal particularly with the use of gas. As the
> debate occurs when it does I might perhaps refer more to the
> terrible incident in Saigon the other day.

The 'terrible incident' referred to here was a terrorist bomb attack. In spite of probing by several back-benchers Mr Stewart made no other reference to the American use of gas during the debate.

Previously at the airport, on his arrival from Washington, Mr Stewart explicitly stated 'Britain wholly supports American policy in Vietnam'.

There has never been any dissociation from this policy. On 21 May 1968 the following exchange took place in the House of Commons between Dr David Kerr MP and the Foreign Secretary: Dr David Kerr (Wandsworth Central, Labour) asked the Foreign Secretary whether he would dissociate Britain from the use of chemical and biological warfare by the United States in Vietnam.

MR. STEWART (Fulham, Labour).—I am not aware of any American activity in this field to warrant our dissociation.

DR. KERR.—Would the Foreign Secretary go back to those people who advise him, and inform them that one Australian officer has died during a gas attack in Vietnam, and that the use of defoliants in Vietnam cannot be characterized as anything other than the use of chemical and biological warfare—warfare which is not against military targets.

Although the excuse is used that defoliation is to expose guerrillas, it is occasioning starvation to an already starving population.

MR. STEWART—Dr. Kerr has given one of the most important reasons for the use of defoliants. If this stops ambush raids it is saving lives. It is inevitable in the course of operations of war there will be interdiction of food supplies. I am not aware of the use of any lethal gases.

The use of gases and chemicals in Vietnam poses many questions both of a scientific and ethical nature. These will be more fully discussed later. Two points in particular, well illustrated in this documentation, should perhaps be mentioned here.

The first of these is the part played by public opinion in the escalation of the use of these agents. The six-month suspension in the use of gas indicates that if public opinion is strong enough it can be effective. The subsequent resumption and escalation show how it can also be manipulated.

The second point is the apparent considerable powers exercised by the military commanders in Vietnam. The delegation of power to authorise the use of gas to area commanders, and the almost unquestioning supply of defoliants to military commanders on the grounds that they know best what is useful, should give rise to some concern. In view of the conflicting reports of exactly which gases and chemicals are in fact in use and even greater discrepancy between the effects of these agents in theory and in practice, this somewhat loose control of their use would seem to be a dangerous precedent.

Vietnam is a problem which is still with us. There are, however, indications that a situation is now growing in the Middle East in which chemicals will be used. The BBC has reported that allegations were made that on 28 July Israel used gas in bombing raids on Jordan, but no reports have appeared in the British press.

There is one thing in common to all these situations, Yemen, Vietnam and Jordan. All are situations which can be described as 'counter-insurgency' or 'guerilla warfare'. This is very significant because no effective means have been found so far of combating this type of warfare. If chemicals prove useful, their use will continue despite any international laws banning them.

2. BIOLOGICAL WARFARE

Any documentation of biological warfare is difficult in so far as all the allegations are based solely on after-the-event eyewitness accounts and circumstantial evidence. The latter must include an assessment of the weapons available at the time. Moreover, the allegations have in most cases been denied by the accused parties.

The first allegations were made against German attempts to employ biological agents during World War I. According to Mr George Merck, in a report submitted to the US Secretary for War on 4 January 1946, there was:

incontrovertible evidence... that in 1915 German agents inoculated horses and cattle leaving US ports for shipment to the Allies with disease-producing bacteria.

The Germans are also accused of inoculating horses with glanders and cattle with anthrax at Bucharest in 1916. (Mentioned by Le Renard 1936, Popescu 1936, Duffour 1937, Le Bourdelles 1939, and fully documented by de Flers 1919.) Similar incidents are purported to have taken place on the French front in 1917. In addition, attempts were also apparently made to spread cholera in Italy (Duffour and Le Bourdelles).

World War II produced several more vague accusations against Germany.

The Soviet Extraordinary Commission established that the Germans took deliberate steps to spread typhus among the Soviet population and the Red Army.

[Statement adopted by the General Assembly of the World Medical Association, 1948]

The Merck report mentions that US intelligence had obtained evidence to indicate that:

the Axis powers were behind the US and Canada in their work on biological warfare.

This, however, did not prevent the allies taking certain precautions.

Late in the war I took 235,000 dosages of a toxoid against one particularly vicious biological to England and we administered it to troops of the US, Britain and Canada. We let the Germans know through their spy channels so they would understand that we were prepared to use biologicals if they started it.

[Dr Brock Chisholm—Major-General commanding the Royal Canadian Medical Corps during the war and first Director of the World Health Organisation]

According to the record of the Nuremburg Tribunal, one of those involved in germ warfare experimentation during the war was Dr Walter P. Schreiber, who was at that time head of the Scientific Department Group C of the Military Academy in Berlin.

The allegations made against Japan seem to have more substance to them. According to the introduction to the Merck Report,

Intelligence reports ... show that Japan had made definite progress in biological warfare ... it is known that the Japanese Army fostered offensive developments in this field from 1936 until as late as 1945. ... Modifications of various weapons developed through research in their laboratories were field tested at Army proving grounds. ... While definite progress was made, the Japanese had not at the time the war ended reached a position whereby these offensive projects could have been placed in operational use.

Somewhat later the same year, the respected war correspondent of the *New York Times* reported:

The Japanese had developed, before the war ended, a crude anthrax bomb, and they had a BW factory near Harbin in Manchuria which was producing toxins or bacteriological poisons.

[27 September 1946]

China accused Japan of using plague bacillus on a number of occasions. This was supported by the Surgeon-General of the US Public Health Service, Thomas Parran, and also by a League of Nations epidemiologist, R. Pollitzer [*Medical Record*, 1942, 155].

Supporting evidence came from the record of the proceedings of the trial held at Khabarovsk in the USSR in December 1949 of twelve Japanese prisoners (Moscow 1950). The following picture emerges.

The Japanese BW programme was largely the responsibility of two detachments of the Kwangtung Army. These were established in 1935 in north-east China. General Shiro Ishii, said to be the main inspiration behind the whole programme, commanded Detachment 731,

> engaged in devising and producing bacteriological weapons intended for the wholesale extermination of human beings.

Detachment 100, under the charge of Jiro Wakamatsu,

> was limited to devising and producing bacteriological weapons of sabotage in the form of exterminating animals and contaminating crops.

Neither of the above-mentioned commanders was captured by the USSR and therefore neither appeared personally at the trial.

Extensive development apparently began in 1931, and five years later two large establishments were built in Manchuria. The main agents mentioned were plague, cholera, typhoid and anthrax, the main vector used was the flea, and the three methods of dissemination discussed were spraying from aircraft, bombing and direct contamination of water and land. Various outbreaks of plague and typhoid were attributed to BW attack.

According to the Report of the International Scientific Commission for the Investigation of the Facts Concerning Bacterial Warfare in Korea and China (Peking 1952):

> From the archives of the Chinese Ministry of Health one of the original reports dealing with the artificial induction of plague at Changte in Hunun province by the Japanese in 1941 was laid before the Commission. Official Chinese records give the number of hsien cities which were attacked in this way by the Japanese as 11, 4 in Chekiang, 2 each in Hopei and Honan, and 1 each in Shansi, Hunan and Shantung. The total number of victims of artificially disseminated plague is now assessed by the Chinese as approximately 700 between 1940 and 1944.

(a) KOREA AND NORTH CHINA

In December 1951 two dispatches, one from Telepress (Rangoon, 5 December) and the other from Reuter (9 December), reported that on the instructions of General Ridgway the three BW experts named at the Khabarovsk trial, General Shiro Ishii, General Jiro Wakamatsu and General Masajo Kitano had been sent to Korea.

In March 1952 the following report appeared in *Time* magazine:

> Dr. Schreiber, it developed, had been brought to the US in a Defense Department scoop-up of German technical men known as 'Operation Paperclip'. His job: consultant to the Airforce in a division with the grandiloquent title 'Global Preventive Medicine' [10 March 1952].

The first official complaint that the USA was using BW in Korea was lodged with the United Nations by the North Korean Government on 8 May 1951. Further allegations were made in 1952, together with a statement by Chou-en-lai, the Chinese Minister for Foreign Affairs, that BW attacks had also been made over north-east China.

These charges were categorically denied by both State Department and military officials. The United States immediately requested both the World Health Organisation and the International Committee of the Red Cross to investigate the allegations. Neither of these organisations, however, was acceptable to China, and in 1952 a supposedly independent commission, the International Scientific Commission, composed of personnel that were acceptable, was set up and invited to Korea and China to conduct the necessary investigations. The report of the findings, which was published in Peking in August, was signed by the following people: *Dr Andrea Andreen*, MD PHD (Director of the Central Clinical Laboratory of the Hospital Boards, Stockholm); *M. Jean Malterre*, Ingénieur-Agricole (Director of the Laboratory of Animal Physiology, National College of Agriculture, Grignon, formerly UNRRA livestock expert); *Dr Joseph Needham*, SCD FRS (Sir William Dunn Reader in Biochemistry, University of Cambridge, formerly Director of the Department of Natural Sciences UNESCO); *Dr Oliviero Olive*, MD (Professor of Human Anatomy, University of Bologna); *Dr Samuel B. Pessoa*, MD (Professor of Parasitology at the University of Sao Paulo, formerly Director of Public Health for the State of Sao Paulo); and *Dr N. Zhukov-Verezhnikov*, MD (Professor of Bacteriology and Vice-President of Soviet Academy of Medicine, formerly chief medical expert at the Khabarovsk trial).

The evidence presented to the commission comprised fragments of bombs and other containers, eye-witness accounts and written accounts and 'confessions' by captured pilots and intelligence agents. Extensive scientific tests were made where possible, and these, together with any other comment, will be detailed in Part 2. The incidents of BW attacks said by the ISC to have occurred in 1951 and 1952 are given below.

Incidents in Korea

Since the beginning of 1952, numerous isolated foci of plague have appeared in North Korea always associated with the sudden appearance of numbers of fleas and with the previous passage of American planes. Seven of these incidents, the earliest dating from February 11th, were reported in SIA/1 (Report of Korean Medical Service dealing with Jan./Feb. 1952) and in six of them the presence of plague bacteria in fleas was demonstrated. Document SIA/4 (Report of the International Democratic Lawyers Commission) added the statement that after a delivery of fleas to the neighbourhood of An Ju on the 18th February, fleas which were shown bacteriologically to contain pasteurella pestis, a plague epidemic broke out at Bal-Nam-Ri in that district on 25th. Out of a population of 600 in the village 50 went down with plague and 36 died.

According to the best information which the Commission was able to obtain, for the past five centuries there has been no plague in Korea. The nearest endemic centres are 300 miles away in NE China.... Moreover, the month of February would be no less than 3 months too early for the normal appearance of plague cases in this climate. Above all, the fleas appearing were not rat fleas, which more usually carry plague in a state of nature, but human fleas.

The Kan-Nan incident (NE China)

On the morning of 5th April 1952, the country folk of 4 villages situated within the area administered from the town of Kan-Nan, awoke to find themselves surrounded by large numbers of a rat-like animal.... During the previous night many of the villagers had heard a plane pass overhead and information provided by the Chinese Air Observer Corps shows that after having crossed the Yalu River just before 10.00 p.m., it was over Kan-Nan about 11.30, it then retraced its course as if its mission had been accomplished. It was identified by the Corps as an American F-28 double fuselage night-fighter plane. In the morning the villagers found many of the voles dying or dead in their houses and courtyards, on their roofs and even on their beds, while others were scattered around the outskirts of the settlement. The total number collected and destroyed in and near the inhabited places of an area measuring approximately 3 × 9 miles was 717. There was an anomaly of season, for small rodents do not usually begin to show themselves in this region until a month later, and then in nothing approaching such numbers. The location was also anomalous, for voles are not frequenters of human settlements. The species concerned also seems to be regionally anomalous. It had never before been seen by the local people.... The Kan-Nan area has never known any form of plague so far as records are available and reasons more than adequate were given to show that a migration of the voles from the nearest endemic areas must be regarded in view of the distance and obstacles involved as highly unlikely. Furthermore, the season was at least a month too early for the normal occurrence of epizootics of plague among rodents in endemic areas.... The principal gap in the evidence consists in the fact that no container or bomb was found. However... in January 1952 there was described in a Japanese journal (*Mainichi*) a container and parachute made of strong paper in such a manner that it would burn away, leaving no trace, after depositing its cargo of infected rats. Other Japanese press reports (*Kowa Shimbun*, August 1952) revealed the existence of a breeding institute directed by Ojawa, a former assistant of Shiro Ishii, which produces a large number of rodents.

The K'uan-Tien incident

On the 12th March, 1952, inhabitants of the town of K'uan Tien, which lies in the south eastern part of Liaotung province near the Yalu River, saw 8 American fighter planes pass over the city about half an hour after noon.... From one of them there was distinctly seen to drop a bright cylindrical object. Immediately afterwards and during the following days, the people of the town including schoolboys organised searches in the region beyond the east gate where the object appeared to have fallen and collected many anthomyiid flies and spiders.

Nine days after the original incident, one of the schoolboys was so fortunate as to discover fragments of a container in and around a shallow crater at the point of impact of the object. The location was a maize field constituted by a small island surrounded by the beds of rivers dry at this time of the year. The largest 'bomb' fragments was of metal, but the most numerous were of a thin porous calcareous substance the nature of which was not immediately obvious.

... The insects and arachnids showed an anomaly of seasonal appearance and the former also a regional anomaly as a zoological species. Competent bacteriological examination by the Chinese demonstrated the presence of the pathogenic organism causing anthrax. The occurrence of this on the arthropods must be considered a highly extraordinary phenomenon.... No cases of anthrax in or around the town were reported as a result of this intervention.

Incidents in Liaotung and Liaohsi

The commission gave exhaustive study to a group of cases in which American planes, coming from across the Yalu River and returning thither were seen to drop objects of various kinds.

(These included beetles, feathers and house flies, all contaminated with anthrax; the planes were usually F-86 fighters and the containers of various types—see Part 2.)

The evidence concerning aircraft, containers, biological objects appearing and bacteriological tests, was now amplified for a number of localities, by concrete and well analysed data concerning human cases of respiratory anthrax and haemorrhagic anthrax meningitis. Five of these were examined, a railwayman, a tricycle rickshaw driver, a housewife, a schoolteacher and a farmer. All of these fell sick of a disease which ran a similar rapid course.... The commission satisfied itself that none of the cases had the customary occupational history connected with anthrax. The beetles appear to have been responsible for two deaths, while the flies and feathers would have accounted for another two ... four out of the five had not only collected the insects and the feathers in the general course of such organised hunts, but were known to have dispensed with the recognised precautions followed by most people, that is to say, had failed to protect the respiratory passages by a mask or had handled the objects without gloves or forceps.

The Dai Dong Incident

Early in the morning after a night (16 May) during which a plane had been heard circling round for an hour or more ... a country girl picking herbs on the hillside found a straw package containing a certain kind of clam. She took some of the clams home and she and her husband made a meal of them, on the evening of the same day both fell ill and by the evening of the following day both were dead. Medical evidence showed that the cause of death was cholera. Further packages of clams were found on the hillsides . . . and bacteriological examination proved that the clams were heavily infected with the cholera vibrio . . . the appearance of marine molluscs contaminated in this way on a hill in the middle of the countryside can only be described as a highly unnatural phenomenon. The human fatalities, moreover, were epidemiologically very abnormal. Evidence presented convinced the Commission that cholera has never been an endemic disease in Korea, for while there have been a number of outbreaks in the last 40 years, it has always been possible to trace them to a maritime point of entry.. . . Light was thrown on the sequence of events when the nature of the locality was examined. The clams were found in a zone some 400 yards from a pumping station at the top of a hill and some 1000 yards from a series of reservoirs . . . distributed, partly for drinking to several coastal settlements and port towns. On the night previous to that during which the clams made their appearance, the purification plant adjacent to the pumping station had been accurately destroyed by American bombers using small bombs, the pumps themselves being undamaged.

The above is a brief synopsis of the incidents mentioned particularly in the Commission's report. The report also goes into detail on the containers used and offers supportive evidence from four American pilots, Lt K. L. Enoch (navigator), Lt John Quinn (pilot), Lt F. B. O'Neal and Lt Paul Kniss, and from intelligence agents including Wang Chi. For reasons of both lack of space and lack of credibility, these will not be detailed here although reference is made to them in Part 2, as the Commission report itself states,

Those who did not wish to be convinced, tended to brush them aside as confessions obtained under physical or mental duress . . .

It continues . . .

The Commission had the opportunity of extended conversation with these men under conditions of free discourse. Its members unanimously formed the opinion that no pressure, physical or mental had been brought to bear upon these prisoners of war. . . .

There is little more that can be said about Korea except that the charges have been emphatically denied by the American authorities, and in most cases those responsible for the testimonials repudiated them on their return to the United States. The whole thing has been written off almost unanimously as Communist propaganda.

Trygve Lie ridiculed the charges. Dr Brock Chisholm of WHO has flatly said that if germ warfare were being waged it would have been known soon enough since millions would die; and Lie offered the services of the UN health organisation to stem any epidemic raging in Korea and China.

Washington issued a series of flat denials ranging from those of Secretary Acheson and General Ridgway to those of the UN delegate Benjamin Cohen in the UN Disarmament Commission. And Warren Austin, chief US delegate to the UN, wrote to Frederic Joliot Curie, the French atom scientist, expressing his astonishment that he gave support to the Communist charges. In these circumstances a Pentagon effort to discredit Communist propaganda photographs created something of a muddle.

On 3 April A. M. Rosenthal, UN correspondent of the *New York Times*, submitted a series of Chinese germ warfare photographs to US experts who denounced them to be fakes. One of these was that of a 'germ bomb ... which for physical reasons is not adaptable even theoretically for carrying germs', Rosenthal went to Washington to check the facts with the Pentagon and was told:

> This is a photograph of the US 500 lb. size leaflet bomb. This bomb does not explode and is used to disseminate leaflets from aircraft.
>
> A Pentagon spokesman [the *Times* wrote] added that the leaflet bomb even theoretically was not adaptable to germ warfare. He said that the leaflet bombs were made with holes in them. Any germs in the bomb would be killed by pressure as the missile descended.

Less than twenty-four hours after the *New York Times* published this story the Associated Press carried a report from Washington of a statement by the Chairman of the House Appropriations Sub-Committee which had held secret sessions on the bacteriological warfare budget. This committee heard testimony from Major-General E. T. Bullene, Chief of the Chemical Corps. Reporter Robert L. F. Sikes, reporting on his testimony, was precise on the matter of weapons.

'Actually,' he said, 'retaliatory bacteriological warfare does not involve some complicated super weapon. The means of delivering germs to enemy territory are simple and involve equipment of the type with which the services are already well stocked ... such as the containers used currently for dropping propaganda leaflets.'

The standard reaction to the ISC report is well illustrated by the following extract from an article which appeared in *Worldview* in June 1965.

The World Peace Council was also used to launch the so-called 'germ warfare' campaign in March, 1952. This worldwide campaign reached a peak of intensity during the Korean War. It was provided a phony but impressive documentary base by an international scientific commission which was hand picked and sent to North Korea and North East China. The report later supplemented by forced 'confessions' of American aviators ... was the key to the whole bacteriological warfare campaign. In spite of the fraudulent nature of the so-called documentation, the hearsay evidence presented, the obviously fake exhibits of bacterial bombs and other paraphernalia the campaign as a whole was a major propaganda triumph.

As with other Soviet propaganda campaigns, the credibility of the charges was enhanced by the support of leading Communists and fellow travellers in the West....

(b) VIETNAM

The inclusion of Vietnam in this section is perhaps open to misinterpretation as no specific charges of biological weapons having been used have been made. Vietnam in this context, however, does serve to illustrate a very important point, which will be discussed in the comment at the end.

The most horrifying aspect of the Vietnamese war is one which so far seems largely to have escaped notice. On 26 October 1966 the World Health Organisation announced that up to October of that year 306 cases of plague and twenty-two deaths have been reported in South Vietnam, and further it was the suspected cause of 2158 cases and 107 deaths.

The *Sunday Times* of 30 October 1966 reported that from January to August there had been 2002 cases and 116 deaths in South Vietnam.

The increase has been relentless. In 1961 only one province in the combat zone was affected. Today 22 out of 29 provinces north of Saigon have been hit by the plague.

Reference was made to the difficulties involved in obtaining any definite figures on plague in Vietnam. The figures quoted are probably very conservative estimates.

Earlier in the same year, on 2 September 1966, *Time* magazine carried the following article:

> War and disease have always been fellow travellers. U.S. troops in Vietnam are fighting Malaria as well as the human enemy, but now, according to a report jointly issued by U.S. Army Medical Research Team in Vietnam and the Institute Pasteur of Saigon, another killer is mounting a virulent attack. Bubonic Plague, the Black Death that slaughtered a third of Western Europe during the 14th Century, has suddenly started claiming casualties by the thousand. In 1961 only 8 cases were reported in South Vietnam, last year some 4,500 cases were recognised and there were upward of 200 deaths. So far this year half the Republic's provinces have registered Plague cases ... the Plague has no significant effect on U.S. troops since every man receives two shots before arriving in Vietnam and Boosters every 4 months. For Vietnamese living in Government-controlled areas vaccine and treatment are always available, but for the enemy V.C., North Vietnamese troops, and those living in V.C. areas the Plague may become a more deadly killer than either side expected.

According to the World Health Organisation's recent report *Epidemiological Situation in Vietnam*, cases of plague have now been reported from twenty-four out of forty-seven provinces in the south and plague infection has been found in rodents in several ports and airports including Saigon, Nha Trang, Cam Rahn and Da Nang.

WHO statistics show no cases of plague in any country surrounding Vietnam except Burma, which has a consistent but steady 100 or so cases a year.

The report cited above mentions that the pneumonic form of plague is now on the increase in the south of Vietnam. Reported in June 1966, it had not appeared previously for more than twenty-five years.

On another aspect of this subject, the following information appeared in an article by Carol Brightman in the June/July issue of *Viet Report* in 1966.

> In early July, a congressional employee had alerted the PSR (Physicians for Social Responsibility) members of a new drive to intensify development of chemical and biological weapons for

Vietnam. They were also informed that a New England firm had contracted a project from the Defense Department to adapt Bubonic Plague for aerial dissemination in South Vietnam. Congressmen Kastenmeier of Wisconsin, Burton of California, and Brademus of Indiana confirmed that similar reports had reached them. Congressman Mathias of Maryland, in whose district Fort Detrick is located, further noted that he understood the budget for CBW was being increased by 25%.

The germ warfare report was confirmed by an executive of the New England firm, Travelers' Research Corporation of Hartford Connecticut, formerly a medical subsidiary of Travelers' Insurance Company. The executive said that since the contract Travelers' operations had become classified, but he stated that it had necessitated a vast expansion in laboratory facilities and personnel (including military personnel). Moreover, he said that the contract was a 'crash program' to produce large quantities of the bacilli that induce Bubonic Plague and Tularemia. PSR members all over the country asked their congressmen to inquire further. Replies came from Harold Brown, Director of Defense; Peter A. Erikson, Director for Information Services, Defense; and Douglas MacArthur III, Assistant Secretary for Congressional Relations, Department of State. Each of them categorically denied the reports. Harold Brown's letter to Senator Edward Kennedy on July 29 1965, was typical: 'We are not advocating the use of biological weapons in Vietnam. . . . There is no contract such as that purported to have been established with a New England concern for the preparation of biological agents in general or bubonic plague specifically. . . .' The PSR Executive Committee, to which Senator Kennedy had forwarded this reply, wrote Brown on August 19 saying: 'We are delighted that not only our fears were groundless, but even more important, that an important agency of our government has reaffirmed the position expressed by President Roosevelt in 1943 that the United States will not initiate bacteriological warfare.' In conclusion PSR noted that in its opinion this position was not generally appreciated. 'We should like permission to distribute your statement widely as a statement of policy of the U.S. Government.' One month passed before Harold Brown's reply.

Meanwhile, on August 27 1965, Jack Anderson (sitting in for Drew Pearson) reported that after receiving his own official Pentagon denial, 'this column told a different story'. In a telephone interview Dr. Ellis, Director of germ warfare studies at

Travelers' Research, acknowledged that the company had contracts with the Air Force's Office of Scientific Research and the Army Materiel Command. He explained that the company was studying the 'behaviour of toxics in the environment', or specifically, the use of air currents for delivery of toxic clouds over a target. 'Other research too secret to talk about' was also being pursued. In view of the earlier denial by the Pentagon, Anderson asked the Air Force to check again 'whether it had a germ warfare contract with the Travelers' Research'. Pentagon spokesmen then admitted that the company was working on germ warfare research, but that this also included a study of 'attitudes within the leadership element of the U.S. Government toward the employment of incapacitating weapons and the reaction of probable public opinion'. Anderson was instructed to add that the 'point is that biological warfare could be humane. Our laboratories have developed germs that can incapacitate a whole nation. . . . The population would be too weak to resist invasion.'

While waiting for Brown's reply, some Washington physicians made contact with a high level State Department Official and a White House Aide, both of whom further confirmed the reports on germ warfare, but added that it was not Bubonic Plague but Tularemia which was being developed. The White House Aide indicated that a final decision to use this weapon had not yet been made, but there was a good chance it would be used and spread in such a way as to enable U.S. forces to deny responsibility and say that it was a naturally occurring epidemic. The 'good chance' for its use, the aide explained, was based on a memo sent from the State Department to the President in mid-June, 1965, in which its long standing opposition to the use of such weapons was reversed.

On September 13th Harold Brown made his reply. He repeated that the 'rumours' reported by PSR 'had no basis of truth' but also, since there might be some members 'who are troubled by these rumours but who have not written to their representatives in Congress' he agreed 'to the distribution to your membership of my letter to Senator Edward M. Kennedy'. To the PSR's real request, Brown answered: 'Since my statements were intended to be a factual response to specific questions rather than a general statement of policy, I do not believe they should be distributed beyond the audience intended, that is, the membership of your organisation.'

And in the *New York Times* of 20 September 1966:

> According to Jonathan Beckwith, Assistant Professor in the Department of Bacteriology at Harvard Medical School 'Work is being conducted in this country to purposefully construct highly pathogenic bacterial strains resistant to anti-biotics.' 'In particular,' he said, 'it has come to our attention that researchers in one of the Government centres studying germ warfare have created amongst others a strain of *Pasteurella pestis* (Plague bacteria) which has been infected with a factor making it resistant to most of the common anti-biotics. Thus not only are we developing ways to spread Plague amongst the enemy but we shall be able to do it in such a way that treatment may be impossible.

The *Sunday Times* on 28 April 1968 said:

> The first indication that the US was in a state of readiness to launch germ attacks in Vietnam slipped by virtually unnoticed last month, following rumours that the storage of American weapons of biological warfare at special bases in Thailand was supervised in an incompetent manner.... The American Navy Department ... denied that germ munitions were to blame. The Navy Department's accompanying comment, however, confirmed that biological munitions stockpiles did exist.

All the above evidence is circumstantial. It serves to illustrate that in our current state of knowledge any allegation that biological weapons have been used, given the appropriate circumstances, is almost impossible to prove or disprove. In this case no official charges have in fact been made. There have been specific allegations, however, that BW has been used against vegetation.

The North Vietnamese News Agency reported on 17 October 1966 that larvae of 'killer insects' had been let loose.

> These larvae were let loose on 30th September 1966 on the Cham Thanh district of In Tan province. Route 21 from Duong Zian Hoi to Vinh Cong was affected.
> All rice, plants, fruit trees in a band of 2 kilometers wide either side of the road have been destroyed.

Similar incidents had apparently occurred in mid-August in the villages of Huong My, Minh Duc and Cam Sun in the district of Ny Cay, Mekong Delta. Around the village of Huong My 40 hectares of young plants were killed.

All the alleged incidents of biological warfare documented here will be fully discussed and assessed later.

2

RESEARCH AND EXPENDITURE

1. THE UNITED STATES

Government interest in chemical and biological weapons is largely dictated by the Army Chemical Corps. The corps is responsible for the various establishments and also for contracting some research work to academic and commercial institutions for the Defense Department.

The Army Chemical Corps

On 28 June 1918 the Chemical Warfare Service was established as part of the National Army by direction of the President, under his wartime powers. Its function was to develop, produce and test materials and apparatus for gas warfare, and to organise and train officers and troops in methods of defence against gas. The cws was an amalgamation of several other organisations. By an act of Congress, dated 11 July 1919, the administrative life of the cws was given statutory basis to 30 June 1920.

By another act, on 4 June 1920, which amended the 1916 National Defense Act, it became a permanent part of the military establishment. This amendment made the cws responsible to the Army for investigation, development, manufacture or procurement of all smoke and incendiary materials, all toxic gases, and all gas defence appliances. It was also charged with research, design and experimentation in connection with chemical warfare and its material. In addition the administration of chemical-projectile filling plants, and proving grounds, the supervision of training for the Army in cw (both offensive and defensive), the supervision of the schools of instruction and the organisation, equipment training and operation of special gas troops were to come under its auspices.

On 9 March 1942, reorganisation of the War Department was effected, placing the cws under Services of Supply (later Army Service Forces). Reorganisation of the Army on 11 June 1946 saw the cws revert to its former position as one of the technical services under the General Staff. On 6 September 1946 the cws became the Army Chemical Corps. The Army Chemical Corps was responsible for research development into cbw for the Army and for the procurement of weapons.

After the war the Army Chemical Corps began its public relations campaign, which has gone on ever since. Pressure has been continually applied to Congress to get more money for cb research and development. The methods and arguments have varied over the years.

In November 1955 Army Secretary Brucker publicly endorsed a study urging that the use of cbr weapons systems be integrated into us military planning. The report was drawn up by a Civilian Advisory Committee headed by George W. Merck.

At the end of the 1950s 'Operation Blue Skies' was launched in an attempt, on the basis of the newly discovered psychochemicals and incapacitants, to make cbw respectable if not humane.

The campaign had some very eminent military spokesmen. According to Major-General Marshall Stubbs, then head of the corps:

> People fear what they do not understand. We can render a great service to our country by removing the cloak of doubt and suspicion surrounding the use of chemical and biological agents in war.... Recently within the Corps we have accelerated our information programme.

The former head of the corps, Major-General William Creasy stated:

> The present funding for CW and BW research should be at least trebled and an adequate program of manufacture of CW-BW munitions be instituted.

Brigadier General J. H. Rothschild, former head of the Corps Research and Development Command, advocated:

> rejecting once and for all the position that an enemy can have the first chemical and biological blow wherever and whenever he wished ...

The existence of research and development in other countries was also used as an argument for increasing cbw spending. Application was made to Congress by the House Committee on Science and Astronautics on the grounds that:

> The United States is spending $35 to $40 million a year on such (CBR) research....
> Increasing this amount over a two or three year period to a

spending level of around $125 million a year is needed, the committee said, to put this country on a par with the Communists.

[*St Louis-Post Dispatch*, 9 August 1959]

In June 1960 the House Science and Astronautics Committee held hearings to investigate this surge of interest in CB weapons. It established that the Defense Department wanted to increase the programme from the existing level of $40 million to 125 million in the coming years.

The sort of arguments which were brought forward to justify this can be seen from the report of the hearings:

> perhaps CBR research for another decade would not alter the general balance of military power. But if it does and the US has not gained the same capability as others the cost to the nation would be beyond calculation.
>
> ... The best immediate guarantee the US can possess to ensure that CBR is not used anywhere against the free world is to have a strong capability in this field too. This will only come with a stronger program of research.

In his suggestions to the committee, Creasy agreed substantially with Rothschild:

> I am not advocating preventive war but we must change our policy which is that we won't hit back until you hit us. ... I would hate to see us enter into any agreement with anybody regarding CBR so that if we are going to fight we are going to do it with our hands tied behind our backs.

Support for the campaign also came from the American Chemical Society, which had a symposium on CBW in 1960.

A lecture by Clifford F. Rassweiler, a former president of the ACS included the following statement:

> Suppose ... Russia forces us to sign an agreement to banish nuclear warfare. ... Suppose ... Russia unmasks its CW and BW potential and demands our compliance with its terms for world domination. Suppose ... we have developed neither CW and BW retaliatory power nor adequate CW and BW defense. If this supposition seems completely impossible to you or if it leaves you complacent and apathetic about this country's present activity in the field of CW and BW defense, then this symposium has failed.

In 1962 a reorganisation of the Defense Department resulted in the dissolution of the Army Chemical Corps and the transfer of its functions to the Army Materiel Command. Shortly after this a Joint Technical Coordinating Group was set up to coordinate the CBW activities of the various services at all levels. The interest in cbw continued as before.

The following extract is from the testimony before the House Appropriations Committee in 1964. The same arguments are being used.

MR. (ROBERT L. F.) SIKES (D.FLA): In the present world situation where there seems to be an effort to find a way to win wars without resorting to nuclear strikes ... there is a possibility that chemical and biological materials will play a much more important part than they have played heretofore. That would be particularly true if the Russians were to demonstrate a very pronounced capability in that field. Does the possibility concern the Department of the Army?

SECRETARY (CYRUS) VANCE (OF THE ARMY): Yes it does concern the Department of the Army and to that end, sir, we are ... additional munitions during the coming years which would increase rather substantially our capability to deliver chemical and bacteriological weapons on target. In addition we are increasing funds for chemical and biological research and development so as to press forward in new types of weapons which may be able to be used in such a situation. . . .

MR. SIKES: Does intelligence tell us what the Russians are really doing in this field?

SECRETARY VANCE: Our intelligence indicates that they are devoting considerable attention to it. . . .

In November 1964 the Army Chemical Corps launched another campaign. Selected reporters were led on a press tour of Fort Detrick in Maryland. Briefings by civilian and military scientists from the nearby Edgewood Arsenal laboratories emphasised the peaceful byproducts of cbw research, such as advances in bacterial genetics, and discoveries of new forms of artificial respiration from work on nerve gases.

One opinion of the Army Chemical Corps was given to Seymour Hersh by a Pentagon official:

[They] were always overselling everything. . . . The Army Chemical Corps is a cult. Those generals all have Billy Mitchell complexes[1] to infinity. Ideas that the White House or McNamara emphasised when they boosted cbw spending would end up getting perverted by the generals.

Nevertheless the success of the pressure continually applied by the

[1] Billy Mitchell was court-martialled in the 1920s for his vociferous advocacy of the aeroplane.

corps (*New York Review of Books*, April 1968) can be seen in the expenditure figures on CBW in the last few years.

In fiscal year 1961 the R and D Budget for CBW for all three military services was about 57 million dollars. By 1964 it had risen to about 158 million dollars with the Army's share being 115 million dollars. It is now roughly at that level or slightly lower. In 1961 only the Army had money for procurement—about 46 million dollars, in fiscal year 1964 the Army received little more than 117 million dollars for procurement related to CBW, the Navy 11 million dollars and the Air Force 8·7 million dollars. Procurement figures for more recent years are classified.

In 1967 Robin Clarke, editor of *Science Journal*, estimated US expenditure on CBW as 'a good deal more than 200 million dollars a year'. Since then Representative R. D. McCarthy (Democrat, New York) has given a figure for 1969 of 350 million dollars.

Edgewood Arsenal

The arsenal is a government-owned and operated installation of the US Army Munitions Command (MUCOM), Dover, New Jersey, which is in turn part of the US Army Materiel Command (AMC) in Washington DC. The commanding officer is Colonel Paul R. Cerar.

In October 1917 the War Department acquired the 10,000 acre, 8-mile-long point of land in Maryland and established Gunpowder Neck Reservation to house the infant gas warfare service.

In May 1918 the name of the installation was changed to Edgewood Arsenal. The Chemical Warfare School organised at Lakehurst proving ground (New Jersey) was transferred to Edgewood in September 1920.

More than 7000 military personnel and 8000 civilians were employed at the arsenal during peak years of World War II. Through their efforts, the Army developed a capability in research, development, procurement and supply of toxic material for use against the enemy, as well as defensive devices for protection from enemy chemical capabilities.

The wartime atmosphere of the early 1940s resulted in the expansion of the installation to its current physical dimensions. In response to wartime requirements, existing industrial and manufacturing facilities were rehabilitated, new construction authorised and utilities further developed. A post airstrip was installed and the rail network expanded. The Chemical Warfare School was enlarged and in June 1942 a modern laboratory was completed to consolidate research and provide a headquarters for the Chemical Warfare Service Technical Command.

Because of this expansion the arsenal's name was changed in May 1942 to Chemical Warfare Center. Extensive organisational changes and the addition of more than 8000 workers enabled the installation to accommodate the Army's growing wartime needs in research, procurement and manufacture in the fields of chemical warfare.

In August 1946, the Chemical Warfare Center became the Army Chemical Center, and in 1963 the name was changed back to Edgewood Arsenal. In a reorganisation approved on 7 July 1966, Edgewood Arsenal was designated as the Army's commodity centre for all chemical weapons and defence equipment research and development. In this category, the arsenal's former administrative control over the biological laboratories at Fort Detrick, Maryland, was relinquished and Fort Detrick was established as a separate commodity centre for biological weapons and defence research and development.

The arsenal's buildings contain 5,500,000 square feet of floor space, with more than 80% of this area in permanent structures. The Amos A. Fries Building, named after Major-General Amos A. Fries, a former Army chief chemical officer, is a $3 million structure providing fifty-three individual laboratories specifically designed for advanced studies of chemical compounds and materials. More than 140 scientists are employed throughout its air-conditioned facilities. Built of structural steel and reinforced concrete, the Fries Building incorporates the most advanced design for safety in laboratory operations.

The John R. Wood Building for clinical research is named after General John R. Wood, first director of Medical Research at Edgewood Arsenal. Costing in excess of $3 million, it is intended to provide new and wider capabilities in the field of medical research.

A number of instrumented test fields, located on the more remote regions of the reservation, provide facilities for testing and development.

Edgewood employs more than 3800 civilians and over 1000 military personnel. More than 900 employees hold bachelor's degrees; over 190 have master's degrees; and seventy-five persons have doctorates.

The total fixed investment in the installation is more than $112 million. A breakdown reveals the following distribution: land (improvements), $9.6 million; buildings and facilities, $75.6 million; and machinery and equipment, $27 million. (The combined gross payroll, military and civilian, for the calendar year 1966 was slightly more than $39 million.)

As of 1 October 1967, the value of the total work programme at

Edgewood Arsenal (not including Rocky Mountain, Pine Bluff and Weldon Spring) was $262 million. A partial breakdown indicates expenditures of $130·9 million for procurement of equipment and missiles (PEMA); $32·3 million for research and development and testing and evaluation; and $28·5 million dedicated to a production base for the installation. The departments are organised into the Research Laboratories, Weapons Development and Engineering Laboratories, Defence Development and Engineering Laboratories, Procurement and Production Directorate, Quality Assurance Directorate, Customer Relations and Commodity Management Office, and Technical Support Directorate.

Its present mission is the operation of a commodity management centre for chemical weapons and munitions, defensive equipment systems, and related test and handling equipment.

According to a fact sheet produced by Edgewood in December 1967:

> Commodity management, briefly defined, is a process wherein the development of an item is controlled by a single agency. This control begins in the concept stage, and continues through research and development, test and evaluation, and finally to adoption or rejection for use in the field.

The organisation is also responsible for any engineering related to the production of these items.

The arsenal, through its technical escort unit, provides technical escort, transfer and shipping for all Department of Defense military chemical and biological materials, and does the same for all Departments of the Army radiological material.

Three sub-posts fall under the administrative control of Edgewood Arsenal. These are Pine Bluff Arsenal, Arkansas; Rocky Mountain Arsenal, Colorado; and Weldon Spring Army Chemical Plant, Missouri.

Rocky Mountain Arsenal (Denver, Colorado) is operated by the Army Industrial Fund as a private corporation. It manufactures nerve gas (mainly sarin, from 1950–57, but now also VX) in addition to mustard gas, incapacitants and anti-crop weapons. It also has storage areas for its products, in particular the nerve gases, and large assembly lines for filling munitions. In 1961 contracts for filling totalled $1·5 m., which increased to $6·9 m. in 1964. The munitions filled include Bolt rockets (with nerve gas) and 750 lb bombs. Facilities are also available for the filling of 155 mm shells and warheads for use on Honest John, Little John and Sargent missiles.

Waste products were originally dumped into settling ponds in the hope that toxic chemicals would sink. Thousands of ducks, geese and other birds died. Sometime later in 1960 many cattle, sheep and several people became mysteriously ill. Autopsies established that animal deaths were due to chemical poisoning, and the government, protesting innocence, had to pay large indemnities.

As a result, in March 1962, poisonous waste began to be disposed of in a well drilled more than 2 miles deep. A month later the area was shaken by the first earth tremor since 1882. 1500 more occurred in subsequent years. Since then 160 m. gallons of waste has been poured down the well. Further land shifts occurred due to the saturation and lubrication of rock faults deep underground. Waste is now disposed of in a sealed lake with an asphalt bottom.

Pine Bluff Arsenal (Arkansas) is involved in the production of biological munitions and toxic chemicals. Many 'riot-control' agents are also produced there. The centre covers 15,000 acres and employs a staff of 14,000. Activities range from the filling and assembly of weapons to the manufacture of intermediates in line production. In 1962 new facilities were added for the filling of munitions with BZ. Munitions are also filled with CS, incendiaries and various biological agents. Seymour Hersh has implied that these biological weapons are shipped to Army storage points around the world, as well as being stored at the arsenal itself.

Weldon Spring Army Chemical Plant (Missouri) is scheduled for the possible production of 2,4D and 2,4,5T for use in Vietnam.

Fort Detrick (Near Frederick, Maryland), set up in 1943 as Camp Detrick, is now the main centre for BW research in America. This centre comprises 1500 acres of land and military establishments valued at $75 million, including 'one of the world's largest animal farms' [employee-recruitment brochure]. Its facilities for study are highly developed, and staff include 120 PHDS, 110 MSCS, 320 BSCS, 34 DVMS and 14 MDS. The research itself can be broadly divided into three categories, defensive, neutral and offensive, much of it falling within the first two. Projects include process development, small-scale production and design. Detrick differs from other research centres in two ways. Its efforts are directed in part towards breeding into pathogenic organisms:

> precisely the characteristics—such as resistance to antibiotics—that medical researchers would like to see eradicated.
>
> [*Science*, 13 January 1967]

In addition, considerable restraint is exercised over its research area. It publishes only about 15% of its findings, and of this 15%

there is nothing to indicate 'the relative degrees of military interest in a particular agent' (*Science*).

From information available, however, Elinor Langer has drawn together a good deal of information about the Detrick research programme.

Diseases that are at least the objects of considerable research and that appear to be among those regarded as potential BW agents include: Anthrax, Dysentery, Brucellosis, Glanders, Plague and Tularemia. . . . In recent years a good deal of attention has been focused on plant diseases also. Recently the Army's Distinguished Service Medal, the highest award the Army gives civilians, was awarded to a Detrick researcher for her contribution to development of a rice blast fungus, a disease that in its natural form has repeatedly damaged Asian rice crops.

Under the circumstances occasional unintentional infection is not surprising. The following selection of reports as early in Detrick's career as 1946/47 may serve to illustrate this point.

25 cases of cutaneous anthrax (*Journal of the American Medical Association*, 13 August 1946).

6 cases of human glanders (*Annals of Internal Medicine*, January 1947).

Acute brucellosis, number of cases unspecified (*New England Journal of Medicine*, May 1947).

Tularemia, number of cases unspecified (*Journal of the American Medical Association*, September 1946).

1 case of psittacosis (*Journal of Infectious Diseases*, January/February 1947).

Another, more recent, accident illustrates the secrecy surrounding Detrick, which is extended to any other institution which becomes associated with it:

On the 1st September, 1959, a 22-year-old enlisted technician named Ralph Powell became ill with Pneumonic Plague. The following day Detrick informed the Frederick County Health Officer, and on the second day it informed the Public Health Service. Its memo to the PHS, classified secret, stated that 'no press release has been made or is contemplated by any DOD agency, unless death occurs. In such a case, the cause of death would not be announced.'

Powell recovered and the report was downgraded to 'for official use only' and on the 6th November the PHS reported the case.

Among the other institutions coming within Detrick's sphere of influence are the National Academy of Sciences and the American

Society for Microbiology. For some years now the NAS has sponsored Resident Research Associateships there, while the ASM maintains a permanent Detrick Advisory committee. Detrick also uses the part-time consulting services of a number of individual researchers. Detrick's influence on the universities is discussed below.

To celebrate the twenty-fifth anniversary of its establishment, Detrick, jointly with the American Society of Biological Sciences, sponsored a symposium in April 1968. This provoked very sharp opposition from some scientists, who contacted colleagues scheduled to speak and urged them not to participate. The reasons given for this action were ethical. In addition the topics were said to be of specific military importance. The two subjects to be discussed were, 'Entry and Control of Foreign Nucleic Acid', the results of which contribute to more efficient biological weapons, and 'Leaf Abscission', which is directly related to plant defoliation. Sixteen scientists refused to participate and on 9 April a demonstration was held by others outside the gates of Detrick. This controversy also caused the ASM to dissolve its advisory committee to Detrick. This has since been reconstituted.

The Dugway Proving Ground (near the Great Salt Lake, Utah), set up in 1944, is a large Army testing ground closely associated with Detrick. It covers about 1800 square miles and employs a staff of 900. Here there is limited testing of non-lethal agents on human volunteers—Army non-combatants—and, according to *Science* (20 January 1967):

> ... occasional experiments have been performed on prisoners. But the military logic of real testing is evidently outweighed by fear of injury and contamination, and field trials are reportedly limited to animals. ...

There have been a number of accidents at the proving ground. According to Dr Kelly Gluber, Chief of Staff of the Tooele Valley Hospital in Utah:

> We occasionally see patients who have got an anticholinesterase (nerve gas) overdose at the proving ground. But will the Army admit it? Never. They refuse to take a realistic attitude.
>
> [*Sunday Times*, 28 April 1968]

Recently, however, the Army were forced to take a 'realistic attitude'. On 4 March 1968 a number of sheep in Skull Valley, about 30 miles north-east of Dugway, became ill and died. They:

> acted dazed, walked in an unco-ordinated manner, with their heads tilted off to one side, urinated frequently and when frightened or pushed often sank to the ground and lay there kicking

unable to get up. . . . The symptoms shown by the sheep are contraction of the pupils, foaming at the mouth and nose, muscular
vibrations and muscular convulsions and rapid short breathing.

[*Science*, 29 March 1968]

Other reports cited symptoms of 'red tears and red urine' (*Newsweek*, 1 April 1968).

Dugway originally denied the testing of any gas or chemicals
which might have been responsible. Later the Army admitted to
testing persistent and non-persistent nerve agents on the afternoon
of 14 March. One of the tests involved dispensing some 320 gallons
of a persistent nerve agent from two spray tanks aboard an aircraft about 27 miles from the affected animals. A weekly demonstration test of firing 155-mm shells containing non-persistent nerve
gas was also conducted. The nearest landed about 15 miles from
the sheep. On the same afternoon 106 gallons of a persistent
agent were disposed of in a burning pit. Lt-Col William L. Black,
Dugway's executive officer, rejected charges that the tests were responsible on the grounds that 'no other form of animal life in the
same area evinced any symptoms whatever'. The wind was also said
to be in a north-north-east rather than an east-north-east direction
on the day in question, although it changed the following day.

The deaths, which eventually totalled between 5000 and 6000,
were investigated by a number of institutions, including Dugway
itself, the University of Utah, Utah State University and the US
Department of Agriculture. Official enquiry was under the direction of the Office of Research and Laboratories of the US Army
Materiel Command. On 18 April the Defense Department issued a
'status report' that 'findings to date have not been conclusive as to
the specific cause of death of the sheep'. There was evidence 'pointing to Army involvement'. Samples of soil, water, snow, vegetation
and wool were analysed for traces of nerve agent, with negative
results, but later traces were found in two samples of vegetation.
This indicated 'that the agent could be present in an area where
the sheep died'. Six days earlier a Public Health Service Report
announced that it had identified a substance 'identical to' an Army
nerve agent in some of the sheep.

The Army speculated that deaths might be attributable to a
number of factors 'of which the agent is only one', that the sheep
may have become 'highly sensitised' to the agent 'through some as
yet unknown mechanism'. A committee was set up to review existing safety precautions. An estimate of the cost of the damage was
more than $300,000.

The end of the story was reached early in 1969, when pressure
from Congressmen forced an enquiry into the incident:

Pentagon witnesses were closely questioned in three separate Congressional hearings on Capitol Hill.

Before a subcommittee investigating chemical weapons experiments, Dr Martin Rothenberg, scientific director of the Dugway proving ground in Utah, was forced to admit under oath for the first time that an open-air test of vx, a nerve gas, had led to the loss of more than 6000 sheep in March 1968.

Previously, although admitting that compensation had been paid to the animals' owners, the Pentagon had never formally gone this far.

Two days of intensive cross-examination revealed that the gas had been tested on March 13 last year. But this was not admitted for nine days, even to the Governor of Utah or State veterinarians.

Instead, as Mr Guy Vander Jagt, a Republican committee member, angrily put it: 'There was a deliberate and systematic attempt to keep the truth from the public, regardless of the hazards to animal and human life.'

... The gas floated in a small cloud for nearly 40 miles before it was brought to earth by a rainstorm.

Asked why it was thought that such gas could be 'spewed all over Utah' without harm to anyone, Dr Rothenberg said: 'Well, it never had in the past escaped from the proving ground.'

The implication that there had been many such tests previously drew gasps from spectators. Mr Henry Reuss, a Wisconsin Democrat, and committee chairman, cut in acidly: 'Doctor, you frighten me.... You really do.'

[Daily Telegraph, 22 May 1969]

The us magazine *Science* ferreted out the truth about the way in which the accident happened. The test called for an aircraft to spray 320 gallons of vx nerve gas from two tanks which were to be jettisoned after use. (This was probably part of the us forces' programme to develop spray techniques suitable for use with fast low-flying aircraft, in this case at just less than supersonic speed.) One of the tanks failed to empty completely, and about 20 lb of vx was still discharging as the aeroplane regained height. The pilot could not stop the flow because, owing presumably to a design fault, no provision had been made to allow the pilot to switch it off.

Other Testing Facilities

There are such facilities in Mississippi. These were established in 1943. Seymour Hersh has alleged that cbw tests have also been carried out in Panama, Greenland and Fort Greely, Alaska. The Pentagon refused to comment on the first two of these locations but admitted that tests had in fact been carried out at Fort Greely and also at Fort Huachuca in Arizona 'for particular climatic conditions', although there was no permanent test station there.

According to the *Sunday Times* 28 April 1968:

Secret efforts are now being made to find a place where CBW agents can be tested with relative safety to humanity. With this in mind the U.S. Government launched project 'Pacific Bird'.

The Pentagon has spent $2,500,000 on this project, which is being handled by the Smithsonian in Washington. Ostensibly the operation is to study the migratory habits of birds in the Pacific, but one factor tends to give the whole business a less innocent appearance. 'Project Pacific Bird' is being substantially financed and directed by Fort Detrick.

At Fort Detrick the answer to queries about the operation is, 'I cannot talk about that project. It's classified.'

Testing of BW agents has been carried out on Eniwetok Atoll in the South Pacific.

Fort McClellan (Arkansas) This establishment incorporates the Army's training school. The activities of this centre are amply illustrated by the following article:

The U.S. Army is quietly teaching Chemical Corps Officers how to use a powerful mind-altering drug called Agent BZ as a possible combat weapon.

A copy of a lesson plan says effects of the mysterious chemical range from giddiness to hallucinations.

Research on mental illness has brought as a by-product a growing list of substances capable of producing 'model psychosis', the lesson explains.

'These brief, controllable, drug-induced disturbances in mental function are often profoundly disorganising and while they last would without doubt be severely crippling to a military group in which they occur.'

The lesson plan discusses the use of marijuana, mescaline, LSD and Agent BZ as possible weapons. Marijuana and mescaline are ruled out because they require such large doses.

LSD, a widely discussed psychedelic chemical, is listed by the lesson plan as having 'great promise', but it is BZ which is described as 'our standard incapacitating agent'.

A Defense Department spokesman described BZ as a delayed acting agent temporarily producing incapacitating physical and mental effects.

The researchers, who declined to be identified, agreed after seeing the symptoms listed in the Army document that the substance probably is related to belladonna, a plant extract which is one of the oldest drugs used in war.

One said he knew Army intelligence was 'very interested' in such a synthetic being developed in the Soviet Union in the late 50s.

According to the lesson plan issued by the Army's chemical centre and school at Ft. McClellan, Ark., the possible symptoms from BZ include giddiness, disorientation, hallucination, drowsiness and maniacal behaviour.

'There is no standard munition for the use of BZ', a Defense Department spokesman said. He would not elaborate but apparently meant there is no specific means of delivering the chemical weapon to an enemy.

The Neuro-Psychiatric centre researchers said, however, that the substance could be sprayed in combination with a faintly oily base, and would be absorbed almost immediately through the skin.

[*New York Herald Tribune*, 13 May 1967]

CBW munitions are stored at Anniston Army Depot, Alabama, and at Blue Grass Ordnance Depot, Kentucky.

The Air Force and the Navy have CBW research programmes of their own, but work under contract to the Army. The headquarters of the Air Force programme is at 'the proving grounds, Elgin, Florida, and of the Navy's at the Ordnance Test Station, China Lake, California.

University involvement

Sixty universities are known to be involved in CBW research in the United States. The following information is taken from the comprehensive survey which appeared in the January 1968 edition of *Viet Report*, edited by Carol Brightman.

Brooklyn College In 1961 the college was involved in a major project on the 'Physical Principles of BW Detection'. The purpose was to 'conduct research applicable to development of BW rapid warning devices', with particular attention to the detection of 'aerosolized BW material'. Brooklyn College held contract no. DA-18-064-CML-2739 with the Physical Detection Branch of the Army Biological Laboratories at Fort Detrick.

University of California, Berkeley In 1961 Berkeley campus held two Army contracts for CW agent research on 'lethal and incapacitating agents'. One project (contract no. DA-18-108-405-CML-188) was intended to 'isolate in pure form and to determine the chemical structure of ryanodine which has an unusual type of pharmacological activity of interest in the search for agents'. The second project (contract no. DA-18-108-CML-5008) was to 'determine the chemical structure of shellfish poison, a highly toxic natural product', as a basis for developing new cw agents. Both projects were supervised by the Agent Research Branch of the Army Chemical Center.

The Office of Naval Research operates a facility at the University of California, Berkeley, known as the Naval Biological Laboratory. There has been considerable speculation that this installation conducts research on biological weapons, as its main concern is the study of contagious airborne diseases. The Naval Biological Laboratory is funded and operated by the Navy, and staffed by personnel from the University of California; it is located at the Naval Supply Depot in Oakland. Among the diseases researched at the laboratory are bubonic plague, valley fever (coccidiomycosis) and meningitis (*Sunday Ramparts*, 12 February 1967).

Although officials of the Oakland installation deny that their research is intended for the development of cb weapons, there is evidence of direct cooperation between the Army's bw laboratories at Fort Detrick and the California laboratory. In 1961 Detrick sponsored a project on the 'stability and virulence of bw aerosols' conducted by the Naval Biological Laboratory in California. The purpose of this project (contract MIPR no. R-56-6-CML-FD) was to 'make basic aerosol investigations on the virulence, survival and behaviour of pathogenic micro-organisms and toxins in particles disseminated from the dry and wet state and to determine the relationships which exist between aerosol virulence ... and such factors as particle size, host, sunlight, relative humidity, temperature, and other environmental factors'. A 1961 task report on this project indicates that:

> research continues on the aero-biology of pathogenic viruses, rickettsia, bacteria, fungi and toxins disseminated from powder and liquids.

Several papers, presumably based on experiments conducted under this project, were presented at the Second International Conference on Aerobiology in March 1966 by staff members of the Naval Biological Laboratory. One paper, for example, concerned 'Physiological Responses of Airborne Bacteria to Shifts in Relative Humidity'. The paper was prepared by M. T. Hatch and R. L. Dimmick (*Bacteriological Reviews*, September 1966).

University of California at Los Angeles In 1961 UCLA held contract DA-108-405-735 with the Clinical Research Division of the Army Chemical Corps at Fort Detrick for research on 'medical aspects of chemical warfare'. The basic purpose of the project was:

to determine, through clinical researches, the effects of selected toxic compounds and of drugs antagonistic thereto: on the US Army and USAF volunteers... also, to advise and assist in the search for more effective toxic compounds.

The research task report on this project stated that:

a three-man expedition to the rain forests of Peru and Equador collected samples of 2,500 plants,

and that:

extracts are being prepared from these plants and screened for biological activity.

University of California Medical School and Center The Medical School was engaged in 1961 on an Army project (DA-18-68-405-CML-755) on the 'pharmacology and physiological chemistry of chemical warfare'. The purpose of the project was:

to develop, through pharmacological research, data for the support of a rational approach to the search for new CW lethal and incapacitating agents.

UCLA's specific task was:

to synthesize and study compounds pharmacologically related to types that have hallucinogenic properties

especially amphetamine derivatives.

The Medical Center in 1966 held contract no. DA-04-495-AMC-791 for research on 'disabling agents on the central nervous system'.

University of Chicago In 1961 the Department of Pharmacology was engaged in research on the 'pharmacology and physiological chemistry of chemical warfare' for the Physiology Division at the Edgewood Arsenal. The purpose of the project was to:

determine the mechanism of action of toxic compounds and their antagonists, seeking concurrently new body systems that may be disrupted by small quantities of compounds to produce incapacitation or death.

Research was rendered under contract no. DA-CML-18-108-61-G8.

According to Chicago's Vice-President for Special Projects, W. B. Harrell, the Chairman of the Microbiology Department, Professor

James W. Moulder, was engaged in BW research for Fort Detrick under a contract which took effect in 1960.

Columbia University   In 1964 Columbia received a $38,000 contract (no. DA-18-035-AML-269(a)) from the Army Chemical Center at the Edgewood Arsenal for research in the field of biological warfare systems. Columbia's task was to 'develop properties of dialyzing membranes for separation of physiologically active products from biological media'.

Cornell University   The Cornell Aeronautical Laboratory (CAL), a division of Cornell University located in Buffalo, NY, is one of the few university-associated installations that have conducted research on the field properties of tactical CB weapons. CAL's involvement in CBW research came to light following disclosures in 1966 of the 'Summit' and 'Spicerack' projects at the University of Pennsylvania. It turned out that Pennsylvania was subcontracting certain aspects of these CBW projects in Cornell. CAL's role was to

> conduct a detailed target analysis to determine anticipated target neutralization requirements. This analysis will consider: (i) protective measures against which a weapon capability should be required; (ii) acceptable time to incapacitation requirements; and (iii) target sizes and content and minimum acceptable casualty infliction to achieve neutralization.
>
> [*Science*, 13 January 1967]

CAL has multiple connections with the Pentagon's CBW laboratories. Three CAL scientists, Arthur O'Conner, Paul Rosenthal and Hiramie T. McAdams, are conducting secret research for the Air Force on 'CB Anti-Material Application' under contract no. AF-08(635)-5400. The 1965 edition of the *Aerospace and Defense Research Contracts Roster* indicates that in 1964 the Cornell Aeronautical Laboratory had received no less than four CBW research contracts from the US Army Chemical Center. Among the tasks assigned Cornell were 'research services on chemical agents munitions systems for tactical employment' (three projects) and 'research services for evaluation and development of test technology'. The contract nos. and values were: DA-18-035-AMC-323(a) $882,000; DA-18-108-CML-6628-(a) $117,000 and $100,000; and DA-18-035-AMC-280-(a) $150,000.

CAL's activities were clarified in a letter from the CAL Public Relations Manager, Harold S. Tolley, to *Science* magazine and dated 23 February 1967.

> The full level of that effort...has run somewhere between $500,000 and $1 million per year. Although few details can be provided, the objective of this programme has been to determine

effective means for delivering chemical agents as a tactical munition.

The emphasis of the Laboratory programme is upon dissemination techniques and does not involve research upon chemical agents themselves. . . . As a classified programme there have been no open publications resulting. However, within the next few weeks a paper will be delivered at a Law Enforcement Symposium in Chicago which deals with the use of chemical agents in riot control. The essential background for this paper stems from the research performed under the Edgewood Contract.

University of Delaware From 1964 to 1966 the university was engaged in research 'on the mechanisms of flow of absorbed particles'. The research, sponsored by the Edgewood Arsenal, was rendered under contract no. DA-18-035-MAC-278(A).

Delaware's Chemistry Department currently holds contract DA-18-035-AMC-342(a) for 'research on an electrochemical detection system'. In 1961 the University of Delaware held two Army contracts. Contract no. DA-18-108-405-CML-525 was intended to support the research effort of the Army Chemical Center 'in the search for new highly incapacitating and lethal types of cw agents'. Contract no. DA-18-108-405-CML-654 was intended to 'perform research in the synthesis of novel heterocyclic systems'. The task report indicates that 'samples of interesting compounds will be submitted to the Army Chemical Corps for screening as incapacitating agents'.

George Peabody College for Teachers Under contract Nonr-1257(01) the project, 'CBR training aid requirements, Army-wide', involved 'basic individual CBR training; advanced individual CBR training; Army Chemical Corps, unit CBR training; courses replacement training; CBR training aid problems; CBR problems of general interest'.

George Washington University Close contacts have been maintained with the US Army Biological Laboratories at Fort Detrick since 1948. From 1954 to 1959, in fact, GW had its own research installation at Fort Detrick, known as the George Washington University Research Laboratory, which was used by GW scientists for research on biological weapons. According to the Annual Report of the Dean for Sponsored Research for 1959:

this project conducts studies, tests, and experimental investigations in a comprehensive research programme relating to the physical and biophysical factors incident to explosive dissemination of biological aerosols.

The report indicated that the GW researchers have had success in improving the efficiency of dissemination of liquids. While it is quite obvious that the end result of this work will be a new weapon, the work of the contract has been kept on a research basis and no development work has been done on it. Most of the research was classified. The value of GW's Fort Detrick research in 1960 alone was $1,202,000 (*Science*, 13 January 1967).

Although George Washington's direct contract work for Fort Detrick was apparently terminated in 1960, the Department of Microbiology still maintains an academic relationship with Fort Detrick, whereby Detrick employees can receive advanced degrees from the university while conducting their research at the Army Biological Laboratories. Since 1959, ten Fort Detrick employees have received PHDS from GW (the Army pays their tuition fees) (*George Washington Hatchet*, 4 April 1967).

Georgia Institute of Technology   The Atlanta Engineering Experimental Station of Georgia Technology holds a classified contract for research on 'toxic explosives' (contract no. W-18-035-CWS-1313). Further details are lacking.

Hahnemann Medical College (of Philadelphia)   The Department of Pharmacology has been conducting research for some years on the 'medical aspects of chemical warfare'. The research was funded by the Clinical Research Division of Edgewood Arsenal, beginning in 1961.

In answer to a *Science* magazine questionnaire, Joseph R. DiPalma, Chairman of the Department of Pharmacology and principal investigator for the project, indicated last year that 'the work concerned mostly the investigation of the oral human toxicity of 2-PAM-Cl (2-pyridine-aldoxime methylchloride) in humans'. According to Dr DiPalma, 'this substance is one of the effective antidotes for the phosphorous type of cholinesterase inhibitors which may be used as war gases'.

Harvard University   Fort Detrick placed contract no. DA-49-007-MD-864 in 1961 for research on the 'laboratory identification of BW agents'. The purpose of the project was to 'devise techniques and material for the rapid identification of BW agents and disease applicable to use in the US Armed Forces'.

In 1961 Dr R. B. Woodward of Harvard worked on an Army project to 'determine the structure of puffer fish poison, a highly toxic natural product, as a model for new chemical agents'. Research was funded under contract no. DA-18-108-61-G-14 with the Army Chemical Center at Edgewood.

In 1964 Harvard received a $35,000 contract (no. DA.18-108-AMC-148(A)) from the Edgewood Arsenal for a study of 'molecular structure and diffusional processes across intact epidermis'.

Illinois Institute of Technology Research Institute The IIT Research Institute is the foremost university centre for research on CBW agents in the United States. The Research Institute's work involves special studies as well as on-going evaluation of tactical CB weapons. The on-going project, 'munitions filling development for new and standard agents', is funded under Army contract no. DA-18-035-AMC-372(A). Recent studies issued under the aegis of this project include studies of chemical bombs and other devices involving G agents and V agents (nerve gases) and CS.

IITRI's major area of specialisation lies in the field of aerobiology —the spread of disease through the atmosphere. IITRI maintains an aerosol laboratory for the study of airborne infections. While some of this, research is naturally of concern to the medical profession, the IITRI's efforts are clearly directed towards the development of biological weapons. This is made clear in a report prepared by John D. Stockham for the Air Force on the 'dissemination properties of encapsulated particles'. According to the author's abstract of this study, the report 'provides information on the feasibility of disseminating microencapsulated biological agents'. The research for this study was financed under contract no. AF-08-(635)-5057. Contract no. DA-18-108-AMC-129(A), from the Army, is for research on the dissemination of chemical warfare agents.

A description of IITRI's research on aerobiology was prepared for the Army in July 1966 by R. Ehrlich, S. Miller, M. D. Schneider and H. M. Yamashiroya. Although the report itself is classified, a description of the report gives some impression of the areas covered. According to the authors:

> this report consists of a series of 7 reports summarising major phases of the research efforts. One report describes IIT Research Institute's aerosol laboratories, including the pathological laboratory and animal holding facilities. Three reports summarise efforts directed toward the development of improved methods for the bioassay of Coxiella burnetii in mice and guinea pigs. . . : The final three reports summarise studies with Venezuelan equine encephalomyelitis (VEE) virus. One of these presents detailed studies on the characterisation of airborne VEE virus.

These reports cover research during the period October 1962 to June 1966 under contract no. DA-18-064-AMC-49(A).

The IIT Research Institute co-sponsored the Second International

Conference of Aerobiology (Airborne Infection), held in Chicago
on 29-31 March 1966, in conjunction with the US Army Biological
Laboratories at Fort Detrick. IITRI researchers prepared several
papers for the conference, and Richard Ehrlich of IIT was one of
the programme chairmen (*Bacteriological Reviews*, September
1966).

In addition to its work for the Army's CBW research installation
at Fort Detrick, IIT has been contracted to the Dugway proving
ground—the test centre for CB weapons in Utah. In 1964 IIT received a $118,000 contract from Dugway for 'the development of
an isokinetic aerosol sampling system'. This project was financed
under Army contract no. DA-42-007-AMC-139.

Iowa State University   Iowa State in 1961 held Army contract no.
DA-18-108-405-CML-269 for CW agent research aimed at the 'Investigation of indole alkaloids'.

Johns Hopkins University   Johns Hopkins has been active in CBW
research over a long period of time: Elinor Langer reports that between 1955 and 1963 Johns Hopkins received over $1 million for
work described as 'studies of actual or potential injuries or ill-
nesses, studies or diseases of potential BW significance and evaluation
of certain toxoids and vaccines'. This research, originally started
under contract DA-18-064-404-CML-100, has been continued at a
reduced level under contract DA-18-064-AMC-104A (*Science*, 13
January 1967).

It is evident that CBW research at Johns Hopkins has covered a
wide range of activities. In 1961, for instance, Johns Hopkins held
two CBW contracts from the Army Chemical Center at Edgewood
Arsenal. The first, on the 'medical aspects of chemical warfare', was
intended 'to determine through clinical research, the effects of
selected toxic compounds... on the US Army and USAF volunteers.... Also, to advise and assist in the search for more effective
toxic compounds.' The research task report indicates that Johns
Hopkins' particular task was the study of V agents (nerve gases).
This research was rendered under contract no. DA-18-108-405-
CML-120.

A second project (DA-CML-18-108-61-G-15) was intended to 'provide basic information in the field of allergy with a view to its
possible utilisation in incapacitation'.

Between 1964 and 1966, Johns Hopkins held a contract for the
'investigation of rapid methods of analysis of aerosol CW agents'.
A report indicates that 'a new approach to collecting compounds in
aerosols and analysing them by gas liquid chromatography has been

developed'. The work was performed under contract no. DA-18-035-AMC-144A.

Kansas State University   Researchers in the Chemistry Department of Kansas State University have been engaged in an Army-financed project involving the scientific analysis of lethal nerve gases. The KSU project, entitled 'ion phenomena', is rendered under Edgewood contract no. DA-18-035-AMC-718(A). According to a description of this project prepared by Robert W. Kiser, the principal researcher, 'a mass spectrometric study of GA and GF was undertaken to obtain more fundamental information of value in determining the processes that occur upon electron bombardment of these organo-phosphorus compounds'. GA is also known as tabun.

University of Maryland   The University of Maryland has held several research contracts with the US Army Biological Laboratories at Fort Detrick. One project, conducted by Professor F. Arne Hansen of the Microbiology Department, was in 'the use of fluorescent anti-bodies for the rapid detection and identification of bacteria'. According to Maryland's President, Wilson H. Elkins, the project was terminated in 1960.

A second project, on the 'vulnerability of man to biological warfare', was continued into the 1960s. The purpose of this project was to 'study infectivity and pathogenicity of potential BW agents in experimental animals and subsequently in volunteers'. According to a 1961 research task report on this project, 'evaluation of volunteers infected with *Pasteurella tularensis* has continued and been expanded. Studies on *Bacillus anthracis* in a variety of laboratory animals infected both by subcutaneous and respiratory routes have continued. Considerable progress has been made in the study of typhoid fever in man.' Research was rendered under contract no. DA-49-007-MD-751.

University of Maryland School of Medicine   Maryland's School of Medicine has also been involved in CBW research involving tests on animals and human volunteers. In 1961 the Medical School held contract no. DA-18-108-CML-6562 for research on 'medical aspects of chemical warfare', to 'determine signs and symptoms of poisoning by selected toxic compounds and devise methods for their detection in post-mortem tissues and fluids'.

These have included the organism responsible for tularemia. At the 2nd International Conference on Aerobiology (Airborne Infection) held in Chicago in March 1966, two scientists who work jointly with the University of Maryland School of Medicine and the US Army Biological Laboratories at Fort Detrick delivered a paper entitled 'Aerogenic Immunisation of Man with Live Tularemia Vaccine'. The scientists were Richard B. Hornick and Henry P. Eigelsbach. Their paper describes experiments conducted with 253 'volunteers' from the University of Maryland Research Ward at the Jessup, Maryland, House of Correction. These men were exposed to aerosolised *Francisella tularensis*, a live vaccine strain. The tests were supervised by W. R. Griffith of Fort Detrick (*Bacteriological Reviews*, September 1966).

University of Maryland Dental School   Even the Dental School has been involved in a project on the 'pharmacology and physiological chemistry of chemical warfare'. According to the 1961 report, the purpose of the research was to 'determine the mechanism of action of toxic compounds and their antagonists, seeking concurrently new body systems that may be disrupted by small quantities of compounds to produce incapacitation or death'. When the report was issued, the Maryland team was studying the effects of ryanodine. Research was rendered under contract no. DA-CML-18-108-61-G9 with the Directorate of Medical Research at the Edgewood Arsenal.

University of Massachusetts   In 1961 the University of Massachusetts was conducting CW agent research in order to 'synthesize potent emetics for possible use as incapacitating agents'. Specifically, the project was designed to 'investigate simple synthetic analogs and other modifications of apomorphine and related alkaloids'. This project was funded under contract no. DA-18-108-405-CML-912 with the Bio-Organic Chemistry Branch of the Army Chemical Center at Edgewood.

Massachusetts Institute of Technology   MIT has been active in a major Army project on the pharmacology and physiological chemistry of chemical warfare, designed to 'develop, through pharmacological research, data for the support of rational approach to the search for new CW lethal and incapacitating agents'. MIT's share of this project performed under contract no. DA-18-108-405-CML-942; according to a report (1961), it was to 'determine the usefulness of servo-analytic information theory concepts and digital computer programs in the assessment of the proposed incapacitating compounds'.

University of Minnesota   Researchers in the Department of Plant Pathology and Physiology of Minnesota's Institute of Agriculture have held two Fort Detrick contracts for work on 'anticrop warfare research'. Both projects continued over several years; according to the Chairman of the Department, Professor M. F. Kernkamp, they were terminated in 1965. Kernkamp was the principal investigator in one three-year project, the purpose of which was to investigate the virulence of certain pathogenic races of *Puccina graminis Iritici'*, a species of wheat rust.

The second project was intended to 'study molds that deteriorate grain in storage'. This apparently is an aspect of an on-going project 'to conduct research on chemical and biological agents capable of destroying the food and industrial crops of potential enemy countries', rendered under contract no. DA-18-064-404-CML-433. The 1961 research task report on this contract revealed that the project 'involved screening, research, pilot plant scale production and field assessment of the following agents: wheat stem rust, wheat stripe rust, rice blast, and chemical agents'. The report also indicates that 'grain yield reduction potential will be determined in areas agroclimactically analogous to potential target areas'.

University of North Carolina The Department of Pathology of North Carolina's School of Medicine has conducted research for the US Army Biological Laboratories at Fort Detrick on the subject of 'industrial inhalation anthrax'. The research team was assisted by Fort Detrick scientists. In a paper prepared by the team for delivery at the Second International Conference on Aerobiology (Airborne Infection) held in 1966, indicates that 'the authors ... developed a protocol to study the clinical course, patho-genesis, and dose-response relationships of experimental animals to a naturally occurring *Bacillus anthracis* aerosol produced in a goat-hair processing mill (*Bacteriological Reviews*, September 1966).

The University of North Carolina is also associated with the Research Triangle Institute of Durham, NC, another CBW research installation.

Ohio State University Dr Samuel Saslow, a Professor of Medicine and Microbiology at the Ohio State University College of Medicine, held a Fort Detrick contract from 3 January 1955 until 31 December 1965 in the field of 'viral and rickettsial agent laboratory research'. The purpose of the project was to 'evaluate the clinical response of monkeys to mixed infections resulting from aerosol exposure to combinations of biological agents ... including *Rickettsia rickettsii*, *Pasteurella tularensis*, influenza virus, and *Coxiella burnetti*'. Dr Saslow's research was funded by the US Army biological laboratories under contract no. FD-GR-61-12. A portion of Dr Saslow's research was described at the Second International Conference on Aerobiology (Airborne Infection), held at Chicago in March 1966 and co-sponsored by Fort Detrick. Suslow and a colleague named Harold N. Carlisle delivered a paper there on, 'Aerosol Infection on

Monkeys with *Rickettsia rickettsii'. (Bacteriological Reviews*, September 1966).

University of Oklahoma   The University of Oklahoma has conducted biological warfare systems research aimed at the potential use of biological agents in 'remote area conflicts', i.e. in situations like Vietnam. In 1964–65 Oklahoma received two contracts from the Army's CBW proving ground at Dugway, Utah, for this purpose. The university's task under these contracts is described as 'ecology and epidemiology research studies in remote areas', including a 'research survey in specified area'. The details of this project are at present unavailable. The numbers and values of the two contracts are: DA-42-007-AMC-121, $134,000; and DA-42-007-AMC-208, $238,000.

University of Pennsylvania   The University of Pennsylvania has received national publicity concerning the notorious Spicerack and Summit projects, but Pennsylvania's involvement in CBW research stretched well beyond those two projects. By 1961 Pennsylvania already was engaged in two major research projects for the US Army Chemical Corps' laboratories at the Edgewood Arsenal. Both these projects were in the field of CW biological sciences research. The first project, funded under contract no. DA-18-108-405-CML-630, was a study of the 'pharmacology and physiological chemistry of chemical warfare'. The purpose of the project was to 'develop, through pharmacological research, data for the support of a rational approach to the research for new CW lethal and incapacitating agents'. The specific task of the Pennsylvania team, led by Drs G. B. Koelle and N. Haugaard, was to conduct 'research on the roles of neuraminic acid in neuronal and of phosphorylases in cardiac activities'.

A second project, on 'basic and applied physiology', was intended to 'conduct research on specific metabolic processes to elucidate the mechanism of action of toxic and other compounds'. Pennsylvania held contract no. DA-18-108-CML-6556 for this project. The Pennsylvania research team headed by Dr A. B. DuBois was directed to research on respiratory and circulatory mechanisms with respect to toxic agents.

By 1965 Pennsylvania was receiving some $1 million a year for applied research on CBW weapons systems, most of it channelled through Summit, an Army contract, and Spicerack, an Air Force contract. Most of the work on these contracts was performed by a semi-autonomous subsidiary of Pennsylvania known as the Institute for Co-operative Research (ICR). In the spring of 1966 it was disclosed that ICR's research on CBW delivery systems included studies for the potential use of CB anticrop weapons in Vietnam. In an interview with *Science* magazine in autumn 1966, Knut Krieger, the chemistry professor who directs the research, indicated that he received Army field reports from Vietnam and that he had evaluated tests on chemical defoliants (*Science*, 13 January 1967).

A description of the *Project Summit Annual Report* for 1965 gives an impression of the kind of research being performed by Pennsylvania. The report, prepared by Frank M. Steadman under contract no. DA-18-064-AMC-2757(A), focuses on feasibility studies on the use of CB agents in counter-insurgent warfare. According to the report's author, project research was concerned with '(A) analysis of the utility of a spectrum of air-delivered hypothetical CB agent-munition combinations in counterinsurgency and limited warfare situations; (B) development of mathematical models for computation of weapons effects'. The report itself carries a secret classification (TAB 67-9, May 1, 1967).

Pennsylvania's parallel contract with the Air Force is entitled 'Situations for Evaluation of Air Delivered Chemical and Biological Munitions in Counter-insurgent Operations'. As in the case of Summit, reports emanating from this project are secret. A description of research performed under this contract, however, gives an indication of what is involved. A report completed by Arthur F. Haney in March 1967 was concerned with counter-insurgent CB warfare in Vietnam, with 'close-support tactical air support', and with armed forces operations military tactics. Pennsylvania held contract no. AF-08-(635)-3597 for its role in this project.

Directors of Pennsylvania's well-known Foreign Policy Research Institute have joined with ICR to provide the Pentagon with basic strategic studies of the utility of CB weapons. J. E. Dougherty, Robert Strausz-Hupe, W. R. Kintner, R. L. Pfaltzgraff, Jr, and R. C. Herber are directing a study of 'the role of biological and chemical weapons in the defense strategy of the United States'. In their abstract of the contract (no. DA-18-064-CML-2757), the investigators state:

> The capability to engage in offensive and defensive biological and chemical operations gives a nation a much stronger position in the struggle for power and provides a powerful deterrent force to bridge the gap between conventional and nuclear weapons capabilities. . . . B/C weapons could provide capabilities for covert and overt strategic and tactical operations of any required intensity in any type of power struggle or warfare without imposing a logistics load beyond the capacities of many of the smaller nations. Effective inspection for control of B/C weapons production appears impractical.

University of Pittsburgh The University of Pittsburgh maintains two research centres, the Army Material Research Staff and the Washington DC Ordnance Research Staff, which conduct CBW research for the Army under contract no. DA-49-186-AMC-214. The Army material centre in Pittsburgh is engaged in secret research on the 'development of weapons and other equipment for special warfare'. The project is concerned with the development of weapons and other equipment for counter-insurgent warfare, including the development of chemical defoliants.

Pittsburgh's Washington DC Research Staff is engaged in a whole range of CBW projects, many of them involving research on tactical CB weapons. One project, specifically connected with the war effort in Vietnam, involves the development of chemical weapons for use in the 'tunnel destruction demolition set XM69'. The project is concerned with so-called 'non-lethal irritant gases', including the gas CS. Pittsburgh's Washington staff has been engaged in other projects dealing with chemical agents like CS. A current project on the 'tactical CS canister cluster, E159'[1] involves the dissemination of CS agents by aerial bombardment. A third project being carried out by this research staff is on the dissemination of chemical agents by a guided missile. The Washington Research Staff recently completed a secret report on the 'chemical warhead, E27, for Lance guided missile'. This was 'an illustrated report on the E27 chemical warhead for the dissemination of non-persistent antipersonnel gas . . . a component of the Lance guided missile system.'
    University of Pittsburgh professors, disturbed about these revelations concerning research being performed at their university, sought to obtain more information containing the two Army-connected research staffs. A spokesman for the Washington staff, a Mr Anderson, informed the professors that the university did not perform any original research on these weapons, but was concerned mainly with preparing technical reports and manuals.

St Louis University In 1961 St Louis University undertook a research project for the Clinical Research Division of the Army Chemical Corps in the field of the 'medical aspects of chemical warfare'. The purpose of the project, funded under contract no. DA-18-108-CML-6601, was to 'determine, through clinical research, the effects of selected toxic compounds and of drugs antagonistic thereto, on the US Army and USAF volunteers . . . also, to advise and assist in the search for more effective toxic compounds.' The specific task of the St Louis team was to 'synthetize, examine by

---

[1] Presumably similar to the recently developed British cluster bomb.

X-ray diffraction techniques, and conduct preliminary biological tests on compounds to test certain hypotheses of drug action'.

Stanford University In 1961 Stanford held a contract with the US Army Chemical Corps proving grounds at Dugway, Utah, for research on the 'meteorological aspects of CBR warfare'. The purpose of the project, funded under contract no. DA-42-007-403-CML-448, was to 'improve the knowledge of meteorological conditions on the behavior of aerosols and particulates'.

Stanford Research Institute The Stanford Research Institute of Menlo Park, California, is one of the principal CBW research centres in the United States. Projects undertaken by SRI in the past few years have involved every aspect of CBW research and development, including the investigation and testing of BW agents, the techniques of CBW dissemination, and the evaluation of airborne CBW delivery systems. A major share of this research is rendered under Army contract no. DA-18-035-AMC-122(A), an on-going project of 'research studies on the dissemination of solid and liquid agents'. Recent studies conducted as part of this project have included investigations of the aerosol dissemination of CB agents, the performance of chemical bombs, mathematical models for CB weapons, CS agents and aerosol generators. Particular studies recently rendered under this contract have included a study of the 'dissemination of aerosol particles by forming clouds', and a proposal for the

secondary injection of CW agents into a supersonic rocket exhaust [which] was directed to the use of a rocket motor for dissemination of chemical agents using the energy from a solid rocket motor exhaust for dispersion.... Heat and turbulence of the exhaust serves to break up and distribute the agent over a wide area.

Dr W. A. Skinner of SRI held two Edgewood contracts in 1961 for CW agent research. One project, funded under contract no. DA-18-108-405-CML-839, was aimed at the 'synthesis of nitrogen-containing heterocyclic compounds possessing physiological activity'. The second project, funded under contract no. DA-18-108-405-CML-587, directed Dr Skinner to 'inform the Industrial Liaison Office (of Edgewood) of those recent European developments in chemical, biochemical and pharmacological research that would be of interest to the Chemical Corps'. This project involved attendance at scientific meetings in Europe, among other duties. Research was simultaneously conducted to study 'the formulation of encapsulated aerosols'. The purpose of this project, financed under Edgewood contract no. DA-18-108-405-CML-746, was to 'obtain fundamental information on the formation of encapsulated aerosols for possible application to the solution of problems on the dissemination of chemical agents'.

University of Tennessee   In 1961 the University of Tennessee was one of several universities associated with the Army's project on the 'medical aspects of chemical warfare'. The overall function of this project was to test selected chemical weapons on animals and then on human volunteers, and to 'advise and assist in the search for more effective compounds'. At Tennessee a research team in the Division of Surgery conducted 'studies of burns produced by mustard gas (HD)'. Tennessee held contract no. DA-18-108-61-G23 for this purpose.

University of Texas, Austin   The Department of Microbiology at the University of Texas has since 1960 held a Fort Detrick contract worth about $15,000 a year for virology research on the production of interferon in tissue cultures infected with virus. The title of the project, funded under contract no. DA-18-035-AMC-391(A), is 'Barrier properties of a group of polymeric materials to VX agents'.

Agricultural and Mechanical College of Texas   In 1961 Texas Agricultural and Mechanical College held an Edgewood contract for 'lethal and incapacitating agent research' to undertake the 'investigation and synthesis of organophosphorous compounds'. The project was funded under contract no. DA-18-108-405-CML-858 with the Army Chemical Corps.

University of Utah   In recent years, the University of Utah has maintained close ties with the Army Chemical Corps' Dugway proving ground, the testing centre for CBW weapons. In 1960 Utah had eight contracts with Dugway, totalling $1,570,000 (*Science*, 20 January 1967). In fiscal year 1965 the University of Utah had contracts for research at Dugway worth $322,000. A summary of Army-financed research in 1961 indicates the kind of services that were being performed by the University for Dugway. Mr E. Dean Vest of Utah was the principal investigator in a project to 'establish endemicity of disease of Dugway proving ground and surrounding areas, to evaluate the hazards arising from biological testing, and to demonstrate absence or spread of biological agents'. This work was rendered under contract no. DA-42-007-403-CML-427.

Utah State University   Utah State University has held a continuing contract with the US Army Chemical Corps' Dugway proving ground since 1960. According to Wynne Thorne, Utah State's Vice-President for Research, this contract is for 'service activities performed by undergraduate students on the campus in counting fluorescent particles as a part of a larger programme in meterological investigation'. The value of the contract for 1966–67 was $92,695.

University of Washington The University of Washington has participated in several Army-financed experimental projects on the clinical effects of chemical agents. One project was intended to 'provide toxicological information required as a basis for selecting new lethal and incapacitating agents'. The project task was to 'conduct research, basic and applied, to discover toxicity of compounds, efficacy of drugs and mechanism of skin penetration of toxic compounds'. Research was supervised by the Toxicology Division of the Army Chemical Corps under contract no. DA-18-108-405-CML-666.

A second project on the 'medical aspects of chemical warfare' (contract no. DA-18-108-CML-6364) was to 'determine through clinical research the effects of selected toxic compounds.... Also, to advise and assist in the search for more effective toxic compounds.' The University of Washington's search for more effective toxic compounds led its scientists to southern Mexico, where plants with psychotropic substances were collected for laboratory experimentation, according to a 1961 report.

More recently, University of Washington scientists have been conducting research on 'liver esterase activity in soman poisoned animals'. This project involves an investigation of the effects of G-agents (nerve gas). This work is funded under contract no. DA-18-035-AMC-384A.

Washington State University A research team at Washington State University has conducted 'anticrop warfare research' for the US Army Biological Laboratories at Fort Detrick. The purpose of the project, funded under contract no. DA-18-064-404-CML-462, was to 'conduct research on chemical and biological agents capable of destroying the food and industrial crops of potential enemy countries'. The specific task of the Washington group was to 'conduct epidemiological studies on stripe rust of wheat'.

University of Wisconsin Scientists at the University of Wisconsin have been involved in several CBW research projects including a project on 'the toxicology of chemical warfare agents', funded by the Army Chemical Corps under contract no. DA-CML-18-108-61-G-12. The purpose of the project was to 'provide toxicological information required as a basis for selecting new lethal and incapacitating agents, for devising techniques for their dissemination, and for the development of therapeutic measures'. A 1961 description of this project revealed that 'animal toxicity studies will be con-

ducted on compounds that are highly active in producing incapacitation or death by inhalation or percutaneous action when
disseminated as gases, aerosols, or gross particles under various
climatic conditions'. The specific task of the Wisconsin team was to
'devise methods for measuring behavioural changes resulting from
the administration of drugs that affect the central nervous system
of rhesus or pig-tailed macaques at several dose levels'.

This project was continued in 1965 with a $103,000 grant from
the Army Chemical Center at the Edgewood Arsenal, under contract
no. DA-18-035-AMC-368-(A). The Edgewood Arsenal financed the
second project at Wisconsin, in the field of 'pharmacology and
physiological chemistry of chemical warfare', under contract no.
DA-CML-18-108-61-G6. A description of the project prepared in
1961 indicates that 'mechanisms of incapacitation and/or of
lethality by selected compounds will be studied, including psychochemical events involved in brain function, the action of respiratory
centres, enzymatic processes and electrical phenomena occurring
during heart action'. The report states that Wisconsin's specific task
was to 'determine the action of vitamins in neurotoxicity, particularly thiamine, and its role in poisoning by tri-cresyl phosphate and
its metabolites'.

A continuing project on 'molecular binding and catalysis' is now
under way, including an investigation of the chemical properties of
the nerve gas sarin. The research is funded under contract no.
DA-18-035-AMC-115.

Yale University When the *New Republic* printed a story by Seymour M. Hersh in its issue of 6 May 1967 which listed Yale among
universities currently engaged in CBW research, Yale officials were
disposed to investigate the charge. Subsequently the Director of
Yale's Grant and Contract Administration, John H. Hoskins, indicated that, 'A review of contracts for research shows that there is
one funded through Fort Detrick. It is an unclassified basic research
agreement supporting research of Dr Jack R. Henderson, assistant
professor of Epidemiology in the Department of Epidemiology and
Public Health. His research is an investigation in the epidemiological properties of viruses.' Among the infections being investigated
by Dr Henderson is the Eastern equine encephalitis virus (*Yale
Daily News*, 8 May 1967).

Commercial Involvement

On occasions anything up to 65% of the total research and develop-
vent budget for CBW is known to have gone to commercial firms.
Many firms are involved, to a greater or lesser extent. Only a few
are mentioned below.

The Muscle Shoals Phosphate Development Works (Alabama) was set up in the early 1950s, at a cost of $50 million, for the production of nerve gas intermediates. At this time the final product was manufactured at the Rocky Mountain Arsenal mentioned above. On discovery of this, the citizens of Denver protested. In 1960 the plant was therefore transferred to a converted Atomic Energy Commission plant in Newport. This is operated by the Tennessee Valley Authority.

The Food Machinery Corporation (Newport, Indiana) operates a major plant for the production of nerve gas (sarin), which is then used to fill land mines, rockets and artillery shells. From here distribution is through normal Army channels. This factory employs a staff of 300 and is reported to have been working 24 hours a day since 1960.

The FMC operates the plant under military contract. Operations began in late 1959 after the FMC had accepted a Pentagon contract for its design and construction worth $13.5 m. Annual running costs, according to 1962 estimates, are $3.5 m.

The Shell Development Company (California) holds a 1952 Army Chemical Corps Procurement Agency contract (CML-4564) for an examination of synthetic cannabis derivatives both for incapacitating and lethal properties.

The Traveler's Research Corporation (Hartford, Conneticut) is an outgrowth of the Traveler's Insurance Company. One of its brochures states:

> The extensive experience of the TRC staff in research on turbulent diffusion and transport of atmospheric contaminants provides a firm base for TRC's participation in the nation's CB weapons analysis program. The center's interest in this field stems not only from the importance of understanding the environmental phenomena involved, but also from our desire to support and assist the United States in acquiring effective, humane, incapacitating (non-lethal) systems for coping with proliferating limited war and counter-insurgency. One study was undertaken for the Army to identify the most effective approaches for contending with difficult military situations with a minimum loss of human life to both sides. Another study conducted for the Navy provided an updated review of the influence of micrometeorological factors on chemical warfare in the form of a technical manual to assist in the identification, observation, and prediction of relevant meteorological factors and processes. In another study for the Army, TRC began comprehensive research on dosage predic-

tion techniques to provide up-to-date knowledge of dispersion processes in the lower atmosphere, and with a critical evaluation of the capabilities and limitations of present quantitative techniques for predicting the behaviour of atmospheric contaminants.

It adds:

> Because modern military planning must often consider technical and strategic goals in relation to their political, sociological and psychological implications, particularly with respect to limited war and counter insurgency, the study was undertaken for the Air Force to assess not only the military potential of non-lethal CB weaponry, but also the psycho-political reaction to its use.

In 1964 this firm was involved in a debate with the Physicians for Social Responsibility about the nature of its work. Since 1965 the TRC has held a contract for the airborne delivery of plague from both the Air Force and the Army. Dr Robert Ellis, the Director of the Bacteriological Weapons Section of the firm, admitted that the study was being made of

> the behavior of these agents (plague and tularemia) and the use of air currents for delivery of the toxic clouds over a target.

(For further discussion of this see Carol Brightman's article quoted in section 1, pp 64–6.)

The Research Analysis Corporation (near Washington) lists in its brochure the following 'research capabilities': study of biological and chemical attacks on crops and some analyses of effects on livestock; covert attack on a food crop; impact of chemical attack on guerilla food crop; evaluation of counter-insurgency requirements in SE Asia; SE Asia environmental data collection; military potential of GB (a nerve gas): the feasibility of chemical warfare in defence of a perimeter in the Naktong Valley basin; and the value of toxic chemicals in ground warfare.

Shock Hydrodynamics Inc. of Sherman Oaks, California, held an Air Force contract for the 'supersonic delivery of liquid chemicals and biological agents'.

Litton Industries were awarded a contract for the 'supersonic delivery of dry biological agents and also a number of contracts dealing with detection systems'.

In addition to these, some thirteen other firms held Pentagon contracts for the development of herbicides and defoliants. This is the tip of a very large iceberg indeed, as probably $200 m. will have been spent on CBW research and development in industry in 1969. This may, however, be the last year of large-scale spending on CBW in the United States. On 19 July 1969 the Senate Armed Services Committee rejected Pentagon plans for a $16 m. programme of offensive CBW development. The total budget proposed was $88 m. Cuts were made in lethal gas and biological capability which the Army wished to acquire.

It is obvious from the information given above that research and expenditure in CBW is quite extensive. The following quotations provide an interesting commentary on all this activity:

> The Air Force budget for the fiscal year beginning next July 1st, now being prepared, will call for the first time for equipping airplanes with nozzles and sprays to deliver 'non-lethal' blows against military installations and population centers.
> [*New York Times*, 2 November 1960]

> *Mr. Sikes:* How far are we going in the way of warning systems and in providing a gas mask and similar defensive measures?

> *Gen. (Earle G.) Wheeler* (US Army Chief of Staff): They are in the hands of troops but we need better types.

> *Mr. Sikes:* I would assume the civilian population was almost completely unprotected in these fields?

> *Secretary Vance:* That is right.
> [US House Appropriations Committee on the 1964 Defence Budget]

> Coincident with the formation of the new airomobile division, the Army is issuing improved new gas masks to its helicopter pilots. A hood to protect the head and neck against mustard and V nerve gases which seep through the skin is also being developed.
> [*Aviation Daily*, 6 December 1965]

2. CANADA

The organisation of CBW research and development is similar to that in Britain and the US. The government department responsible is the Defence Research Board (DRB), which operates eight specialised research and development establishments, three of which are concerned with CBW, and 'organises and supports research on problems of defence interest in universities and other agencies' (*Canadian Almanac and Directory*). Annual expenditure is between $30 and $40 million.

Suffield Experimental Station, Ralston, Alberta is the largest of the government establishments, and covers about 1000 square miles of flat prairie land. The area is surrounded by high wire fences.

From 1941 to 1947, when it was taken over by the DRB, Suffield was the responsibility of the Army.

In 1942, a chemical warfare school known as S-11 was established at the station under the command of Lt.-Col. J. Roberts. This school which was originally set up for the training of mortar companies also conducted experimental field trials with mortars and rockets using CW-filled shells.

[*Canadian Almanac and Directory*]

A new laboratory was opened in 1955 at a cost of $1,500,000, and there are currently three wings under the Chief Superintendent at Suffield, the Administrative Wing, the Research Wing and the Field Wing.

The Research Wing is divided into six sections; physics and meteorology, chemistry, radiation, physiology, animal and bacteriology.... The Field Wing consists of a field experimental section which conducts the field trials and a munitions and toxic stores section.

[*Canadian Almanac and Directory*]

Research has been carried out into nerve gases and botulinus toxin, amongst other things. According to Dr Brock Chisholm:

During the war, the method of testing was to clear large areas of prairie in the Canadian West and to stake out prairie dogs, chickens, pigs and other animals at various points, widely distributed throughout the area. The fatalities were extraordinary— almost unbelievable and with very small quantities of botulinus toxin being used.

A toxoid was subsequently developed and 235,000 doses administered to troops in the US, Britain and Canada.

Mr Archie Penney, the deputy chairman of the DRB, has stated publically that Suffield is engaged in the development of new weapons.

Other centres   The other two centres are the Defence Research Kingston Laboratories at Barriefield, Ontario, and Defence Research Chemical Laboratories at Ottawa, Ontario (*Canada Year Book 1962*).

There is at present no information available as to the extent of university or commercial participation in CBW research in Canada.

3. BRITAIN

Britain's centre for chemical and biological weapon defence research is at Porton Down in Wiltshire. It was established in 1916 after World War I at a cost of £4 million. At this time the emphasis was obviously on chemicals alone. After World War II the field of study was extended to biological weapons and a small unit was set up under Sir Paul Fildes to consider this aspect.

The establishment was originally under the Ministry of Supply, but when this was disbanded in 1960 it became the responsibility of the War Office and is currently under the Army Department of the Ministry of Defence. The total area inside the 22-mile long wire fence surrounding Porton is about 10 square miles. Of this, 7000 acres are used for testing. Apparently, 1300 acres of Allington farm are used for conventional farming. There is in addition a school at Winterbourne Gunner.

Allington Farm   The main function of the farm lies in its Animal Breeding Centre. The Superintendent has described it as:

> a small production department providing biological aids for MRE and CDEE and other Ministry of Defence establishments. The only experiments as such are the production of serum for Dr. Smith's establishment.
>
> [*Select Committee*]

Surplus guinea pigs are supplied to the Public Health Laboratory Service on repayment ... rats ... are supplied to the Nuffield Department of Clinical Medicine at the Radcliffe Infirmary Oxford ... at a charge of 11s. per pair....

[*Hansard*, 29 May 1968]

The Chemical Defence Experimental Establishment

The annual cost of the CDEE is £1·6 million, about £90,000 of which is accounted for by services provided to the MRE and Allington Farm. The staff includes seventy scientific and engineering grades (including medical) and 120 experimental officers (including medical) thirteen of whom are service officers. The function of the last mentioned is:

> to represent and interpret in detail the functional requirements of their service's equipment in the CW defence field and to inform and advise their service of technological advances in these fields which can influence policy and functional requirements for equipment.
>
> [Report of the Select Committee on Science and Technology, 6 May 1968]

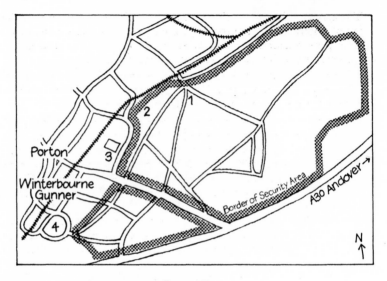

PORTON DOWN

1. Allington Farm.
2. Chemical Defence Experimental Establishment.
3. Microbiological Research Establishment.
4. School of Nuclear and Chemical Ground Defence.

In addition to permanent staff the CDEE have:

> visits from the Advisory Board, that is the Chemical Defence Advisory Board of the Scientific Advisory Council.
>
> [Select Committee Report]

This has

> 9 members excluding crown servants. No member ... receives a grant for research.
>
> [*Hansard*, 21 June 1968]

There are also:

> consultant visits from scientists and technologists either from industry or from the universities ... and a system of vacation consultations. This involves scientists ... from professors down to lecturers and research people who come to the establishment normally during the summer vacation and work here on average for 2 months.
>
> [Select Committee Report]

The exact percentage of the CDEE's work which remains unpublished is not known but it is probably about 30% to 45%. Activities vary from pure research to commercial transactions with industry.

According to Mr G. N. Gadsby, Director of the CDEE:

We are neither staffed nor financed to undertake purely civil work on any significant scale. This should not be taken to infer that we have no interest in civil/industrial type problems.

Pure research covers aerosol physics, physical chemistry, bio-chemistry, micrometeorology and study of particle size. Applications of research done include several different specialised respirators, a portable resuscitator, air filtration units, protective clothing, alarm equipment, a needleless injector for the delivery of atropine injections and an oxime tablet to be taken to reinforce atropine as an antidote to nerve gases.

Some of these things are of interest to industry. The portable resuscitator is manufactured under licence by an industrial firm, which has sold over 8000 to fire brigades and rescue services. The needleless injector has been in commercial use for about a year (*Hansard*, 22 May 1968). In 1967–68 between £15,000 and £30,000 was earned in this way. Much of this is done through the National Research and Development Corporation.

We also undertake certain services in support of industry under the aegis of the Board of Trade and the Ministry of Labour.

[Select Committee Report]

Direct services to other government departments, such as the Ministry of Overseas Development, Ministry of Technology and the armed forces, yielded an income of about £7000 last year.

Other Ministry of Defence patents have relevance to the development of certain insecticides and aerosols.

There remain two aspects of the CDEE's work which have very little relevance to industry. These are work on the nerve agents and the development of the riot control agent CS. Patents are currently held by the Ministry of Defence in respect of both of these.

According to the Select Committee Report:

Basic work on organic phosphorous compounds has been done here in relation to the G agents and the V agents,

(off the record)

... In the case of the G agents these came from German developments during World War II. The V agents which were identified in the UK stemmed directly from work which was done by a large chemical organisation in this country working on insecticides.

(This is referred to later in the section on nerve agents.)

Research on the application of insecticides is now the responsibility of the Ministry of Overseas Development. The v agents were subsequently developed further in the USA, and are now stockpiled. Considerable work is also done on the riot-control gas CS. This gas was developed at Porton as a less dangerous alternative to other agents currently in use. Newer methods of using these agents are continually being prepared; 1969's innovation is a cluster bomb. Much work is in progress on 'technical chemistry' on pyrotechnics and smokes, and on dissemination methods. There is an active munitions section which is concerned with various aspects of design and assessment of the effects of CW in the field.

Nancekuke pilot plant

The Army Experimental Station at Nancekuke is situated between Portreath and Portowan in Cornwall. It is an outstation of the CDEE, dealing with processing. It was first established in 1925 as the Chemical Defence Research Establishment on the site of a first world war gas factory at Sutton Oak in Lancashire. In 1949 it was transferred to a disused airfield at Nancekuke and in 1962 became the Processing Research Division of the CDEE.

Expenditure and staff are not known. Facilities are available

for exploring manufacturing processes on a smaller than pilot plant scale.

[Mr Gadsby, Select Committee Report]

The most convenient source of fresh water is the local mineshafts, in particular Williams mineshaft which supplied 14 m. gallons in 1965, 13.6 million in 1966 and 5.6 million in 1967. [*Hansard*, 8 May 1968]

It has been suggested that waste materials are disposed of in the same way. If this is so, then the earth tremor experienced by Cornwall in 1965 may well be explained, in view of the occurrences at the US plant in Colorado, although officials at Nancekuke insist that sterilised effluent is piped out to sea.

It has also been suggested that there is an underwater sonar screen around the station as protection. The screen is undoubtedly there but that particular function has been denied:

The transmissions referred to which are being carried out by the Navy Department for oceanographic research purposes have no connection with the CDEE.

[*Hansard*, 8 May 1968]

The largest single activity of Nancekuke is the production of CS. Its production capacity is apparently 5 tons per year, according to

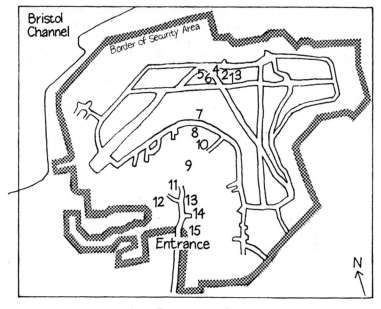

ARMY EXPERIMENTAL STATION
NANCEKUKE, PORTREATH, CORNWALL

1. Offices and safety building.
2. Process building.
3. Charging building.
4. Laboratories.
5. Boiler house.
6. Generator.
7. Laboratory.
8. Refuse disposal unit.
9. Substation—switchroom.
10. Laboratories.
11. Substation—drawing office.
12. Store.
13. Police unit.
14. Laboratories.
15. Police Lodge—dog kennels.

Mr Gadsby. (Some newspapers, however, reported it to be 60 tons.)
The amount manufactured is not constant, it seems; only a ton was
made in 1967 and none in the first six months of 1968. At the same
time, 1½ tons p.a., according to the Ministry, is transported to
Schermuly Ltd, Dorking, Surrey (see below). Occasionally cs is sold
in bulk to overseas governments, but there are no details available to
identify these.

Four rail wagon loads of cs were transported from Cornwall to
Surrey between May 1967 and May 1968 (*Hansard*, 30 May 1968).
The gas left:

in powder form packed in polythene liners in sealed steel drums.
The drums were then loaded into specially lined wagons.

The drums hold 134 lb. In case of accident

> the gas would not be harmful unless it was kicked or there was a high wind.
>
> The only result would be, in the words of the Ministry spokesman, 'a tickle on the end of your nose'.
>
> [*Surrey Advertiser*, May 1968]

Apart from CS, the Nancekuke establishment is concerned with the production of antidotes to the nerve gases, especially the production of P2S (on antidotes, see below pp 212–23, esp. 215–17). It is rumoured that P2S is produced by a commercial firm in this country in tablet form. Research into the production of British anti-Lewisite and CN is also studied.

The functions of Nancekuke are listed as:

1. the assessment of large-scale production;
2. limited supply for trials;
3. production for protection and detection;
4. storage characteristics.

Papers on work done have been published on occasions, but 'a significant part of the role of the station is secret' (*Hansard*, 8 May 1968).

Testing

Some 7000 acres of Porton are used for testing, and a small area of this is permanently sealed off—where small-scale tests with nerve gas take place.

The remaining area is used to test smokes and riot-control devices. This contains many features of archaeological, botanical and zoological interest. It is periodically open to parties of the public with special interests, such as natural history societies. There is also a small unit where experiments are carried out on volunteers, under strict medical supervision. This includes tests with nerve gas.

On 16 March 1960 the following article appeared in the *Daily Telegraph* under the headline 'Nerve Gas tests on Servicemen':

> Nerve gas experiments on British Servicemen have been carried out in great secrecy at the Army Chemical Defence Experimental Establishment at Porton near Salisbury.... The War Office has confirmed the use of nerve gases and the fact that servicemen have been acting as voluntary 'guinea pigs'.

Perhaps there has been a change of policy since 1960. On 19 June 1968, Mr Tam Dalyell asked the Secretary of State for Defence:

> What experiments are being conducted in defence research establishments involving the use of atropine?

MR JOHN MORRIS: 'None.'[1]

(Atropine is the antidote to nerve gas poisoning.)

Moreover, on the same day Mr Dalyell asked:

How many British soldiers volunteered last year to be subjects for experiments in the use of the gas BZ?

MR. JOHN MORRIS: ... In practice servicemen volunteer, not for specific tests, but for any tests which may be necessary to carry out in future. When the need arises servicemen are told beforehand of the nature of the test and are then at liberty to withdraw if they wish. Four volunteers took part in BZ tests in 1967. The tests were carefully controlled and there was no danger to the men concerned.

[*Hansard*]

Nevertheless, accidents do occur, and probably more than are actually publicised. On 9 June 1953 the Minister of Supply, Mr Sandys, stated:

I regret that on 6th May LAC Ronald Maddison died from the effects of asphyxia after taking part in a trial with war gas at the Chemical Defence Experimental Establishment at Porton. In addition to the coroner's inquest, I ordered a full technical investigation into the circumstances of the accident. The report shows that all the same precautions had been observed as in the many thousands of previous trials carried out over a considerable number of years.... Further trials of this kind have been suspended.

On 22 June 1953 Mr Driberg asked:

How many fatal accidents have occurred since 1954 in consequence of war gas and other trials at the CDEE Porton and other chemical and biological establishments; how many men have been disabled for considerable periods of time; what percentage of those taking part in the trials are servicemen; how far participation in them by servicemen is compulsory and whether it is proposed to resume the trials suspended after the fatal accident of 6th May.

Mr Sandys replied:

Apart from the case of 6th May there have been no accidents of the kind referred to in the first and second parts of the question.

---

[1] The authors know of several experiments conducted in 1968 involving atropine. This answer is wrong.

Almost all those taking part have been servicemen and all have been volunteers. The question of the resumption of the trials must await the completion of the study of the cause of the recent accident.

There have apparently been 'no cases of accident or illness among workers engaged in research at Nancekuke in the last three years' (*Hansard*, 8 May 1968). According to a report in *Peace News* on 3 December 1965, prior to that date, 'Over a four-year period, on two occasions poison gas has actually escaped and gas masks have had to be worn.'

The Microbiological Research Establishment

The MRE was set up in 1951 and its annual cost is about £900,000. The staff includes forty-eight scientific officers and seventy-six experimental officers. The Biological Research Advisory Board consists of eleven members, excluding Crown servants.

About 10% of the budget comes from civil sources and 80–90% of the results of all work done is published. As with the CDEE, there is a considerable range of activities. The two principal functions, according to Dr C. E. Gordon Smith, the Director, are:

> to assess the risk to the British people and armed forces of attack by biological warfare and to devise means of protection against such attack.
>
> [*Nature*, 22 June 1968]

To this end the MRE laboratories are extremely well equipped and have facilities which are in some respects the best in Europe. These include the ability to produce large amounts of certain organisms.

One international seminar on continuous culture has been held to which were invited delegates from Russia and Czechoslovakia.

Research into antigens and the production of vaccines is also a function of the MRE. Anthrax vaccine is supplied to the Ministry of Health through the Lister Institute [Select Committee Report]. The MRE facilities are useful in abnormal circumstances. Over three-quarters of a million doses of vaccine were produced for the Asian 'flu epidemic.

Just recently a great deal of useful work has been done on the Vervet Monkey Disease which caused seven deaths in Germany. Reports of progress were:

> sent to 40 Laboratories all over the world; 9 of these have been supplied with infective material and/or antisera: 4 in the USA,

and one each in Germany, Panama, South Africa, Uganda and the USSR. A non-infective complement fixing antigen has been prepared for distribution to the WHO reference laboratories.

[*Hansard*, May 1968]

The MRE has also:

been making studies for and in collaboration with the Animal Virus Research Institute into the survival of foot and mouth disease, disease virus in the atmosphere, the meteorological conditions favourable to its transmission and into the possibility of its transmision to animals by way of infected milk tankers.

[*Hansard*, 15 May 1968]

A study of the ecology of mosquitoes in Tanzania is being undertaken by one of the entomologists at the MRE who has been seconded there for 3 months to the World Health Organisation.

[*Hansard*, 22 May 1968]

In addition the establishment:

assists by being represented on the Basic Research Committee of the Water Pollution Research Laboratory and also provides supplies of bacterial tracer as required.

[*Hansard*, 22 May 1968]

Work has been done on the development of penicillin for the NRDC.

A mobile laboratory pathogen unit has also been developed, the details of which have appeared in technical literature. It has been demonstrated at a meeting of the Society of Applied Bacteriology and will be sold on the commercial market.

The establishment also has:

a programme of research on decontamination. . . . On a number of occasions the Establishment has assisted in the testing of sterilisation techniques.

[*Hansard*, 22 May 1968]

Stringent safety precautions are observed at all times.

It is said by eminent scientists that these are the most stringent in the world. Both staff and public are protected by the use of air filters that have been especially designed to remove all bacteria and viruses from the air leaving fume cupboards, safety boxes and laboratories. The effluent water is also sterilised and tested for sterility before ejection to the establishment's drainage system.

[*Daily Telegraph*, 10 August 1962 (letter from J. E. Firman, former engineer at Porton)]

In spite of this, and the security measures, accidents do occur. In June 1959 an Indian rhesus monkey escaped while being transported from Porton to another centre. It took cover in Patcham Woods, Sussex. The order was given to shoot the animal on sight. Armed men who took part in the search were told that the monkey was 'dangerously contaminated'. This was later denied.

In August 1962 Mr Geoffrey Bacon, a research scientist at Porton, died of pneumonic plague. The disease was given on his medical certificate as 'virus infection'. He was admitted to the Salisbury Royal Infirmary on the day this certificate was received at Porton. The following afternoon two doctors arrived at the hospital from Porton and diagnosed plague. Mr Bacon died that evening. A secret inquiry was held by the War Office at which the local Medical Officers of Health were present only as observers.

This incident caused much concern. Councillor Austin Underwood, then a member of Amesbury Rural District Council's Public Health Committee, attempted to make public the dangers he felt that Porton held for the area. Explosions (there have been two) could release massive amounts of bacteria into the atmosphere. He also pressed for Porton to have its own isolation hospital to minimise the danger of any more accidents like that of Mr Bacon. According to a film shown by BBC on 6 June 1968, there is, in fact, now an isolation hospital at Porton.

It is obvious that a lot of the work done at Porton is in fact extremely valuable. For several reasons there is nevertheless still a cause for concern about the existence of the establishment in its present form and also about some of the work done which is not so well publicised.

A great many of the papers published from Porton concern plague and aerosols.

In the *New Scientist* on 8 December 1966, Dr Bernard Dixon considered the implications of these. He concluded that:

> The knowledge and techniques required to accomplish this entire programme (i.e. development, large-scale manufacture, and means of dissemination of bacteria suitable for CBW) are reflected either explicitly or implicitly in the hundreds of papers which have been published from Porton. Much of the work can be interpreted as the preparation for offensive biological warfare. Much of it can equally well be explained as prudent defensive research.

More recently a paper was published in the *Journal of Microbiology* by W. D. Lawton of Fort Detrick and B. C. Morris of Porton. This concerned experiments involving the transfer of genes between strains of bacteria closely related to plague. This will be discussed in Part 2.

It has also been rumoured that Porton is currently exporting large amounts of plague vaccine to America.

University Involvement

In answer to a question asked by Mr Dalyell in the House of Commons on 19 May 1968, details of research sponsored by the CDEE and the MRE were given as follows.[1]

CHEMICAL DEFENCE EXPERIMENTAL ESTABLISHMENT

Nature of Research	Location
Research on fluorohydrocarbons	University of Birmingham
The isolation purification and structure determination of physiologically active peptides	University of Exeter
The development of ultra-microbiochemical techniques to explore the mode of action of drugs	University of Liverpool
Synthesis of components of pharmacological or therapeutic interest	University of Manchester Institute of Science and Technology
A study of the processes concerned with the metabolism of drugs and toxic substances	St Mary's Hospital Medical School
Determination of the structure of pharmacologically active compounds	University of Sheffield
Studies in the chemistry of organo-phosphorous compounds	University of St Andrews
Synthesis of 4 hydroxy 1,2,3,4 tetrahydrisoquinolines	London University
Histopathological studies in neurotoxicity	London University Institute of Neurology
Research on the optical properties of aerosols	University College of South Wales
The absorption and removal of hydrocyanic acid gas by solids	University of Bristol

[1] Any errors in terminology are due to *Hansard*. Some of the more obvious ones have been corrected.

Nature of research	*Location*
Metabolism and toxicity of highly fluorinated cyclohexanes	University of Birmingham
Effect of prolonged inhibition of cholinesterase in animals	Middlesex Hospital Medical School
A combined behavioural electro-physiological and biochemical investigation of the central action of certain drugs	University of Birmingham
Investigation of the preparation and properties of fibrous absorptive carbons	University of Bristol
A physico-chemical investigation of the reaction of nucleophiles with unsaturated systems	King's College, London
An investigation of the ability of some biological systems to inactivate acetylcholine and of the mechanism of such inactivation	Chelsea College of Science and Technology
Genetica factosa and the effect of infantile stimulation on the activity of the acetylcholine—cholinesterase and other systems in the brain of the rat	University of Southampton
Nucleophilic catalysis in relation to the treatment of organophosphate poisoning	University of Kent
Some aspects of the biochemistry of the skin	Queen's University, Belfast
Factors influencing the gelation of liquids with special reference to organic liquids and gels without chemical cross-links	Welsh College of Advanced Technology
The effect of drugs on neuro-muscular transmissions and contractile force of mammalian skeletal muscle	University of Bristol
Studies relevant to the reactivation of organo-phosphorus inhibited enzymes	University of St Andrews

MICROBIOLOGICAL RESEARCH ESTABLISHMENT

Nature of Research	*Location*
Investigation of fluorocarbohydrates	University of Oxford
Diffusion controlled electrodes for use in biological systems	Birkbeck College, London University
Investigation of the use of hydrated calcium phosphate and related materials for the purification and fractionation of viruses and viral compounds	Oxford College of Technology

| Fractionation of compounds of microbial origin important in the pathogenesis of infectious diseases | University of Birmingham |
| Electrophoretic behaviour of bacteria | University of Liverpool |

This was verified by the Select Committee report, which added that these contracts:

> did not put the university into a position that they did not want themselves. They voluntarily enter into this.

Further research produced some more details of defence contracts.

Birmingham University Study is being conducted into the fractionation of compounds of microbial origin important in the pathogenesis of infectious diseases.

Bristol University The Chemistry Department has three contracts. These concern the basic physical measurements of the absorption of gas by porous carbons; the absorption of gas on solids; and antidotes for gases (lapsed).

Exeter University Research is under way into the isolation, purification and structure determination of ricin.

King's College, London Dr Mary Whittaker is studying isoenzmyes of cholinesterase in blood and tissues. (Nerve gases are anticholinesterase agents.) Dr Whittaker told the *Observer* (26 May 1968):

> I work for a Medical Department. If Porton withdrew their support I should seek a grant from somewhere else to continue the work or re-apply to Porton at a later date.

Dr Whittaker was working on insecticides in 1937 and over two years developed symptoms similar to those now resulting from nerve gases. This process continued for seventeen years, resulting in permanent handicap (BBC programme 6 June 1968).

Institute of Neurology Research is being conducted into certain pesticides and insecticides known to cause paralysis.

University of Liverpool The Department of Inorganic Physical and Industrial Chemistry held a contract from April 1967 to April 1968 worth £1200 for Electro-phoretic behaviour of bacteria. The Department of Pharmacology over this period had a contract for 'ultra microbiochemical techniques for exploring mode of action in drugs'.

The University of Liverpool *Recorder*, No. 48, October 1968, carries the announcement:

> The Council has gratefully accepted the following research grants:

From the Ministry of Defence:

> A further grant of up to £1545 for a period of 10 months from 1 March 1968, in continued support of the research into the developments of ultramicro analytical techniques to study the local actions of drugs being carried out in the Department of Pharmacology.

In May 1968, the Registrar of the University made the following statement in answer to the concern expressed about these contracts:

> The work being done in our Chemistry Department, and which is partly supported by the Chemical and Biological Establishment of the Ministry of Defence, Porton, is entirely fundamental and academic in character. It relates to the investigation of the chemical and physical structure of the surfaces of biological cells, using harmless bacteria, by the technique of micro-electrophoresis (which was discovered and developed in this laboratory). This work has been in progress in the laboratory for the past fourteen years. It is not in any way secret and the findings have been published without restriction in the leading chemical and biological journals. In fact, eight papers have already been published. The theses of the graduates who have carried out this work are all freely available in the University Library for reading.
>
> In undertaking these studies we have been entirely free to choose the direction of the research. The financial assistance has merely helped in carrying out research which would have been done irrespective of the Ministry's support.

St Mary's Hospital Medical School   Work is being done on the metabolic fate of toxic substances.

Oxford College of Technology   A contract is held for the separation of protein and nucleic acids to obtain these materials in a highly purified form.

These contracts are all financed by the Ministry of Defence and they are all pure, not applied, research. The results of the work are published in open literature. This is by no means a comprehensive list of relevant defence contracts, but it serves to indicate the level at which the university is involved.

On the whole it seems that very little objection can be raised in so far as the research is at such a fundamental level. There are, however, exceptions. On 13 February 1968 in answer to a question asked by Mrs Ann Kerr, Mr Benn stated that of the contracts the Ministry of Technology had placed for defence purposes, thirty-seven had a security classification. These were not identified so there is no way of knowing whether any of them is relevant to CBW.

Commercial involvement

Information on this subject is difficult to find. The firms themselves do not broadcast their activities in this field unless it becomes necessary, and with respect to contracts the government consistently refuses to provide any details.

22 May 1968

> Mr Dalyell asked the Secretary of State for Defence if he will publish the terms of the commercial agreement between the MRE Porton and the Wellcome Foundation in relation to the development of pharmaceuticals.

> MR JOHN MORRIS: 'It is not our normal practice to publish commercial agreements of this kind.'

19 June 1968

> Mr Dalyell asked . . . what are the terms of his Department's contract for the manufacture of gas with Schermuly Ltd, Spar Works, Newdigate, Guildford, Surrey.

> MR JOHN MORRIS: 'It is not the practice to disclose the terms of contracts.'

> Mr Dalyell asked . . . what contracts Her Majesty's government have with the Charterhouse group of companies or their subsidiaries in relation to the manufacture and packaging of CS gas.

> MR JOHN MORRIS: 'It is not the practice to disclose details of Government contracts with commercial firms.'

Schermuly Ltd—subsidiary of the Charterhouse Group This firm is located in Dorking, Surrey. For the last eight years about 1% of the turnover has come from the packaging of CS gas which arrives from the pilot plant at Nancekuke.

Four CS products are assembled: (i) a 460-gram hand-grenade, with a range of up to 35 m, which continues to emit its contents for 16 sec after detonation; (ii) a 135-gram cartridge (which can be fired from a standard 38-mm Webley & Scott signal pistol), with a range of 70–90 m, which continues to emit for 10 sec; (iii) a port-fire—about 20 in long, which is used for demonstrating the effects of CS fire when training troops and riot police, and (iv) a training pellet, which is used for the same purpose.

The CS is mixed into a composition containing 25% CS, 30% potassium chlorate, 30% sucrose, 3% kaolin and 2% zinc oxide. This composition has a high efficiency: 90% of the CS is vaporised and only 10% lost in the process.

The mixture is pressed into hollow pellets: 194 grams for the grenade, 54 grams for the cartridge. These are then assembled and dispatched in ammunition boxes containing ten grenades or forty-two cartridges.

There are two kinds of contractual arrangement: an embodiment loan, whereby the casing and detonator remain the Ministry's property and are simply lent to Schermuly to be filled with a CS mixture and assembled, the finished product being sold by the Ministry to police forces inside Britain: and an export licence, whereby Schermuly buys the casing and detonator from the manufacturers, fills them with a CS mixture and sells them direct to police forces abroad. The Ministry refuses to disclose all the names of overseas governments to which CS weapons have been sold by Schermuly. They include a number of NATO and Commonwealth countries, among them Hong Kong, Singapore, Ceylon, Malaya, Cyprus, Bermuda and Jamaica. They do not include France or the US.

The finished tear gas canisters are packed into ammunition boxes and transported from the factory by lorry—in respect of exports, to Southampton. Boxes are reported to have been packed for South Africa, Vietnam, Australia and Ghana.

On June 14 1968 several Army lorries arrived at the CS packing section and left fully loaded with an armed escort. During the loading procedure, one man with rifle and binoculars positioned himself on a 'tower' inside the plant. The CS laboratory was boarded up that afternoon. It is possible that a militant demonstration was expected and the factory stocks had been removed to an Army storage depot. However, laboratory work continued.

Because of adverse publicity one of the directors of Schermuly, Mr M. D. Fairbrother, made the following statement:

> In the past few weeks much publicity has been given to the anti-riot agent known as CS. Both CS and the name of Schermuly Ltd were included in a long article in the Sunday Observer on May 26—the following week the BBC elected to show a film on chemi-

cal and biological warfare in which there was specific reference to cs—*Sanity*, the voice of CND, thought fit to take up the cry in their June issue; the organisation has apparently decided to attract further publicity by one of their marches on this factory. My company has been involved with cs for the past eight years. This is a substance of which we have no fear and it is incomprehensible that it should be linked with any CND campaign....

Those of the public who know our company, a company already known to mariners throughout the world, are aware that practically the whole of our production covers pyrotechnics for the purpose of saving life.

cs smoke generators and cartridges produced by this company are basically pyrotechnics and are categorised by us as items designed for dispersing rioters without those responsible for law enforcement having to resort to methods which might inflict injuries and even worse. There would never have been a Sharpeville episode if cs had been available.

Now let us deal with the ingredients of cs. This we acquire from the Ministry of Defence and it arrives properly packed in sealed drums by British Railway goods and carrier services. We treat it with similar respect as applied to other pyrotechnic chemicals and ingredients and store it in the same manner. It is a powder which looks like sugar and you can handle it with bare hands. If you blow a little into the air the reaction is that of taking a good dose of snuff—perhaps a slight overdose and admittedly without any satisfaction that may be gained by this form of powdered tobacco!

In fact, light-heartedly we say in the factory that if you want to cure or keep free of colds spend an hour or two in the cs section. Mixing and pressing operators working with it all the time have quite average protective clothing and masks. When management or foremen or even visitors visit the sheds where mixing and pressing are carried on, no special clothing or masks are worn but all are prepared for some discomfort including a good cry or a sneeze or two if free particles are inhaled or enter the eye. This procedure has been going on for the full eight years.

cs is mixed with normal every-day pyrotechnic chemicals to obtain its final form of a cs smoke composition. As smoke it generates fast and its effect is immediate—this has been put to the test by many of us in this factory—recovery from its effect is rapid and complete. Because these stores generate smoke fast and with immediate effect, it dissuades rioters from attempting to pick them up and throw them back as is done so often with an-

other product, CN (ω-chloro-acetophenone), better known as tear
gas, an anti-riot agent which has been used for the best part of
this century. This is generally recognised as relatively harmless
but CS is authoritatively considered to be even less harmful.

This explains the CS as seen, handled, known and supplied
from our factory.

Now we ask ourselves, why this apparent concerted attempt to
discredit CS and all those connected with it. British CS anti-riot
grenades and cartridges have been used effectively for years without any evidence of harm to anyone—and this also applies to
CN. Among many territories in which CS has been used effectively
and without recrimination is Hong Kong—had it not been so
effectively used by properly trained British police there might
otherwise have been serious bloodshed with grave consequence
to its inhabitants and world opinion.

One final authentic piece of evidence indicating that there need
be no concern about danger from CS smoke. In addition to the
grenades and cartridges referred to above we make what is called
a training generator which has the identical filling. This is used
by the forces not only for testing respirators but for demonstrating
the effects of CS to the troops.

CS as used by the British and as mixed, filled, assembled and
supplied by Schermuly is unadulterated by any chemical or irritant which might induce the appalling effects which recently
have been ascribed to it.

It may have been noticed that apart from the heading [?], I
referred to these stores as CS smoke generators. This is a far more
accurate description than is the sinister word 'gas' which undoubtedly became tagged to CS because of its being similar
to that of CN which has universally been known as tear gas over
the decades.

I am confident that the majority of people treat with a certain
scepticism the more sensational reports they may read.

Very little is known about other firms, but some information appeared in a pamphlet published by the Stop It Committee in 1968.

Imperial Chemical Industries produce dialkylthiolphosphonic
acids—components of nerve gas. They currently hold US patent
2863901 for this and have held a British patent, 797603 in the past.

A subsidiary, Plant Protection Ltd, produces 2,4-D-2,4,5-T and
MCPA.

Albright and Wilson holds a US patent for the manufacture of
phosphorus-containing pesticides which are toxic to man.

Other sources have alleged that Albright and Wilson are producing a mustard gas in crystalline form packed into canisters to be exploded by an impact detonator, the heat of which turns the crystals into gas.

There is undoubtedly a great deal more commercial involvement, but this is as far as our knowledge extends at present.

4. WEST GERMANY

The following description of research and development in c and b weapons was given by Dr Ehrenfried Petras, the former Director of the Laboratory for Microbiology in the Institute of Aerobiology in Grafschaft Sauerland.

The statement is quoted as given on 6 December 1968 before an International Press conference in East Berlin arranged by the East German Foreign Ministry.

The West German military research potential in the b and c weapon sector comprises a wide range of highly pathogenic microorganisms and virus aerosols, v substances, g gases, toxins, psychoactive war agents, algogens and phytotoxic war agents.

The scientific treatment of these problems in special research establishments, university institutes and in laboratories of the chemical industry in West Germany gives predominance to the following considerations:

1. Further research into and the new development of biological and chemical war agents and the possibilities of applying them as aerosols.
2. The investigation of optimal procedures for detecting these toxic agents and rendering them harmless, including the development and production of antidotes.
3. Investigation into combined injuries arising from the simultaneous action of various forms of ABC weapons.
4. Research into all the problems concerned with individual and collective protection, as well as medical provision for the victims of poisoning and radiation.

These research complexes form a necessary unity within the West German Federal Defence Ministry's conception on the comprehensive preparation of atomic, biological and chemical (ABC) warfare and for this reason cannot be regarded independently of one another.

The current West German armament program in the b and c weapon sector is carried through as a tightly organized system of research, testing and preparations for production under the supervision of the Federal Ministry of Defence. The central administration of military research and development work in this field is to be found in the Military Technology Department of the Federal Ministry of Defence.

This relates to conferring of contracts, coordination, and the financing of work. At the same time this department exercises a decisive influence on the selection of the highly-qualified scientists needed to carry out the required work.

Recently a special 'ABC Study Group' was set up on the initiative of the Federal Ministry of Defence for the immediate direction of preparations for biological and chemical warfare. This is made up of representatives of the sections of the Federal Ministry of Defence which are concerned with this work.

A special role as an advisory and coordination body of the Bonn Ministry of Defence in the ABC sector is played by the 'Scientific Advisory Board for the Medical and Health Services of the Bundeswehr', which is also referred to as the 'Advisory Council on Military Medicine'.

Apart from these bodies the Federal Ministry of Defence has its own research establishments, such as the ABC E 53 proving ground of the Bundeswehr in Münsterlager in the Lüneburger Heide, the ABC Defence School at Sonthofen, as well as the Institute of Aerobiology in Grafschaft. Furthermore, it also directly concludes research contracts with individual persons or scientific work teams, or, for purposes of camouflage, via the Fraunhofer Society.

Because of various political and economic considerations, as well as for purposes of maintaining secrecy and camouflaging its activities, the West German Ministry of Defence has from the very beginning of its rearmament placed value on having its military research conducted in such a manner, largely in the existing civilian research establishments of West German chemical trusts, university institutes and other research bodies, that its real character was not immediately evident. One of the main prerequisites for this method lies in the fact that, under the conditions of modern research and industry, there is a large amount of overlapping of research work for civil and military purposes. This results in substantial advantages for the West German Ministry of Defence, such as a better camouflaging of its work for offensive military purposes in civil research currently being conducted, and the saving of time, personnel and funds.

Even today the West German Ministry of Defence has already secured a dominant influence on the corresponding West German potential in research and industry so that there are many scientists who do not dare to reject research contracts of the Federal Ministry of Defence.... The Institute of Aerobiology in Grafschaft, Sauerland, was founded in 1959 with the aim of carrying out research for the West German Ministry of Defence on preparations for b and c warfare. At first it was thought of directly subordinating the Institute of Aerobiology to the Federal Ministry of Defence as a federal institution. But this idea was rapidly dropped and instead the Institute was formally subordinated to the Fraunhofer Society for purposes of camouflage.

Thus the responsibilities of the Institute were from the very beginning determined by technical military projects of an offensive character. As early as spring 1961 the Federal Ministry of Defence took over the direct management and control of the Institute. The special interest of the Federal Ministry of Defence in the Institute was also made very plain by the fact that the Federal Defence Minister of that time, Franz Josef Strauss, made an appointment to visit the Institute on 10 January 1961.

The conferring of contracts for the Federal Ministry of Defence is conducted by section T II 2, formerly section T II 4 of Department T (military technology). The responsible consultant for the Federal Ministry of Defence was Ministerial Counsellor Dr Glupe until last year. Since 1967 the Grafschaft Institute has been directly responsible in scientific matters to the instructions of Ministerial Counsellor Dr Strathmann in the Federal Ministry of Defence, whereby Dr Engelhard (the son of Professor Engelhard of Göttingen University) is working as his assistant.

In accordance with the statute of the Fraunhofer Society, a board of trustees was assigned to the Institute director. This board has the task of specifying the special responsibilities of the Institute in close cooperation with the Federal Ministry of Defence. Prominent scientists belong to the board, who at the same time maintain connections with other institutes and thus establish an expansion of the scientific potential to implement the aggressive objectives laid down by the Federal Ministry of Defence.

Until 1963–1964 the most important representatives were:

Professor Lendle, of the Institute of Pharmacology and Toxicology of the University of Göttingen

Professor Kliewe, at that time Director of the Institute of Hygiene and Microbiology of the University of Mainz

Professor Langendorff, Director of the Radiological Institute of the University of Freiburg.

The Federal Ministry of Defence exercises its influence through

Government Counsellor Dr Bollinger, and the Fraunhofer Society through its general secretary, Herr Epp.

On the instruction of the Federal Ministry of Defence a new board of trustees was called into being for the Institute, consisting of the following professors:

Professor Westphal, Director of the Max Planck Institute of Immunebiology of Freiburg

Professor Lüttringhaus, Director of the Organic Chemistry Institute of the University of Freiburg

Professor Kimmig, Director of the Skin Clinic and Polyclinic of the University of Hamburg.

The authority of this board of trustees is sanctioned by the Federal Ministry of Defence. Its composition guarantees a high level of scientific work within the framework of research on biological and chemical warfare as conceived by the Federal Ministry of Defence.

This military research work at the Grafschaft Institute is conducted in the following three departments:

1. In the Medical-Biological Department, to which the B 1–7 laboratories and the hot cell belong.
2. In the Chemical Department with laboratories 1–4.
3. In the Physics Department with laboratories 1 and 2 as well as the laboratory for particle accelerators.

In addition, there was the Laboratory for Microbiology, which was under my direction.

At present some 70–80 staff belong to the Institute. A considerable increase in personnel is envisaged. The conditions upon which staff are employed at the Institute are alone indicative of the importance that the Federal Ministry of Defence attaches to this Institute. Only such personnel can be employed who are acceptable to the Federal Ministry of Defence. A new requirement introduced in spring this year is that scientists applying for employment to the Institute should personally call at Department T II 2 of the Federal Ministry of Defence. All personnel working at the Institute are obliged to maintain secrecy, whereby the system of levels of secrecy and the regulations of the armed forces are in force.

As much as attempts are made to maintain a cohesive system of personnel, internal and external security, the management of the Institute takes pains in conjunction with the Federal Ministry of Defence to make the true character of the scientific work being performed impervious to the uninitiated through the use of cover-up terminology and through the decentralised treatment of research work for offensive military purposes.

Extensive work has been carried out, for example, on the following problems:

1. Aerosol research. In this investigations were carried out on the production of aerosols with b and c poison content of prolonged effect. These investigations were conducted—in so far as they concerned the b sector—in the laboratory headed by me, while the investigations with chemical substances were carried out in close cooperation with the Chemistry and Physics Departments.

The production and investigation of this war material is conducted only with regard to the envisaged sudden and long-term contamination of large sections of country, which can only be of interest in case of a war of aggression.[1] The results of this research serve the Federal Ministry of Defence in making assessments for large-scale operations in case of war. The introduction of these into practical technology is then conducted on proving grounds E 53 in Münsterlager, among others, under the direction of Senior Government Counsellor Dr Lockau. On the basis of these scientific findings and supplemented by the experience of other institutes and industrial laboratories, the modern chemical industry of the West German Federal Republic (e.g., the successor undertakings of the IG-Farben trust, the Farbenfabriken Bayer AG, BASF and Hoechst) is in a position to produce and supply large quantities of the war material required by the Bundeswehr at short notice.

The Grafschaft Institute receives instructions for its work both in the scientific and military respects in the field of b and c aerosol research through the German-American Professor Alexander Goetz from Pasadena (USA), among others, who stayed in Grafschaft twice for six weeks in 1961 and 1962 at the instigation of the Federal Ministry of Defence. Professor Goetz had previously worked for many years in the field of aerosol research on behalf of the Pentagon. The copy of an extensive report on part of the relevant research work, which was kept secret for 10 years, is on hand in the Grafschaft Institute.

2. The determining of toxicity and the nature of poisoning after injection and, characteristically enough, after the inhalation of known and newly-developed organic phosphorous com-

---

[1] It is impossible to accept this statement, JC, JN.

pounds. These investigations are carried out by the Medical-Biological and Chemical Departments, whereby staff of the Physics Department can be called in if needed. Because of its dangerousness, a special laboratory, the so-called bunker, was built for this work. In this special laboratory a certain amount of security is provided for the service personnel working with highly toxic substances by the creation of differences in gas pressure. This laboratory is for all practical purposes a small gas chamber which is only available to the departmental heads and the director of the Institute. This research work is connected with the problems mentioned under 1. and can be judged accordingly.

3. The determining of the permeation capacity of newly-developed organic phosphorous compounds such as vx substances, specifically in experiments on animals and on human skin. In this connection it must be pointed out that vx substances are tested and prepared for production for military purposes and for no other reason on account of their high toxicity.

4. Work on the theory of ultra-poisonous synthetic substances and technical preparations for handling them.

5. The solving of problems concerning the technology of applying aerosols of organic phosphorous war agents in experiments with animals. This research work is conducted to derive knowledge for the military application of organic phosphorous war substances.

6. The preparation of experiments with highly pathological micro-organisms and breeds of viruses as well as with the bacteriological toxins, especially with the botulinus toxin, the most effective of all known poisons. In strict seclusion, my former colleague, Dr Salomon and I had to prepare a study for the Bonn Federal Ministry of Defence, in which it was to be worked out in which way military establishments could be paralysed in a short time by means of biological weapons. In this work a distinction was made between disease viruses of vary[ing] pathogenity and incubation times, as well as between the ... opportunities for their use. In order to do away with the moral qualms in the carrying out of such work, this study was declared by the management of the Institute to be defence work for the protection of the Bundeswehr. This study is today still 'top secret'. All of the material available in its preparation, even scribbled notes, had to be given up to security officials

of the Institute on leaving the workrooms. The prepared work was then finally taken from our hands.

On the basis of this study I later on had to work out a program for the building up of an extensive collection of highly pathogenic breeds of micro-organisms. Furthermore, a virus centre for the entire sphere of NATO Forces, Central Europe, was to be installed in the Grafschaft Institute, i.e., for experimental purposes a collection of hundreds of typhus, paratyphus and enteritis viruses was to be set up.

Although I am not a physician, but a microbiologist, I received special permission to handle such highly pathogenic breeds of micro-organisms.

For the realisation of this, corresponding safety precautions, e.g., the immunisation of the staff of my laboratory, were prepared and carried out. The first highly pathogenic breeds had already arrived in my laboratory. On account of the explosiveness of this project, the Bundeswehr, in fact, took over the further processing.

So much for a number of research themes from the work of our Institute. Certain experimental results were and are to be placed under the protection of secret patents for schemes which seem particularly important and worth-while. For this purpose the Fraunhofer Society in Munich has a special patent centre. For example, a project worked on by me was given a secret patent with the names Bisa, Zach and Petras.

A number of titles of research reports which have been prepared over the past few years in Grafschaft for the Federal Ministry were:

1. The injury caused by inhalation of aerosols of esters of phosphoric acid. Through this work for the first time operational methods for the production of highly toxic aerosols of phosphoric acid esters were developed and their high effectiveness studied on apes and rats.

2. Experiments with phosphoric acid ester TP 59 and the effect of antidotes on rats, as well as the checking and examination of o-secondary-butyl-methylfluorphosphoric acid ester.

This work involved the all-round testing of newly-developed and up-till-now unknown organic phosphorous compounds with regard to their military usefulness and applicability.

In the case of TP 59, it is a highly toxic compound which is structurally somewhere between Sarin and Soman.

3. Histo-pathological investigations on rats injured by TP 60.

The cover-term TP 60 stands for the comprehensive testing of the chemical war agent soman to determine its effect and the extent of its effectiveness from the point of view of putting it to use.

4. The qualitative and quantitative registration of the biological effects of fast neutrons as the basis for investigations on combined injuries.

Through this work methods were developed and studied which bring nuclear radiation and chemical war agents in operation at the same time in combination, in order to increase effectiveness in military operations.

On 27 March this year a colloquium was held in the Institute of Aerobiology in which well-known scientists from a whole series of West German universities and representatives of the Federal Ministry of Defence as well as officers of the Bundeswehr took part. Here the academicians working in the Institute reported on the results of their investigations. Here I shall only mention two subjects which are particularly characteristic:

'The Soman intoxication' and
'Mechanism of retardation and reactivisation on esterases'.

A few remarks on the activity of the Physics Department. This department is, in addition to its specific work in the field of atomic warfare, involved in the total work conception of the Institute for B and C war preparation. Since the beginning of 1968 this department has dealt with the problems of combined injuries to a special degree.

The Grafschaft Institute maintains relations with other research establishments with which there is either direct cooperation, or to solve problems on behalf of the Federal Ministry of Defence whose scientific results are made available to the Institute for further use.

In the minutes of a colloquium that was held on the occasion of a work session in the Institute on 5 November 1965, among others, the close cooperation between the Institute, the Federal Ministry of Defence, the board of trustees as well as with other institutes, as, for example, with the Institute of Cellular Physiology of Professor Leiner (Finthen near Mainz) was shown. In the presence of Professor Kimmig, Professor Lüttringhaus and Professor Westphal a thorough discussion was conducted at this colloquium on tests with chemical war agents and their effect on human skin.

A whole series of further institutes in the West German Federal

Republic in addition is working directly on research commissions on the various problems of B and C war agents and their employment placed and financed by the Federal Ministry of Defence, for example, with the Pharmacological Institute of the University of Göttingen headed by Professor Erdmann. Professor Erdmann gives the Grafschaft Institute regular detailed indications about future test arrangements and questions to be posed which arise out of its own work, after checking with the Federal Ministry of Defence.

The Grafschaft Institute for its part supports the research activity of Professor Erdmann. For example, on the occasion of a work session held on 13 or 14 January 1967, 500 milligrams of Soman were given through Dr Oldiges, the present scientific head of the Institute of Aerobiology, to Professor Erdmann on behalf of the Federal Ministry of Defence.

The Grafschaft Institute in practice regularly has stocks of Soman available delivered by the Federal Ministry of Defence. After the dissolution of the Institute of Cellular Physiology of Professor Leiner the stocks of war agents available there were transferred to the Grafschaft Institute on instructions of the Federal Ministry of Defence.

Along with the already mentioned relations the Grafschaft Institute maintains such relations, among others, with university institutes in Bonn, Münster, Saarbrücken and Kiel.

However, not only the work carried out on its behalf by the West German Institutes is made available to the Institute by the Federal Ministry of Defence, but at the same time the scientific results of work carried out on behalf of the US Army by West German institutes (for example, the Institute of Veterinary Physiology of the Goethe University (Frankfurt-on-Main) and the Chemical Institute of the University of Bonn) also.

In addition to close cooperation with university institutes there is also close cooperation with the chemical industry. In one of the first series of tests of the chemical department of the Institute, for example, the preparation Zephirol taken over from the Farbenfabriken Bayer AG was tested for its usability as a general field disinfectant. For some time there has been cooperation with the Farbenfabriken Bayer AG through Dr Clarmann, head of the detoxification centre of the Federal Republic in Munich, 'Krankenhaus rechts der Isar', for the purpose of camouflage.

Especially for the last two years there has been close contact with the ABC testing centre E 53 of the Bundeswehr, which is of great significance for the direct military utilisation of the scientific findings made in the Grafschaft Institute. The members of the staff of the testing centre as also of the Grafshaft Institute carry on a close exchange of experiences. That was not always the case. Since, however, the security regulations in the Institute were tightened up the Federal Ministry of Defence has approved this closer cooperation.

There was an absolute prohibition on publications up to three months ago for practically all work carried out on behalf of the Federal Ministry of Defence.

It should be noted that Dr Herbert Oldiges, the head of the Institute, has admitted that CBW research is performed there, but says it is not concerned with the production of weapons. According to Dr Oldiges, the agents used are supplied by other western countries.

The Institute and the Fraunhofer Gesellschaft, a large non-government organisation, were reorganised in 1968, and a space biology programme of Dr Petras' was scrapped. Dr Petras refused to work on a new CBW assignment. Further comment on these allegations is reserved for Part 2.

Commercial involvement

Dr Petras gave the following information on industrial activity in West Germany on CBW.

Within the framework of West Germany's military research on chemical warfare agents (particularly organic compounds of phosphorus) the Farbenfabriken Bayer AG in Leverkusen take first place among the successor companies to the IG-Farben trust in West Germany.

On the basis of internal contractual research highly toxic organic esters of phosphoric and phosphonic acid and the corresponding fluoric compounds were tested for the possibilities of their military application and efficiency at institutes of West German universities. It is known that these toxic substances are partly by-products of the Bayer AG's research on plant-protective agents and pesticides which are obtained from the research workers involved against the payment of high premiums. The research workers, in turn, have to give a pledge of secrecy. The substances are then tested amongst other places at the

Pharmacological Institute, Physico-Chemical Institute and Radio-Biological Laboratory of Göttingen University, by Professors Lendle, Erdmann, Deuticke, Friedberg, Engelhard and Drs Zeck, Bosse, Franke, etc.

Pharmacological Institute (Toxicological Department) of Bonn University, by Professor Klimmer and others.

'Krankenhaus rechts der Isar' (Isar Hospital).

Toxicological Department of the Faculty of Medicine of the Munich Technical College, by Dr M. von Clarmann and others

Mainz University by Professor emeritus Leiner
(formerly worked in the Institute of Cellular Physiology at Finthen near Mainz), who works directly for the Federal Ministry of Defence

Fraunhofer Society in Munich, Institute of Aerobiology at Grafschaft in the Sauerland, through its head, Dr Oldiges

Technical College in Hanover, by Professor Schiemann and others

Institute of Veterinary Pharmacology and Toxicology, by Professor Kewitz

The entire organisation of the placing of orders and control is centralised in the Bayer AG in three persons: Professor Kurt Hansen (general director of the Bayer AG), Dr Walter Salzer (manager of the Wuppertal-Elberfeld works and member of the board of directors of the Bayer AG, plant protection branch) and Dr Richard Wegler, director in charge of chemical research at the Wuppertal-Elberfeld works and head of the scientific commission on plant protection).

Instead of entering the picture itself the Bayer AG—as it did in the past—uses these directors of institutes as dummies for the implementation and safeguarding of its military interests and goals in the field of chemical warfare agents. This is particularly borne out by the fact that men like Professor Klimmer, Lendle and Kewitz were installed in the 'Advisory Council on Military Medicine' of the Federal Ministry of Defence or in the toxicological surveillance system, the central file of poisonous substances and the toxicological commissions. Within this military research system of the Bayer AG the origin of the highly toxic agents to be tested is disguised, the institutes naming foreign allies as the suppliers. The Bayer AG's branch in the USA, the Chemagro Corporation in Kansas City, Missouri, is of military importance. This enterprise which has its own modern research facilities and installations for the production of plant-protective agents and pesticides, has been set up in such a way—as regards its location and production methods—that it can change over to the production of organic phosphoric agents (systemic gases) within a short period. The same conditions have been provided in the Bayer AG's Dormagen branch.

5. INTERNATIONAL COOPERATION

There is a considerable amount of international sharing of information and facilities in CBW research and development. In particular, Britain works closely with the USA, Canada and Australia. There is a quadripartite agreement which covers this. There are agreements also with NATO.

Britain and the USA

A series of questions asked in the House of Commons during the last eight years throws some light on the extent of the cooperation.

23 March 1960

Q.

MR ZILLIACUS asked the Minister of Defence by what authority official information regarding a powerful nerve gas developed in this country has been supplied to the Defense Department of the USA.

A.

MR WATKINSON: Details of a British discovery relating to chemical warfare were passed to the US authorities at the research stage under the arrangements for the exchange of defence information between the UK and the US.

30 March 1960

Q (1).

MR ALLAUN asked the Minister of Defence why information regarding new methods of chemical or germ warfare were supplied for purposes of mass production and stockpiling by the USA, which is not a signatory to the Geneva Convention on Poison Gases.

Q (2).

MR WARBY asked the Minister of Defence to what extent it is a condition of any agreement for the exchange of information regarding the results of chemical warfare research with the USA that full-scale production shall take place only with the consent of the country supplying the information.

A.

MR WATKINSON: Information of this kind is exchanged with the US authorities at the research stage under normal arrangements in order to assist the development of an effective defence. No restrictions are placed on the use which either country may make of the information for its own purpose.

An article in *The Times* of 8 February 1967 stated that:

> The US and Britain have an arrangement whereby British Army officers are kept up to date in American developments in chemical and biological and radiological warfare. An annual course is held for about 12 senior British officers who are sent to the United States each June. The course is held at the United States Army's Dugway proving ground in Utah. The lessons learnt at Utah are passed on to the British Army's own more modest chemical warfare school at Winterbourne Gunner, Wiltshire, where unit instructors are taught. Training in chemical warfare is not widely practised in the army, but Rhine Army exercises are held which include the use of defensive measures against that kind of attack.

This was substantiated by the Select Committee Report, when the question was asked, 'How often do people go to Dugway?' The reply to this is as follows:

> Very occasionally, I would say on average once every 3 or 4 years. I think we get more visits to them. The main reason for going to Dugway is that they run a short training course for the American Services and this is of interest to us. From time to time we have someone attend this course to find out what the military are being told.

Cooperation extends to standardisation. The Select Committee Report states:

> the USCBR representative is a member of the staff of the US Standardisation Office, UK. . . . He is here primarily in the role of liaison officer for standardisation interests and in this context he operates not only with CDEE although he is located physically in this building, but also with the other two establishments.

Britain and Canada

During World War II cooperation was understandably very close indeed. According to the *Canadian Almanac and Directory* there was at that time:

> a joint US–Canadian research project known as the War Disease Control Station at Grosse Ile, Quebec, and a Chemical Warfare Experimental Station at Suffield, Alberta, which had for most of the war been a joint responsibility of Canada and the United Kingdom.

Further on the *Almanac* states:

> in February 1941 the Canadian Government and the Government

of the United Kingdom provided for the sharing of all operating costs at Suffield on a fifty-fifty basis for the first two years.

British financial support was terminated in 1946, but Suffield still does an important work.

Much of the work done at Suffield is of course of a classified nature, for the facilities of the establishment have been used very freely by both of Canada's major allies. In 1950, for instance, after a lapse of some years most of the field trials of chemical warfare agents which were conducted in the free world were done at Suffield. Throughout 1952 the chief emphasis at Suffield was on the testing of CW ammunitions for both the United Kingdom and the US equipments.

[*Canadian Almanac and Directory*]

Britain and Australia

Very little is known about Australia but some things can be deduced from the *Australian Year Book 1966*. The Department of Supply includes a research and development division which has as part of its work the operation of a joint UK–Australian 'weapons research project', which most probably includes some CBW investigation. Britain also uses the testing facilities at Innisfail. These are apparently not very extensive.

The Agreement

13 May 1968

> MR DALYELL asked the Secretary of State for Defence: (1) if he will publish the terms of the quadripartite agreement between Great Britain, Canada, Australia and the United States on biological warfare; (2) if he will publish the terms of the quadripartite agreement between Great Britain, Canada, Australia and the USA on chemical warfare.

> MR REYNOLDS: I assume that my hon. friend is referring either to the Technical Cooperation Programme or to the Basic Standardisation Agreement of 1964. In neither case is there a special agreement covering chemical or biological warfare.

17 June 1968

> MR JAMES DAVIDSON asked the Secretary of State for Defence to which countries the results of any research, at the Ministry of Defence establishment at Porton Down, Wiltshire, into any deadly germs have been sent.

Mr John Morris: There are arrangements for the exchange of information on defence research and development with the us, Canada and Australia and with other members of NATO. These include information on defence against biological warfare.

The quadripartite agreement was finally officially admitted to exist in the Select Committee Report. When referring to standardisation between the USA and Britain the report remarks:

> This is conducted under the aegis of the quadripartite agreement between the US, the UK, Canada and Australia.

Elsewhere the report states:

> there is a clause in the agreement which enables you not to disclose any information virtually that you do not want to disclose in the national interest.

NATO

On 23 March 1960 Mr Warbey asked the Minister of Defence

> What discussions have taken place in NATO regarding the equipment of the forces of the member countries with chemical and biological weapons.

The answer was short and to the point:

> I cannot give details of confidential discussions in NATO.

According to *Der Spiegel* (8 May 1966):

> ... even in the framework of NATO exercises, the US army operates with all available chemical and biological weapons.

30 March 1960

> Mr Malcolm Macmillan asked the Minister of Defence to what extent facilities are to be available in this country for the training of NATO military personnel and civilian specialists from other countries in the use of chemical and biological weapons.

> Mr Watkinson: Facilities have been available for some time and will remain so for training limited numbers of NATO personnel in defence against chemical and biological attack. No facilities are made available to NATO by the UK for training in the offensive use of chemical and biological weapons.

The Select Committee Report affirmed that:

> We have an agreement with NATO as NATO. We also have co-operative agreements bilateral and trilateral with specific NATO and WEU countries.

West Germany

The West German position is an ambiguous one. West Germany is very active as a coordinating centre for research and development in this field but her capacity is not so clear.

The West German Federal Ministry of the Interior and the Federal Ministry of Public Health, the Federal Office for the Protection of the Civil Population, the German Research Community and the Federal Health Board set up in West Berlin, are concerned with the organisation of the system and central office of toxicological surveillance, the file of poisonous substances, the decontamination centres, the setting up of the toxicological commission and information centres. Though officially declared to be institutions for the protection of the population, they form an extremely important part of the West German preparations for B-C warfare. The central file of poisonous substances serves to collect data on all significant toxic agents already existing or being developed in West Germany's partner countries within the Common Market. The aim is to create a second centre (alongside the USA) for all problems of toxic agents and their military use to give West Germany hegemony over its NATO partners. This programme is carried through with active support from the United States.

The specialists who play a key role in the implementation of this concept include Professor Klimmer, head of the Toxicological Department of the Pharmacological Institute of Bonn University, Dr H. Tombergs of the Federal Ministry of Public Health in Bad Godesberg, Dr W. Pietrulla of the Federal Health Board in Berlin-Dahlem, Dr K. H. Beyer of the Provincial Office of Food, Pharmaceutical and Forensic Chemistry in West Berlin, Professor Koller of the Institute of Medical Statistics and Documentation at Mainz University, Professor Lendle, former director of the Pharmacological Institute of Göttingen University, Professor J. Schunk of the Federal Office for the Protection of the Civil Population in Bad Godesberg and Dr Carl-Heinz Schiel of the German Research Community.

There has been close cooperation since 1960 between the Bonn Ministry of Defence and especially the US Chemical Corps and the centres subordinate to it in the USA. In addition, since 1960 there have been regular visits by leading staff members of the US Chemical Corps, including, among others, Dr Wolf, who is certainly generally known.

Detailed conferences with employees of the US Chemical Corps have been and are being carried out in Grafschaft, and undoubt-

edly elsewhere as well. In addition there was a direct guidance of
the Grafschaft Institute on the occasion of two visits lasting six
weeks each of the German-American Professor Alexander Goetz
of Pasadena, who was for many years a member of the war research
team of the US Chemical Corps and who was employed at the
California Institute until a few years ago. He was also employed
as an American secret service agent in the years following World
War II, during which he made use of German patents in Göttingen and on the strength of that the Milipore Filter Corporation
was constructed on behalf of the Pentagon. It is today a giant
undertaking which receives up to 50% of its orders from the
Pentagon. Production is under the strictest military secrecy. In
Grafschaft Professor Goetz was active twice for six weeks each,
especially for the aerosol sector, for both the B sector and the C
sector. The visit in Grafschaft of Solly Zuckerman from England
was announced for 28 November [1968]. In World War II Zuckerman was an adviser of Winston Churchill in the field of ABC warfare.

A whole series of West German firms, for example, IG-Farben
successor Bayer Leverkusen, or West Berlin firms supplied herbicides to the United States and these were in turn used by the USA
for so-called retaliation actions in South Vietnam.

[These statements are included in the published proceedings of
the East Berlin press conference referred to on p. 123.]

Universities

Finally, there is the question of international cooperation and the
universities. This can be illustrated with respect to Britain. In
answer to a question on 13 February 1968, Mr Benn, the Minister of
Technology, replied:

The United States Department of Defense, Army, Navy and Air
Force currently sponsors 130–140 research contracts at British
universities. Their estimated nominal value over the past five
years has been £395,000 per annum. My Department does not
exercise financial control over these contracts, which are chan-
nelled through my Department only so that duplication with
United Kingdom Government-sponsored research may be
avoided. . . .

The United States Department of Defense is currently financing
research work at 27 British Universities—Aberdeen, Bangor,
Queen's (Belfast), Birmingham, Bristol, Cambridge, Cardiff,
Durham, East Anglia, Essex, Glasgow, Hull, Keele, Kent,

Leicester, London, Manchester, Newcastle, Nottingham, Oxford, Salford, Sheffield, Southampton, Strathclyde, Sussex, Swansea, York.

The fields of research covered are bio-sciences, chemistry, earth-environmental sciences, electronics, materials mathematics, mechanics, metallurgy, molecular physics, physics, physical sciences and propulsion.

All of the research contracts are unclassified.

This caused considerable protest at Manchester, a month earlier. The *Guardian* reported on 27 January:

The possibility that Manchester University may be aiding the Americans in their campaign in Vietnam is to be debated on Thursday at an emergency general meeting of the university union.

If an emergency motion is carried, the Vice-Chancellor, Sir William Mansfield Cooper, will be asked to make an immediate statement about research at the university for the Dow Chemical Company, which manufactures napalm, and for the United States Army and Air Force.

The motion states: 'This EGM, being aware of the fact that departments of this university have received finance for research from the USAF, the US Army, and the Dow Chemical Company (the manufacturers of napalm used in Vietnam) expresses strong concern that it is likely that an institute of higher learning is directly aiding the American war effort in Vietnam.'

It reaffirms the university union's policy in demanding withdrawal of US troops, a cessation of the bombing and an end to British Government support for America's actions. It continues: '... This EGM demands that the Vice-Chancellor makes an immediate statement giving full information on the nature of the research financed by the USAF, US Army and the Dow Chemical Company, and reveals the source and quantity of the finance, and that the university shall end all research activities which can, in any way, aid the American barbarism in Vietnam.'

The Vice-Chancellor's statement read:

Research Grants received from the U.S.A.

Over the last 10 years the University has received $1,452,839 from American sources, of this sum $1,420,039 has been paid by the American Armed Forces (including the National Aeronautics and Space Administrations), for work in support of space research programmes at Jodrell Bank and in support of the lunar programmes of Prof. Kopal. From private American sources the University has received over a 10-year period $32,800. More than half this came from the California Institute of Technology and enabled Prof. Kopal to evaluate spectrometer instruments. The remainder was in support of research in the field of high-polymer chemistry. The Dow Chemical Company is currently making a grant of $7,000 for research in the general area of polymerisation.

All the above grants, without exception, are for work in fundamental science; all are for work the nature of which is determined by the University. All lead to free publications, the fact that some processes or materials on which scientists work could be applied in war is entirely coincidental. No work in the University of Manchester has any conceivable connection with any such application.

US financing of research abroad should give rise to some disquiet. Some of the contracts, even if not those in Britain, are classified. The situation has grown up in the US that some university departments have come to rely for finance on military contracts, and with increased dependence has come a greater say by the military in the direction of research. It is not impossible to imagine a similar situation in Britain.

From what has been said above, it may be seen that international cooperation is extensive, and operates at a variety of levels, commercial, university, as well as through the military establishments themselves. This complexity makes it very difficult to get an overall picture of what is being done in research, development and deployment of these weapons. It also complicates the legal position with regard to the possession and use of such weapons. An attempt to assess the relative positions of interested countries with regard to CBW is made in Part 2.

3

INTERNATIONAL DECLARATIONS AND NATIONAL POLICY

As a result of a conference held at the Hague in 1899, The Hague Gas Declaration was signed by several nations, who thereby agreed not to use projectiles which disseminated poison gases. The second such conference was held in 1907, resulting in the Hague Convention, which runs as follows:

> Regulations concerning the Laws and Customs of Land Warfare Annex to the Hague Convention of 18 October 1907:
>
> Art. 22. The right of belligerents to adopt means of injuring the enemy is not unlimited.
>
> Art. 23. Besides the prohibitions provided by special Conventions it is especially prohibited: (a) to employ poison or poisoned arms; (b) to employ arms, projectiles or materials of a nature to cause superfluous injury.

Both the US and Britain were bound by this, as were Germany, France and Russia.

Both the Versailles treaty of 1919 and the subsequent treaties with Bulgaria, Austria, Hungary and Turkey prohibited the manufacture of chemical and biological weapons. The prohibition only extended, however, to the defeated powers of World War I. After this international policy was the responsibility of the League of Nations, and in 1920 the League's Permanent Advisory Commission for Military, Naval and Air Questions reported (1) that the use of an asphyxiating gas was no more cruel than other methods of warfare as long as it was not used against non-combatants; (2) that preventing or limiting manufacture of CB weapons in peacetime would not automatically prohibit their use in war.

The Geneva Protocol of 17 June 1925 is still the most important international treaty for the restriction of chemical and biological warfare. It was respected throughout World War II despite the considerable stockpiles of these weapons held by many nations at the time. The protocol reads as follows:

The undersigned plenipotentiaries in the name of their respective governments:

Whereas, the use in war of asphyxiating, poisonous or other gases and of all analogous liquids, materials or devices has been justly condemned by the general opinion of the civilised world: and

To the end that this prohibition shall be universally accepted as part of International Law binding alike the conscience and the practice of nations;

Declare:

That the High Contracting Parties, so far as they are not already Parties to Treaties prohibiting such use, accept this prohibition, agree to extend this prohibition to the use of bacteriological methods of warfare and agree to be bound as between themselves according to the terms of this Declaration.

The High Contracting Parties will exert every effort to induce other States to accede to the present Protocol.

Twenty-nine countries signed the protocol originally but six failed to ratify it. At present it has been ratified by forty-four nations. The exceptions are Brazil, Japan, Nicaragua, Salvador, the USA and Uruguay. Iceland has neither signed nor ratified the protocol. Most of the signatories retained the right to retaliate.

After the war, in 1945, the United States, together with France, Britain and Russia, drafted the Nuremberg Charter defining war crimes and responsibilities. The relevant articles to this discussion are 6 and 7, although they do not relate specifically to chemical or biological warfare. The US can definitely be held to be bound by this charter, if not by the Geneva Protocol,[1] and to that extent it is important. (The relevant passages are in italics.)

Art. 6. The following acts or any of them are crimes coming within the jurisdiction of the Tribunal for which there shall be individual responsibility:

(a) Crimes against peace: Namely, planning, preparation, initiation or waging of a war or aggression or a war in violation of international treaties, agreements or assurance of participation in a common plan or conspiracy for the accomplishment of any of the foregoing:

(b) War Crimes: Namely, *violations of the laws or customs of war.* Such violations shall include, *but not be limited to,* murder,

---

[1] Whether the US is bound by the Geneva Protocol though not a signatory is a matter of discussion. It has been persuasively argued that the Geneva Protocol is an accepted part of international law and therefore binding on all states.

ill-treatment or deportation to slave labour or for any other purpose of civilian population of or in occupied territory; murder or ill-treatment of prisoners of war or persons on the seas, killing of hostages, plunder of public or private property, *wanton destruction of cities, towns or villages or devastation not justified by military necessity*;

(c) Crimes against Humanity: Namely, murder, extermination, enslavement, deportation and *other inhumane acts committed against any civilian population before or during war*, or persecutions on political, racial or religious grounds in execution of or in connection with any crime within the jurisdiction of the Tribunal, whether or not in violation of the domestic law of the country where perpetrated.

Art. 7. The official position of defendants, whether as Heads of State or responsible officials in government departments, shall not be considered as freeing them from responsibility or mitigating punishment.

The Potsdam Conference of 1945, like the Versailles treaty, forbade Germany to manufacture, amongst other things, chemical weapons. In 1946 the United Nations adopted a resolution calling for 'the elimination from national armaments of atomic weapons adaptable for mass destruction'. This was extended to cb weapons in 1948. In 1954 the Paris Protocols established the Council of the Western European Union the duties of which included ensuring Germany did not manufacture abc weapons and controlling the level of these weapons held by other members. International inspection teams were set up.

On 5 December 1966, the United Nations adopted the following resolution:

Guided by the principles of the Charter of the United Nations and of international law;

Considering the weapons of mass destruction constitute a danger to all mankind and are incompatible with the accepted norms of civilisation. Affirming that the strict observance of the rules of international law on the conduct of warfare is in the interest of maintaining these standards of civilisation;

Recalling that the Geneva Protocol for the Prohibition of the Use in War of Asphyxiating, Poisonous or Other Gases and of Bacteriological Methods of Warfare of June 17th, 1925, has been signed and adopted and is recognised by many states;

Noting that the Conference of the Eighteen Nation Committee on Disarmament has the task of seeking an agreement on the cessation of the development and production of chemical and bacteriological weapons and other weapons of mass destruction and on the elimination of all such weapons from the national arsenals as called for in the draft proposals on general and complete disarmament now before the Conference,

(1) Calls for strict observance by all States of the principles and objectives of the Protocol for the Prohibition of the Use in War of Asphyxiating, Poisonous and Other Gases and of Bacteriological methods of Warfare, signed at Geneva on 17th June, 1925, and condemns all actions contrary to those objectives;

(2) Invites all states to accede to the Geneva Protocol of 17th June 1925.

1. UNITED STATES POLICY

In 1899 at the first Hague Conference the US delegation was instructed to oppose the declaration and neither signed nor ratified it. The reasons given by Captain Mahan, the head of the delegation, were that there was at the time no proof that the weapons were either inhumane or barbaric and they might be a decisive factor in a future war. On the other hand the 1907 conference was in fact instituted by President Theodore Roosevelt and the US subsequently signed and ratified the Convention.

After World War I a proposal supported by the US Navy to ban chemical warfare was introduced by General J. Pershing, an adviser to the Naval Board, to the Washington Naval Limitations Conference held from 1921 to 1922. Article v of the resultant treaty stated that as most of the major powers were already bound by agreements condemning 'the use in war of asphyxiating, poisonous or other gases and all analogous liquids, materials or devices' this should become part of international law. This treaty was never put into effect.

In 1924 The International Conference of American States attended by the US and seventeen other South American States issued a policy recommendation that 'the governments reiterate the prohibition of the use of asphyxiating or poisonous gases'.

A year later the League of Nations held a conference on international trade in arms, ammunition and implements of war. The US tried to get a CBW prohibition clause incorporated but the committee decided this did not fall within the field of reference of the conference. As a result the US suggested that a protocol be added to Article v of the Washington treaty. The result of this was the Geneva Protocol of 1925 which, ironically, in spite of favourable reception by the Departments of War and Navy and the Senate

Foreign Relations Committee, was refused ratification by the Senate in January 1926.

In 1943, during World War II, President Franklin D. Roosevelt made the following statement:

> From time to time, since the present war began, there have been reports that one or more of the Axis powers were seriously contemplating use of poisonous or noxious gases, or other inhumane devices of warfare. I have been loath to believe that any nation, even our present enemies, could or would be willing to loose upon mankind such terrible and inhumane weapons. . . . Use of such weapons has been outlawed by the general opinion of civilised mankind. This country has not used them, and I hope that we will never be compelled to use them. I state categorically that we shall under no circumstances resort to the use of such weapons unless they are first used by our enemies. [U.S. Senate Committee on Foreign Relations—'Chemical Biological and Radiological (CBR) Warfare and its disarmament aspects' (1960)]

The US was thus to abide by the principles of the Geneva Protocols. The President subsequently refused advice that CB weapons should be used. Pressure must have been strong because the Merck Report of 1946 stated:

> Only the rapid ending of the war prevented field trials in an active theatre of synthetic agents which would, without injury to human or animal life, affect the growing crops and make them useless.

From this time on the Army Chemical Corps played an increasingly important part in US policy. The type of pressure applied by the corps has been described above.

On 8 April 1947 President Truman withdrew 'from the Senate 19 old pigeon-holed treaties including the 1925 Geneva Protocol against gas and bacteriological warfare' (Facts on File, Vol. VIII, No. 337).

A proposal introduced to the UN Security Council by the USSR during the Korean War calling for complete ratification of the Geneva Protocol was not accepted by the US. An alternative was offered asking for a proposal to limit all weapons of mass destruction. In November 1955 the Army publicly endorsed the report of the civilian advisory committee which recommended the development of CBW 'to the fullest extent the human mind can encompass' (see above).

The 1956 Army Field Manual FM27-10, 'The Law of Land Warfare', states quite explicitly:

'The United States is not party to any treaty now in force that prohibits or restricts the use of warfare of toxic or nontoxic gases, of smoke or incendiary materials or of bacteriological warfare.[1]

The hearings of the 1959 House Appropriations Sub-Committee on Defense contain the following interesting dialogue.

GENERAL CREASY: First I will start off with the national policy.
(Off the record)

MR FORD: May I ask how long that policy has been in effect?

GENERAL CREASY: Since about October 1956, about a year and a half ago. The National Policy has been implemented by a Department of Defense Directive.
(Off the record)

On 3 September 1959 Congressman Robert W. Kastenmeier (Wisconsin—Democrat) introduced a resolution into the House which read in part:

That the Congress hereby reaffirms the longstanding policy of the United States that in the event of war the United States shall under no circumstances resort to the use of poisonous or obnoxious gases unless they are first used by our enemies.

[US H. of R. 86th Congress, 'House Concurrent Resolution 433']

The resolution was rejected. The government expenditure figures for research development and procurement in this field rise dramatically from this time onwards. The subsequent opposition to the resolution both from the State Department and the Defense Department is not therefore entirely surprising.

In September 1960 the State Department officially replied:

As a member of the United Nations the United States ... is committed to refrain from the use not only of biological and chemical weapons but the use of force of any kind in a manner contrary to the Organisation's Charter. Moreover, the United States is continuing its efforts to control weapons through enforceable international disarmament agreements. Of course we must recognise our responsibility to our own and the Free World's security. These responsibilities involve, amongst other things, the maintenance of an adequate defence posture across the entire weapons spectrum, which will allow us to defend against acts of aggression in such manner as the President may direct. Accordingly the Department believes that the resolution should not be adopted.

---

[1] This is evidently a departure from a manual of 1954 quoted by Hersh, which stated: 'Gas warfare and bacteriological warfare are employed by the United States against enemy personnel only in retaliation for their use by the enemy.'

The Pentagon's reply was as follows:

It must be considered that biological and chemical weapons might be used with great effect against the United States in a future conflict.

Available evidence indicates that other countries, including Communist regimes, are actively pursuing programmes in this field. Moreover, as research continues, there is increasing evidence that some forms of these weapons, differing from previous forms, could be effectively used for defensive purposes with minimum collateral consequences. These considerations argue strongly against the proposed resolution which appears to introduce uncertainty into the necessary planning of the Department of Defense in preparing to meet possible hostile action of all kinds.

In January 1960, however, between the resolution's being introduced and its being opposed, President Eisenhower, referring to CB weapons, and their possible use, stated at a press conference—'so far as my own instinct is concerned, it is not to start such a thing as that first'.

In 1965 a White House aide stated in an interview with the Physicians for Social Responsibility that in May President Johnson received a memo from the State Department reversing its long-standing opposition to the use of biological weapons. (See Carol Brightman's article quoted above, p. 66.)

In December 1966 at the United Nations General Disarmament Conference the United States endorsed a resolution put forward by Hungary asking all countries to abide by the intent of the Geneva Protocol. The original version also condemned 'any actions aimed at the use of chemical and bacteriological weapons'. It referred to such action as an 'international crime'. This was amended, however, because of American opposition on the grounds that it was 'subject to contention, misinterpretation and distortion'.

The United States, although not bound as a signatory, is thus still obliged in some way to show that her actions in Vietnam are not contrary to the principles of the Geneva Protocol. The arguments used are basically three: plants and crops are not covered by the protocol and therefore defoliation and crop destruction are admissible; secondly, the US is not officially at war in Vietnam and the protocol limits the 'use of weapons in war'; and, finally, the gases being used are not 'asphyxiating or poisonous'.

Since Roosevelt's affirmation of the policy of no first use of these weapons there seem to have been two changes of policy, first, towards the offensive use of chemical weapons, in October 1956, and second, the State Department's abandonment, in 1965 (if Brightman's account is accurate) of its objections to the first use of biological warfare.

In the face of increasing opposition to CBW in the US, President Nixon has ordered a review of CBW policy. This information was given in a letter to Representative R. D. McCarthy, one of the principal opponents of CBW in the USA, from Gerard Smith, Director of the US Arms Control and Disarmament Agency:

> Within the US Government the control of chemical and biological agents is a subject of major concern. The President has directed the executive branch to undertake a detailed review of chemical and biological warfare, including the US position on arms control and the ratification of the 1925 Geneva Protocol.

2. BRITISH POLICY

Britain is bound by both the Hague Convention of 1907 and the 1925 Geneva Protocol, but with respect to the latter retains the right to retaliate. The purpose of research is therefore officially purely for defence. Membership of NATO and the signing of other agreements tends, however, to complicate the issue somewhat.

On 10 February 1955 the Prime Minister was asked:

> whether, in view of the disquiet caused by provisions in the Paris Agreements which permit the stockpiling in Germany of chemical weapons, and of biological weapons he will renew the pledge which he gave to the Soviet people through Marshal Stalin that if German forces used against them weapons prohibited under the Geneva Convention, British Forces would retaliate in kind against the German Forces concerned.

To which he replied:

> I cannot accept the premise of the Hon. Member's question. The Paris Agreements need cause no disquiet except to those who seek to destroy the unity and defensive strength of the free nations. The essential purpose of these Agreements is to provide for international limitation and control over the level of stocks of these as well as other weapons which may be held by member countries on the Continent of Europe.

On 6 April 1960 Mr Silverman asked the Secretary of State for Foreign Affairs:

> Which of our allies in NATO has not as yet signed the Geneva Convention on chemical and biological warfare, and having regard to the embarrassment with possible legal complications of joint armed forces, some of whom are bound by these conventions and some not, what representation will he make to

NATO Council to ensure that all NATO countries renounce use of these weapons.

MR PROFUMO replied:

All our NATO allies are parties to the convention except Iceland and the US. President Eisenhower has recently made it clear that he is not contemplating any change in traditional US policy of not being the first to use chemical and biological weapons.

With regard to the second part of the question, NATO Supreme Commanders act under the political direction of the North Atlantic Council. There can therefore be no question of such weapons being used without the approval of member governments. No representations are, I think, necessary.

MR SILVERMAN added:

Does the Right Hon. Gentleman agree that the difference between a declaration by President Eisenhower and the signing and ratifying of the Convention is that whereas a declaration by President Eisenhower binds his administration, it does not bind his country and a formal act of ratifying the Geneva Convention would be binding. . . .

MR PROFUMO replied:

. . . The Hon. Member will appreciate that I cannot be responsible for any action the US Government may or may not take whether it is this Government or the next.

In view of subsequent actions by the US administration and the quadripartite agreement described in the last chapter the present position of the British government is difficult to defend.

The precise extent to which British research is entirely defensive is difficult to determine from available evidence. Mr Parkin's question quoted above indicates that the British government at some time gave a pledge to the USSR to protect her from Germany with respect to CBW. This implies offensive capabilities. The following answers to questions in the House of Commons over the last ten years perhaps give some indication of the British position:

2 April 1958: 'The purpose of the research is defensive, but in order to study defensive methods one has to study what the other fellow can do to you.'

[Mr Sandys]

26 January 1959: 'The Ministry of Supply Establishments at Porton are *mainly* engaged in carrying out research on defensive problems of microbiological and chemical warfare. The researches are essentially directed towards assessing the threat and providing defence against it. . . .

I can only repeat that their purpose is *almost* entirely defensive.'

[Mr Aubrey Jones (emphasis added)]

8 December 1959: '... it has proved to be wise to consider both defence and retaliatory power. ...'

[Prime Minister]

23 March 1960: 'We are not stockpiling these weapons. We are of course bound by the Geneva Convention and our only purpose in the matter is ... that we must assess the threat in order to prepare defences.'

[Mr Watkinson, Minister of Defence]

30 January 1963: 'We are bound by the Geneva Agreements as to the use of these weapons. We are however entitled to defend ourselves or retaliate.'

[Mr Thorneycroft, Minister of Defence]

1 May 1968: 'We neither develop nor produce bacteriological weapons and no question of a role for them in our deterrent strategy arises.'

[Mr Healey, Secretary of State for Defence]

The following extracts from the Select Committee Report on Science and Technology (8 July 1968) provide more insight:

Question 1060: Suppose this country was—I can only ask for your view on it, I appreciate that these things are not ultimately under your control—the victim of a germ war attack, in your view would it be possible for us to fairly quickly retaliate?

Answer (by Mr Gordon Smith of the MRE): No Sir, we should need a good deal of development work before we could retaliate.

Question 1062: Thinking in the context of research it is possible to develop the chemical, or be aware of how to prepare the chemical or the biological agent; over and above that there is the question of its dispersal and of its use in either battlefield or assault combats?

Answer: We have to understand how the organisms would be grown. This does not mean that we would have necessarily the plant to do this on the scale which would be required to make an offensive weapon but, of course, we do have equipment for the growing of micro-organisms. On the other hand if you want to mount an attack, you have to have systems which disperse the agent from some sort of vehicle. We have made no attempt to develop this sort of equipment.

The same question was put to Mr Gadsby of the CDEE. His answer was as follows:

> It is one thing to know how to produce a chemical agent in a laboratory, the next critical phase is to know how to produce that in quantities appropriate for the filling of delivery systems. This is not really a question of using larger test tubes, it involves the whole complex business of chemical engineering. First of all you would have to produce the agent in the appropriate quantities, having produced the agent you then have to design the weapon systems—and I intentionally use the word in the plural—necessary, effectively to deliver, disperse and disseminate these chemicals under operational conditions. We have at Nancekuke the facilities for exploring manufacturing processes on a smaller than pilot plant scale, so we have in the past worked out the procedures.
>
> (Off the record)
>
> Considerable development work would be necessary in order to develop the necessary aerial and ground weapon launching systems.

Question 1064: In the opening remarks that Mr Gadsby made to us this morning he did refer to how other nations interpret the Geneva Convention so far as training in this field is concerned. I am wondering to what extent a scientific assessment has been made here, and what in fact are the realities of disbursement between nations, in particular our own and others in this field, bearing in mind what the Chairman has said about sidelining.

Answer: First of all let me comment about scientific assessments. Certainly we have carried out assessments, but unless one has reliable factual data, these cannot be called scientific in the strictest sense of the term, since they incorporate a degree of judgment.

(Off the record)

Question 1068: One of the roles of the establishment you said earlier was to assess the threat. Does this mean that it is part of your duties to provide the services in the kind of conflict in which the chemical or biological warfare might be used? Would you not agree that the existence of stock piles does not necessarily prove that countries would use their stock piles in a given time of war any more than the Germans used gas weapons, although I believe they possessed large stock piles, but they chose to use high explosives instead. Is it your function to look at the type of conflict in which these weapons could be used?

Answer: Naturally when we are carrying out an assessment of the threat it is our job to see that these are looked at in a realistic context. If it comes to the question of a thorough operational assessment then this would go to the Defence Operational Analysis Establishment at West Byfleet. We have not the facilities here for wargaming.

Question 1069: (Off the record)

Answer: (Off the record)

Question 1070: Following that point further we would certainly not have the stock pile?[1]

Answer: No.

Question 1082: (Off the record)

Answer: (Off the record)

Question 1083: Does it represent a breach in the Geneva Convention to have the attack capacity in this field?

Answer (Mr Gordon Smith): No, because the Geneva Convention permits retaliation in kind, not only retaliation against aggressors but also retaliation against allies of aggressors.

Question 1086: For this type of warfare—which we hope will for ever be avoided—is large stock piling necessary?

Answer: This again depends on the scale with which you wish to wage it. If you were considering, as General Rothschild did, attacking the whole of China then considerable stock piling would be required. If, on the other hand you were considering an attack on a military objective such as an airbase or a vessel at sea—both of which are highly susceptible objects—then you could make enough and just use it more or less straight away.

Question 1087: (Off the record)

Answer: (Off the record)

Question 1088: (Off the record)

Answer: (Off the record)

Question 1089: I would like to go back a little Mr Chairman, and ask in the light of what you have already told us, can I take it you are in a position to devise vessels or agents and weapon systems which are already available to potential enemies or other nations.

(Off the record)

---

[1] This question and No 1083 are extremely important as they seem to indicate the existence of a specific stockpile and a specific attack capacity. Probably, since NATO possesses chemical, if not biological, weapons, they refer to NATO stocks kept in West Germany.

Answer: If in broad terms intelligent sources advised us of the basic outlining characteristics of a weapon then we would naturally be called upon to assess the effectiveness and the implications of such a weapon. The other general point which I might make is the responsibility of the two establishments here is to some degree a little wider than those of other defence R and D departments in so far as you have no chemical corps, or its equivalent, in the services. You have no body of professional users who spend their lives giving attention to the operational aspects of this particular form of warfare. Therefore, it falls upon the establishment to do assessment work and to formulate and put operational ideas to the service staff, so that perhaps more than in any other R and D establishment we are consulted on the operational aspects, more than might be the case in other fields.

Question 1090: It is quite clear that you are in a position to advise and advance procedures for known systems, so other people would also be in a position to give advice on how to use other people's systems?

Answer: Other people's defensive?

Question 1091: No, other people's offensive.

Answer: Yes, in general terms.

Question 1092: You are perfectly well informed from the point of view of work and responsibility to advise British forces how to use equipment already in possession of others?

Answer: Provided we had the complete weapon systems to do this.

The indication seems to be that even if Britain is not developing weapons, the knowledge, some of which is classified, is there to do so should it be necessary.[1] The existence of Nancekuke implies a more than theoretical knowledge of this kind, as do the facilities of the MRE described in the previous chapter. This will be discussed more fully in Part 2. It would seem, moreover, that Britain has access, through NATO or the quadripartite agreement, to already existing stockpiles of weapons should the need for them ever arise.

Doubt about Britain's actual capabilities and potential are not allayed by the intense secrecy which surrounds the subject of the CBW in Britain.

On 30 July 1951, Mr J. Morrison asked the Minister of Supply:

What has been the cost of the new research building at Porton: what was the cost as in the original estimate?

[1] As will be shown in Part 2, offensive capacity need not be based on British resources alone.

Mr G. Strauss: It would not be in the public interest to give this information.

14 July 1952:

Mr Emrys Hughes asked the Minister of Supply what is the nature of the work being carried out by his Department at Porton: how many persons are employed there: and what has been the expenditure incurred there up to the nearest available date.

Mr Duncan Sandys (the Minister of Supply): The Ministry of Supply establishments at Porton are engaged on chemical and microbiological research. It would not be in the public interest to give the figures asked for in the question.

27 October 1952:

Mr Emrys Hughes asked the Minister of Supply if he will arrange a visit of Hon. Members to the bacteriological and chemical research station at Porton.

Mr Sandys: Various establishments of the Ministry of Supply are from time to time visited by the Select Committee on Estimates. Should this or any other Committee set up by the House require to visit the establishments at Porton, I shall be glad to afford all necessary facilities.

Mr Hughes: Could not these facilities be extended to ordinary Members of Parliament who are not on these committees? Could the Minister tell us why there is this iron curtain of secrecy round this bacteriological research station? Is he aware that last week the Prime Minister complained that a large amount of public money had been spent on the atom bomb without Parliament knowing anything about it? It this being repeated in the case of the bacteriological research at Porton?

Mr Sandys: Visits to any of these establishments inevitably interrupt the work of the senior staff, who have to show people round. I am sure that the House will support me in trying to limit visits to those which are really necessary.

This type of response continued until comparatively recently. On 26 May a report of the Select Committee proceedings appeared in the *Observer*. Mr Tam Dalyell, who passed the report to the press before publication, was as a result referred to the Committee of Privileges. The report was several weeks late in publication.

In its final form, the report, which starts at question 1004, has five complete questions and answers off the record (1069, 1082, 1087, 1088 and 1105). In addition, parts of nine others are missing (1004,

1005, 1028, 1040, 1063, 1065, 1071, 1089 and 1099). From the context it would appear that these deal primarily with statistics of expenditure and Britain's potential capabilities (possibly offensive) in any future conflict.

The Ministry of Defence's letter advising which parts of the report should not be published read in part:

> we have thought it proper to give very careful consideration to the sidelining...in order to strike a proper balance between the material which we regard as quite unsuitable for publication and that which it would be permissible, even desirable to publish.

Because of the leak of the report to the *Observer*, some of the intended deletions were retained. In particular, question 1063 was not meant for publication. This is quoted in full above and deals with the CDEE's work including its 'pilot plant' at Nancekuke. Part of the answer is in fact still omitted. The information which is provided in this answer, taken together with the context in which other questions have been entirely omitted, makes it easy to speculate that Britain's power to retaliate may not be quite so hypothetical as it at first seems.

According to Vice-Admiral Sir Norman Denning (secretary to the Services Press and Broadcasting Committee of the House of Commons), with respect to Porton:

> The only D-notice which might conceivably be applied to it is in the event of any weapon development of chemical and biological warfare.

The *Observer*, it seems, was in possession of an unedited copy of the report. In view of the omissions in the report as finally published, the article which appeared on 26 May showed considerable restraint. The article dealt in particular with questions 1077 and 1080 which concerned university involvement. The Ministry's recommendation on these was:

> There can be no objection on security grounds in the normally accepted sense of that expression to publication of this information. Indeed, I think there have been references elsewhere to the University contracts.

If it was the existence of a D-notice which prevented the *Observer* from publishing information on Porton's work and capabilities, whether potential or actual, then this gives serious cause for concern. In fact it implies that the deleted parts of the report deal to some extent with weapon development of chemical and biological warfare. If this is the case, then Britain's defensive brief looks rather ridiculous.

If D-notices were not a consideration in the data published by the *Observer*, the failure to discuss Porton in more detail was an unfortunate omission in the present atmosphere of secrecy and consequent confusion about the establishment's function.

A full account of the Select Committee proceedings could do much to allay doubts on this subject. The present edited report on the other hand may even confirm for some people what were previously only suspicions.

On 1 June 1968 a four-day demonstration began outside Porton held by several peace and religious movements. On 19 June, as a consequence, Mr Dalyell found it necessary to ask:

> For what purpose an Army van and two photographers took pictures of demonstrators outside Porton on Whitsunday, 1968.

> MR JOHN MORRIS: Photographs were taken in view of the possibility that damage might be caused to Government property. However, I have now given instructions for the photographs to be destroyed.

On 6 June the BBC showed a film concerning CBW research and development. The necessary films of experiments had to be obtained from Sweden because of an Act of 1867 on cruelty to animals.

All the publicity at this time meant added pressure, and on 12 June 1968 the following exchange occurred in the House of Commons:

> Mr Dalyell asked the Secretary of State for Defence if he will consider arranging a number of open days in 1969 at the Microbiological Research Establishment, Porton.

> MR JOHN MORRIS: Yes, sir.

> MR DALYELL: I thank my Hon. Friend. Would it then be possible to bring this forward to 1968? May I say that I welcome this answer, in so far as a full open day would help to remove part of the mystery from biological warfare activities?

> MR MORRIS: I am glad of my Hon. Friend's words of welcome for my reply. I hope that the open day will be held in the autumn of 1968, or possibly early 1969.

> SIR G. NABARRO: Will the Hon. Gentleman explain what value he considers that open days can have in the examination of microbes at Porton?

> MR MORRIS: What I am seeking to do—and I hope that this meets the wishes of the Hon. Gentleman—is to balance national security and public interest. I have been to Porton myself recently and I have concluded that there is merit in my proposal, and I commend it.

On 19 June there were signs that the government was changing its mind.

Mr Dalyell asked the Secretary of State for Defence if he will arrange for the Microbiological Research Establishment and Chemical Defence Experimental Establishment at Porton to issue regular reports describing the general character of their classified work.

MR JOHN MORRIS: No.

On 22 and 24 June the Advisory Boards of the MRE and the CDEE respectively wrote letters to *The Times* to justify amongst other things the secrecy concerning some of the work of these establishments. The Boards consist of twenty-three professors and eminent scientists. From the MRE Professor Sir Charles Dodds, FRS, and others, wrote:

Because of the recent attacks made on the scientists and on the work of the Microbiological Research Establishment at Porton, we, members of the Biological Research Advisory Board, consider that attention should be drawn to the following.

1. We have full access to all the work of the establishment and are satisfied that it has no military offensive objectives.

2. We are aware of the basis on which any work is classified and are convinced that publication is withheld only if it involves a risk to national security.

3. The staff is of high scientific calibre and their work, which is of outstanding quality, contributes extensively to medical science, public health and industry. Their motives both social and scientific are beyond reproach and no justifiable moral stigma can be attached to their working for the establishment. Statements to the contrary, especially by their fellow scientists, are both deplorable and irresponsible.

4. The animal experiments at the establishment are conducted entirely according to Home Office regulations and differ in no essential way from experiments in other institutes and in industry concerned with medical research. The Littlewood Committee inspected the establishment's animal facilities and were satisfied that these were among the best they had seen.

We endorse the view expressed in your leader of June 6 that 'in the present state of the world the work carried out at Porton Down is a source of reassurance, not a cause of panic'.

From the CDEE Dr J. M. Barnes and others wrote:

The doubts which have been cast on the nature of the work of the Chemical Defence Experimental Establishment at Porton imply that the scientists working in the establishment are socially irresponsible. We are scientists who know the work and the staff of the establishment well, and we know that both are devoted to the protection of this country from a real threat.

No one has yet produced a global disarmament plan that will work, and the rate of progress is so slow that it may be a very long time before disarmament becomes a reality. Until there is effective disarmament there must be effective protection against chemical attack.

The work of CDEE is directed to finding out what we must protect against and how to create the protection. Without this work we might have no breathing space in which to strive for a less menacing world.

On the question of disarmament the British government, though advocating it, has been singularly ineffective until recently in actually doing anything about it. On 11 May 1959 Mr Philip Noel-Baker suggested in a question concerning CB weapons addressed to the Secretary of State for Foreign Affairs:

> Ought not the government now to institute a very close study for their abolition?

> MR ORMSBY GORE: I think that that would be very wise and we are quite prepared to do so, but as the Right Hon. Gentleman is aware, at present those weapons are prohibited altogether. They are banned. What we have to do is to see that their abolition becomes part of any disarmament programme.

23 March 1960:

> MR HENDERSON: ... Are [our government] putting a firm plan forward at the disarmament conference with a view to controlling these weapons if an agreement is reached?

> MR WATKINSON: ... Nobody will be happier than Her Majesty's Government if ... biological weapons are banned along with all others.

Strong pressure was applied by Mr Dalyell to try to get some action by Britain at the February 1964 Conference.

17 December 1963:

> Mr Dalyell asked the Prime Minister whether as a step towards reaching an agreement on chemical and biological weapons he will propose to President Johnson and Mr Krushchev an exchange of information between Great Britain, the USA and the USSR.

> PRIME MINISTER: Both the American and Soviet disarmament plans put forward at Geneva contain proposals for the elimination of chemical and biological weapons. I think the best way

to proceed is to discuss these matters at Geneva in context of
these two plans.

MR DALYELL: Will the Prime Minister prepare the ground by
taking suitable technical advisers?

PRIME MINISTER: We usually have them with us at Geneva. . . .
Certainly I will see if this might be done.

MR NOEL-BAKER: Would the Prime Minister consider the possibility of making a proposal to abolish biological warfare preparations in advance of a general agreement?

PRIME MINISTER: I should like to discuss this very interesting
question with the Americans, our allies, and other allies to
see whether we can make any progress before the actual stages
of a disarmament agreement are put into practice. I am not
sure that this is possible. It raises all sorts of security issues,
for one thing.

20 December 1963:

Mr Dalyell asked the Prime Minister whether he will make an
approach to President Johnson to the effect that proposals for
an agreement on the control of chemical and biological weapons
should be placed on the Agenda of their February meeting.

PRIME MINISTER: I will bear the Hon. Member's suggestion in
mind.

16 January 1964:

Mr Dalyell asked the Prime Minister what recent initiatives
had been taken by the UK representatives at the Geneva Disarmament Conference to propose an exchange of information
on chemical and biological warfare between Great Britain, the
USA and the Soviet Union.

PRIME MINISTER: The subject has not yet come up for discussion
at Geneva but the US disarmament plant which we support
makes provision in Stage I for examination of the problem of
chemical and biological weapons. . . .

MR DALYELL: . . . does this not represent a missed opportunity?

PRIME MINISTER: This must form part of the general problem of
disarmament. . . .

21 January 1964:

Mr Dalyell asked the Prime Minister how many technical advisers, experts in problems of chemical and bacteriological warfare, will be travelling with him to the US in February 1964?

PRIME MINISTER: None, sir. I do not consider this necessary. I
have recently consulted the Americans or other NATO powers

represented at the Geneva Conference on these matters and shall continue to do so as necessary.

Following publicity, similar pressure was applied with respect to the eighteen-nation Disarmament Committee which reconvened on 16 July 1968. This time it was more successful.

1 July 1968:

> Mr Tam Dalyell asked the Secretary of State for Foreign Affairs if he will explore the possibilities through the United Nations of establishing an international treaty similar to the Nuclear Test Ban Agreement, to cover chemical and microbiological warfare.
>
> Mr Mulley: I would refer my Hon. Friend to what I said in the House on 19th June. We think that when the Eighteen-Nation Disarmament Committee reconvenes, it should work for further measures in the nuclear field to follow up the Non-Proliferation Treaty, but that it should also give serious consideration to non-nuclear disarmament problems.
>
> A priority here will be for the Committee to consider what can be done in regard to chemical and biological weapons, with a view to strengthening and bringing up to date the existing agreement in this field, the 1925 Geneva Protocol.

4 July:

> Mr Dalyell: When the Geneva Conference reconvenes on 16th July shall we be raising these complex problems of inspection and verification?
>
> The Prime Minister: It is certainly our intention when the Committee reconvenes on 16 July—we are now examining all the issues that we think it should consider and we have been devoting particular attention to the question of chemical and biological weapons.

11 July:

> Mr Philip Noel-Baker: Will the Prime Minister bring some realism into the matter by ordering his experts to prepare some plan so that it may be ready when a disarmament treaty is being made?
>
> The Prime Minister: I think my Right Hon. Friend knows that this matter can be handled only on a multilateral basis, as indeed can the nuclear problem, and that we are examining the whole question of what proposals we should make when the 18-Nation Disarmament Committee reconvenes next week. We have been devoting very close attention to the question of

chemical and biological weapons in our study of arms control and disarmament matters.

On 16 July 1968 in Geneva Britain called for an international ban on chemical and biological weapons. This was followed by detailed proposals at the 1969 conference. These are discussed in Part 2.

The final word is with Mr Dennis Healey, who stated on 17 July 1968, after a visit to Porton:

'I am not only satisfied it is genuinely defensive, I am also satisfied of the reasons why it should remain secret.'

He thought a great deal of public anxiety could be allayed if more information was given about the nature of the work which had to be kept secret and why it should be secret.

To this end they would have the open days already promised. Some would be of highest scientific level for scientists with special knowledge in that area. Others would be for informed opinions, such as journalists and defence correspondents.

Mr Healey claimed the policy of sharing with the Americans had not resulted in any increase of American offensive capabilities.

'The British Government is searching for means for effective international control of biological weapons—a total ban with effective verification. . . .'

A good deal of work done in both of these establishments was on the way in which a potential enemy known to possess these weapons might use them to attack Britain and which targets would be the most vulnerable.

'For us to publish this information would be absolutely absurd and very dangerous to the country's security.'

'Again some work is being done at Porton on the properties of agents which a potential enemy is known—and other people—to possess.'

'If we revealed what we know, this could be prejudicial to our intelligence resources, and encourage him to develop other agents we don't know about.'

'Further, in the course of defensive work you find out how weapons might be prepared.'

'To publish this information to the whole world would enormously reduce the security of the world as well as this country.'

3. WEST GERMANY

Like Britain, West Germany is party to both the Hague Conventions and the 1925 Geneva Protocol, as well as being a member of NATO and the WEU.

Bonn's declared policy is defensive only, and officially West Germany has renounced the right of manufacture of CB weapons.[1]

The Federal Republic of Germany renounced the manufacture of nuclear, biological and chemical weapons as early as 1954, when it was admitted to membership in the Western European Union and the North Atlantic Treaty Organisation, and it submitted to the corresponding international controls.

[*Friedenspolitik in Europa*, Herr W. Brandt
(West German Foreign Minister)]

Herr Brandt is referring to Protocol No. III, 'On the Control of Armaments', of 23 October 1954, which in annex I contains a commitment of the West German government (announced by Chancellor Konrad Adenauer) not to manufacture such weapons on the territory of the Federal Republic. This Protocol forms part of the Paris treaties.

In November 1968 Dr Petras, Director of the Laboratory of Microbiology in the Institute of Aerobiology in Grafschaft, defected to East Germany. In a television interview shortly afterwards he explained that he felt morally obliged to take such action in view of the build up of CB weapons and the intensification of research in West Germany.

This provoked denials from Bonn. There was much talk of protective clothing and gas masks. At the same time:

the spokesman of the West German war ministry, Herr Domröse, in one of these denials, clearly said that it was a question of biological and chemical means of destruction for deterrent purposes.

On 6 December 1968 a press conference was held in East Berlin at which Dr Petras answered questions. On being asked what had finally decided him to leave he replied as follows:

The last impact was given by the reorganisation of the Institute undertaken at the end of March of this year in Grafschaft. It was substantiated in detail by the former head of the Institute, Dr Bisa, that now extensive development work on the B and primarily on the C sectors was to be undertaken. Of course, I did not immediately make a firm decision after that. Something like that requires time.

Before I left, ten colleagues had already voluntarily resigned from the Institute. In addition, two colleagues, Dr Zoch and Dr Bisa, were removed from the Institute by force. Of at least five resigned colleagues, I know that they openly, even though not

[1] But she has not renounced the right to stockpile weapons if these are supplied by another power.

publicly, explained that moral scruples played the decisive role in their step. The other voluntarily resigned colleagues without exception adduce limitations on their personal freedom and other grounds for their action. In addition, however, among these colleagues, too, there was a distinct uneasiness to be noted about the work carried out in Grafschaft. I can of course not give more details here in view of the methods practised by the Federal Ministry of Defence. The Federal Ministry of Defence had obviously included the mentioned conflicts of conscience in its calculations right from the outset. Strict security examinations were therefore carried out. There was constant spying and deliberate diversion from the true character of the work. It was repeatedly said that our work is of a purely defensive nature, and many colleagues allowed themselves to be led astray by this for some time. From 1961 the Jesuit priest and biologist, Dr Haselpater, in the meantime he has left the Institute, served as a signboard for the 'peaceful' character of the Institute. Externally, precisely for Catholic circles the presence of this Jesuit father was to guarantee that no illegal research or research in contradiction to international law was being conducted. I consider him a man of integrity. After the reorganisation of this Institute his resignation also puts him among those who had the courage to express the conflict of conscience openly.

He was also asked about the military aspects of his work in the Institute.

Under my direct management we carried out preparations for B warfare. Under strict secrecy my former co-worker Dr Salomon and I had to prepare a study for the Bonn Ministry of Defence. On the basis of this study I later had to draw up a programme for the building of a comprehensive collection of highly pathogenic microorganism breeds. In addition a salmonella centre for the entire NATO sphere of Central Europe was to be installed in the Grafschaft Institute. Further, preparations for C warfare were carried out. I have already reported extensively on this. As was said, V agents have already been tested. Because of their experimental toxicity they are suitable only for military purposes.

Two important points should be made here. Dr Petras has not made a very convincing case for his assertion that West German preparations are other than defensive. However, the presence of US and NATO forces prepared to use CBW makes the position of the West German government difficult to defend. The existence of 'defensive' research, part of which is secret, must give rise to serious disquiet. It must make disarmament talks with the Communist powers doubly difficult. If the reorganisation referred to involved an increased interest in offensive research, West Germany could possess weapons potentially as effective as nuclear ones.

The defection of Dr Petras and seven other West German scientists was widely reported in the Continental press, particularly in Sweden and Holland. The British press gave it little attention.

There are two main points which have emerged from this discussion of policy. The first is justification of use of chemical weapons, *vis-à-vis* international law. The second is the existence of secret research, which may or may not be purely defensive, in face of national declarations of no first use. The former is well illustrated by the USA, the latter by Britain. Both will be discussed further in Part 2.

We finish Part 1 of this book with a description of Swedish defence policy. Sweden has no stockpiles of chemical or biological weapons. An extensive programme of research into defence procedures is, however, pursued at the Swedish Defence Research Institute. None of the information which results from this programme is classified. The institute is expected to spend £6½ million on research in 1968.

The results of the programme are tangible and cost an additional £12 million. All buildings in main cities are equipped with gas and aerosol proof shelters in the basements. This includes airtight steel covers for the windows and airtight steel doors. In periods of extreme international crisis washing machines are removed from laundries and replaced by filtration plants. All main cities in addition have well-stocked public shelters which are used as garages during peacetime. These are primarily for government personnel.

Publicity is purposely given to the subject. Each household should have a leaflet giving details of first-aid techniques against CB weapons. There are nerve gas antidotes for 900,000 civilians and a large stock of gas masks.

According to Dr Magnussen, the Deputy Director of the Institute:

> We also want the public to know that the institute is working on chemical and biological warfare so that they feel they are getting proper protection.

The Swedish government offers 'defence' as justification for CBW research, a policy not dissimilar to Britain's.

The Swedish government provides the civilian population with concrete proof that in the event of attack they will be protected.

The Swedish government reserves no right to retaliate with CBW.

The Swedish government is party to no information-sharing agreements. The results of any research are freely available to all.

Part 2

Analysis

John Cookson

The preceding section has been a review of the documentation of CBW. The intention was to give an idea of the efforts involved in CBW research, the interest and the application. Official attitudes were also discussed. This section attempts to inform and provide a basis for rational examination of the preceding data. For this a knowledge of how CBW systems work is necessary. An explanation of this is what is attempted here. The writer of this section has few illusions about the difficulty of the subject. He can only say that to the best of his ability he has made it as simple as possible. In fact, in retrospect, he can see two possible sources of error. The first of these is oversimplification, the second is due to the limitations of the author's ability in explanation.

CBW is a fusion of physics, meteorology, pharmacology, toxicology, microbiology, chemistry, genetics and many other fields of study. The author's training was in biochemistry and genetics. Herein lies the problem, especially where conflicts arise between the 'experts'. The best people to work out these difficulties, unfortunately, because of security restrictions, are not able to be of assistance. The author in advance apologises for the errors.

Some of the data are obviously more comprehensible to scientists and doctors. Where possible we have indicated where this is so, where a previous knowledge of biology would be useful. In such cases the conclusion rather than the discussion may be of more interest, for example, in the section on the production of the biological weapon. In some cases, to describe what happens, scientific terminology must be used; this we have attempted to explain.

The section dealing with how lethality is measured is perhaps one of the more difficult ones to grasp. The writer would suggest that the reader should, however, make every attempt to understand it as it is critical to the comprehension of some of the later information.

The subsequent discussion is divided into two sections, chemical weapons and biological weapons. What may have become obscured is the fact that these agents may be difficult to distinguish, e.g. the defoliants, which are synthetic chemicals, are classed by the Americans as biological weapons; most psychochemicals are extractable from natural sources but classed as chemical agents. This very difficulty of distinction is the reason why the chemical and biological weapons must be considered together. Another reason is that, like nuclear weapons, they both affect large areas. Napalm is a terrible weapon but unlikely ever to jeopardise large numbers of the world's population. It is impossible to argue from qualitative considerations of how a weapon acts. It is the quantitative effect which is of importance. (This is discussed in more detail later.)

The section on chemicals is the first to be considered. Defoliants are dealt with at the end of the discussion of chemical agents. It is the writer's opinion that they are chemical rather than biological weapons.

Defence, disarmament and other considerations where a separation of c and bw was considered undesirable or not worthwhile have been considered after a description of the weapons and the history.

4

ASSESSING THE EFFECTS OF CBW AGENTS

Before any discussion of the use of chemical and biological agents it is necessary to clarify some of the terms in which the quantitative data are expressed. Several of them are present in the text.

Lethality

The Median Lethal Dose—LD_{50}   This is the dose which results in death for 50% of the animals under attack. It may be expressed in terms of mg/kg body weight or as mg/person (in this case one assumes a 'standard man' as usually 70 kg or 100 kg). The former measure is more useful. The LD_{50} is useful for comparative toxicities and is the best measure available for solids and liquids.

(Analogous to this is the LC_{50}, which is the concentration required to produce 50% fatalities when victims are exposed to a gas for a specific time. There are severe limitations to the use of this and a better measure is shown below.)

The $L(Ct)_{50}$ This is the product of the concentration and the time of exposure necessary to produce death in 50% of the subjects attacked. This is the best available means of assessment for gases, aerosols, etc. It is expressed in terms of mg-min/cu m. This assumes a standard aerosol size and a rate of breathing.

The Average Lethal Dose   This is the average dose required to cause the death of a member of a population. It is not an accurate measure and is met especially in the discussion of agents effective in minute quantities where $L(Ct)_{50}$ is less practical. It may be expressed in mg/animal or mg/man or mg/kg body weight.

The Average Lethal Inhaled Dose   This is the average dose which on inhalation causes the death of a member of a population. This is met with in connection with the same group of compounds previously mentioned—those effective in very small amounts. The specification of *inhalation* is of considerable importance. Some agents can be effective through both skin and lungs, or might have different effects by ingestion. The average lethal inhaled dose may thus differ from the average lethal dose.

The above is a simple description and definition of the terms used; a more detailed and critical assessment follows. The utility of any definition depends on the validity of the assumptions made in its formulation and experimental assessment. The following questions have to be asked.

1. How useful are the definitions themselves (median lethal dose, etc.) as means of measuring and comparing the effects of agents? What assumptions are made?
2. What problems are there in obtaining this information from laboratory animals?
3. Can the experimental data be extended to other situations— can the effects of agents on man be predicted on the basis of animal experiments?
4. Can the data obtained for a 'standard man' bear any relation to the effects on a real, heterogeneous population?

1. *How useful are the definitions? What assumptions do they involve?*

This first point involves the separate treatment of each definition. The other points effect every means of lethality estimation in a similar way.

The Median Lethal Dose—LD$_{50}$ The major difficulties in methods of estimating lethality arise from the complexity of the dose/response curve. As the amount of an agent increases from zero, at first very few deaths occur per unit dose of agent added (say from 0 to 5% mortality). Then the number of deaths per unit dose of agent added rises rapidly (say from 5 to 95%). When the dose is very high (95–100% mortality), then the increase in mortality per unit dose falls again. This results in an 'S' (sigmoidal) curve if a graph is plotted of mortality against log. dose.

Usually in giving graded doses one finds the following types of data: 10%, 27%, 35%, 65%, 80% mortalities. The difficulty is to find a dose which produces 50% mortality in the animals treated. This is done by adjusting the data on dosage/mortality to the form of a straight-line graph instead of a curve. The advantage of this is that scattered points due to the variation expected in the experiment can be fitted in more easily. The LD$_{50}$ can thus be assessed by an interpolation which is easier for a straight-line graph than for a curve. The accuracy of this assessment is reasonable. Calculation can usually be made of the possible difference which might be expected from repeating the experiment several times. There is bound to be an experimental variation. The limits of this are usually indicated.

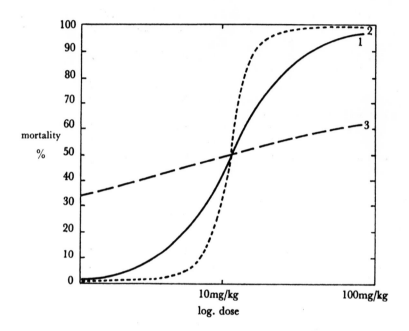

Three dose/response curves

same LD$_{50}$ {
1. illustrates the sigmoidal curve

2. a compound with a small difference between LD$_{50}$ and LD$_{100}$

3. a compound with a large difference between LD$_{50}$ and LD$_{100}$

Having obtained an LD_{50} which is valid, and fairly accurate to within defined limits, it is now important to consider if this is comparable with other LD_{50}s, and how far it is an assessment, for any agent, of the lethal effect. To go further it is necessary to consider the sigmoidal response curve again.

Dose response can vary in many ways. Obviously the range of doses for comparison of two agents may be different, one being effective, say, from 0·1 mg/kg to 0·2 mg/kg and another from 0·001 mg/kg to 0·002 mg/kg. In addition, the very form of the 'S' shape may change. For one agent the 'S' may be flattened, which would mean that the difference between 50% and 100% death in dosage is less than when the 'S' is less vertical. In the latter case the difference between the LD_{50} and the LD_{75} is small. In the first case it may be large. If so, a much larger dose would be necessary to produce an effect. For example, in the first case, if, say, three times the LD_{50} is applied, 88% mortality may result. In the second case it may be 100%.

For LD_{50}s to be of any real use, the agents compared should have similar dose/response curves. Probably the only case where they have any real meaning is when dealing with ratios of LD_{50}s in the order of 100:1. For closer figures comparisons are not likely to be very useful. It is possible, by using refined statistical methods, to produce a reasonably comparable measure of relative LD_{50}s for two agents. This analysis is difficult and requires careful consideration, as all the features of the result cannot be explained. Strictly, for comparison by this measurement, dosage response curves should be similar in form and ranges of effect should be well separated.

One point about LD_{50}s is that there is no particular significance in these numbers. An LD_{75} could just as easily be used. The reason for such an arbitrary unit is that the LD_{100} cannot be determined unambiguously, as one may gather from the dose/response curve mentioned. Thus a purely arbitrary measure is used. This should be remembered when considering effects. LD_{50} is of comparative use only. It cannot predict at which concentration a different proportion of the animals will die.

As with the data on chemical agents, LD_{50}s for biological agents are met in some sources. These are subject to much greater imprecisions than estimates for chemicals. In the latter case the agent is assumed to be stable and the population is considered to produce a variable response to it; for the biological agents, however, variation is also certain within the group of agents (for example, bacteria) themselves. The same statistical difficulties are also encountered. These have already been considered in detail. In the case of microbes, to calculate the LD_{50} dose and effect must be estimated.

For virulence measurement there are two ways. (Virulence refers to an effect within strains of a species; pathogenicity is a characteristic of the species.)

1. Finding the dose of each type of organism which will produce a particular effect in the experimental animal.
2. Varying the dose and measuring the effect produced.

The possible effects measurable in this fashion are lesion counts and mortality data. Lesion counts are the less useful. Both measure the effects of a living organism, which is assumed not to vary and which, of course, does. Mortality data are used in the LD_{50}.

The Median Lethal Concentration—LC_{50} This suffers from the same statistical difficulties as the above. Time must be specified.

The $L(Ct)_{50}$ This measure is on the same statistical basis as those mentioned previously. It differs in that the effects of exposure to the agent for a particular length of time are taken into account. Ct is the Haber factor. It is the product of concentration and time. It is assumed that exposure to an agent in high concentration for a short time is equivalent to exposure to a lower concentration for a longer time. If the $L(Ct)_{50}$ of a gas is 500 mg-min/cu m, this means that:

$$50 \text{ min} \times 10 \text{ mg exposure} = 500 \text{ mg-min/cu m}$$

gives death of 50% of the population.

$$25 \text{ min} \times 20 \text{ mg exposure} = 500 \text{ mg-min/cu m}$$

gives death of 50% of the population.

Haber's law states

$$Ct = K$$

where C = concentration; t = time for effect on 50% of the population; K = a constant.

This formula holds quite well for the lung irritants and the blood gases. For other gases effects are not strictly cumulative. It is necessary to consider the nature of the gases, the reason for toxic effects and the non-applicability, in some cases, of the above formula.

One important case where exception to the above rule occurs is phosgene. In very high concentrations the gas kills by an action which produces an effect described best as 'cooking' on the lungs. For a lower dose, death is due to accumulation of fluid in the lung. The two toxic effects are quite different.

It is important to realise the fundamental differences between a discussion of solids or liquids and a discussion of gases. The latter must be considered more carefully. There are three types of 'gases':

1. True gases—these occur in the gaseous form at normal temperatures, e.g. chlorine or phosgene.
2. Vapours—e.g. carbon tetrachloride, benzene and the mustard gases.
3. Aerosols—airborne solid particles and liquid droplets.

In dealing with poisons inhaled by an airborne route, one cannot simply extrapolate from the results, for example, of intravenous injections. The similarity which often exists between oral and inhalation $LD_{50}s$ is an illustration of how effectively poisons are absorbed by the lungs. This similarity cannot always be assumed. The toxicity of airborne poisons is dependent on the amount of material retained in the respiratory tract (some material will not reach the lungs. Some may be rapidly exhaled and will hardly be absorbed at all). For true gases and vapours (1 and 2 above), reliable calculations can be made of the amount absorbed if the nature of the substance, concentration in the atmosphere and the amount of contaminated air inhaled in the period of exposure are known. The amount of vapour absorbed can be predicted from Ct, because the rate of diffusion into the blood stream is proportional to the concentration in the atmosphere.

For aerosols, however, size is an extremely critical factor. Aerosols are discussed with respect to particle size later. There is a critical requirement for aerosol particle size to allow penetration of the nose (where larger particles are trapped) to the lungs where absorption occurs (there is also a lower limit). Further variations, not only particle size, occur owing to individual differences in the geometry of the respiratory passages. It will also depend on loss in the nasal passages, the amount lost by the impingement on the bronchiolar tree, the rate of settling and the impactibility of the particles. All affect $L(Ct)_{50}s$, and as they differ between species they complicate extrapolation to man.

Toxic action may be enhanced or depressed by the type of solvent employed. Solutions of poisons in oils, organic solvents (e.g. tabun in 20% chlorobenzene) and aqueous solutions are usually absorbed much more rapidly into the blood stream than solid ingested particles. Toxicity depends on the rate of absorption, rate of detoxification and rate of excretion. For dosage over a long period of time, detoxification may have important effects on the toxic action. This is a cause of the inaccuracy in $L(Ct)_{50}s$ for gases effective by other portals than the lungs. For arsenic and cyanides in small doses detoxification may have considerable effect.

It is also possible to estimate lethal doses from $L(Ct)_{50}s$ by the following formula:

$$(VaC - c)t = k$$

where k is effective dose (mg); V is volume of inspired air (l./min); c is rate of detoxification (mg/min); t is time of exposure (min); a is percentage of absorption; C is concentration in inspired air (mg/l.).

V, a and c vary with the concentration and nature of the poison. Other factors affecting these are mental and physical activity (it is usual to specify V in $L(Ct)_{50}$ determinations), reflex stimulation and inhibition of respiration, the health of the individual and the physical and chemical properties of the inhaled materials.

The $L(Ct)_{50}$ is the best means of assessment for the harassing gases which attack the lungs. Certain chemicals (e.g. toxins) are effective in such small concentrations that average lethal dose and other such less precise methods are acceptable.

Average Lethal Dose As has already been mentioned above, this is of special use for the measurement of agents effective in very small quantities. It is, however, limited to some extent. It can give no estimation of variability of response to an agent's action within a population. If, for example, one group within a population is able to withstand a much higher dose than normal, this will inflate the overall average figure. This 'weighting' effect does not appear in the estimation. In the estimation of median lethal dose it is to a certain extent eliminated. These same restrictions apply for inhaled doses.

Other terms may be met in the text, but they are usually self-explanatory. A *fatal dose* is that expected to result in death. This is mentioned in relation to agents whose effects show significant variation from individual to individual. Some people seem to have fantastic resistance to certain poisons. Others may possess a hypersensitive response, referred to as idiosyncrasy.

Toxicity Ratings

Description	LD_{50} for oral dose	Estimated lethal dose for man
Extremely toxic	up to 1 mg/kg	1 grain (a taste)
Highly toxic	1–50 mg/kg	1 teaspoonful (4 cc)
Moderately toxic	50–500 mg/kg	1 oz (30 gm)
Slightly toxic	500/1000 mg/kg	1 pt (250 gm)
Practically non-toxic	5000–15,000 mg/kg	1 qt
Relatively harmless	above 15,000 mg/kg	above 1 qt

*2. What problems are involved in obtaining this data from labora-
tory animals?*

Such assessments depend on two things:

1. The agent tested.
2. The population on which it is tested.

With chemical (as opposed to biological) agents it is usually
assumed that the first is not variable to any significant extent. It
should be noted, however, that the lethality data depend upon the
way in which a particular agent is effective; percutaneously (through
the skin), through the gut, or by inhalation (through the lungs).
The $L(Ct)_{50}$ (and other measurements) is often found to be different
through the different portals of entry. Alteration of the solvent
used can often radically affect the apparent toxicity of a compound. New estimates have to be made for any alteration in the
agent.

Usually in the case of chemicals it is possible to administer
accurate doses. The same cannot be said for biological agents. The
difficulty is to know how many live organisms are being administered.

To quantify the virulent effects of a pathogenic organism it is
necessary to measure the dose of organism and the number of infective units required. For protozoa, the number of organisms which
have been administered can be counted. In many cases it is possible
to assess how many are alive. For bacteria the same process can be
used, but there is no method of discovering the number of live pathogenic organisms among those counted. Thus estimates of numbers of
infecting units, especially in the lower range, are very approximate.

An example will show another difficulty in the estimation of virulence. If pneumococcus type 1 strain B is disseminated in aerosol to
mice, no infection occurs. If only a few organisms are injected into
the peritoneum, pneumonia develops and the animal dies. This
illustrates the difficulty of dealing with organisms where the reason
for virulence is not known. It is thought to be affected by several
factors and the nature of microbial pathogenicity is thought to be
very complex. Thus LD_{50}s and other measures can only be rough
guides.

Variations arising from the second point, the population, are
obviously of importance. In laboratories an attempt is made to
maintain the animals in the optimum condition. Exactly what constitutes the optimum condition, however, varies with the laboratory.
One man's excellent healthy specimens are another's undersized,
undernourished runts.

There is yet another difficulty concerning assessment. Does one use a large number of animals when it may be impossible to maintain them in optimum condition, or does one risk statistically less significant results with a smaller population more easily maintained in good condition and which may be observed with more precision? In the latter case autopsy on the animals may be possible, so that internal changes can be examined. With some poisons, internal changes examined under post-mortem can be great and may be of importance. Individual organs can then be analysed for concentration of poison.

The animals used for research are usually highly inbred and do not differ greatly genetically within a particular line. Differences between laboratories' assessments of the same agent may be due to some strains possessing partial resistance or idiosyncrasy to the agent being tested. This is of greater significance for the biological than for the chemical agents. Many results are reasonably reproducible, however. This has been shown by testing with a standard agent and comparing data.

A more serious cause for concern, perhaps the most serious, is the variation in lethality results from the different species of animals under test (from rats to porpoises). These can be compared by relating dosage to body weight (mg/kg). Some wide variations can occur. It is usual to assume for man that the dose in mg/kg lies somewhere between the extremes found in experimental animals. This will vary with the species and it is common to use as many different species as possible.

In view of these variations, attempts should be made to test the agent on as wide a variety of animals as possible. This may not be deemed necessary in an agent destined for military use, where the chief interest may be assumed to be in the effects on troops in the field. Use on heterogeneous populations, including pregnant women, children, the old and the sick, may be expected to have diverse effects on the different groups.

3. *Can the effects of agents on man be predicted from animal experiments? Can this data be of use apart from the situation in which the agent was applied?*

So far there has been variation of a statistical nature (point 1). This is usually estimated and expressed in the results based on assessments from experimental animals. There is also variation due to the physiological state of the population. Under-nourishment frequently makes the agents more effective, as do pregnancy and extremes of age. Variation arising out of differences in lethal dosages for different species must be added to this. In extending these data to man it is assumed that the lethality for man lies within this range. On the basis of the figure thus obtained the dosage in terms of kg body weight may be extended to a 'standard man' of 70–100 kg body weight.

Obviously a single figure cannot represent a very accurate assessment of the lethal effect even on a 'standard man'. No statements are made about the degree of confidence or the variation which can be expected in figures quoted. In assessments for military use the testing is likely to be on the best male and female specimens of the species.

A further point in this assessment is that in experimental determination for the gases, techniques of 'precision gassing' are used. How far this represents a true test of effects in field use may be judged from the reports in the text of the actual use of the gases. The effects of several agents used consecutively or together are very rarely considered.

Extrapolations from animal experiments to man in the case of micro-organisms are notoriously inaccurate. This is one of the reasons for using plague experimentally in the laboratory. In the rats the plague produces a disease similar to that produced in human beings. An illustration for the commoner difference: in cattle *Brucella abortus* causes spontaneous abortion; in man it causes a fever. This is also admirably illustrated by the unsuccessful attempts to use animals in vaccine tests. Apart from tests on the higher primates, tests on animals are of very little use in assessing effects on man. Thus any prediction of the effects of biological weapons unless they are tested on man, which may be impermissible, must be guesswork. This has particular relevance later.

4. *Can the data obtained for a 'standard man' bear any relation to the effects on a real heterogeneous population?*

There are two main points here. In natural conditions some people will receive larger doses than others, depending mainly on their occupation at the time of attack, response to attack (running, for example, increases the intake of agent into the lungs), and their physical condition. The second point is the possible variation of groups within the population. The worst affected are usually the very young, followed by the very old, adolescents, pregnant women, women in general and finally adult males. Obviously assessments based on the response of adult males could not be expected to be valid for the other groups mentioned. L(Ct)$_{50}$s may, with all the inaccuracies, possibly be acceptable assessments for adult males but the same figure can certainly not be applied to children under two years old. A consideration of the effects of the use in Vietnam of certain of these agents, the author believes, supports this view. Descriptions of gases as 'harmless' by lethality calculations based on adult males are misleading when the agent is used indiscriminately against a whole population comprising men, women and children.

Thus all the figures for assessing lethality of agents seem to be of limited usefulness. While they can, with varying degrees of accuracy, give information on relative toxicities, they cannot be quoted to describe the effects on a real population. All assessments of lethality are subject to inaccuracy. For quotation in the usual military context concerning tactical use against opposing troops, they may provide some guide. For use against a civilian population they are misleading.

Incapacitance

Incapacitance is defined as the concentration of an agent at which 50% of the population is no longer able to offer resistance or fulfil military duties. In *Science Journal* it is defined in the same manner as $L(Ct)_{50}$ and LD_{50}. In the text the source is quoted or $I(Ct)_{50}$, and ID_{50} is used. This is subject to inaccuracies to the same extent as lethality estimates, although the possibility of field testing makes incapacitance figures more reliable than those for lethality.

Field testing has been performed on volunteers in Britain and on volunteers, prisoners and conscientious objectors in the USA (*Science*, January 1967). In Britain some experiments with nerve gases have been performed on service volunteers (Associated Press, 14 March 1960, reported in the *Chicago Sun Times*, 5 March 1960). These gases are not recommended as incapacitants.

Such studies of the subject in 'ideal' or near ideal conditions are probably only of limited value for application to real situations. They are unlikely to reveal the effects of a given agent on a population in a very poor health, the effects of repeated doses or of massive concentrations. For riot-control agents the estimates would have some validity, but even then would provide only a rough guide. Military assessments should strictly be applied only to the specific situation for which they are intended. Extension to non-military situations is not valid.

Persistence A gas is defined as persistent if it remains in effective concentrations for more than 10 minutes after dissemination. Dispersal will, however, depend to some extent upon prevailing conditions like wind, humidity, etc., and where and how the gas is applied. The above refers to open situations.

All the above terms will be met in the text. Reference to this section should make it clear which particular term is being used. Other measurements found in older literature refer to the minimum lethal dose. This is the minimum dose required to cause death. It should now be clear that to assess such a dose is very difficult, and that it is a much poorer measure of toxicity than the LD_{50}.

Similarly, where toxicity data are very sparse a 'lethal dose' is sometimes referred to. This usually means that too few tests have been performed to assess an LD_{50}. This often occurs in cases of human poisoning, where the dose which caused a fatality is known, but not how much of an overdose was applied.

5

CHEMICAL AGENTS

The basis of almost all modern warfare is chemical. Napalm, high explosives and practically all our methods of remote killing are based on chemicals. The distinguishing feature of napalm and explosives is that their primary effect is the physical consequence of a chemical reaction. The expansion of gases provided by a chemical reaction drives a shell. The heat due to combustion results in the primary effects of napalm (a secondary effect is the production of carbon monoxide, which is toxic).

Chemical weapons are those which produce their effects on a living target, man, animal or plant, by virtue of their toxic chemical properties. This is correctly described as toxic warfare. It is important to note that chemical weapons need not be aimed specifically at men but also at crops. Anti-personnel chemical weapons have been in effective use since World War 1. It is only with the advent of air power that anti-crop chemical weapons have been seriously considered.

The anti-personnel weapons discussed here can be placed in several arbitrary categories:

1. Riot control and harassing agents; including lachrymators (causing tears), sternutators (causing sneezing) vomiting agents and orticants (causing itching).
2. Blood and nettle gases and choking agents.
3. Vesicants.
4. Incapacitating agents.
5. Psychochemicals.
6. Nerve agents.

There are, in addition to these, the anti-crop and defoliation agents. The necessary attributes of a chemical weapon are now considered.

Many compounds which in terms of their high toxicity would seem on paper to be excellent agents may not prove their worth in practice. To be useful as a weapon an agent must be stable in storage under a variety of conditions. Any deterioration is to be avoided as this could cause a catastrophic loss of effectiveness. In dissemination any agent must be active in small enough quantities to affect a reasonably large area. There is obviously a limit to the amount of chemical which can be placed in any munition, along with the propellant and high explosive. Maximum area must be effectively covered if any advantages are to be gained over conventional weapons. Some at first sight suitable agents cannot be used on account of their extreme volatility or involatility. A good agent must retain its potency for some time. For riot control agents this should be short. For lethal agents it can vary depending on the situation. Occupation of the area treated may be desired, in which case a non-persistent agent like hydrogen cyanide could be used. In other cases a persistent agent like vx may be more suitable. For some agents decontamination presents a problem.

Once an agent has been disseminated it is beyond the control of the disseminator. For this reason the technology of dissemination and the importance of meteorological conditions cannot be over-emphasised.

Another important aspect of these weapons concerns defence. Ideally, the attacker should be protected against the weapon physically (a necessity for handling and manufacture) and medically (antidotes being available in case of accident). At the same time this protection should be denied to the enemy. This can be done by using an agent together with another substance which will prevent or inhibit the activity of an antidote.

Essential to any nation concerned in chemical warfare is ability to detect enemy gas attacks. Chemical detectors for nerve and mustard gases are available in the usa. There is a chemical pad available for British troops which gives a colour indication of the presence of nerve gases. Unfortunately, there is so far no system which is rapid enough to prevent a high number of casualties before masking in the event of a surprise attack. Protection against gases has an interesting history which is more fully discussed later, as are the other points mentioned here.

There is thus a considerable difference between possessing a range of toxic chemicals and a useful weapons system. A necessary feature of such a system is that all the various components should be integrated. Environmental conditions, munitions, agents and delivery systems must be dove-tailed. If, for instance, a burning grenade is to be used, then a substance which is inactivated by heat is useless. Again, there is a critical requirement for particle size if an agent is to be absorbed effectively by the lungs in an aerosol. Because of this complexity chemical weapons systems are more difficult to devise than might be first imagined.

The history of toxic warfare illustrates many of the points so far made. It is also instructive as to the current state of development in toxic warfare, providing a perspective and indicating possible future developments.

In his book *On Guard against Gas*,[1] H. A. Sisson says:

> To avoid being overwhelmed by the horror we may as well concentrate on the scientific interest of the subject and on such humour as can be extracted from it.

This provides an apt introduction to chemical warfare.

1. RIOT CONTROL OR HARASSING AGENTS

The harassing agents, lachrymators, sternutators, vomiting agents and orticants, have a history dating from World War I, including the use of 'tear gas' by police forces. Several of the above classes of agents have multiple effects; for example, CN, a 'tear gas', can in some instances cause nausea.

It is essential here to clear up a point which emerges both from press reports and even from the proceedings of the House of Commons. In some cases these agents have been described as 'non-lethal'. This is patently untrue. None of these agents is non-lethal. All these gases are characterised to a greater or lesser degree by a large difference between the concentration needed to incapacitate and that needed to kill. Some of these can produce casualties in riot control operations. It is difficult to assign a gas any particular description like 'harassing' or 'lethal'. The line drawn between these is purely arbitrary.

It is an important characteristic of riot control agents that they should cause few casualties in riot-control situations. It must be emphasised, however, that this does not apply if they are not used in open conditions. In closed spaces the casualty rates may be expected to be higher. This is especially true if the people affected are unable to react in the normal way and get out of the gas. With some of these gases, damage may be caused if the eyes are rubbed. It must also be emphasised that the effect of these gases in extremely high concentrations is not clear. Most of the literature on these gases deals with the lethality data and the effect of incapacitance. In some cases the effects of exposure to high concentrations for considerable periods of time are also of importance.

The representative classes of this type of agent discussed here are the vomiting agents and the lachrymatories.

[1] London 1938.

The lachrymatories

The gases considered here are:

CA   α   Brombenzylcyanide (Camite)
CN   ω   Chloracetophenone (CAP)
CS
CSl   } Ortho chlorbenzalmalononitrile

(The letters are military codes.)

The principal requirements of these agents for field use are a lack of persistence and an effect which does not last much longer than the period of exposure. Under these circumstances smoke-generating grenades are preferred because smoke is very quickly dispersed. Some of these agents can also be spread as crystals which generate gas when disturbed. They are mainly characterised by the fact that they produce tears. This effect is probably due to their activity on the thiol groups of enzymes. These agents were first used in warfare in World War I. They were found on the whole not to be very effective. Later they were used as riot control agents.

CN—chloracetophenone

At room temperature CN takes the form of white crystals. To be used effectively it must be vaporised or made into a very fine (micronised) powder. It was first produced in America in 1918. Until the advent of CS it was probably the most widely used tear gas in the world. The major reason for the ineffectiveness of CN is not its toxicity but dissemination difficulties. After production the 'gas' has a tendency to condense rapidly, and for this reason smokes are preferred.

The effects of this agent and those of the other common lachrymatories of this time are very similar. At field concentrations between 1 and 10 mg-min/cu m they have their incapacitating effect. These cause, as their first effect, watering of the eyes. This may be followed by tightness of the chest, nausea, retching and vomiting and pain in the epigastrium especially on exposure to high concentrations or low concentrations over a long time. The primary effects are due to irritation of the eyes and mucous membranes. This affects nerve endings, and causes the body to secrete fluid, tears, saliva and other secretions in the respiratory tract.

In addition to the properties mentioned above the effects on workers exposed to these agents during manufacture are informative. Several effects were noted among workers in England who were preparing one of the lachrymatories, ethyl iodoacetate, after prolonged exposure or very high doses. It was noted that coughing, tracheitis and oedema of the lungs could occur from exposure to the fumes. Pneumonia was reported to be a possible consequence. A large quantity in contact with the skin caused blistering. Autopsy on a casualty from the factory who had been standing near a shell when it exploded revealed acute inflammation of the respiratory tract and severe pulmonary lesions. Necrosis of the lung membranes was extensive. Some damage to the kidney tubules was also noted. The effects of the other lachrymatories are reportedly the same. The $L(Ct)_{50}$ for CN is 8500 mg-min/cu m. The incapacitating dose (i.e. the $I(Ct)_{50}$) is 5–10 mg-min/cu m.

It should be emphasised that these figures are consistent with the expectation of a low level of casualties when used in open situations. Damage may result to the eyes if they are rubbed or if people affected are unable to get away. Field use in World War I showed a number of fatal casualties had occurred. Protection is, however, adequate. Cases of conjunctivitis frequently recovered completely. The proportion permanently blinded by lachrymatory agents was very low—in the order of a few per cent.

The words of M. Dixon, who worked on CN in World War II, are of interest:

> Lachrymation . . . ceases when exposure is terminated. After sufficiently long or repeated exposure it ceases and can no longer be elicited at which point signs of damage (conjunctivitis) make their appearance.
>
> [*The Chemical Warfare Agents*, Biochemical Society Symposium
> No. 2, London 1949]

This is significant for the cases of use given later. It was also found at Porton during World War II that if troops were sufficiently motivated they would not be significantly affected, even by quite high concentrations of the gas. They would still perform military functions quite adequately.

CA—'Camite'—brombenzylcyanide

CA was first used in the first world war. It has the same properties as the other lachrymatories, but produces more severe effects. Under normal conditions similar effects to those on the ethyl iodacetate workers may be seen. CA is 'a potent irritant and is lethal to animals when the concentration is high or the exposure is long'.[1]

---

[1] F. W. Oberst, J. W. Crooks, F. Swain, F. P. Ward, W. S. Koon, N. P. Musselman, 'Toxic effects of brombenzylnitrile vapour in various animal species', *Abstracts of the 8th Annual Meeting of the Society of Toxicology*, March 1969. (The authors of the paper are members of the Department of Toxicology at the Medical Research Laboratories, Edgewood Arsenal, Maryland.)

$LD_{50}s$ for animals are 4,900 mg-min/cu. m. for pigs, 18,900 mg-min/cu m for rats. The LD_{50} for man has been given as 3,500 mg-min/cu m.

Confusion is sometimes caused by the incorrect assignment to CA of the code BZ.

CS—orthochlorbenzalmalononitrile

CS was first prepared in 1928 by B. B. Corson and R. W. Stoughton (hence the code CS). Its current use by the Americans stems from work conducted in Britain. In 1956 a (British) War Office policy statement made it clear that a more effective, preferably less toxic, riot control agent than CN was required. Scientists at the CDEE screened 191 possible replacements and found CS and its near derivations (e.g. orthonitrobenzalmalononitrile) most suitable.

This work was described in a document declassified in June 1968 called 'Agents for riot control: the selection of T.792 as a candidate agent to replace CN' (Porton Technical Paper No. 651). In 1959 the CDEE prepared an internal report on the toxicity of CS (Porton Technical Paper No. 672). This was also declassified in June 1968. By injection CS was found less toxic, for a monkey, rabbits, guinea-pigs, rats and mice, than CN. Injections wherever made (at 100 mg/kg) were insufficient to kill some of the animals. By inhalation doses of 13,200 mg-min/cu m were the highest averages used. Of the twenty-one animals tested only one guinea-pig died, probably from a previously contracted pneumonia.

Scientists from the Armed Forces Chemical Centre, Maryland (in *Toxicology and Applied Pharmacology*, 4, 656–662, 1962, C. Punte et al.), give the approximate LD_{50} for mice as 8 mg/kg by intravenous injection (twenty-two animals used). The Porton report states that intravenous injection of 25 mg was insufficient to kill the majority of the animals. The American $L(Ct)_{50}$ figures are:

mg-min/cu m
32,500 for rats
43,500 for mice
8,300 for guinea-pigs
17,300 for rabbits

'An occasional animal' developed pulmonary oedema and haemorrhage in the adrenal glands at 20,000–30,000 mg-min/cu m.[1] These figures would, in the classification now generally accepted, of Gleason Gosselin and Hodge in their work on the toxicology of commercial products, rate CS as moderately toxic compound.

[1] The article also says that necrosis of the respiratory and gastro-intestinal tracts occurred if particles of the 'gas' were absorbed.

As yet the CDEE have published no $L(Ct)_{50}$s of CS because 'it was never envisaged that the agent would ever be used in concentrations within several orders of magnitude of its estimated toxicity'. American workers at the Edgewood Arsenal have made numerous studies of CS toxicity. An early estimate of $L(Ct)_{50}$ for man was given as 25,000 mg-min/cu m, later 61,000 mg-min/cu m (now the US official figure). The British minister of defence on 11 March 1968 gave the toxic dose for large animals such as man at 150,000 mg-min/cu m. An American report had quoted this for monkeys. The official US figure is rather less.

The dose to disperse rioters is 0.75 mg-min/cu m. The dose tolerated by man is quoted at 10 mg-min/cu m. These are the sort of concentrations obtained in riot control situations. This should be qualified with a consideration from the above figures of toxicity in confined spaces. One US technical paper admits the possibility that under such circumstances $L(Ct)_{50}$ figures could be approached. *Science Journal* (August 1968) gives the following as an example using the lowest toxicity figures given: 'Personnel in a tunnel 1 m in radius, 20 m long, would stand a 50:50 chance of death if 150 grams of CS were introduced and they stayed for an hour.' This needs qualification. First, usually all the aerosol would settle out within a fairly short time. A second point is that the figure is an estimate for a 'standard man'. Use on a tunnel with children, old people, etc., may be expected to have more severe results. Standard US grenades are 250 grams. Use of such devices as the 'Mighty Mite' (see section on use in Vietnam, pp 18ff) could rapidly produce lethal concentrations in confined areas. It is in this context that toxicity data should be considered.

Its effects have been described in an Army publication as 'impressive, CS produces immediate effects even in low concentrations'. The British government patent on its use states:

A concentration of between one part in 10 m and one part in 1 m is enough to drive all but the most determined person out of it within a few seconds.

This is equivalent to a field concentration of between 1 and 8 mg/cu m. The Americans have stated that it is effective for from 10 to 20 mg/cu m.[1] The lethality data have been given above.

The effects of CS are immediate and their duration is usually five to ten minutes more than the time of exposure. It causes an extreme burning sensation of the eyes with copious tears, difficulty in breath-

---

[1] Effectiveness depends also on how efficient the grenade or means of producing 'gas' from powder is. Variability in this respect would account for the disparity in these figures.

ing and tightness of chest, involuntary closing of the eyes, sinus and nasal drip, nausea and vomiting. The US Army claim that their tests show that it has no effect on the eye resulting in a temporary conjunctivitis and no corneal damage. It has been tested on, for example, monkeys and goats ill with pneumonia. High concentrations were said to have no significant lethal effects. The same is said to be the case for repeated exposure (EASP 600–1). This should be compared with the data above from toxicological study. To date, according to the US Army, no deaths have been caused by cs despite its widespread use. One may dispute this on the basis of the reports from Vietnam (see the section on use in Vietnam). The above are the effects as reported by British and American official sources (especially *Edgewood Arsenal Special Publication*, EASP 600–1).

A less useful piece of evidence is also available. Dr M. F. Kahn gave a toxicological report to the Conference on CBW in London (February 1968). This alleged that cs caused a variety of more serious effects. He stated that in most cases the effects were relatively mild. Nevertheless he alleged that fatal cases had occurred in Vietnam. A report was mentioned of an investigation by members of the North Vietnamese Commission on US War Crimes. Their findings were that cs was lethal for monkeys at a concentration of 12,500 mg-min/cu m. Pathological findings were severe polyvisceral lesions, mainly of liver, brain or kidneys. (The reported American findings on the 'occasional animal' may be noted.) For a cat the lethal concentration was found to be 45,000 mg-min/cu m. (This is not unreasonable in view of the above.) In France Professor Ag. A. Roussel used mice of white pine strain CFI, of which two-thirds died on exposure to 200–2500 mg/cu m for 10 hours.

Several points are significant about these reports. Although we have described these in terms of $L(Ct)_{50}$s the conversion has been performed for purposes of comparison. As the French and Vietnamese workers failed to give accounts of the number of animals used and in some cases definitely did not use sufficient, little credence can be placed on the accuracy of figures given. Our description in terms of $L(Ct)_{50}$ units is only to allow comparisons with previous data; it is not a valid $L(Ct)_{50}$ statistically. In addition, two points made by the French workers themselves are important. First, they failed to volatilise or make the gas into a fine enough powder for the effects noted to be referrable to concentrations of 'gas'. As it is disseminated, a very fine powder is produced, the form in which it has maximum effect. Apparently the French workers used bulk powder. The pathological effects noted by these workers suggest that the toxic effect they observed was due to the intake of powder rather than very fine particles or smokes (cf Punte). The US forces use powder whereas the British riot control grenades produce smoke (see the section on Vietnam).

Recently the British at Porton have begun to re-examine the toxicity of cs. The results of this should be very interesting, particularly with respect to the previously quoted figures. There is some disparity between the statement of EASP 600–1, a sheet of facts for non-Department of Defense enquirers, and quoted literature effects. The Edgewood publication, in view of the toxicological findings (which are not as yet complete) would seem to be misleading. Its whole tone is calculated to give an impression that cs is almost completely harmless. In view of what we have described here and the data from Vietnam (even accepting the inaccuracies and distortions), this is clearly incorrect. This gas has a relatively low lethality; it is not non-lethal. Its effect depends on the situation and how it is applied. The reader can make his own judgement from considering the above and the methods of application in Vietnam. The fact is that it is not the weapon which kills; axes can be used on trees just as easily as heads. It depends on how it is used whether it is a weapon. It is difficult to argue against the use of gas in police operations against dangerous criminals. This is not warfare. Military use of the same gas in Vietnam is abuse. Murderers are determined by their intentions rather than their methods; a vase can kill as surely as a bomb. It is a matter of the intention of the user.

The vomiting agents

These agents have been described incorrectly as being riot control agents. A. M. Prentiss in his book *Chemicals in War*, a history of gas warfare written in 1937, described DM as a respiratory irritant. To the best of the author's knowledge no nation or body other than the US Armed Forces uses it as a riot control agent. In their search for a replacement for CN the British considered DM, but the Legal Branch of the War Office ruled it out. They stated that in view of its poisonous nature 'the use of DM must be proscribed in accordance with the provisions of the Geneva Gas Protocol'. The Americans have admitted using it in Vietnam.

Three agents were developed during World War I. These were:

DM Diphenylaminochlorarsine, or more correctly 10 chloro-5, 10-dihydrochlorphenarsazine.

DA Diphenylchlorarsine.

DC Diphenylcyanarsine.

The last of these compounds was first used by the Germans in the later stages of World War I. According to German reports, its effects are more severe than those of DM or DA. This agent and DA have some vesicant (blistering) properties. The effects of DM and DA are almost the same. Towards the end of the war, DA was replaced by DM, which was easier to prepare. It was stockpiled as 'M' bombs by the allies, but they were never used. The Germans tried to use DA in a glass bottle in a shell with an explosive charge. This was not in any way successful and illustrates the problem of effective dissemination. This is discussed in more detail in the section on use.

DM—'Adamsite'

DM is available for use with US troops. It may be used in combination with CN. In a CN/DM formulation the immediate effects of CN may be coupled with the delayed effects of DM.

The effects of DM may be delayed for up to 20 min. They may become more severe even after exposure has finished. A. M. Prentiss describes DM thus:

> One is not aware of breathing this gas until sufficient has been absorbed to produce its typical physiological effects. It irritates the nose and throat in concentrations as low as 0·00038 mg/l. and causes irritation of the lower respiratory tract at a concentration of 0·0005 mg/l. A concentration of 0·65 mg/l. is lethal at 30 min exposure, while the lethal concentration for 10 min is 3 mg/l.

These figures when converted to $L(Ct)_{50}$, accepting the approximate nature of this in this case, are very interesting. Mr Julian Perry Robinson (*Science Journal*, April 1967 gives an $L(Ct)_{50}$ of 30,000 mg-min/cu m. This is in agreement with the figure for the shorter exposure time in the above description. For the longer exposure time this figure is 19,500 mg-min/cu m.

The US Army manual, *Field Manual 3–10*, states that:

> DM alone is not approved for use in riot control operations where deaths are not acceptable. Excessive and possibly lethal or completely incapacitating dosages can be developed from its use. However, it may be used in military or paramilitary operations, counter insurgency operations or in limited or general war where control of target personnel by the incapacitating effects is desired and where possible deaths are acceptable.

The effects of this gas resemble those of the lachrymatories but are more severe. Lachrymation, salivation, nasal drip and epigastric pain are experienced. Retching and vomiting (hence the name) follow. Giddiness, mental disorders and faintness were noted in World War 1 as effects of these gases. The pain, headache and tightness of the chest are worse than for the lachrymatories. The pain in the nose has been described as 'agonising'.

Both American and British physicians examining casualties during World War 1 noted that exposure to DC and DA produced certain motor disturbances. These they attributed to a form of toxaemia. This caused acute pain in the joints. These effects were thought to be a result of impairment of the function of the central nervous system. Some muscular twitching and ataxia to a greater or lesser extent was observed.

We have given the available toxicity figures of the agents under discussion. Those for CS are not readily available. From this data it may be seen that DM is given as the compound with the lowest toxicity. In view of the statement given in the manual this seems strange. It may be that the form in which DM is disseminated,. i.e. an 'arsenical smoke', may be more effective in producing casualties than the lachrymatories, which are spread as micronised powder and which rapidly condense. Quantitative data given in the *Military Chemistry and Chemical Manual* are, as no times of exposure are given, of little value.

Special publication 2–31 (1960) from Edgewood Arsenal states (Mr B. P. McNamara):

> Very severe exposures to tear gas or adamsite can produce damage to the respiratory tract. Adamsite is arsenical and although remote, there is the possibility of systemic arsenical poisoning. This may be recognised and differentiated from effects of teargas by marked nausea and vomiting which may persist for an hour or more after poisoning.

The effects of arsenical poisoning will be dealt with under herbicides and defoliants.

We hope that the above may have proved informative especially in view of the interest in these agents at present. It is clear from the above that the description 'non-lethal' is clearly wrong. In addition, it is apparent that the effects of these gases depend on the mode of use. The tear gases used against crowds may be expected to have few, if any, permanent effects. The same cannot be said for DM, which can cause casualties even in riot control operations. Use in confined spaces will cause fatalities. How far this is realised in practice can be seen in the section dealing with use in Vietnam.

A compound of CN/DM is a weapon currently available to American forces. The two gases used in this fashion would reinforce each other's effects. In this case the result would be more severe than the use of one alone or separately.

Another formulation available to the US Army is CNS, which consists of CN with chloropicrin and chloroform. Chloropicrin,

trichlorethylchloroformate, phosgene and chlorine were the main
lethal agents of World War I.[1]

A continuous spectrum of agents of varying effectiveness and
toxicity is available. The question of when an agent is describable
is lethal is a difficult one. Some statements have been made to the
effect that even the mustard gases are considered more 'harassing'
agents than lethal. The line may be drawn at as high as 20% expected fatalities. It is impossible to say. Most of the data refers
mainly to fit healthy men. Limited testing of gas on human volunteers with diseases, for example, pneumonia, has occurred. This is,
however, in precisely controlled conditions. The field effects, those
of high concentrations, repeated exposure, cannot be tested in this
way. The effects on a massed population cannot be predicted. The
only test for field effect is field use. In recent years Vietnam and the
Yemen have provided information on this aspect.

2. Blood and nettle gases and choking agents

Some of these agents have a long history in gas warfare. The blood
gases and choking agents were first used in World War I. The
nettle gases are a more recent formulation and have never yet been
used in war. The first considered are the blood gases.

The Blood Gases

The first one of these to be developed for use in war was prussic
acid (hydrogen cyanide). The French put great faith in this, which
at first sight would not seem unjustified. At the time it was one of
the most deadly poisons known and would seem on paper to have
been an ideal agent. Starting with the battle of the Somme on 1 July
1916, the French fired more than four million shells containing over
4000 tons of a prussic acid, arsenic tri-chloride mixture (Vincennite)
against the Germans. This surprisingly had very little effect, much
to the consternation of the French.

British experience of prussic acid (using shells) indicated that its
effects were very poor. The French, in similar experiments, got excellent results. One explanation of this disparity was that the French
used dogs in their experimental shots while the British used goats.
Dogs are much more sensitive to prussic acid than are goats. The
problem then was to determine which of the animals most closely
resembled man. From captured documents and other information,
the British concluded that man was more like the goat. The French
would not accept this. To settle this dispute, Professor (later Sir

[1] The Wall Street Journal report quoted on pp 18–19 uses the terms 'non-
lethal' and 'nonpoisonous' in connection with CNS.

Joseph) Barcroft, without a gas mask, entered a chamber in which a dog was exposed to a high concentration of prussic acid and stayed there until the dog died. Sir Joseph reported that the only long-term effect he suffered was a momentary giddiness when he turned his head quickly, which vanished after a year.

It was also realised that hydrogen cyanide as used in the field was dispersed so rapidly that it was totally ineffective. The Russians, however, had managed by the time of World War II to compound hydrogen cyanide into a form which could be successfully sprayed from aircraft. This was a considerable achievement as hydrogen cyanide has a strong tendency to polymerise (i.e. the molecules tend spontaneously to form long chains). In addition, hydrogen cyanide and cyanogen chloride replaced phosgene in certain types of munitions in the US arsenals in World War II.

The blood gases, though not as toxic as phosgene, are very quick-acting and are difficult to protect against (special respirators have to be used). Thus, in spite of earlier failures, research continued until an effective means of using the gas was developed.

The effects of prussic acid are due to its affecting oxidation processes, especially the absorption of oxygen by haemoglobin. In high concentrations such as might occur in confined spaces, it could be considered a fulminant poison.[1] In the words of the *Medical Manual of Chemical Warfare*, 1955: 'It may cause death with dramatic rapidity through paralysis of the respiratory centre in the brain.' In low concentrations it may be detoxicated as swiftly as it is absorbed. Liquid prussic acid attacks through the skin and the eyes and may be effective in causing death in this fashion.

It is not an irritant to eyes, nose or throat. In high concentrations the first signs are uneasiness and vertigo, palpitation and deep heavy breathing. Unconsciousness and convulsions follow. Death occurs through paralysis of the respiratory centre in the brain which controls nerves concerned in breathing, and also circulatory failure. Sub-lethal concentrations usually cause no long-term ill effects. Cobalt salts have been suggested as a form of therapy for extreme cases. Prolonged unconsciousness as a result of this form of poisoning could cause permanent mental damage.

In future applications the gas would probably be used as a spray. The American Army had this gas (designated AC) in stockpiles. The munitions included balloons, and it was recognised that its function would be mainly in tunnels and similar confined spaces.

The second blood gas considered is cyanogen chloride, which may be evolved when decontaminating solutions are used on tabun. It is unlikely to be of much military use, as, unlike hydrogen

[1] I.e., a poison with an extremely rapid action. Death is almost immediate.

cyanide, it has an irritant action and this gives warning of its presence. The only warning given by AC is the experience of symptoms. Cyanogen chloride causes stinging in the nose, lachrymation and blepharospasm (convulsive blinking) in low sub-lethal concentrations.

Cyanogen chloride in the lungs reacts with the haemoglobin to liberate hydrogen cyanide. Its effects are therefore very similar to those of AC. In non-fatal cases pulmonary oedema can occur as a fairly common complication. Cyanogen chloride is probably one of the war gases least readily absorbed by gas masks and thus protection is difficult.

The nettle gases

In 1956 Edgewood Arsenal published a report on the properties of war gases in four volumes. It is classified secret. Volume 2 deals specifically with the blood and nettle gases. The latter are mainly skin irritants. These are a step up from the orticants and take the irritancy of the latter to a much more painful level. Exposure to them has been likened to being thrown naked into a bed of stinging nettles, hence the name. These were first seriously considered in the 1930s by the Germans. These were sometimes referred to as 'Red Cross' agents.

A typical gas of this category is dichloroformoxime. This was said to have been stockpiled by the Russians during the second world war. It causes lachrymation and skin irritation at low concentrations. At high concentrations it causes vesication (blistering) and penetrates the skin to enter the blood circulation. Unlike many other agents which have these properties, it has fairly lethal effects percutaneously. It causes the very heavy oedematous response characteristic of its phosgene residue (see choking gases). An Edgewood Arsenal report in 1945 quoted a lethal percutaneous toxicity in guinea-pigs of 25 mg/kg body weight, about twice that of lewisite. In the words of Mr Julian Perry Robinson to the CBW Conference in London, February 1968: 'Its combination of highly painful skin attack with the possibility of a lingering death by asphyxiation (due to oedema) undoubtedly makes it one of the nastiest agents available.'

It is difficult to see any particular use for these gases tactically at present against trained and protected troops. The ideal lethal agent would be imperceptible and therefore non-irritating. Riot control agents must be non-lethal. The nettle gases could have possible application against ill-protected guerillas or in counter-insurgency operations.

The choking agents

Of these gases, phosgene is the most important. This gas and the related di-phosgene were both used in World War I. Phosgene was used in some late gas cloud attacks and in shells. It was so dangerous that it even survived as a weapon in World War II, when it was one of the four main gases stockpiled. It was partially replaced for some purposes by hydrogen cyanide. The earlier chemical warfare agents mainly had their effect by contact irritation of the respiratory tract or by effects on the skin and eyes. Phosgene has a systemic action. Phosgene and chlorine, another member of this group, have their main action on the lungs or the respiratory passages. They cause pulmonary oedema. In the case of phosgene, these effects may be considerably delayed. With chlorine, however, immediate irritation occurs. The action of phosgene on the respiratory tract is typical of this type of agent.

Phosgene carbonyl chloride

Phosgene is not persistent at normal temperatures and its effect is therefore very dependent on meteorological conditions. Phosgene may, however, be used effectively with, for example, chlorine or mustard gas. It has a very characteristic odour even in low concentrations, rather like musty hay. On exposure an immediate irritation of the respiratory passages and smarting and watering of the eyes occurs. Irritation of the respiratory passages causes catching of the breath, coughing, tightness, constriction and pain in the chest. After the initial pause, breathing continues in a gasping fashion. There are violent fits of coughing. Nausea, retching and vomiting and profuse expectoration also occur. Headache and a sense of fatigue prostrate the victim. The severity or otherwise of these conditions cannot give any indication of the subsequent fatality. There usually follows a latent period which may be of several hours' duration. This particular property of phosgene gave rise to a rather macabre tale. A German soldier was captured by the British and claimed that the British gas was useless as, despite exposure, he was still perfectly fit. He remained so for 24 hours—and then died. Severe exertion following exposure can cause serious or even fatal cardiac or respiratory symptoms.

After the latent period, breathing becomes rapid, shallow and difficult, the cough returns and much frothy white or yellowish fluid may be expectorated. Several pints may be coughed up in a few hours. Haemoconcentration begins and may be considerable.

Pulmonary oedema increases and acute oxygen lack becomes apparent. This is due to de-oxygenisation of the blood and the greater number of corpuscles resulting from haemoconcentration. There is a florid generalised cyanosis which later changes to a leaden pallor. There is a weak running pulse and respiration is shallow (cf. use in Yemen, pp 6–14). Restlessness and anxiety or semi-coma or a muttering delirium follow closely, attended by collapse and death. In the first 24 h, 80% of the fatal cases die. Those dying after the third day usually die from broncho-pneumonia. If the pallid state is not reached, recovery frequently occurs. Absorption of the oedema fluid occurs very rapidly and within a week considerable recovery may be noted.

Percussion of the chest despite the oedema may give resonance. Breath sounds are weakened and may be harsh in character but never tubular. Fine râles are heard; rhonchi may be noted occasionally. Inflammation complications such as those of pleurisy, bronchitis and broncho-pneumonia may be seen. Convalescence may be impeded by lassitude, dyspepsia, precordial pain, dyspnoea and persistent tachycardia.

The mode of action of these agents is twofold; firstly bronchial constriction and even severe bronchospasm may occur as it is inhaled. The permeability of the alveolar capillaries is increased and oedematous fluid fills the alveoli (the finest part of the lung where oxygen is absorbed). This prevents oxygen and carbon dioxide exchange. The patient compensates by increased respiratory effort which results in localised emphysematous areas. Oxygen want becomes urgent and there is impaired heart function.

The second effect is on the circulatory system. The oedema fluid is lost from the blood into the lung tissues; this causes a higher concentration of blood corpuscles (haemoconcentration); this causes increased blood viscosity, which, with poor respiratory exchange, causes difficulty to the heart. More work has to be done to maintain the circulation and there is less oxygen for respiration; carbon dioxide accumulates. The combination of these increasingly aggravates the anoxia, resulting finally in heart failure.

As may be expected from the above, the major lesions are pulmonary oedema, rupture of the alveoli and haemoconcentration. The fluids mentioned as being produced may be seen escaping from nose and mouth. The lungs are voluminous, oedematous and congested. Usually, the sooner death occurs after gassing the greater the oedema (accumulation of fluid). The trachea and bronchi are usually normal in appearance but contain the frothy yellowish fluid previously mentioned. With chlorine and chloropicrin, the trachea and bronchi may show serious damage. On removal from the chest, the lungs are heavy with oedema which alternates with areas where there is emphysema and distension together with small areas of collapse. When the lung is sectioned, fluid drips from the cut surface and very dark viscid blood exudes from the vessels. Most of the other organs are generally normal apart from in some cases dilation of the right side of the heart.

The toxicity of phosgene is given as 3200 mg-min/cu m. In World War I phosgene was the nearest thing to an offensive gas developed. It does, however, lack multiple effectiveness. It attacks the lungs only, it reacts with moisture in the air to form a visible mist; it is decomposed rapidly by water, and its boiling point is too low for satisfactory use. A 1944 report from the Dugway proving ground in Utah refers to a 1000-lb M79 phosgene bomb. Similar weapons may still be available to the American forces. It is unlikely that they are stockpiled on any large scale. Phosgene is unlikely to have very much future application except in situations like that in the Yemen. It is of no interest to the major powers.

3. VESICANTS

The design feature of these agents which characterises them is their property of causing blistering. In the history of chemical warfare these agents were among the first used in World War I by the Germans. It is an indication of their effectiveness that they are still in the US armoury fifty years after their first use.

The original mustard gas was first prepared in 1859 by Guthrie and Niemann independently. It had been first discovered probably in 1854. In 1876 Victor Meyer first prepared it in a pure state and described its properties. The Germans used Victor Meyer's method as the basis for industrial production on a large scale, and were the first to use mustard gas. The original gas was five times as toxic as phosgene, and many of the more modern derivatives are even more toxic, some even almost as toxic as the older nerve gases. The vesicants were one of the major breakthroughs of World War I. They differed from other gases in that they combined lung irritation with powerful systemic effects. They also by-passed the gas mask. This was a considerable breakthrough and an interesting parallel with the V nerve agents, which were later to do the same for the nerve gases.

The multiple effects of the vesicants, and their significance, were not realised at the time of their first use. Between the wars, however, mustard gas was considered to be the most serious threat in the event of a future conflict. The significance of its systemic effect was to remain largely unrealised, although it was well documented, until World War II. It was then that the organised search for agents with powerful systemic effects became serious and resulted in the lines of development expanded and continued today.

It is tempting to speculate about what would have happened had mustard gas been used first by the Germans instead of chlorine, or possibly in combination with it. Undoubtedly, because of the insidious and horrifyingly spectacular effects, panic on a much larger scale could well have resulted. This could have caused complete breakdown of allied resistance. As it was, for three days there was a gap in the line which the Germans failed to exploit. The German Higher Command seemed unable to understand the havoc that had been wrought. It was an opportunity that was never to arise again from the use of this technique.

The first use of mustard gas was in shells, not in the gas cloud method. On this occasion, because it was not very detectable and its effects were delayed, many soldiers had removed their gas masks. These, of course, succumbed to the effects of the gas later. Because of their insidious and delayed effects, the sulphur mustards (the original mustard gas and derivatives) are most effective in a defensive action.

The *Medical Manual of Chemical Warfare* lists four types of vesicant:

1. Mustard gas (H). The 'Lost'[1] or 'Yellow Cross' agents of the Germans, known as 'Yperite' by the French.
2. The nitrogen mustards. These are the nitrogen analogues of the sulphur mustards. Their current use is in the treatment of various cancers.
3. Lewisite (named after Professor W. Lee Lewis, the inventor, an American, like the inventor of 'adamsite', Professor Roger Adams of the University of Illinois). This is what was picturesquely (and inaccurately) known as the 'Dew of Death'.
4. Ethyl dichlorarsine was used by the Germans in 1918. It was not as strongly vesicant as mustard or lewisite, but was, like lewisite, very irritating to the respiratory tract. These are discussed in more detail later. The effects of the mustards may be gathered from the effects of the original mustard.

Mustard gases

The following sulphur mustards are currently available. These and their properties are detailed below:

1 The name 'Lost' comes from the names of the two German chemists, Lommel and Steinkopf, who independently suggested that H might be a useful weapon.

Army code	Name	Toxicity (by inhalation $L(Ct)_{50}$)
H	Mustard gas ⎫	Both are reported about 700–
HD	Distilled mustard ⎭	1000 mg-min/cu m
T	No trivial name	400 mg-min/cu m
Q	Sesqui mustard	200 mg-min/cu m
	Tabun (the oldest nerve gas)	150 mg-min/cu m

It will be seen that of the standardised agents, a variety of toxicity effects are possible. These range from fairly low lethality to approaching that of the older nerve gases (by inhalation).

It is possible that the less volatile agents under examination, e.g. the alpha omega-bis (beta-chloroethylthioalkanes) are not considered to be of great military significance. They have probably been superseded as persistent agents by the highly effective v nerve gases which are much more lethal. Even the most potent of the vesicant agents has a much lower toxicity than the new v agents. At the concentrations in which the nerve agents are lethal (50–200 mg-min/cu m) the mustards have their irritant effect. For Q these can include severe incapacitation (or even death at 200 mg-min/cu m). The other agents cause eye damage at 200. With Q, skin burns and eye damage occur at concentrations even as low as 50 mg-min/cu m. In future tactical use they will probably be used for skin attack.

It will be realised that the manufacture of these agents and putting them into munitions poses special problems. The extent of the problems is illustrated by the accounts from the factories. The casualties of the US Chemical Warfare Service staff at the mustard gas factory at Edgewood Arsenal in Maryland in the month of August 1918 exceeded the casualties of any unit of the same size during the same period on the Western Front. Similarly, for the British mustard gas factory at Avonmouth, practically every one of the 1100 men in the factory was more or less severely gassed during the few months the factory was in operation. Many were admitted for treatment several times. More modern factories provide good protection against such hazards.

A further aspect of this problem is the recent revelation that occupational exposure to mustard gas can be cancer-inducing. This has arisen out of study of the effects of mustard gas exposure experienced by workers in a factory which produced this in Japan during the war. This research is not conclusive yet, however, and more information is necessary.

This is the history of the 'king of the battle gases', as it was described prior to the advent of the nerve agents. The effects of the original mustard gas are discussed in some detail below.

Mustard gas (H)

This has a long and notable history in war. It was stockpiled with T as a 60/40 HT mixture in World War II. Its effects are as follows:

A concentration of 1 in 10 million causes eye irritation. It has little or no smell and may be undetectable as concentration of this order and even greater. Its faint garlicky smell may also be disguised by smoke, etc.

Lachrymation and irritation occur after 2-3 hours and severe conjunctivitis, nasal drip and sneezing also begin at this time.

Nausea, retching, vomiting and epigastric pain follow. The official medical history of World War I refers to this as being prolonged in some convalescent cases, where gas poisoning was not suspected. A duration of three years was mentioned where gas poisoning had not at first been diagnosed.

Conjunctivitis becomes worse, the blood vessels become more congested, the cornea becomes misty. The throat feels dry and burning; the voice is hoarse and there is a dry harsh cough.

On exposure to liquid the effects are increased. Intense burning pain, blepharospasm and swelling of the eyes results. These close within about 8 hours. Secretion of a watery fluid from the eyes follows, sight is impaired and secondary infection may develop. Amongst other effects, oedema of the eye occurs, which may take three months to subside. Convalescence is slow and the lachrymation and the eye damage may persist for several months. In very severe cases, vascularisation may occur and secondary oedema may set in. These effects may occur for months or even years with progressive impairment of vision. This may even recur after some fifteen years after apparent cure.

Complications noted from World War I casualties included corneal ulceration, blepharitis, styes and Meibomian abscesses. Secondary infection is the likely cause of most of the damage. The devitalisation of tissues, especially if damage is increased by rubbing, is the major complicating factor.[1] In cases of very severe exposure the chances of secondary infection are very high because the tissue takes a long time to heal owing to damage done to the finest blood and lymphatic vessels. It is only when the effects are localised and superficial that rapid healing occurs. The largest cause for convalescence among affected soldiers preventing their rapid return to duty was the eye damage.

The effects on the skin are quite striking. Some hours (up to twenty-four) after exposure, a diffuse erythema (a rash) develops on

---

[1] This is also true, though to a lesser extent, of the riot-control agents.

the face and neck in the axes of the limbs but most of all in the genital area.

Twenty-four hours after gassing a typical picture is of acute headache and pain from the eye effects mentioned. In the words of the *Medical Manual*, these 'render the patient temporarily blind, apprehensive and completely miserable'. No further symptoms other than the ones previously detailed make their appearance. Forty-eight hours after exposure the condition is worse. The reddened skin begins to form blisters. These coalesce to form huge blisters (blebs) possibly several inches across. These may occur anywhere on the body except the palms of the hands. They have been reported on dorsum of the hand, abdomen, arm, buttock, thighs, legs or feet, and genitals. The vesication of the penis may be acutely painful especially when the victim is urinating.[1]

The basis of the percutaneous attack is the ready solubility of the agent in lipid and lipid-like substances in the skin. The inability to recognise that this has happened (because the effects are delayed) precludes treatment until the damage has been done. Upon puncture, the blebs release a clear fluid. The blisters may be delayed in appearance for even up to one week. At this time the skin turns a coppery black. Unlike mechanical lesions, as these are concerned more with the underlying tissues, the results may take weeks or even months to heal.

After forty-eight hours the temperature rises, as do the rates of the pulse and respiration. It is now that the damage to the lungs and respiratory tract has its significance. As one would expect from the above, effects on the delicate membranes of the respiratory system are spectacular. The mucous membranes are covered with a yellow membrane or slough under which is a granulating surface. The post-mortem examination of the lung reveals collapse of small areas of the lungs and compensatory emphysema. The finer branches of the lungs and even the bronchi may be filled with a thick heavy exudate. There is an important distinction between mustard gas and phosgene gas poisoning. In phosgene poisoning there is a massive oedema, the lungs are filled and drip on sectioning. With mustard gas the lungs are voluminous and become congested but present an entirely different picture (see the section on use in Yemen), and there is no massive oedema.

In addition to the gross pathological changes some others are apparent on microscopic examination. These are mainly congestion in the lungs and some other organs. This may also be visible in the

[1] The degree of incapacitation depends heavily on how much, and which parts, of the body are exposed to the agent. Vesication of the penis is much more painful than vesication of the buttocks.

stomach and small intestine. The other main region of damage is the bone marrow. There may be an increased production of polymorphs; in very severe cases usually associated with a severe leucopenia. It may be pale yellow instead of red. In the words of the medical manual, 'should leucopenia develop the outlook is grave'.

In World War I cases of haemorrhagic nephritis were attributed to severe gas poisoning. In addition lesions were noted in the liver. If a fatal dose is received through the lungs death can occur within a few days but may be delayed for up to two or three weeks. Rare complications such as abscesses of the lung, bronchiectasis or even gangrene may occur. These are the result of secondary invasion by bacteria. More usually the non-fatal cases develop a bronchitis with an abundant expectoration of muco-pus. Sloughs of tissue from the trachea and lung may be seen in the expectorated matter. Broncho-pneumonia is one of the more serious possible consequences.

Despite early suggestions that dark skin was more resistant than light skins to mustard gas effects this now seems unlikely. An idiosyncrasy may, however, develop if a second exposure occurs even some considerable time after the first.

Chronic effects include debility, gastric pain, mental inertia, breathlessness, errors in refraction and amnesia. Aphonia (inability to speak) may occur but is transient and may be psychosomatic. Later effects on the lung and respiratory tract have also been noted. In the words of the *Medical Manual*:

> In a small but definite number impairment in health was evident. The symptoms were chronic cough and breathlessness due to chronic bronchitis and fibrosis. Some had bronchiectasis. Their condition was always worse in winter. Owing to steady deterioration in the health of these men their value in the labour market progressively declined.

The incidence of pulmonary tuberculosis (contrary to the arguments of many of the early anti-CW campaigners) was not significantly higher in the soldiers gassed with mustard than those who had not been gassed at all.

It is true that most of the mustard gas casualties were in fact superficial ones. One suspects this to be due rather to the ineffective dissemination rather than the lack of potential of the agent itself. Some 0·5% were permanently injured as a direct result of gas action. The chronic cases which developed later are excluded from this estimate. Also, this applies to protected soldiers. It would have been useful to have some data from the Italian use to see how it worked on unprotected people. It has been described as highly effective.

Of mustard gas casualties in World War I only some 2·5% died. Lest anyone should take any comfort from this, it is subject to some qualification. In World War I the use of mustard gas was in shells. In future wars aerial dissemination is likely to be of some importance. Spraying could be very effective. Mustards may be used in shells where the intention is to convert some of the liquid to vapour and some to liquid droplets to contaminate ground and produce severe skin effects. Shells capable of doing this have been developed.

In World War I it was also undoubtedly true that some of the mustard gas wounds were self-inflicted. This is unlikely in future wars. It is probable that German losses due to this cause were greater than allied ones owing to the allied use of propaganda from the air and the greater disaffection among the Germans.

The more persistent mustards would be of more interest but still mainly because of skin action, although Q possesses, in addition to the severe vesication of the more persistent agents, a high inhalation toxicity. To quote the words of an Edgewood Arsenal report MLRR 403, September 1955, the lung action is 'a bonus effect'.

The mustards are particularly useful as they penetrate clothing, even rubber. They are almost ideal defensive agents. In the German retreat in World War I use of mustard to halt the allied advance was highly effective. Some parts of the Argonne forest, and other areas where the gas was most likely to persist, were impassable for some weeks. This effort almost totally exhausted the German gas shell stocks. They are also useful in counter-insurgency (cf the Yemen). One fact which militates against their use if re-occupation is desired, or the population is not to be permanently antagonised, is that they cause a characteristic soft scar. Such scars, especially on children, like the keloid scars of A-bomb survivors, would form a semi-permanent reminder of the attack. This may be politically undesirable. The effects of vesicants may be accentuated in hot climates where the skin is more receptive. Chemical-impregnated protective clothing may be difficult to wear in these circumstances. Vaporisation would also be easier which would make dissemination more effective.

It is strange that significance of the systemic effects of mustard gas were not realised until 1943. The circumstances are quite interesting. A ship carrying mustard gas was sunk in Bari harbour. The survivors who swam through the liquid mustard had an abnormal condition of shock. This was due to damage to the blood cell producing system of the body (the haemopoietic system). These particular effects are highly characteristic of the next group of mustards to be considered, the nitrogen mustards.

The nitrogen mustards—HN-1, HN-2, HN-3

These are nitrogen compounds similar to the sulphur compounds. The reason for their action is still unclear. Mustards do cause cross-linking of DNA (the hereditary material in cell nuclei). The reason for the cytotoxic action is still, however, unknown.

The vesicants are essentially defensive, but the nitrogen mustards are the nearest to an offensive vesicant which has been produced. Their effects are delayed usually only 20–30 min as opposed to a delay of up to many hours for the others. They are hydrolysed but the products are also toxic. Some have a fishy smell. Some have no smell at all. Skin symptoms may not appear. After severe exposure there is erythema and mild but fairly rapid blister formation. The effects on the respiratory tract are much as those of the other mustards. The most marked effects are on the lymphatic and haemopoietic tissues. The effects may follow absorption through skin or respiratory tract. These may vary between a mild transient leucocytosis (increase in white blood cell leucocyte count) to severe leucopenia, thrombocytopenia and anaemia.

Had these gases been used in World War II, they would probably have been sprayed from aircraft. They have no war potential today, but because of their cytotoxic effects are used in cancer chemotherapy.

The arsenical vesicants

These consist of lewisite and the Dicks. The vesication is the same but complications arise due to arsenic poisoning. The hazards from these have been reduced by the discovery in World War II of an antidote. This was known (to the Americans) as British Anti-Lewisite (BAL,2,3 dimercaptopropanol). It has considerable use in the normal treatment of poisoning due to arsenic and some related metals.

Lewisite-chlorovinyl dichloroarsine

In its pure state lewisite has the aggressive effects of the lung irritants, the irritant effects of the lachrymators and orticants, and vesication similar to the mustards. Its vesicant action would normally predominate. It smells slightly of geraniums.

The effects of lewisite are shock and haemoconcentration from heavy contamination. It causes severe burns to skin and eyes which are acutely painful. Lewisite vapour causes erythema rather than vesication. This develops within 8 hours. The lewisite blister is sharply defined. It covers most of the erythematous area and is filled with an opaque fluid. Lewisite causes severe eye damage within a short time. Within 15 minutes there is sub-conjunctival haemor-rhage, intense chemosis and oedema of the cornea. Other eye damage such as corneal ulceration and sloughing, and complications such as iritis, etc., can occur.

A. M. Prentiss has the following to say about this so-called 'Dew of Death'.

The future rôle of lewisite is uncertain.... In cold and hot dry countries it would be very effective, but in wet rainy countries much less effective.

A further point acting against its use is in its sharp odour, which causes it to be easily detected. In addition, lewisite vapour does not penetrate clothing quickly (though more quickly than mustard gas), and wet clothes afford fairly complete protection. Its rapid destruc-tion by water also makes its use seem unlikely. This gas was the subject of much passionate and inaccurate propaganda before World War II. It has now been relegated to its proper position—a historical footnote.

In view of recent advances in toxic warfare this gas is no longer considered for use.

The Dicks

Typical of this group is ethyldichloroarsine. The Germans had much faith in this gas at the end of World War I. They have low persistency (about 2–3 hrs). They are of no practical use in future war in any situation. Their effects are similar to those of the other vesicants. German faith in them in World War I was virtually as misplaced as was that of the Americans in lewisite.

The reason for the fairly detailed consideration of mustard gas and other gases (for example phosgene) is so that the reader may make comparisons especially where, as in the section on use, there is controversy about which agents were used. It is hoped that from the data given the effects, features of use, possible future and his-torical significance of these gases as weapons may be seen. This will also aid the comprehension of the section on toxic substances in war.

4. INCAPACITATING AGENTS

Incapacitating agents may be placed in two categories:

physical incapacitants,
psychotomimetic agents.

These have been more picturesquely referred to as the 'on the floor' and the 'off the rocker' agents, respectively. The two are considered separately here but later it will be realised that to some extent they overlap.

Of the 'on the floor agents' there is only one which has been standardised for use by the Americans. It has also been tested on British servicemen at Porton. This is the agent called BZ. There are several reasons for thinking that it is this type of agent rather than the 'psychochemical' which has the greatest attraction for the military. Brigadier-General Graydon C. Essman, commanding general of the Chemical Corps, Research and Development Command, has stated in a speech given before the Rocky Mountain Arsenal Chapter of the Armed Forces Chemical Association (US):

> Psychochemicals are not the whole story. In some cases they could be the lesser story. Physical incapacitating compounds could also be used, perhaps to better advantage, in many situations. Since a soldier must think, see, hear, stand, lie or move as needed and manipulate his weapons or tools, it is possible to incapacitate by interfering with any one of these functions. Other compounds are known which produce respiratory irritation, temporary lowering of the blood pressure, severe vomiting, laxation, or temporary anaesthesia. These effects in contrast to the psychological agents are truly incapacitating in a military situation since they produce a result that is militarily measurable. Anaesthesia or hypotension may ultimately prove to be the most useful type of incapacitation, since the individual is physically immobilised.

It is probable that the agent BZ is of the type to which General Essman was referring. Many abnormal bodily conditions can be induced by chemical means. We will cite here several of the more likely examples.

Hyperthermia—heat stroke or exhaustion   There are several means by which this can be accomplished. It has been suggested that studies of hibernation mechanisms may form a means of discovering how to increase body heat production or decrease heat loss. The way in which the heat production of animals coming out of hibernation is increased fifty-fold has a chemical basis. Tri-iodothyronine increases heat production in very small doses in man as does a material isolatable from salmonella cultures. BZ shows some evidence of this type of activity. The effects of DNP and DNOC are of this type but these are not effective in small enough doses.

Orthostatic hypotension—inability to remain standing without fainting   Several chemicals are available for this purpose. The results from use may be variable. There is as yet no agent of CW potential but interest lies in certain enzyme inhibitors. Monoamine oxidase inhibitors such as 2-phenylisopropylhydrazine are likely to be of interest. Other compounds of interest include 2-(2,6 dichlorophenylamino)-2-imidazoline hydrochloride. This may be effective within the range of compounds of CW utility. The activity of hypotensive drugs is not understood and some are known which reduce hypertension but have no effect on normal patients. Harmine and harmaline derivations among MAO inhibitors may also be mentioned; all of these have no doubt been of interest. A problem arises in that the effects of most of them may be delayed for up to several days.

Muscular hypotonia—inability to operate many of the voluntary muscles It is a characteristic of the organophosphorous esters that they cause loss of control of voluntary muscle function. In some cases this may result in a paralysis of the flaccid type. This is separable from the high lethality characteristic of some of these compounds. Triorthocresyl phosphate is an example. In this case incapacitance may last for some time, depending on the dose. No clinical agent, however, is effective enough for CW use. In 1959 the Director of Medical Research in the US Army CW laboratories reported that a compound was known which in 'minute' quantities causes an ascending spinal paralysis. It is claimed that the respiratory muscles at no time cease to function and the victim recovers spontaneously within 24 hours. Evidently this compound was not entirely suitable as nothing has been heard of it since. This compound may have been O-succinylcholine iodide which produced effects like tubocurarine. It affects the eyes at concentrations of 0·20–0·25 mg-min/kg. It does not cause respiratory failure until very high concentrations are used but is similar in effect to the substance the general was referring to. The Swedish defence establishment was examining this in 1953 (L. E. Tammelin, *Acta Chem. Scand.* 7, 1953). Drugs for the treatment of rheumatoid arthritis, etc., are also of interest here: e.g. certain benzothiazoles and benzoxazoles. Most of these, however, need too large doses to be effective. Other examples are enamine derivatives of malonic acid.

Muscular tremors There are some agents which will produce this effect and much research is known to be in progress. The tremor-causing agents 'tremorine' and 'oxotremorine' are of CW interest. (The active metabolite is 1-(2-oxopyrrolidino)-4-pyrollidino-but-2-yne.) Amine derivatives of this have been prepared and tested by Porton workers (Bebbington and Brimblecombe, *Advances in Drug Research*, II, 143, 1965). A quantity of 0·05 mg/kg by intravenous injection produces tremor in mice. Some of the amine derivatives may be even more effective. The effects of oxotremorine start within five minutes and may last for several hours. It is effective almost within the dose range within which it could be used as an agent.

Other effects of interest include laxation, for which an agent has been developed, physiological blindness and vomiting. It is extremely doubtful whether an effective anaesthetic agent could ever be developed. One drug of potential interest as an anaesthetic agent is Etorphine M99, 6:14 endoetheno-12-(2hydroxy-2-pentyl) tetra hydro oriparine. This causes narcosis at a dose 1500 times less than the LD_{50}. Even the medical use of anaesthetics can give rise to deaths in some circumstances. One suspects that the military utility of these agents is small. It is very improbable that they are a serious military consideration in any large conflict. Adequate protection would not be difficult by means of conventional gas masks, etc. It is also probable that few could be made to be effective through the skin. It is a requirement for cw use that these agents be effective in very small quantities. There is very little chance that an agent which is effective in small concentrations would not prove lethal if used in battle conditions in high concentration.

The Americans have extensive stockpiles of the gas BZ. Having considered the above it seems unlikely that this is contemplated for use in conventional gas warfare. It is more likely to be used in counter-insurgency operations or against guerillas.

BZ

The formula of this agent is totally unknown. It was thought at first to be derivative of a potent psychochemical. It has since been disclosed by Mr G. N. Gadsby, director of the CDEE, that BZ is a glycollate. It is therefore an anticholinergic psychomimetic agent. (This means that it shows some of the properties of the nerve gases.) These were developed by Abood, Biel and others at the University of Chicago in cooperation with a commercial firm. Of these substances the glycollates of 3($\pm$) quinuclidinol are the most potent, according to Abood. It is in the glycollates of this series, or alternatively of the substituted 3-piperidyl glycollates, that BZ will probably be found. Especially potent esters are the N-methyl 3-hydroxypiperidyl glycollates with one substitutent on the glycollic acid phenyl, the others being phenyl, cyclohexyl, cyclopentyl, cyclobutyl or cyclopropyl.

A possible antidote to the piperidyls is 1,2,3,4, tetrahydro-9-amino acridine. They cause death in high concentrations owing to the anticholinergic effect, similar, in some respects, to the nerve agents. The effects of BZ are still shrouded in mystery. The *Army*

Technical Manual TM3-215 gives the following description of symptoms:

> Interference with ordinary activity; dry, flushed skin; tachycardia; urinary retention; constipation; slowing of physical and mental activity; headache; giddiness; disorientation; hallucinations; drowsiness, maniacal behaviour (sometimes); and increase in body temperature.

The *Weapons Employment Manual* warns that there are 'critical limitations' to its use. It is a general criticism of BZ and psychochemicals that the unpredictable and possible maniacal behaviour may be undesirable in certain circumstances, e.g. if the enemy commander has nuclear weapons in his control. It is probable that BZ incapacitates at a dosage of less than 0·01 mg/kg by intravenous injection, or at concentrations less than 100 mg-min/cu m.

The Americans have been notably silent about the effects of this agent in other than minute concentrations. This must give rise to some fears about its effect in high concentrations. Until 1963, this was the only standardised incapacitant of the US forces.

A suggestion has been made that this compound is the STP of the hippies of California. A sample of this STP on analysis was shown to be 2,5 dimethoxy-4-methyl amphetamine. Subsequent research has shown that this compound possesses about one-fiftieth of the activity of LSD, and it is therefore not of great CW interest.

5. PSYCHOCHEMICALS

Psychochemicals are associated in the public mind with war without death. It is unfortunate that this ideal is a long way from realisation. To many people the terms 'psycho gas' and 'incapacitant' are synonymous. These weapons have been the subject of a vigorous publicity campaign, mainly in America. For this reason they have been described as more a weapon of public relations than of war. The reason for their popularity is that their effects can be demonstrated in the laboratory and these quickly wear off. The other sides of these are not shown. Any agent which is powerful enough to produce these effects in small enough quantities for CW use will be almost certainly lethal in the doses met with under field conditions. The other main reason for their popularity is their effect even in very small doses. One bomber could carry enough doses of LSD 25 to incapacitate the population of the whole world. However, this does not make it a weapon.

General Creasy has said that given enough money it would be possible to develop a psychochemical weapon within five to ten years. This would probably mean that, if such a substance could be developed, and, as the General says, 'there could be no positive assurance that you could have it ready' (*Chicago Sunday Tribune Magazine*, 13 March 1960), it could be available by 1970. The psychochemicals affect the mind rather than the physiology of bodily function although, as in the case of BZ, mixed effects are possible.

In congressional testimony released in March 1959 by the US Armed Services Committee, Assistant Army Secretary Finn J. Larsen stated that both the US and the USSR were developing a new gas 'capable of neutralising a population', one which makes its victims 'incapable of realising what they are doing for hours but which, once the effect wears off, leaves no permanent injury'.[1] In earlier press releases Army officials were quoted as expressing the belief that it might be possible to direct such gases against entire cities, preparing the way for their seizure without damage to the buildings and with no harmful effect on the population. Whether the officials were correct or not can be determined from the accounts of the psychochemical of most current interest.

All of the psychochemicals have a bizarre and interesting history. They are nearly all derivations of naturally occurring compounds, many of which were isolated from fungi. Among these are the 4-hydroxydimethyltryptamines (psilocine and psilocybine), pantherine, and ibotenic acid. These and related substances stimulate the peripheral nervous system, causing disorientation and hallucination. Other hydroxy indole substances with psychotropic effects have not yet been completely isolated and tested. The dosage level for dimethyl tryptamine is about 1 mg for medicinal use. This is much too great for chemical warfare.

Amongst muscarine-like compounds TM-10 xylocholine is of interest. In addition to its muscarine-like effects it causes vomiting, salivation and lachrymation. Others include 1,2,3,4 tetrahydroisoquinoline, which has a moderate activity. This is of interest to the CDEE, to judge from published details of contracts with universities. Some benzyl quaternary ammonium compounds are also studied. Some have toxic side effects. Most of these have effects on laboratory animals in doses of 1–10 mg/kg or less. Some amidines and amidoximes have also been examined.

The derivatives of mescaline, the mescalinic phenylethylamines, are isolatable from cacti. These are active in doses of 30–50 mg, which is much too large. Methedrine, psilocin (discovered by the same chemists who developed LSD 25, Stoll and Hoffmann) and its

---

[1] Almost certainly BZ. Work on the glycollates was started in the 1950s, and their high potential was evident as early as 1959.

ester psilocybin suffer the same disadvantages. Psilocin is effective in doses of 4–8 mg.

The only current substance of cw interest is LSD 25. This was discovered by the Swiss chemists Stoll and Hoffman in 1943. In isolating it Hoffman noticed that he had been comatose for half an hour; he later gave himself the first trip ever. He administered several times the required dose.

LSD 25—(d(+)lysergic acid di-ethylamide)

Behavioural changes are induced by LSD (the + isomer) with a quantity of as little as 0·0005 to 0·001 mg/kg. This places it well within the range of effect of drugs useful in chemical warfare, i.e., effective in doses of less than 0·01 mg/kg. The LD_{50} for man is not known, but estimates vary between 0·2 mg/kg and 3 mg/kg. The intravenous LD_{50}s for various species are given below:

mice	46 mg/kg
rats	16·5 mg/kg
rabbits	0·3 mg/kg

An elephant was killed with a dose of 0·1 mg/kg. The lethal dose for man remains uncertain as no deaths have been ascribed to its use. LSD poisoning in animals results in mydriasis, pilo erection (the hairs being caused to rise as when the animal is afraid), increased reflex activity, ataxia and spastic paresis. Death is caused by respiratory failure. Haemorrhage occurs if anti-coagulants are given beforehand.

The difference between lethality and incapacitance on these figures is acceptable (several hundred fold) for cw application. LSD is, however, much less effective by inhalation than ingestion, and it is very expensive (£1000 a lb). Its apparent usefulness as an agent is thereby diminished. There is no evidence of chronic toxicity.

A variety of serious side-effects do occur. LSD has caused convulsions in man in a few cases. The long-term effects are a horror story. It was established some time ago that LSD caused chromosome breaks (damage to the hereditary material). In a number of animal species increased rates of abortion and the production of congenital malformations have been demonstrated. A possible teratogenic effect of LSD has been postulated for two human embryos. More recently the suggestion has been made that LSD may be associated with an increased incidence of leukaemia.

The LSD psychosis is of considerable interest. Of 225 adverse reactions to LSD reported before 1967, 142 were cases of prolonged psychosis. These usually do not need more than a few weeks' treatment, but for some it may be a matter of months. The effects include paranoid delusions, schizophrenic hallucinations and overwhelming fear. A few victims may take some years to recover from the effects.

There are two aspects to the problem: are the psychoses induced in people already disturbed or in normal people? Psychotic conditions are aggravated by LSD and, although there is not complete proof, it seems likely that this can cause serious derangement, even in apparently normal people. A surprisingly large proportion (30–50% of those with the long-term psychosis had this reaction after only one application of the drug. A further complication is that spontaneous recurrence of the hallucinations may occur days or months after the last dose of LSD administered, usually in the case of habitual users.

Suicide has been reported as a consequence of LSD, though it is unlikely to be a true effect of the drug. LSD can cause the deaths of people taking it indirectly, as a result of the delusions it produces, for example, the delusion that one can fly. In one case a young man stepped into traffic, shouting 'Halt,' and was duly mown down. In certain people LSD has caused attempted homicides and at least two successful ones. A small proportion of those exposed to LSD become violent, as in one test on thirty soldiers in which one had to be restrained.

The disadvantages of LSD as a weapon, in addition to its possible long-term effect and possibly unpredictable results, are several. LSD acts through the lungs. Current respirators give complete protection against it. Complete recovery is possible without the use of an antidote. For nerve gas poisoning, antidotes must be given within a few minutes. In the case of LSD an antidote can be given at any time. Even a few individuals unaffected could rapidly redress the effects of an attack. Antidotes are now becoming available against LSD; one compound of possible use is azacyclonol. It also seems likely that the commanders concerned in large-scale deployment of long-range weapons will be well protected. Ordinary troops will also be protected. The only effect, one suspects, could be against civilians.

6. NERVE AGENTS

It is with the advent of these gases that the classical arguments for and against chemical warfare are largely invalidated. These substances changed the application of chemical warfare from the tactical to the strategic. Previous applications and thinking in this field had been restricted to tactical situations in which two armies used these weapons locally to gain a military advantage. The incredible toxicity of the nerve agents makes it feasible to attack populations. In this they are less effective than biological weapons, however.

The novel means whereby these substances have their toxic action has been elucidated. Organophosphorous poisoning, which is caused by them, is due to their inhibition of certain enzymes of the nervous system, amongst which is acetylcholinesterase. The way a nerve gas acts on the body is best illustrated by a consideration of what happens at a nerve ending which goes to a voluntary muscle. At the point of insertion of motor neurones into muscles a substance, acetyl choline, is released after stimulation. (The motor neurones are the nerves which cause the muscle to contract.) Normally at the nerve ending acetyl choline is released, which acts as a chemical messenger to cause the muscle contraction. The acetyl choline is then removed by acetylcholinesterase. If the acetylcholinesterase is prevented from working the muscles can be 'switched on' but cannot be 'switched off'. As a result the victim may be described as having been stimulated to death. The accumulation of toxic acetyl choline occurs.

The above is a simple picture of how this system works in one particular case. It should be emphasised, however, that this is not a complete description of the process. Acetylcholinesterase is not the only enzyme that is affected; so also are, for example, some dehydrogenases and pseudocholinesterase. There will be a fuller description and discussion in the section on long-term effects.

The effects of these agents may be described as spectacular. The symptoms of nerve gas poisoning are as follows. In the case of sarin: at 15 mg-min/cu m, for a fairly inactive man, the vision becomes dim, the eyes hurt and become hard to focus, there is pinpointing of the pupils. These effects may last for a week or more. At 40 mg-min/cu m the chest feels tight, breathing is impaired, coughing, drooling, nausea, heartburn and twitching of the muscles is experienced; excessive sweating also occurs; the penis erects. At 55 mg-min/cu m there is a strangling tightness in the chest; vomiting, cramps, tremors and involuntary defaecation and urination occur. At 70 mg-min/cu m severe convulsions are experienced. These are usually closely followed by collapse, paralysis and death. Death is usually due to asphyxiation caused by paralysis of the respiratory muscles.

It is the voluntary muscles which are first affected. These, due to their inability to become de-activated, go into a state of vibration and then become paralysed (fibrillation). This causes the muscle twitching, etc. For the involuntary muscles which control the blood vessels, gall bladder and other internal organs, the delicate sequence of activation and de-activation of the various systems is upset.

The rate of development of these symptoms depends on the state of activity of the person affected. Exposure to high concentrations may cause death almost immediately in a man under battle conditions, i.e. moderate to strenuous exercise. One inhalation would be sufficient to give a lethal dose. Acute effects may follow 30 minutes to 1 hour after exposure. Death usually results within 5–10 minutes. Some of these substances given to laboratory animals at doses near to the LD_{50} may kill very slowly.

The long-term effects of these agents are not as yet clear. The US Army has stated that survivors of an attack are not likely to suffer disablement. This is open to some dispute. It has been discovered from work on insecticides that two types of paralysis may result from exposure to certain organophosphorous compounds. For the tri-tolyl phosphates and their derivatives, e.g. TOCP, a flaccid paralysis may occur if doses less than the LD_{50} are applied. The severity of the effect is dependent on the dose. Usually recovery is complete within a matter of months—at the most a few years. These are not CW agents.

It was also discovered that severe paralysis could develop after exposure to an insecticide, Mipafox, NN'Di-isopropyl phosphorodiamidic fluoride. Two cases of paralysis due to this were known in England in the early 1950s. Paralysis was different in character and severity from that due to TOCP. This was of a spastic type. Degeneration of the axons of the nerves occurs and the chance of complete recovery is slight. The effects are progressive. This has now been shown to be due to the effect of this agent on an enzyme in the central nervous system not affected by other agents. It had previously been thought that the paralysis was caused by hydrofluoric acid released in the nerve cells.

Experiments on animals have yielded some interesting results. DFP acts upon the hen to produce paralysis. This does not occur in man and illustrates the difference between animals and man in response to certain agents. Further researches on the hen have shown that the compounds that can cause paralysis, e.g. the nerve gas sarin, all have a certain chemical structure. It is not known if sarin has any long-term effects in man. The characteristics of these compounds which is diagnostic of paralysing agents of this type is that all possess a phosphorus-fluorine bond. If this is the case then one may expect that soman could possess paralysing capabilities and tabun would not. Thus it is known that some of these compounds can have paralysing effects on man and it seems likely from animal experiments that some of the CW agents may also have this property. The case of DFP illustrates the difficulty of extrapolating directly from animals to man.

As all the compounds which showed a spastic paralysis result are characterised by acute toxic effects, it is difficult to assess what the effects of less than lethal concentrations are because these are so small. Experimentally, the animals are given an antidote before being exposed to a concentration less than the LD_{50}. A further experimental difficulty arises from the fact that effects may be progressive and delayed in appearance.

Therapy

There are five means by which the effects of the nerve agents can be treated, and to some extent cured:

1. Artificial respiration techniques. The usual cause of death in nerve gas poisoning is asphyxia. Death may be delayed for some time, however, by use of a respirator. Porton has been instrumental in producing an excellent one. This is a temporary measure to allow time for chemotherapy to become effective. By this means and the use of atropine, cats have been kept alive after receiving 8–10 times the LD_{50} for sarin. They subsequently died. Probably the limit of usefulness of this technique is about half an hour, depending on the dosage.

2. Use of atropine. Atropinisatión blocks the acetylcholine which accumulates at parasympathetic nerve endings. This blocking is not complete. In treatment care has to be taken to balance the dose of atropine against the nerve gas since atropine is a powerful poison in its own right. This compound has the effect of doubling the LD_{50}. It relieves central nervous depression.

3. Use of tubocurarine. This relieves the action of the nerve agent in the nerves to the voluntary muscles. It also blocks the action of acetylcholine. D-tubocurarine in just below the lethal dose has been shown to have some value in support of the atropine effect. Further work is needed before this could be of operational use.

4. Treatment with pentamethonium. Use of this compound or hexamethonium affects the action of acetylcholine of which it is an antagonist at ganglia.

All of the above treatments mitigate the effects of the acetylcholine produced which poisons the body. These techniques are temporary, they cannot affect a cure. The following method is curative in effect.

5. Reactivators. The effect of nerve gases is by a chemical combination with acetylcholinesterase. If this process can be reversed then the enzyme will become functional again, and will remove the poisonous acetylcholine. Several compounds will cause

this, certain enzymes, water (very slowly), hydroxylamine and some oximes.

Historically, the first of these oximes to be considered was pyridine-2-aldoxime methiodide (P2-AM). This removes the phosphate groups bound to the enzyme. The shape of the molecule is of considerable importance. P3-AM is not active at all. The most effective compounds are derivatives of P4-AM and others possessing the hydroxyiminomethyl group. The success of oxime therapy depends on how strongly the nerve gas is bound to the enzyme. It is for this reason that tabun is difficult to treat.

It has been suggested that the success or otherwise is connected with the ability of the oxime to get to the brain. A word of warning concerning the use of oxime therapy. It is not a panacea for organophosphate poisoning. Use of P4-AM with sarin produces a compound of greater toxicity than the original. Hydroxime acetone is, however, effective. It should also be noted that P2-AM is a weak inhibitor of acetylcholinesterase. This does not matter in most circumstances. In some cases (e.g. with the substance parathion) the picture can be further complicated by the fact that the substance administered is metabolised to a more toxic form.

Russian workers have found that the reactivation of acetylcholinesterase inhibited by nerve gas can be slowed down by thiourea. This could cause difficulties in chemotherapy to be accentuated.

For the best results, a combination of these therapeutic techniques has been shown experimentally to be most effective. In an experiment in which 8–10 times the LD_{50} of sarin (or tabun) was applied and the antidotes P2-AM and atropine were used, two out of three dogs so treated survived. This technique, it should be emphasised, in conjunction with tubocurarine, is a long way from universal field application. Doses usually have to be precisely calculated. A possible future development in this field would be the production of a substance which without affecting any other function would remove nerve gas residues from the enzyme. Toxogonin is a compound in which there is considerable interest. The problem with existing chemotherapy is that the chemotherapeutic agents are poisonous themselves.

In our original description of the nerve gas action, we described the activity of acetylcholinesterase at a nerve ending in a voluntary muscle. Attempts to correlate acetylcholinesterase activity with the toxic effect have not been entirely successful. The closest correlation between toxicity and acetylcholinesterase level is for the voluntary muscle—hence this was the example we chose. Despite the amount of research which has been done, the theory of nerve gas poisoning by affecting AChE remains a theory. Attempts to correlate blood AChE levels with toxic activity have been unsuccessful. If rats are fed small doses of nerve gas for a long time then blood AChE level falls to 50% without death. A single dose of the same amount causes death. In some cases no symptoms appear until the AChE level is 40% of the normal. Thus things are not as simple as it would at first appear. It seems possible that the toxicity of these compounds for insects is not based on this system at all. Hence the use of some organophosphate compounds as anti-helminthitics (against a form of worm like parasite) and selective insecticides. Cows may be injected with a substance which will kill a parasitic insect which lives beneath the surface of the skin without harming the cow.

There are two classes of nerve agents. These are the G agents and the V agents. The G agents were the first to be discovered and will therefore be considered first.

The G agents

There are five major G agents. These are:

GA	tabun
GB	sarin
GD	soman
GE	no trivial name
GF	CMPF

The first type of agent prepared was DFP in 1932. Interest in these agents as weapons of war began when it was realised, following work on organophosphorous insecticides, that in addition to being potent insecticides they had a high toxicity for mammals. This was due to the work in 1934 of Gerhard Schrader in the Leverkusen laboratories of I. G. Farben. Biological effects were investigated by his colleague Kukenthal. In 1937 esters ('organic salts') of some of the dialkylamidophosphorocyanidic acids were subject of a patent application which was treated with the highest military security. One of these was the first effective nerve gas, tabun. More toxic compounds were later discovered. In the following year esters of the alkyphosphonofluoridic acids were found and one of these was another of the nerve gases, sarin.

It seems likely that intelligence reports and captured prisoners furnished the British with information concerning the German military interest in these compounds. Identical reports were concerned with DFP, di-isopropylphosphorofluoridate, on which, in the initial stages of their effort, the British concentrated. This team was led by B. C. Saunders at Cambridge and started operation in 1941.

The toxicity of DFP was no great improvement on the conventional chemical warfare agents available at that time, for example, hydrogen cyanide. This is just as well, because in the earlier days the researchers at Cambridge subjected themselves to doses of DFP both accidentally and deliberately. A DFP pilot plant became operative in 1945 at Sutton Oak near Manchester. Another pilot plant for DFP production was started in America. Much of the pioneer work was done at the biochemical division of Edgewood arsenal.

The German effort was much more successful. German security had been so complete that the allies had little idea of the direction of the work going on. Tabun and the other new agents were given the code name trilon, a well-known detergent. Some of the work done by Schrader's team was in fact published during the war. This was in reference to the successful development of insecticides. Results of Schrader's group were also described in Barth's *The Chemistry of Fluorine*, published by Springer at this time. Two types of potential compounds of high effectiveness were being examined, the nerve gases and some fluorine derivatives (which were also examined by the British team). The fluorine compounds are considered later.

At the end of the war, British research had developed agents at the laboratory stage comparable with the Germans. Germany, however, had started large-scale production of tabun in April 1942 at Dyhernfurth near Breslau. This was jointly controlled by I. G. Farben and the German war administration. By April 1945 12,000 tons of tabun had been made. This was about one-tenth of the total weight of chemical warfare agents used from 1915 to 1918.

Soman, the third war gas to be developed and to have the characteristics of a suitable weapon, only reached the laboratory stage by the end of the war. It was discovered in Heidelberg in 1944. The British also had agents of similar toxicity at the laboratory stage by the end of the war.

Of the G agents, tabun was the only one which could be produced readily on a large scale. The industrial preparation of sarin attempted by the Germans failed in its last stage due to the fact that fluorine, a highly corrosive and chemically active element, had to be used. At this time, despite strenuous efforts, no really satisfactory means of handling this substance on large scale had been devised. However, the Germans had got as far as having two plants for the production of sarin under construction when the war ended. This problem has now been solved by both the British and the Americans. The Americans are producing sarin on a large scale.

The degree to which the Germans were ahead of the allies at the end of the war was amazing. A really fantastic effort had been made by Schrader and his colleagues. This was revealed in the British intelligence objectives sub-committee's evaluation made under H. Martin at Long Ashton research station. These were published in BIOS report 1095 followed by Schrader's account in BIOS report 714. It is possible that some of the more modern nerve agents had their origin in this work. It is only now that the significance of the compounds then discovered is becoming clear.

Further research has yielded two more war gases, GE and GF. These are apparently not stockpiled as the Americans seem to prefer the older agents. Their chemical properties and details of their toxicity are still not available. They may have their origin in some of Schrader's work.

GA—tabun (Ethyl-N-dimethylphosphoroamide-cyanidate)

Tabun is the least toxic of the G agents considered for warfare use. Its toxicity is twenty times that of phosgene, one of the major lethal gases available in World War II. The $L(Ct)_{50}$ by inhalation is 150 mg-min/cu m. Tabun is reputedly an agent which the Russians have stockpiled. The German nerve gas plant which was transported to Russia at the end of World War II is said to have made at least 50,000 tons. This is about half the total weight of the chemical warfare agents discharged in the whole of World War I. Tabun is commonly a colourless or light brown liquid. The Germans prepared to use this in a solution of 20% chlorobenzene for aerosol dissemination. GA suffers from certain disadvantages. It is readily absorbed by gas masks and in comparison with the more modern agents has a low toxicity. It is also comparatively more quickly destroyed by moisture (hydrolysis). The hydrolysis product, hydrogen cyanide, is also highly poisonous. Treatment of tabun with decontaminating solutions such as calcium hypochlorite causes the evolution of cyanogen chloride, another highly poisonous gas. Tabun possesses a greater persistence in the field than many of the other G agents, and it has been suggested that this could be useful in certain situations. One suspects that this may be incorrect, because more powerful persistent agents (V agents) are now available. Vapour may be a hazard for some time after dissemination. The effects of tabun are not as amenable to oxime therapy as those of sarin. This is not likely to be an important consideration because other more toxic G agents are even less amenable. For these reasons tabun is no longer stockpiled in the West, although other nations may possibly still consider it useful.

GB—sarin (Isopropylmethylphosophonofluoridate)

This was originally named Samarin after Samara Province where the Russo-German 'Bersol' factory was situated after World War I.

Sarin is twice as toxic as tabun. The $L(Ct)_{50}$ of this compound is 70 mg-min/cu m. The LD_{50} of sarin by mouth is 0·28 mg/kg; in the eye it is 0·05 mg/kg. This is the major G agent stockpiled in the West. Despite the difficulties in its manufacture the Americans have been producing it on an extremely large scale. It is the only agent admitted to be available in chemical warheads for missiles. The Honest John, Sargent and Lance missiles possess chemical warheads. These explode, releasing smaller bomblets. (This will be considered in more detail in the section dealing with munitions.)

The Germans made some hundreds of tons of intermediates in its manufacture but were unable to produce more than half a ton of the gas. However, two plants with an annual production of 7200 tons were under construction towards the end of the war. Sarin is a colourless liquid. It is less persistent than tabun, and in general it would seem the more effective non-persistent nerve agent.

GD—soman (Pinacolylmethylphosphonofluoridate)

Soman is approximately three times as toxic as tabun. The $L(Ct)_{50}$ of this compound is 40–50 mg-min/cu m. It seems not to be stockpiled to any large extent. It is a colourless liquid and may be disseminated as vapour, liquid or aerosol. It is characterised by being highly resistant to oxime therapy. As its toxicity is not significantly greater than that of sarin it would seem to present no very great advantages.

GE and GF

The formula of GE is completely unknown. GF is cyclohexylmethylphosphonofluoridate, CMPF. There is no data as to their toxicity or persistence. It is unlikely that they are stockpiled.

All of these agents, in addition to being effective by inhalation, are effective through the skin. It had been found that by altering the solution in which the agent is disseminated, the percutaneous toxicity and effectiveness through the lungs may be enhanced. Canadian workers have shown that the percutaneous lethal dose for guinea pigs of 50% solution of soman in dimethyl sulphoxide is six times smaller than that of pure soman. The toxicity through the skin for these agents is approximately between ten and thirty times the $L(Ct)_{50}$, depending on the persistence of the agents.

The next class of agents to be discussed is characterised by an extremely high percutaneous toxicity; these are the V agents.

The v agents

The history of these agents is of particular British interest. They were discovered by Imperial Chemical Industries in the early 1950s. This was subsequently confirmed by Dr C. E. Gordon Smith, Director of the MRE at Porton. Mr Julian Perry Robinson reported to the conference on CBW in London that ICI applied for a patent in 1955.

> ... certainly it was ICI who in 1955 applied for a patent to cover the phosphonothiolates mentioned earlier. They thereby prevented Bayer from getting one on their rather later application. One of the inventors named in the Bayer application was the same Gerhard Schrader who was responsible for the nerve gases in the first place.
>
> [Steven Rose (ed), *CBW*, London 1968, 24]

The v agents are the result of further work along the lines which produced the G agents. Two agents are standardised, VE and VX. Both of these, as has been publicly confirmed by Mr. G. N. Gadsby, are O-alkyl (-2-dialkylamino ethyl thio) alkyl phosphine oxides. Early reports on these compounds were produced by Ghosh and Newman of ICI in 1955. US work on these compounds seems to have started to appear in the literature in 1957. Workers at both Edgewood Arsenal and Suffield have reported various results relating to them. The Russians may have prepared the compounds before the ICI workers, since the Germans had already done so. Swedish work was also reported in 1957, and the first accounts of toxicity the author has been able to find after Ghosh and Newman are in Swedish work.

The more toxic members of this group, such as methyl ethoxy- (2 dimethyl amino ethyl thio) phosphine oxide, have LD_{50}s in the range 0·02 to 0·05 mg/kg for intra-peritoneal injection (that of the compound just mentioned is 0·05 mg/kg). The LD_{50} of sarin by the same route is 0·45 mg/kg. These compounds are thus approximately ten to twenty times more toxic than sarin. The $L(Ct)_{50}$ for the v agents is given as 10 mg-min./cu. m. As little as 2–10 mg of vx on the skin is likely to be fatal. This amount is so small that it could hardly be seen. The inhalation toxicity is about five times that of soman. The v agents are therefore several hundred times more toxic than the most lethal chemical weapons before the advent of the nerve gases. They are about 2000 times as toxic percutaneously as mustard gas, and about 300 times as toxic through the lungs.

It seems unlikely that VE is being stockpiled. Extremely large American stockpiles of vx are known to exist. These agents are colourless and odourless.

We have already discussed the gas/gas mask deadlock. In the history of the development of chemical warfare this has been broken many times. The G agents were one such breakthrough. The V agents represent another. For the G agents, a gas mask forms adequate protection of a temporary nature. This is not so for the V agents, and they thus represent a considerable advance. At Porton, special suits of chromium impregnated micro-porous polyurethane have been developed. In addition special decontamination procedures and chemical detectors are in use with British forces. Special casualty stations have also been developed. No way has yet been found in which a soldier can function normally under battle conditions where heavy concentrations of the agents are present. Protection is expensive, prohibitively so for a civilian population. This presupposes the early detection of nerve gas attack, which at present is very unlikely until the first casualties have occurred.

This ends the section on nerve gases as weapons. We now consider other lines of research and work on possible successors to the V agents. At the same time as work was proceeding in Germany on the nerve gases, some other very promising agents were also being examined. These were the fluorine compounds referred to previously, the fluoracetates. These possess many advantages as CBW agents.

The history of these as weapons of war is an interesting one. The natives of Sierra Leone use fluoracetate obtained from ratsbane to contaminate the water supplies of hostile villages. For a long time the native product was not isolated from these highly poisonous plants. When it was isolated, it was found to be a member of the group.

These compounds were first prepared by Zwarts in 1896. It is interesting to note that he failed to publish any data on the high toxicity of these compounds. In 1943 Polish chemists fled to England with information concerning the toxicity of the methyl esters of fluoracetic acid. The figures given were for oral doses:

horse   1 mg/kg
sheep   0·3 mg/kg
man   2·10 mg/kg

The toxicity for man was generally less than for animals. Compounds with ten times the toxicity became known as a result of further work.

In their favour as CW agents are the following. They are insidious and are not sensibly detectable even at lethal concentrations; they are highly toxic. They have no immediate symptoms; no medical treatment is available. In addition they are very stable in dissemination. Their detection and protection against them is also difficult. The volatility of the compounds can be varied by choosing the appropriate esters, from the volatile and ethyl methyl fluoracetate derivatives to persistent fluorocarboxylate esters.

Probably because of the great promise of the nerve agents and the lower toxicity of the fluoracetates, the fluoracetates have been neglected. A further factor against them is that no therapy is known. This makes their large-scale handling difficult. The number of recorded accidents involving nerve gases runs into hundreds. If no therapy was possible, then there would have been a very high fatality rate. If suitable chemotherapy could be found, then the fluoroacetates could be useful agents. They may still be considered as possibilities as some of the work done on these agents in America during the war is still not published—to the authors' knowledge.

Shortly after World War II a concentrated search was made for further anti-cholinesterase agents. The French examined over 300 aryl carbamates. Some of these were more toxic than the nerve gases but do not seem to have been developed as weapons. The most recent developments in the field of nerve gas research are the production of compounds similar to those of Ghosh and Newman with the sulphur replaced by selenium. These are among the most toxic synthetic agents known. As an example, O-ethyl Se-(2-diethyl amino ethyl) phosphonoselenoate, has an LD_{50} of 0·021 mg/kg by sub-cutaneous injection. As a rule, these compounds are more toxic than their sulphur analogues (which include the v agents).

7. DEFOLIANTS

The defoliants, their effects and their use in Vietnam are considered here together. It is difficult to discuss these topics separately and it is instructive to consider them in the context of their use and in the special conditions of Vietnam. Indeed, as will be apparent later, this is the only valid way to discuss these data at all.

As we have said previously, to the US Army the defoliants are biological weapons. Therefore BW is, in their eyes, already being waged in Vietnam. This must mean that escalation to biological weapons proper (the present writer does not consider defoliants biological weapons), for example, rice blast fungus and other epidemic diseases of food-producing plants, is very possible. Some American military men are known to have exerted pressure to permit the use of these. Fortunately this possibility is probably quite remote.

In Part 1 an idea of the extent of anti-crop operations was given;

this is an attempt to gauge the possible effects. First, the effects of the defoliants on:

1. plants,
2. animals,
3. the soil and the environment,

are discussed. A consideration of how they are used in Vietnam follows this. In conclusion some of the American data and the Department of Defense's defoliation study is criticised.

The compounds admitted by the Americans to have been used in Vietnam are:

2,4D
2,4,5T
Cacodylic acid
Picloram

Others alleged by other sources:

Arsenic trioxide
Various arsenates (lead, etc.) and arsenites
Calcium cyanamide
Sodium cyanide (and other cyanides)
DNP and DNOC
Maleic hydrazide

Suggested for use by the Americans have been: CMU and other substituted ureas. These are discussed in turn with respect to their action.

Before going into a detailed examination of the chemicals used and what they do, some important points should be made. To many people it may seem that, in a particularly barbarous war, the defoliation programme is one of the lesser aspects. This we believe to be incorrect. The use of gas, fragmentation bombs, etc., affects a proportion of the population of Vietnam at present. The use of herbicides and defoliants could well have significant effects on the future of Vietnam, even for generations to come. In terms of their effects they are more important than the gases currently admitted to be in use.

To understand this statement it is necessary to consider not simply the effects on plants, but the effects on the whole environment. Any habitat which includes animals and plants, from a pool of rain water to a tropical rain forest, is in a dynamic state. Its condition at any moment is due to the interaction of influences of which we as yet know little. The balance of these is a situation which may have taken hundreds, thousands or even millions of years to develop. The effects of plant killing cannot therefore be seen in isolation from possible effects on the rest of the environment. In the past man's unintentional interference with these influences has had catastrophic results, for example the creation of the dust bowl in America, and currently the rapid ageing of the Great Lakes.

The use of defoliants in Vietnam constitutes a massive assault on a complex natural system. This is a deliberate intrusion into a little understood environment, and the results are impossible to predict. The upset resulting from such use could cause an irreversible deterioration of large parts of Vietnam.

The agents used have been described in two classes, herbicides and defoliants. The defoliants are employed with the intention of removing leaves from the trees. Herbicides are effective in poisoning the plant so that it dies. The distinction between the two is one of degree. The effects of defoliants depend on the strength of solution which is used. In very low concentrations the defoliants may act to stimulate growth. In higher concentrations they may act as selective weed-killers, particularly against broad-leaved plants. It is only in this restricted sense that they are selective. In higher concentrations still they cause the death of other plants.

Herbicides may be described under several headings:

Contact herbicides:
    selective
    non-selective—which kill all top growth

Translocated herbicides:
    effective against deep-rooted annuals and perennials (these are moved about in the vascular system of plants)

Soil sterilants:
    act by direct contact

1. Effects on plants

2,4D and 2,4,5T—2,4 Dichlorophenoxyacetic acid, and 2,4,5 Trichlorophenoxyacetic acid

These compounds act by accelerating normal leaf fall. A plant hormone (auxin) is produced by the plant in the leaf blade. As long as this is kept at a reasonably high level the leaf remains on the plant. Slowing of the rate of production of auxin or its cessation causes the formation of an abcission layer where the leaf stalk joins the plant. This consists of a layer of weaker cells which are easily ruptured so that leaf fall occurs. Auxin has many other functions in the normal life of the plant.

Understanding of the nature of leaf fall is very incomplete. Many other classes of hormones have now been discovered in plants. How they are related to auxin and each other in leaf fall is not known, but it seems likely that auxins act through the control of ethylene synthesis. Ethylene is a simple organic molecule which is very effective in small doses—several parts per (us) billion.

Professor Arthur Galston has suggested that substances such as 2,4D and 2,4,5T might cause a greatly increased ethylene production. Ethylene is a gas, and could therefore drift to other plants not touched by defoliant, such as crops, and have serious effects. The exact mechanism by which ethylene acts is unknown.

Drifting is also a considerable problem with 2,4D as this is fairly volatile. In Part 1 we cite numerous cases of damage due to this in Vietnam. In view of this hazard very precise instructions for use are usually issued by manufacturers.

2,4D has been used extensively in the USA and Britain. In Britain there are many suggestions concerning its application. Situations where drifting is liable to occur are mentioned (e.g. in the *Weed Control Handbook*) as being undesirable. The same goes for the contamination of drainage ditches. Both types of contamination are occurring in Vietnam.

These defoliants are only defoliants in a very limited sense.

2,4D and 2,4,5D have other uses than defoliation. They have been used to kill trees by cutting the bark and inserting the herbicide into the vascular system which translocates water and food in the plant. Thus they can be effective as herbicides.

Even applying the correct dose of chemical may not have the desired effect; the toxicity of 2,4D and 2,4,5T is also dependent on the soil. Toxicity to plants is generally higher in sandy soils than in clay soils. The exact result in soils such as the acid–sulphate 'dat–phen' of the Mekong Delta is almost completely unpredictable. In heavy soils 2,4D and 2,4,5T tend to be retained longer. (Further important data relevant to this is mentioned in the section on effects in the soil.)

It is essential to realise that the description of a weedkiller as selective or non-selective is very dependent on conditions. How they are used in Vietnam is discussed later.

Cacodylic acid—Dimethylarsenic acid

Cacodylic acid is an organic arsenical. It is a herbicide. It seems that this substance is not very dangerous to plants, in most applications. Cacodylic acid is said to show almost no activity after a few weeks when applied to soil in quantities of 50–100 lb/acre. It is rapidly inactivated by ion exchange and surface adsorption. This inactivation is very rapid in soils of high moisture content. Over the last few years, however, it has progressively fallen out of favour in America, partly because of fears of long term effects. When cacodylic acid is applied to rice crops at 5 lb/acre some toxic residues are retained. Rice will not grow again in treated fields, which indicates that in such conditions, widespread in Vietnam, cacodylic acid in some form is persistent.

Picloram (4 amino 3,5,6 trichloropicolinic acid)

This is a compound unrelated to any other herbicide. Its action on the plant bears a superficial resemblance to that of the hormone weed-killers. Its mode of action at a molecular level is as yet unclear. It is water soluble and possesses the severe disadvantage for normal use that it is highly persistent in the soil. The dichloro-derivative is similar in action and is also of great persistence, which is highly variable with soil type. It is ineffective against grasses.

It is apparent that there is an appalling ignorance of the effects of even those compounds admitted to have been used. The effects in a tropical environment are altogether unknown.

This ignorance is more serious in the case of other compounds which could be used, or are alleged to have been used, in Vietnam. Some of these have undoubtedly been employed, but in the absence of official confirmation there is little comment one can make. North Vietnamese officials have made detailed claims of damage, and some scientists have supported these with their own observations, although the present writer feels that there is no case in which the people concerned can be considered free of political bias. Nevertheless, the persistence of some of the claims, for example, of the use of DNOC, is sufficient to merit attention. The least one can say is that there is no lack of credibility in the alleged application of most of these compounds in Vietnam.

Substances allegedly used in Vietnam

The arsenates, arsenites and arsenic trioxide

These compounds are very highly toxic to plants (phytotoxic). Toxicity is dependent upon solubility in water. The more soluble the compound, the more damaging the effect. Thus the compound sodium arsenite is highly toxic, and calcium arsenate is more toxic (and more soluble) in most conditions than lead arsenate. Arsenic effects (in the form of arsenite or arsenate) are highly dependent on the form of administration.

Arsenic may be effective on plants through the leaves, trunk, twigs, or through the roots. Permeability is enhanced by moisture, high humidity, lime, leaf or bark wounds or insect damage.

The mode of action of arsenic on plants is still not fully understood. If arsenic is applied to leaves it is not translocated to the roots, but application to the roots results in the translocation of arsenic to the leaves, where it may reach very high concentrations and produce its toxic effects. Arsenic causes yellowing of leaves, burning, necrosis, discolouration and leaf drop. The chlorophyll of the affected plants is rendered inactive, with the result that photosynthesis stops and the plant is unable to build up food. Damage may vary according to the plant organ affected, but may occur in fruit, stem or roots. Damage also varies with plant type. Drupes, beans, cucumber, oats and lettuce are sensitive to arsenic, but grasses are on the whole resistant.

Other factors enhancing plant damage are temperature (especially above 80°F), humidity, slow drying conditions, application time and high carbon dioxide or salt concentrations—all commonly found in the tropics. Even an ineffective application of calcium arsenate one day may the following day cause considerable damage owing to change in the environmental conditions. Calcium arsenate may form more soluble products with greater damaging effects.

Sodium arsenite produces direct damage at the point of contact; systemic action is not important. Arsenic trioxide is also highly phytotoxic; even a concentration of one part per million causes the death of leaf tissue and chlorophyll poisoning.

Perhaps the most serious aspect of the use of arsenic compounds on plants is the long-term effects. Arsenic trioxide accumulates in the soil. In the soils of old orchards concentrations of 4–12 ppm may be built up in the upper layer (particularly in sandy soils which are poor in humus), which then becomes unproductive. Even some plants concentrate large quantities of arsenic; for example, *Pentia incana* can concentrate as much as 355 ppm in the aerial parts of the plant. Plants of this sort obviously present a hazard to grazing animals.

Arsenic compounds are very good soil sterilants. Calcium arsenate in particular inhibits germination in various plants. The variation of effect with different soil types is shown below, where the amount required to cause a 50% fall in crop-yield is given.

quartz sand	4 lb/acre arsenical	As
20% colloid content	192 lb/acre arsenical	As_2O_5
60% colloid content	2112 lb/acre arsenical	

As little as 30 ppm of arsenic is sufficient to be effective as a soil sterilant.

Of particular interest with regard to Vietnam is the effect of calcium arsenate on rice plants.

Soil type	Dosage (lb/acre)	Effect
Silty clay	50	yield down 45%
Sandy loam	150	yield down 65%

It has been argued that cacodylic acid (an organic arsenical) has none of these effects. Its manufacturers point to its extensive use in the United States. Without further data on the action and effects of these compounds it is impossible to comment. As a rule, all the inorganic arsenicals are accumulative and persistent. As an example, the arsenic content of soil around a barberry bush treated with 2 gal of commercial sodium arsenite declines from 0·676% at treatment to 0·04% over fourteen months with a 30-in rainfall. Organic arsenicals tend to be less persistent. Six to twenty-four months is the figure quoted for the persistence of arsenic in temperate conditions.

Some 12 million pounds of sodium arsenite are used per year in Malaysia for weed control. This is quite effective, and in tropical conditions persistence is greatly reduced. It is applied by hand to control undesirable plants on rubber plantations.

The greatest objections to using these compounds are their persistence and their toxicity to man and other animals. More will be said about this later.

Calcium cyanamide

The use of calcium cyanamide as a herbicide has an interesting history. In 1896 Sir William Crookes caused great concern when he warned that unless man was able to make nitrogenous fertilisers from the air, widespread starvation would occur. In the early 1900s calcium cyanamide was used as a fertiliser under certain conditions and its herbicidal activity was noted. It is used nowadays in certain cases to inhibit the germination of plants. Its application as a herbicide is restricted because it is noxious and poisonous. Except in special cases, its use as a herbicide has fallen off since the production of the hormone weedkillers. Its major use was during and before World War II.

For its application to be really effective close attention must be paid to soil conditions. For some applications a moist soil is necessary. It is essential that in use cyanamide should not decompose for some time after application. It breaks down to form cyanide, which is rapidly inactivated in the soil. This explains the critical effect of soil conditions. The effects of the compound can be radically diminished by heavy rainfall and good drainage. Tropical rainfall conditions could render it ineffective but could also cause it to contaminate water supplies.

Sodium cyanide

This compound is used as a soil sterilant. Because it is highly toxic to man and animals its use is very restricted. It possesses the advantage that it is very rapidly inactivated in the soil.

2,4 dinitrophenol (DNP) and 4,6 dinitro orthocresol (DNOC)

These compounds both act in similar fashions on plants. The main use of DNOC is as a non-selective herbicide. It may in certain cases be used selectively, but this requires careful application.

More is known about the toxic action of these herbicides than is the case with many others. DNOC and DNP act at a fundamental level to interfere with respiratory processes, hence their general toxicity to both animals and plants. These substances act in less than lethal amounts to increase the rate of respiration. They do this by preventing the build-up of energy in the form of high-energy phosphate compounds. In higher concentrations in plants they have the effect of denaturing and making inactive proteins, particularly the flavoproteins. DNOC also inhibits fermentative reactions. It is a translocated herbicide which leaves no toxic residue.

DNOC is essentially equally toxic to plants in any soil. There has been some debate about its cumulative effects but it leaves no toxic residue. That such effects are important in agriculture in most circumstances is unlikely. DNOC and DNP are highly soluble. They are therefore quickly leached through the soil, the faster the more porous the soil. They may thus cause damage by affecting the roots of trees and other plants.

Maleic hydrazide (1,2 dihydropyridazine 3,6 dione)

This is a highly persistent herbicide. It is very effective against grasses. It can act on tissue in two ways; it inhibits respiration and it inhibits cell division (mitosis) in the plant. Experiments with broad beans showed considerable damage to chromosomes.

Maleic hydrazide is very persistent in plant tissues. It can be extracted from Bermuda grass as long as one year after application. It retards crop growth at a concentration of 100 parts per million in the soil. In North American and European soils it is rapidly broken down. It has been shown experimentally that in North American conditions it is retained only in kaolinitic clay loams.

It is interesting to note that the use of maleic hydrazide and 2,4D together has less effect than using either alone. The reason for this is that maleic hydrazide penetrates through the leaves and is translocated around the plant, while 2,4D removes the leaves so that less· absorption occurs. If, however, 2,4D is used two weeks after maleic hydrazide, the effectiveness is greatly enhanced.

Compounds suggested for use by American official sources
CMU (*3-p chlorophenyl 1,1 dimethyl urea*)
CMU as a herbicide has a fairly short but fascinating history. It was discovered in 1950 by Dupont de Nemours Co. in the USA. The researchers were searching for a compound to treat coccidiosis, an intestinal complaint of poultry. CMU was found to be of no use for that, but is an amazingly effective soil sterilant.

One trial of this substance in Britain to compare its effects with those of TCA was so spectacular that the workers gave up the comparative study and changed to an examination of the recolonisation of sterilised soil. The apparently low toxicity to man of this class of compounds would seem to make it ideal for use in Vietnam. These compounds exhibit a very high persistence—about two years —under North American conditions. Normally it is applied at the rate of 24 lb/acre and has been suggested as an alternative to arsenates and chlorates.

The apparent suitability of CMU for use in Vietnam was mentioned above. At this point the distinction between tropical and temperate conditions becomes important. Attempts to use CMU in Malaya as an alternative to arsenates have shown that in tropical conditions it is much less effective and its persistence is considerably reduced. The reason for this is the heavy rainfall and rapid leaching. To have any useful effect it needs to be applied in four times the quantity needed in temperate conditions. If it has been used, it is unlikely to have been very effective. This illustrates very well the difficulties and dangers of extrapolating from one particular set of conditions to another.

CMU is very rare among herbicides in that its mode of action is definitely known. It interferes with the Hill reaction in photosynthesis (the process by which plants use the sun's energy to build up their own energy stores). The particular reaction in question is probably concerned with the utilisation of oxygen and the substance inhibited is probably a cytochrome.

2. Effects on man and animals

As before, the compounds are treated in the order in which they were mentioned in the text (p. 224). It should be emphasised that in many cases LD$_{50}$ values can only give an indication of acute effects. For some substances chronic effects are of importance. Similarly teratogenesis (production of congenital malformations), carcinogenesis (production of cancer) and other long-term effects may not be noticed in animal experiments. It will be illustrated later that even the most careful animal experiments may not permit extrapolation to man (see the section on DNOC).

A second point particularly deserving of emphasis is that the effects on the indigenous flora and fauna of Vietnam are impossible to predict. As far as the writer is aware, no toxicological data are available for tropical earthworms and insects. This statement may seem trivial and irrelevant, but in reality animals such as these have important functions in the ecology of tropical forests. They are particularly important in the maintenance of a healthy soil. (This is discussed in more detail later.)

The toxic effects of herbicides on the smaller animals (mammals especially) are unknown. Defoliation or the use of herbicides may deprive the animals in a particular area of valuable food supplies or cover to protect them from enemies. Thus without any direct toxicological effect on the animals damage to some species has undoubtedly occurred. An illustration of this is the action of 2,4D on aquatic vegetation (see p. 235).

Rare animals could become extinct, not through the direct effect of these compounds but because their sources of food supply (animal and plant) had been killed off. As an example of this sort of interaction one may consider the Australian koala bear. This animal lives only in eucalyptus trees. Killing the eucalyptus would not directly harm the koala but would lead to its extinction none the less.

There is no change so remote that it does not affect some aspect of the complex economy of living systems. Living systems are so interwoven that even the tiniest disturbances cause chain reactions, even if these may not be apparent for years, decades or even centuries.

It is impossible for anyone to say what the full effects of defoliants will be. So far everyone is guessing. No one before has had the temerity to influence an unknown environment on such a scale. The interactions within an environment are quite unbelievably complex. It will be realised that toxicology data cannot help the appreciation of such effects. One thing is certain: what has happened is not reversible. We could not return the land to the *status quo* before defoliation and the use of herbicides, even if we knew the appropriate strategy. That irreversible changes have taken place we know. One known example is that there has been an increase in bamboo and certain grasses. What the results of this, and the myriad of more subtle changes that have occurred, will be it is impossible to say. We will certainly never know, because we knew insufficient about the ecology of the stricken areas of Vietnam before defoliation to make a valid comparison.

The effects of specific compounds on man and animals
2,4D and 2,4,5T
The effects of even these, the best known of the herbicides and defoliants used in Vietnam, are not very well known. The impression given by all American official sources seems to be that these are totally innocuous weedkillers. Quoted below are the manufacturers' warnings to users. The Dow Chemical Company have issued the following warning with the product described below.

Esteron R 245 O.S.
For the control of trees, brush and broad leaved weeds (67·7% 2,4,5,T mixed with Diesel oil, No. 1 or No. 2 fuel oil or kerosene for spray application. For certain circumstances water sprays are recommended).

The label states:
WARNING. Do not contaminate irrigation ditches or water used for domestic purposes.

CAUTION. May cause skin irritation. Avoid contact with eyes, skin and clothing.

It further states:
Do not graze dairy animals within 7 days after treatment (to avoid contamination of milk).

Another Dow preparation of alkanolamine salts of 2,4D for the selective control of many broad-leaved weeds in non-crop areas and in certain crops carries the warning:
Causes irritation of skin and eyes. . . . In case of contact, flush eyes with plenty of water for at least 15 minutes and get medical attention; wash skin with soap and plenty of water. Remove and wash contaminated clothing before re-use. Do not wear contaminated shoes.

The *British Weed Control Council Handbook 1965*, states that:
Prolonged exposure, notably to oil solutions, may cause skin or eye irritation to some individuals. Plastic gloves and light goggles

should be available to personnel mixing spray materials. Also, for some types of mist spraying, a face mask is desirable to avoid prolonged breathing in of oil droplets.

It is quite plain from the above that these chemicals are noxious and to some extent could cause damage, especially to the eyes.

Toxicity

These agents are not highly toxic. Cases of poisoning resulting from use in America are extremely rare. In England occasional fatalities occur.

On the basis of the known fatalities, the lethal dose for man has been estimated as 50–100 mg/kg. Toxicity seems to vary markedly with the method of application. Injection of quantities of 2–3 gm into men results in severe toxic reactions, coma, fibrillary twitching, and urinary incontinence.

2,4D formulations have on rare occasions caused peripheral neuropathy. A progressively increasing paralysis, pain and paresthesia have been noted in a few cases. These disabling effects may last for several years. It may be expected that aerosol application of 2,4D and 2,4,5T would be more effective in producing deaths and incapacitance than ingestion, owing to the higher efficiency of absorption of toxic materials into the blood through the lungs. (The LD_{50} of 2,4D is halved for rats by aerosol dissemination.)

As a rule, it seems that toxic effects by ingestion are not very likely. 2,4D and 2,4,5T have little effect on life span or reproductive capacity when fed to a variety of animals. Further data are, however, urgently needed on inhalation toxicity.

In high concentrations the Merck Index reports that 2,4D can cause gastro-intestinal upset and eye irritation. It has been alleged by the North Vietnamese that these effects may be serious.

We have quoted elsewhere the detailed allegations of the North Vietnamese concerning the effects of 2,4D and 2,4,5T on cattle. It seems likely that the North Vietnamese have exaggerated the effects of 2,4D and 2,4,5T or that these were not the compounds which caused the damage. (This point is discussed further in the general consideration of the use of herbicides in Vietnam, pp 246ff.)

Of interest with respect to environmental effects are the effects of 2,4D on fishes. It is known that concentrations of as little as 3·0 ppm in water can be lethal to rainbow trout over a period of 24 hours (in temperate conditions), and 2·2 ppm is lethal to fish over 48 hours (in both cases the estimate is a LC_{50}). The level at which damage is likely to occur even after a short time of exposure is in the region of 1 ppm or even much less. Fish form an important protein supplement to the diet of the Vietnamese. There have been innumerable reports of fish dying as a result of defoliation. This can only have serious effects on the health of the population, which is already poor.

Of particular significance is the removal of water vegetation through the use of 2,4D. If a small amount of water vegetation is removed, it is beneficial to fish; the removal of larger quantities has quite a different effect. According to the *Weed Control Handbook* (4th edn), 1965:

1. Fisheries. Fish may not only be killed or rendered inedible by a chemical but also by deoxygenation of the water resulting from the decomposition of dead weeds.

For use of 2,4D in water. Amine and sodium salts are recommended because the oils of ester formulations may be toxic to fish.

(In Vietnam the n-butyl ester is used.) 2,4D in such formulations is toxic to the organisms fish feed on. Herbicides in water, then, may have three effects: a direct toxic one and two indirect ones due to deoxygenation and killing fish food. This is another illustration of the problem of assessing the effects of herbicides. Quantitative data on toxicology may be practically useless.

Without further work it is possible only to express the gravest fears of what may be the effects of defoliants and herbicides on the flora and fauna of Vietnam. The above can only give an indication of possible effects. The only way to know for certain is to examine what is happening in the field. Even then in the absence of baseline data the effects may be difficult to judge. It should be remembered that 2,4D and 2,4,5T are the best known compounds used in Vietnam. The lack of data on other compounds is due to the lack of published information. This does not mean that the compounds are innocuous, although some probably are, but simply that nobody knows.

Cacodylic acid

This substance is an organic arsenical which the Merck Index describes as containing 54·29% of arsenic. There is some controversy about the significance of this and its effects.

The toxic effects are due to arsenic, which is discussed later. Figures have been given for the LD_{50} of cacodylic acid by injection. These are:

	mg/kg
dog	1000
rat	900

It will be realised from this that the toxicity of this compound is less than that of 2,4D and 2,4,5T; however, the LD_{50} values for inhalation are not given. Whether cumulative affects due to arsenic poisoning do occur from the use of this compound is a matter of debate. Much evidence has been obtained to suggest that arsenic from cacodylic acid does not accumulate in animal tissues. It is also thought not to be passed in milk but to be excreted in the normal way. Excreted products, however, may be toxic and possibly persistent.

This whole question of cumulative nature is unclear. The fact remains, however, that men, and especially their animals, could become sufficiently contaminated for a proportion of fatalities to result. This would be particularly likely with children. Again, more toxicological data are needed. The published effects of cacodylic acid are summarised below.

Cacodylic acid does not cause serious eye irritation. It does, however, if fed to rats, reduce the life span and weight gain after prolonged dosage. It has no effect on cattle and little effect on fish. More worrying are the reports that it is teratogenic. In feeding experiments with rats reproductive organs were damaged. Other studies have confirmed the action of cacodylic acid as a cytotoxic agent affecting cell division, and limited experiments have shown it to produce congenital abnormalities.

Picloram

Toxicity figures for this compound indicate that it hardly constitutes a hazard for man at all. Its LD_{50} is about 8200 mg/kg. It is non-corrosive and relatively harmless, as far as is known. Experiments which involved feeding a variety of animals with picloram have shown that it does not have chronic toxic effects. It is excreted in the urine unchanged. Its toxicity to fish is variable, but it is generally low enough to be insignificant in open water. As the MRI report admits, however, it does constitute a hazard to wildlife through its indirect effects.

The arsenates, the arsenites and arsenic trioxide

These compounds are highly toxic. The minimum lethal dose for a man is about 138 mg. It may be expected to be considerably less for a child. LD_{50} values for various arsenic compounds (oral doses) are given below.

Animal	LD_{50}	Compound
Rabbit	20 mg/kg	Arsenic trioxide As_2O_3
Rabbit	100 mg/kg	Lead arsenate
Rabbit	50 mg/kg	Calcium arsenate

Pig
Cow
Horse
Sheep
} 500–2000 mg/animal is the minimum lethal dose for these animals of arsenic ingested

Generally it is found that arsenites are more toxic than arsenates, and that the more soluble calcium and sodium compounds are more toxic than lead or other compounds. In general terms, two or three teaspoonfuls of any of these compounds should be sufficient to kill a human being.

Sodium arsenite has an oral lethal dose for mammals of 10–50 mg/kg. In drinking water amounts ranging from 0·21 to 10 ppm have caused deaths. A toxic dose on fairly short exposure is 12 ppm. Long-term exposure to doses of 0·21 ppm has also been fatal. The minimum dose tolerable without grave risk of poisoning is probably much less than 1 ppm. In this context the use of arsenic compounds in Vietnam would seem very serious. The onset of chronic arsenic poisoning may take from two to six years in man.

The effects of arsenic poisoning on livestock are also quite impressive. A single feeding of 0·1 grain of arsenic/oz of feed has killed chickens and pigs. This is quite a small amount.

Sodium arsenite is extremely toxic to wildlife. Its use in locust control in Africa has caused heavy fatalities among game. Usually animals are kept away from arsenite-sprayed areas for at least three months in dry conditions. Birds have been known to die from eating insects poisoned by arsenite.

Low concentrations (less than 3 ppm) of arsenic (in the form of arsenic trioxide) have caused the deaths of fish food organisms in water. Chironomid larvae, fresh-water shrimps and mayfly larvae are killed at these concentrations. Sodium arsenite at 1 ppm kills Daphnia magna, a pond organism and typical fish food. Even if smaller organisms and water plants are not killed, with the additional result of deoxygenating the water, arsenic compounds have a fairly high direct toxicity for fish. Concentrations of 4–40 ppm kill off most species.

A significant problem with arsenicals is the danger of persistence. Alfalfa fodder for cattle containing 650 ppm of calcium arsenate has proved fatal. Sodium arsenite is the most dangerous of the arsenicals from this point of view; absorption of as little as 4·2 grains in food has caused the death of cattle. Residues of arsenic on fruit would prove fatal to children. Arsenite is present in the milk of poisoned animals, and this could create a further hazard.

Arsenic probably acts in the body by converting to arsenite, which then inhibits certain enzymes in the metabolism essential to the build-up of energy (notably pyruvate oxidase).

The symptoms include tightness in the throat and severe pains in the stomach within 1 hr of intake. Continual vomiting of blood and bile follows, with diarrhoea and excess urination (both fluids containing blood). The skin becomes cold and clammy, blood pressure falls, and there is a characteristic thirst. Coma and death occur within the day.

About one case in twenty shows severe cerebro-spinal depression. Less severe nervous effects are seen in about one-fifth of those affected, usually tremors, cramps and fits resembling epileptic fits. The more serious cases typically demonstrate vertigo, headache, sensory disturbances, spasms of the muscles to the extremities, delirium and general paralysis.

Chronic poisoning can be caused by repeated small doses, although arsenic is not a strictly cumulative poison. This effect is increased if excretion is interfered with. Early signs include faintness, loss of appetite, weight loss, abdominal pains and diarrhoea occurring together or alternately. Later symptoms include puffy eyelids, calluses of the skin, yellowish pigmentation, eruptioris or exfoliative dermatitis, peripheral neuritis with numbness or tingling (paresthesia). There is generally apathy and dullness of mind. This is followed by paralysis, muscular atrophy, nephritis and liver damage. Death is due to cardiac weakness associated with fatty degeneration of the heart muscles, liver and kidneys. The effects can be treated and alleviated by BAL 'dimercaprol'.

The symptoms of chronic poisoning in livestock resemble those in man. Skin thickens and peels, there is stiffness in the joints, and symptoms like diarrhoea are similar. Arsenates cause greater pathological changes than arsenites, but in neither case are they very marked. Ulceration and necrosis of the gastro-intestinal tract is notable in cows. Calves show a characteristic ascending paralysis from the hind limbs towards the head.

Similar effects to those of arsenic are produced by lead and manganese. Manganese poisoning resembles arsenic in its chronic effects. Lead is a true cumulative poison, and builds up in the tissues.

Chronic poisoning from manganese results in sleepiness, muscular twitching, cramps in the legs, increased tendon reflexes, a characteristic spastic gait and a fixed mask-like expression. There is no effective therapy. Lead poisoning results in symptoms similar to those caused by arsenic. The damage to the nervous system may be so severe as to be irreversible. This is characterised by peripheral neuritis, pains in the extremities, especially in joints, paresthesia and paralysis. Muscular atrophy does not occur. There are considerable changes in the levels of certain cells in the blood.

Compounds of lead and manganese with arsenic are alleged to have been used in Vietnam. The concentration of the first two substances is likely to be very small in comparison with that of the arsenic, but they may contribute to its toxic effects. However, without a more detailed analysis of the proportions and quantities it is impossible to say definitely which component has the greatest effect or indeed place great faith in the assays.

DNP *and* DNOC

The action of these compounds is probably very similar in all living organisms. The toxicity of dinitrophenol was realised in World War I when it was used in the manufacture of explosives. Despite warnings against its use, it was put on the market as a slimming agent in 1933. In fifteen months 100,000 people took it. The many deaths and cases of lens opacity (leading to blindness) which followed made its therapeutic limitations quite clear.

The toxic dose of DNOC for man is not known, but is estimated at about 29 mg/kg. In man, but not in laboratory animals, it is a cumulative poison. The rabbit can metabolise DNOC and so counter its effects. Ingestion of single 75 mg doses by human volunteers produced no damaging effects. Death occurred in a human volunteer who ingested repeated doses when the level of DNOC in the blood was 70 ppm.

Characteristically, the tissues, organs and fluids of victims are stained yellow. Lung congestion, oedema and certain types of haemorrhage occur.

DNOC and DNP affect the enzymes in respiratory reactions. Acute toxicity data are given below.

Compound	LD_{50} mg/kg	animal	how taken
DNOC	25	rat	orally
DNP	30	rat	orally
DNP	200	rabbit	orally
DNP	20–30	dog	orally

The chronic toxicity of these compounds is about thirty times less than that of sodium arsenite.

When a lethal dose of DNOC or DNP has been taken symptoms develop rapidly. Death may occur within 10–60 min and usually death or recovery has taken place within 24–48 h. The symptoms are nausea, gastric distress, restlessness, heat flush, sweating, deep, rapid respiration the rate of which increases until distress occurs. Cyanosis follows, then collapse and a quiet death from heat-stroke (hyperthermia) or cerebral oedema. The transition from apparent well-being to death takes about an hour. The effects are increased by high environmental temperature. Men die in a very similar fashion to laboratory animals, and both exhibit a highly characteristic stiffness (rigor) immediately after death.

If large sub-lethal doses are given to animals at long intervals no deaths occur. If small doses are given frequently they may have an effect. If 100 ppm of DNOC is given to young rats in their food for six months there is no impairment of growth. At 500 ppm growth is impaired. In the case of man, since he is unable to metabolise DNOC, as little as 1 mg/kg per 24 h given over a period of time is sufficient to cause a dangerous rise in the concentration of DNOC in the blood. There is no method of detoxification for DNOC and DNP in man. There is no antidote.

In some cases from the 1933 period important chronic effects were noted. Skin lesions were common, as were angioneurotic oedema, otitis media (inflammation of the middle ear) and leucocytosis (an increase of certain blood cells). Neuritis and various changes in the cardiovascular (heart and blood vessel) system were also noted. Most characteristic in about 1% of the patients treated with DNP was the development of lens opacity in the eye, leading to blindness. This often occurred over a period of many years even after the treatment was discontinued. In some cases the blindness took fifteen years to become complete. This was an effect which it was very difficult to demonstrate on laboratory animals, which indicates the difficulty involved in extrapolating from animal experiments to man.

People exposed particularly to DNOC are tired, hot, breathe rapidly and display an exaggerated euphoria. This condition is one of the clearest diagnostic features of the action of this compound. By the time it occurs a potentially toxic dose is present, and further exposure leads to a quick death.

Even today in the United States DNOC, which is used as a crop spray, causes a significant number of deaths in summer.

Maleic hydrazide

This compound has an LD_{50} for rats of 4000 mg/kg. This means that it is relatively non-toxic. Of more interest than the toxicity data is a report by Darlington and McCleish that maleic hydrazide could cause cancer in mice. Extensive tests were performed by Barnes and Magee, and their report, published in 1957, showed that this was not so. This case is important as the carcinogenic effects of most chemicals are not known, and teratogenesis and chronic effects may be difficult to determine. LD_{50}'s only give an indication of acute effects. In the case of many of these compounds insufficient data are available to allow the exclusion of some chronic effects.

CMU *and* DCMU

This class of compounds has an extremely low toxicity, but the discovery that they caused chromosome breaks in plants led to suspicions that they might be carcinogenic in man. A long series of tests, during which rats were fed graded doses (25 ppm, 250 ppm, 2500 ppm) showed no decrease in life span or increase in cancer incidence over two years. The LD_{50} figures for CMU (and the related DMU) are given below.

CMU   N'N' (4 chlorophenyl) N'N' dimethylurea
       3600 mg/kg   rat

DCMU   N' (3,4,dichlorophenyl)—N'N' dimethylurea
       3400 mg/kg   rat

Toxicity would provide no barrier to application of this as a soil sterilant in most conditions. It has been noted, however, that DMU effects sheep at high dosages, seriously if only temporarily at doses so far used. Some toxicity to fish is quite possible, even at the doses used in Vietnam.

3. Effects on the soil

To many people soil is simply what you walk on or put plants into. They think of it as a relatively inert material. This is far from true; soil is an environment of incredible complexity and interest.

'Soils', according to V. V. Dokhuchaev in 1879, 'result from the combined activity of the following agencies: living and dead organisms (plants and animals), parent material, climate and relief'. The various elements are so bound to each other that variation in one has a profound effect on all the others, and thus on the whole soil structure.

Far from being amorphous, soil, if it is fertile, has a well-defined crumb-like structure. This allows good aeration and drainage, which encourages plant growth. Bacterial activity is necessary to maintain a healthy interchange of materials in the soil. Substances excreted in the roots, waste matter and carrion, all are utilised by the bacteria. The bacteria die, fertilise the soil and are degraded. Their waste products are of great importance. Soil bacteria are a fundamental part of the cycles of interchange of carbon and nitrogen in nature.

Formation and preservation of the soil structure is due to the activity of plants and soil organisms. Plants push roots through the soil, and these act mechanically to break the soil up. The crumb structure is preserved to some extent by substances secreted by bacteria which keep the particles intact.

It may now be seen that herbicides and defoliants act in two ways, firstly by directly affecting the organisms within the soil and secondly by removing the plants on the surface. The consequences of both will be considered here. It should be emphasised again that all the data currently available refer to North American, and European (including Russian) work. Little work on a similar scale has been done in the tropics. The first effect to be considered is the action of defoliants and herbicides on soil organisms.

2,4D and 2,4,5T

In the soil acids such as 2,4D usually disappear in temperate climates between two weeks and four months after application. 2 chlorphenoxyacetic acid may remain for a year, while 3,4 dichlorphenoxyacetic acid does not disappear at all. Disappearance is due to the micro-organisms in the soil, especially the genera *Nocardia* and *Arthrobacter*. The rate of disappearance depends on the water content, temperature and the amount of organic material present. It is not known what compounds are produced by microbial action in this way. Professor Galston suggests that 2,4 dichlorphenol and 2,4,5 trichlorphenol may be produced. These cause destruction of natural auxins when applied externally or internally. It is thus possible that while breakdown is occurring (in the case of 2,4,5T this can be a considerable time) further toxic products, or even some of greater effect, could be produced.

2,4D has very great persistence in certain soils. Application of 2,4D causes the number of soil bacteria to be diminished. This decline in numbers is greater in the case of spore-forming bacteria than in the case of non-spore forming ones and fungi. Thus not only are the absolute numbers of bacteria present reduced, but so also are the relative numbers of different types. Also, those bacteria which break down 2,4D and 2,4,5T are encouraged by natural selection, since these substances are present in the environment.

Breakdown is rapid in warm moist soils. These compounds are readily leached out of light soils. In some they are retained in the clay fraction where they may remain for some months. This is important since they have some action as soil sterilants. The persistence of 2,4D can be greatly increased in anaerobic environments (lacking in oxygen), where there is little bacterial action of the right type to break it down. Thus it has been reported that in rice paddies 2,4D has accumulated in the mud, causing a continuing hazard. DDT and many other insecticides also accumulate in the same way.

Cacodylic acid

The present writer has been able to find little relevant data about the effects of cacodylic acid on micro-organisms.

Inactivation of cacodylic acid in plants is fairly rapid, especially in soils with a high moisture content. It is impossible to predict what the effect on the soil organisms of Vietnam would be. The use of cacodylic acid in the United States is lessening as better non-arsenical alternatives are available.

Picloram

Picloram is extremely persistent in the soil. The Dow Chemical Company's journal *Down to Earth* quotes a case in which a decrease of only 3% was observed over a period of 400 days. Its effects on micro-organisms in tropical conditions are not known. Little is known of the effects of picloram in temperate climates. It is known, however, to cause gross changes in the soil micro-organisms and their metabolism. It is not broken down by microbial action.

The arsenates and arsenites

The arsenates and arsenites are soil sterilants and are bactericidal (arsenites especially). They usually become fixed, mainly in the topsoil layer. They could cause radical changes in the bacterial population.

Calcium cyanamide and sodium cyanide

Calcium cyanamide and sodium cyanide are also toxic to soil bacteria. The cyanide is rapidly inactivated. In the degradation of the cyanamide cyanide may be produced. This too has a bactericidal action. Interestingly enough, when cyanamide is first applied there is, in temperate conditions, a rise in the number of soil micro-organisms. This is dependent on the concentration of hydrogen ions. Many soils in Vietnam are highly acidic.

DNP *and* DNOC

DNP and DNOC act as soil sterilants, but the significance of this in tropical conditions is not clear. It depends to some extent on the temperature of the soil, as toxicity is increased with rising temperatures. It should also depend on the rate of leaching. Damage may be caused by DNOC being leached to the rooting zone of plants.

Maleic hydrazide
Maleic hydrazide is extremely persistent in plant tissues. What its effects are on soil organisms the author has been unable to discover.

CMU *and* DCMU
CMU and DCMU are soil sterilants, and as such one would expect them to be bactericidal. The author has no information about their effects.

The second important level at which the plant killers act is that of the plants themselves. We have already discussed the effects of defoliants on plants, and it is now necessary to discuss the consequences of this removal of vegetation. Two consequences in particular are of importance to our discussion, erosion and laterisation.

Erosion can occur if the covering vegetation which stabilises the soil and holds it together is removed. Erosion is a process which occurs all the time in soils. New soil is also constantly being formed, by weathering and deposition of rocks and the action of soil organisms. Normally these processes are more or less in balance. Removal of vegetation eliminates the main obstacle to erosion.

There are two types of erosion, sheet erosion and gully erosion. *Sheet erosion* occurs when a thin layer of topsoil is removed. The process is continuous and practically unnoticeable. It occurs when the soil is in bad condition, with reduced porosity impairing drainage. Water then runs off the surface, taking soil with it. Since soil is abrasive, the process is cumulative. The effects of this type of erosion can be partially mitigated by good husbandry of areas affected.

Gully erosion involves the formation of channels scoured out of the earth. The process is irreversible, and can be an extremely powerful force. In one case in the United States reported by Chase the point onto which water dropped from a barn roof in Georgia started this type of erosive process. A rivulet formed which produced a canyon which eventually became 200 ft deep and covered 3000 acres. With the action of tributaries of the main stream, a total of 40,000 acres was affected.

The immediate consequence of the removal of vegetation is that the soil dries out. This begins the erosive process, as the crumb structure breaks down and the small soil particles are then more easily transported. The soil may at this stage be still capable of reclamation, before erosion has really set in. Once it has set in, little can be done as the process is effectively irreversible. Another process which may take place is laterisation, often before gully erosion.

Laterisation may affect certain—though by no means all—red soils in the tropics when these have been exposed through the removal of vegetation. The surface of the soil is burnt to a brick-like consistency. The process bears a rather dubious relationship to laterite, a type of rock which, it has been suggested, may have been formed by this process. Laterite and so-called laterite soils occur widely in Asia. Practically any parent material, but particularly sandstone, can undergo laterisation. One theory of laterite formation postulates that it was the result of deforestation. This may very well be true. Vietnam may be useful in telling us.

The temples of Siam and Cambodia, at Angkor Wat for example, have been constructed out of laterite. If this is the ultimate fate of some of the soil of Vietnam, it is obvious that it is of little agricultural use. Laterite soils are very poor from an agricultural point of view. They are extremely porous and liable to weathering and need very careful husbandry to be fertile. The onset of laterisation in Vietnam could lead to serious erosion. The consequences of this we have already mentioned.

The only real necessity for laterisation is that the parent material must be rich in alumino silicates. The characteristic red colour is due to weathering and the addition of iron oxide to the soil (the Mobius rubefaction); the end result of increasing the amount of iron oxide in the soil is laterisation.

Several factors make discussion of the effects on the soil difficult. In tropical soils animals larger than micro-organisms are significant in maintaining soil structure (more perhaps than in temperate regions). One Madagascar worm, *Geophagus darwinii*, can excrete 100 grams of earth in half an hour. The effects of a large number of these the author leaves to the reader's imagination. This is quite a large worm, 3 ft long and 1 in. in diameter. The 'thousand leg' *Julus corralinus* of the island of Reunion eats huge quantities of fallen leaves. Ants, termites and similar insects are all of considerable importance. Without knowing the contributions of all these to the economy of the environment, and the effects of the chemical, it is impossible to predict what will happen. Present data are totally insufficient.

A second major problem is the effect of climate.

Climatic influences are more active in the tropics than in temperate regions: temperatures are higher, rain occurs in the form of torrential downpours, storms are often of great severity and violence. Vegetation growth is extremely rapid when moisture conditions are favourable while . . . changes in the soil occur with corresponding speed. It is this dynamic quality of the tropics

which distinguishes them particularly.... It is necessary to take
all factors into consideration as well as their interactions and not
to be unduly influenced by any single factor.

[Tempary and Grist, *An Introduction to Tropical Agriculture*,
1959]

In view of the above, it will be interesting to examine more specifically the agents in use in Vietnam. The major compounds used
have already been discussed, and all that will be necessary here is
some qualification. The formulae of compounds in use are given
below:

Agent orange A 50:50 mixture of n-butyl esters of 2,4D and
2,4,5T. Used against heavy jungle and crops.

Agent white Also known as Tordon 101. This is a mixture of
2,4D and picloram in an alkanolamine formulation. It is used for
woody plant control.

Agent blue This is neutralised cacodylic acid used for grass control and the destruction of rice crops.

Agent purple Various butyl esters of 2,4D and 2,4,5T, interchangeable with Orange.

In discussing the effects of defoliants in Vietnam we shall follow
our previous practice, and divide the subject into the effects on
plants, animals, the soil and the environment.

In what follows the agents whose use has not been proved will not
be discussed. It is, however, apposite to refer here to points previously mentioned. Mr Cyrus Vance may have confirmed the use of
arsenicals and cyanides. Secondly, many of the reports from Vietnam would be explained if more toxic compounds had been used
than those officially acknowledged. The description of the 'deadly
yellow powder' and other reports of powder applications are sugges-
tive of arsenic trioxide or other arsenic compounds. Once it is
admitted that cw is being used, it becomes impossible to reject out
of hand even the most improbable allegations.

Data on the effects of defoliants in Vietnam are scarce, and come
from two main sources, Fred Tschirley, who went to Vietnam for the
us Department of Agriculture, and E. W. Pfeiffer and G. M. Orians,
sent to Vietnam by the Society for Social Responsibility in Science.
Neither party spent a long time in Vietnam, and facilities for
examination were restricted by the war conditions.

The effects in Vietnam

Agent orange, which constitutes 50% of the herbicide used in Vietnam, and agent white (35%) are used largely on trees, and it is the

effect of these which we shall consider first. It should be remembered that examples from other situations may not apply to Vietnam.

Agent white is the main agent around Saigon because of its lower tendency to drift. In other regions, where there is little agriculture, Orange is used.

Different responses to defoliant may be seen in different types of forest. Mangrove forests are highly susceptible; one application is sufficient to kill a large proportion of the trees. Areas treated in 1962 showed little regeneration even in 1968. Some of the lower vegetation, for example, the saltwater fern, was also removed, and had not grown again in 1969 (Orians and Pfeiffer). The majority of mangrove species, with some exceptions, are susceptible to Orange and White. Prediction of the prospects for regeneration is very difficult, but one estimate which seems reasonable is twenty years for treated mangroves (if full regeneration does occur). The effect of dead trees and of their diminished ability to hold soil particles is difficult to assess. The greater the amount of soil removed, the greater the difficulty of regeneration. Thus all estimates are extremely risky, and one of twenty years errs on the side of caution. The favouring of certain species by the removal of the dominant vegetation and the effects of water movement could considerably extend the time needed. Certain species of crab attack seedlings and thus may entirely prevent regeneration.

In the semi-deciduous forest areas the picture is different. One spraying causes a modest kill of the trees of the upper canopy. A second application (and about 25% of the broad forested area has received two applications) before the canopy has recovered gives a heavy kill of all woody plants. If only one application is made seedlings and saplings survive, since they are protected by the canopy vegetation.

Many grasses are resistant to the herbicides used in Vietnam, and invade treated areas, making regeneration more difficult. Unfortunately no data at all are available on the regeneration of forests in Vietnam. The indications are, however, that complete regeneration will take many decades.

The major problem with regard to fresh growth is the incursion of bamboo. Bamboo very quickly exploits areas where trees have been killed. Few seedlings can survive among the bamboo, assuming they are there to survive. The most serious direct danger from herbicide application is that seedlings may be killed and re-seeding delayed. It is Tschirley's opinion that this will retard fresh growth, if it was not for the bamboo, fresh growth might be fairly rapid.

Similar assessments have been made for the pine forests and the small area of rain forest. Dr C. Minarik of Fort Detrick has said that the major use of White (picloram) would be in controlling conifers. Enough White has been procured to spray the whole of Vietnam's pine forest twice over. (It should be noted that White is also used in other situations, for example near Saigon.) Although only 35% of the defoliant used in Vietnam is White, the proportion of the area treated may be higher, since areas treated with Orange generally need a second application. No data is published on the persistence of picloram in Vietnam, and there must inevitably be fears that it is dangerously high. Picloram is not metabolised by bacteria, and inactivation in heavy soil may be expected to be slow. It is likely to be retained in the upper layers of the soil. No information is available about the effect of picloram on rice plants.

According to spokesmen of Chemical Operations, US Army, defoliation damage cannot kill rubber trees. Research in Malaysia has shown that the n-butyl ester, at all concentrations used, killed rubber seedlings in six weeks. Accidents in Vietnam have shown that trees younger than seven years die; older ones generally recover. One notable exception was the defoliation of 250 acres of rubber plantation Ben Cui, where all the trees, which were thirty-three years old, were killed. Necrotic damage to rubber trees has also been reported.

The Rubber Research Institute of Vietnam has concluded, according to Orians and Pfeiffer, that repeated defoliations are threatening the very existence of rubber culture in Vietnam. Defoliants may also assist the spread of plant disease by causing damage, as has been noted on at least one occasion. Damage to or destruction of manioc, guava, mangoes and jack-fruit has been reported. Latex-producing trees seem to be heavily affected, as are vegetables.

The use of agent blue (which contains cacodylic acid) is a further cause for serious concern in view of its possible persistence in rice paddies in mountainous regions.

The main worry with regard to the toxicity of these agents is that the effects on man of high doses, and the conditions under which severe reactions to, say, 2,4D and 2,4,5T occur, are not known. Despite data from animals which would indicate a low toxicity for 2,4D, the MRI report states that the toxic dose for man is 50–100 mg/kg, which would make it a moderately toxic compound. On the basis of this figure some fatalities might be expected from its use in Vietnam. In the face of this figure, and of the total lack of information on inhalation toxicty, the MRI's conclusion (Report, 193) that 'the risk of human and animal toxicity is very, very low,' appears unwarranted.

Similarly, although picloram has a high LD_{50} orally, as Tordon 101 its LD_{50} is much lower, putting it into the mildly toxic rather than the non-toxic category. Again, picloram is not an irritant, whereas Tordon 101 (agent white) caused mild to severe blepharitis, severe swelling, mild to severe iritis and mild to moderate corneal opacity in 39· out of 67 rabbits in one test. These symptoms had completely cleared up at the end of twenty-eight days. Picloram in combination with 2,4D has caused the death of a sheep at a dose of 36 mg/kg (according to the abstract of an article from *Scientist and Citizen*). The effect of mixtures may thus be worse than that of individual agents on their own. The $L(Ct)_{50}$ figure for rabbits exposed to Tordon 101 is 150,982 mg-min/cu m. This is the only aerosol study quoted in the MRI report, which deals with herbicides applied in aerosol form. While the oral toxicity figures for a few mixtures are available, more data on these and on inhalation toxicities are essential.

Another worrying aspect is the use of agent blue (cacodylic acid). In view of its long-term effects it would seem a criminal act to use it on rice crops, where there will be a maximum of human contact with it, and where it might be persistent.

The effects on the soil are, as yet, impossible to evaluate. Little of the data presented by the MRI is relevant to tropical conditions, and there is an almost complete lack of information on this subject. The risk of laterisation is difficult to assess. Some 30% of the soils of Vietnam are liable to laterisation. Two types of laterite are already found there. Tschirley does not think that defoliation would hasten it. In certain cases, for example, around Special Forces' camps, the process may be accelerated by the almost complete removal of vegetation. Tschirley noted that flooding as a consequence of erosion was taking place. A change in the water-holding properties of the soil is a distinct possibility.

Finally we come to the ecological effects. As might be expected, data on these are very scant indeed. According to Pfeiffer, serious changes have occurred in the treated mangrove areas. With the exception of migrant birds, insectivorous and fruit-eating birds were totally absent. Fish-eating birds were reduced in number. It seems likely that the aquatic ecology was less severely affected than the terrestrial. Rare species restricted to mangrove areas may be in danger of extinction. No relevant data on the effects on forest species are available. That serious ecological changes have occurred is beyond doubt; their significance may well take a long time to appreciate.

Our summary shows that although the Midwest Research Institute did a good job in collecting data, their conclusions are of dubious value, for example, their statement that herbicides were not mutagenic, which was based on their lack of effect on organisms without chromosomes but with a much simpler genetic apparatus (see above,

p. 51). Other conclusions throughout the report give the Department of Defense the benefit of the doubt. When the MRI's report was studied by the National Academy of Sciences' Science Research Council, the council had some reservations. Firstly, they implied that the report was not comprehensive, and secondly, they made the point that much of the work reported had nothing to do with Vietnam. (The first hundred pages, in this writer's opinion, are largely irrelevant.) In particular, no details are given on the ecological consequences, which are perhaps the most important aspects of the use of defoliants. Yet beside the Department of Defense's summary report the MRI document seems a masterpiece of scientific objectivity. The summary states: 'Only a few scientific reports are available from the areas of operational use in Vietnam as to the vegetational response to the defoliation chemicals.' This is a serious under-statement. We have already discussed the dangers of applying data to different conditions from those to which they originally referred. This is what drawing firm conclusions about Vietnam from this report would be. Undeterred, the Department of Defense's summary lists several 'conclusions':

1. Destruction of vegetation is the greatest direct consequence of using herbicides.... Secondary growth or replacement vegetation invades rapidly under the tropical conditions of Vietnam, and partially killed or defoliated trees exhibit rapid recovery.

This is completely untrue, as the account above has shown. Neither is there any basis for such a conclusion in the MRI report. Tschirley, an expert in this field, says:

The time scale for the regeneration of semi-deciduous forest is unknown. Available information is so scanty that any prediction would have no validity and certainly no real meaning.

2. Long term effects on wildlife may be beneficial or detrimental. In many temperate zone areas, herbicidal treatment of the forest has improved the wildlife habitat and favoured animal production through increases in wildlife food plants. Destruction or modification of the habitat may greatly influence fauna that are rare or in danger of extinction.... Animals such as the rare kouprey, an ancestral bovine, may be favoured by the increase in bamboo and grasses following defoliation.

This is open to a number of objections. It is a very strange view of ecology which assumes that an increase in animal numbers is necessarily beneficial. In many cases increases in numbers can later have catastrophic effects on the survival of species. Overcrowding, falls in the food supply available, the spread of disease among animals forced into close contact by their numbers, a whole range of disadvantages, may face animals which are suddenly able to increase in number. Usually it means that if they are normally preyed upon the predators have a field-day; or if the animals in question are themselves predators, some starve. If increases in the number of particular animals are associated with multiple changes in the environment, including the other animals, the results may be far from beneficial. On balance, any introduction of foreign matter into a complex ecological system is detrimental. To view what must be very short-term effects and pronounce on their beneficence is foolish. Defoliation has been practised in Vietnam for less than ten years. The effects of defoliants on the flora and fauna of the country may take decades or even centuries to become apparent. The Defense Department's summary does admit that 'many unknown factors, including feeding habits of many indigenous animals, make specific effects on wildlife difficult to predict.' This must surely rate as quite a remarkable understatement. Knowing the feeding habits of indigenous animals would not in any case help to predict herbicide effects. There are countless interactions between animals and plants, some more, many less, critical to the animals' survival than their feeding habits.

This conclusion was not supported by Orians and Pfeiffer, who went to Vietnam to see for themselves. Probably the nature and extent of these effects will only be realised long after the Vietnam war is over.

3. Herbicides now in use in Vietnam will not persist at a phytotoxic (poisonous to plants) level in the soil for long periods.

The reader is referred to the previous discussion of this question. Only ignorance or wishful thinking could be responsible for such a statement.

4. The probability of lethal toxicity to humans, domestic animals, or wildlife by use of herbicide is highly unlikely. Direct hazard to people and animals on the ground is nearly non-existent.

For reasons given in a previous discussion (pp 231–41) it seems to us that the MRI report's conclusion on this point is unjustified, and based on insufficient evidence. It may be relevant to remark here that people who have been sprayed with defoliants have a different opinion from the Department of Defense.

5. Unlike many insecticides, herbicides seldom persist in animal or insect tissues. Transfer of herbicides to the next animal in the food chain in defoliant-treated areas is negligible. Most herbicides,

including all of those used in Vietnam, are readily excreted and do not accumulate in the human body.

Of all the Defense Department's conclusions this seems to be the most reasonable, until one asks what is meant by 'seldom' and which herbicides are referred to. If the only herbicides in use are the four previously referred to, then this conclusion is largely correct. If other herbicides suggested have been used, this conclusion is as false as, in the present writer's opinion, are all the others.

> 6. Indirect effects of herbicides resulting from destruction of aquatic vegetation may produce changes in the biota of the aquatic environment. Direct toxic effects on fish and aquatic organisms are negligible. Destruction of specific plants used for fish-foods will lead to changes in the food chain in the aquatic ecosystem. Applications of herbicides to remove floating aquatic weeds will provide important benefits because their presence depletes the oxygen content of the water.

The indirect effects have already been discussed. The question of toxic effects on fish is too complicated for a firm answer to be possible. Fish species show a wide variety of response to the agents used, and it is impossible to assess the effects without performing experiments on species indigenous to Vietnam. Reports from Vietnam contradict the assertion that herbicides are harmless to fish. The MRI's report is based almost entirely on North American studies.

The present writer does not understand the last statement. Surely floating aquatic weeds would produce oxygen by photosynthesis, rather than depleting the oxygen content of the water. One might suspect that deoxygenation would occur if the weeds carried out little photosynthesis and clogged the water.

The Pentagon's summary finally concludes that 'reliable judgements could not be made with respect to the effects of defoliants on water quality, on mammals and birds in danger of extinction, on climate and the hydrologic cycle, or on soil erosion'. The Defense Department's criteria of reliability seem rather odd.

8. CHEMICAL WEAPONS SYSTEMS AND THEIR DEVELOPMENT

The early large-scale uses of chemicals in war began a history of continuous development of ever more ingenious and effective weapons. It rapidly became clear at the outset that to have a highly toxic chemical was not the same as having a weapon. Some of the early problems are still not solved today.

Many lessons of permanent value were learnt from the use of gas in World War I. The first type of attack used was the 'cloud' attack, in which a cloud of gas was released and allowed to drift over the enemy lines. On the occasion of its first use, by the Germans, it was very effective, but the effectiveness of the new weapon gradually became less. A number of factors were responsible for this. First, the Allies soon developed a primitive form of gas-mask. A second factor was the weather. The wind blew more often from the Allied to the German lines than in the opposite direction, making retaliation more of a risk than had been foreseen. The reversal of wind direction could also make gas blow back on the disseminators. Gas attacks of this type took immense preparation which could not easily be concealed. In this form gas was an unwieldy and uncertain weapon.

The next significant development was the introduction, again by the Germans, of the gas shell. Once again, despite initial success, the weapon soon came to seem less fearsome than it had first appeared. This was due both to the development of anti-gas drill and other methods of protection by the Allies and to the neglect by the Germans of certain important principles.

The development of shells for gas warfare is a fascinating history of blunders and breakthroughs. In general, the British seemed to be able to produce good agents but poor shells, while the Germans produced shells which were good from a mechanical point of view and had a high capacity for carrying agents, but rarely filled them with the right agents. The complexity of marrying the right agent to the right shell had not yet been fully realised.

Among the early mistakes was the use of hydrogen cyanide, which, although one of the most toxic substances then known, was volatile and quickly dispersive. The use of lachrymatories in shells was also abortive, because it proved impossible to maintain a sufficiently high concentration of the agents to be effective. The German use of DA and DC in shells was also ineffective because the agents were destroyed when the shell exploded. The British later prepared more effective means of disseminating arsenical agents (like DA and DC) in 'smokes' and not as vapours.

Chemical munitions are designed to spread lethal or incapacitating doses of agent over fairly wide areas. For this to be achieved, the agent has to be converted into a vapour, gas or smoke, droplets, or a combination of these. It is necessary to find the form which best uses the toxic properties of the particular agent. It was a long time before the problems involved were understood.

Perhaps one of the most effective weapons of World War I period was the trench mortar. This was of short range but could project large quantities of agent. The Livens projector is a good example of this type of weapon. The trench mortar was very effective in producing very high localised concentrations of gas. This was a technique in which the British excelled but which the Germans never mastered.

The most significant feature of chemical munitions was not appreciated by researchers until late in the war. This is the fact that whatever system is used there is a limit to the proportion of the total weight of the carrier which is available for the agent. These limits were 10% for shells, 40–50% for trench mortars and 90% for aerial bombs. The use of aerial bombs was suggested during World War I, but they were never used. It has been said that commanders considered them 'inhumane'.

From the crude systems of the early days, so much at the mercy of environmental disturbances, there were gradually developed more precise ways of building up gas concentrations in particular areas. At the same time, many of the techniques of the static war fell out of favour, and trench mortars and gas clouds could not be used effectively in more mobile types of war. Shells and aerial methods of dissemination therefore became the foundations of chemical warfare technology until the end of World War II. The only uses of cw between the wars were by the Japanese against the Chinese (aerial bombs) and by the Italians against the Abyssinians (aerosol sprays from aircraft).

During the period since 1939 the principles underlying the design of weapon systems became better appreciated. At the London conference on cbw Mr Julian Perry Robinson summarised the considerations which go into the making of an effective weapon.[1] These were the knowledge distilled from the errors of the past. The factors are:

1. The agent
2. The munition
3. The weapons system
4. The environment (meteorological conditions, terrain, etc.)

In chemical warfare the main requirement with regard to the agent is very high effectiveness. The most toxic or incapacitating agent available is used. Lachrymatories and sternutants were used in World War I because they were the most potent agents then known. The most effective gas of this period, H, mustard gas, is now considered a harassing agent. The chemical properties of an agent have to include suitability for storage and a reasonable degree of stability on dissemination. In modern warfare the main gases used will be mustard derivatives and nerve gases. These agents have been fully discussed above.

The critical importance of the second factor, the munition itself,

[1] See Steven Rose (ed), *CBW*, London 1968, 19-34.

should be apparent from the first part of this section. The easiest gases to use in munitions are non-persistent gases such as phosgene, which disperse when allowed to escape into the air. Problems arise, however, with a gas like hydrogen cyanide AC, which is too easily dispersed in gaseous form. If the agent is to be released over a wide area in a lethal or incapacitating concentration, care must be taken to match the agent with a munition which makes the best use of its toxic properties. The ideal munition will produce particles of the right size and at the right velocity, and vapours or liquid droplets in the right proportions, to utilise the contact and inhalation properties of the agent. Agents which have no effect through the skin would be ideally produced as 1–5-micron particles which would penetrate the lungs. Droplets or larger particles would be a wasteful use of the agent.

The most difficult agents to disperse are the toxins, such as ricin. Ricin is a fairly heat-stable vegetable protein some 8–10 times stronger than the older nerve gases on a weight for weight basis. It was the filling of the British w bomb in World War II. It is not suitable for explosive dissemination in shells. More suitable is spraying or aerial bombs which split into small bomblets which release toxin as they fall to the ground.

The most effective modern chemical weapons are the nerve gases, which can be formulated with a variety of properties, from volatile 'gases' to fairly involatile liquids. They are reasonably stable under heat and storage, and are a near-ideal chemical warfare agent.

The wide variety of chemical agents means that few standard munitions can be made for all the fillings available. At present there are only a few fillings in actual use. The principal ones are the nerve gases GB and VX, which are used by the United States. The composition of the Russian munition fillings is not known, but they are mainly in the nerve gas category.

The weapons system is another part of the problem of chemical warfare. Chemical weapons are available in a wide range, from grenades to large strategic missiles. It should be remembered that a weapons system which has no use in a European situation, such as spraying from aircraft, may be important in other conditions, in this case, in counter-insurgency or anti-guerrilla operations. A number of particular weapons systems will be considered in detail later. A great advantage of chemical weapons is their flexibility. It is a small matter to put a chemical warhead on a missile instead of a high-explosive (or nuclear) one. Similarly, chemicals shells are interchangeable with high-explosive ones.

The greatest obstacle to a general adoption of CBW weapons is our fourth point, the effect of the environment. The effectiveness of chemical weapons depends on temperature, humidity, wind speed, terrain and many other factors. Reducing the variability in performance caused by the environment is as important an object today as it was when shells were substituted for gas clouds because of their greater precision. One modern aerial bomb splits into 264 submunitions, which disperse a rising cloud of gas on reaching the ground. A gas cloud higher than a man has no useful function.

We shall now consider some modern weapons systems. Since most chemical weapons are probably deployed in Europe, we shall consider the systems which are most important in these conditions. Of the early weapons systems from World War I, the shell remains an extremely effective disseminator of chemical agents. With the advent of the missile, aerial dissemination seems unlikely to be much used. In a modern war manned aircraft are unlikely to have an important role. The manned aircraft may still be a feasible proposition if experiments being carried out in the United States into high speed dissemination systems are successful. It was an accident during a high speed test of vx dissemination which killed the 6000 sheep in Utah. It seems quite possible for freeze-dried biological material or toxins to be used in the same way from jet aircraft. Current interest, however, is still mainly in shells and rockets. Future chemical warfare will probably use shells and missiles for offensive purposes. There may also be a limited role for devices such as landmines.

We shall now briefly consider a shell, a short-range missile and an intermediate-range tactical missile.

The artillery shell

We shall consider the M121 series of 155-mm shells. This has been in production since the early 1950s with a choice of fillings, non-persistent or persistent nerve gas (GB or vx). It is about 2 ft long and contains a heavy explosive charge. The weight of chemical carried is 6 lb (6% of the total weight). The performance figures for a GB-filled shell are quite impressive. In good conditions, if the shell bursts in the air 15 ft above the ground a concentration of 3500 mg/m^3 is produced over an area of 20 yd radius. This concentration may kill in a couple of inhalations. At about 50 yd from the burst a concentration is built up in 25 sec which is sufficient to kill in less than 10 sec exposure. This is a long way from the gas shells of World War I. In view of the existence of such weapons it is amazing that arguments can still be brought forward, based on World War I statistics, to show that the use of gas is humane. Gas in World War I was not so much humane as ineffective.

A shell filled with GB produces droplets which rapidly vaporise. With vx part of the liquid becomes an aerosol which penetrates the lungs; the rest becomes droplets, which act through the skin. This method utilises very well the dual effect of the v agents.

Short-range rockets

A second system of considerable interest is the missile made for the American M55 rocket launcher. This is a descendant of a German World War II rocket known as the *Nebelwerfer* ('cloud-thrower') which was developed to carry tabun.

This equipment was ready for operational use in 1960. It consists of forty-five 6-ft 'Bolt' rockets in a multiple tube launcher, all of which can be launched in 30 sec. It can be mounted on a truck or a helicopter. Orders for many thousands of missiles were placed in 1960. Performance figures available indicate that two such launchers could spread half a ton of nerve gas on a square kilometre within thirty seconds, causing 30% casualties almost immediately.

Intermediate-range missiles

These have a range of 5–200 miles. The Little John (LJ) has a fairly short range, but the Honest John (HJ) and Sergeant have a range of up to 125 miles, or perhaps more for the Lance. The details of chemical and biological warheads for these missiles are still secret, but it seems likely that the warheads will contain numerous bomblets which will be dispersed by explosion above the target. The bomblets are vaned to make them rotate; rotation stabilises them and activates the fuses. Different types of bomblet are standardised for different types of agent; some for explosive dissemination (for nerve gases), others as gas propellants, etc. There are bomblets designed for labile material such as ricin, one of which splits on reaching a predetermined height. The agent then disperses and spreads as it falls to the ground.

It has been said that the Sergeant or Scud (the Russian equivalent) could produce 30% casualties on a fully deployed battle group of 1400 men within a short time under practically any conditions. This assumes, of course, that no protection is available and that significant proportions of the battle group are not contained in armoured personnel carriers or other CBW-proof equipment. Probably performance figures like these bear only a slight resemblance to the real situation on the battlefield. Anti-gas drill, the terrain, and the protective equipment available could reduce these figures drastically. It seems probable that even nerve gas will eventually be considered only a harassing agent, and will be effective more in reducing military efficiency than in causing significant casualties.

The final point to be discussed is the effect of the environment on any chemical weapon. Variations in effectiveness of between ten and fifty times may occur if environmental conditions are unfavourable (see Julian Perry Robinson's paper in Steven Rose, *CBW*, London 1968, 29, 34). This applies more to older systems than to modern ones, and it may be significant that realistic data on modern weapons are much harder to come by. High winds, humidity, rain and other factors can render chemical weapons less effective. Despite the logistical difficulties, the effects of cw are predictable enough for it to be used as a supplementary weapon. Some us Army manuals have suggested as possible situations the edge of areas hit with nuclear weapons, where chemical weapons could exploit confusion and the possible lack of gas-mask discipline among troops partially affected by the explosion. cbw might also be used on small targets not considered worth a nuclear attack.

A major factor in any such use would be surprise. In cases where large bodies of troops are dug in and may be surprised, cw could be very effective, as could attacks on fortified positions where troops might feel they were relatively safe. The main advantage of these weapons is that accuracy is not as important with them as with other weapons. Most of the us data seen by the present writer has emphasised the usefulness of cw in shell form, and it is in this form that cw munitions make their most important contribution to military capability; shells form the bulk of the cw munitions available to the major powers. It is in this form that they could be most effectively used to supplement nuclear weapons on the battlefield.

It is unlikely that even in a strategic situation, as opposed to the tactical ones described previously, cw or bw would be used alone. The suggestion that cbw might be used on cities and nuclear weapons on missile sites is not persuasive. cbw has a supportive role in total war or the limited war situations discussed here. It would of course be possible to mount clandestine cbw attacks as a preliminary to a nuclear one in order to reduce the effectiveness of retaliation. On the whole, however, cbw is not a war-winning weapon, except where retaliation is not possible, as in the case of a cbw attack by one non-nuclear power on another.

In the case of the clandestine use of cbw in Europe, nuclear weapons would be used as soon as the effects of the cbw attack became apparent because the logistical difficulties of occupying stricken territory would be enormous, and the preparations for invasion would almost certainly alert the enemy. The need to prevent retaliation would also argue for an immediate nuclear strike in order to neutralise the enemy completely.

None of these considerations can give anyone much comfort. Unfortunately many people think that cbw is unlikely to be used. As things stand, however, if war comes it will be used, quickly and with terrible effect.

6

BIOLOGICAL AGENTS

Biological warfare is the intentional use of living organisms or
their toxic products to cause death, disability or damage in man,
animals or plants. The target is man, either by causing his sick-
ness or death, or through limitation of his food supplies or other
agricultural resources. Man must wage a continuous fight to maintain and defend himself, his animals and his plants in competition
with insects or micro-organisms. The object of BW is to overcome
these efforts by deliberately distributing large numbers of organisms of native or foreign origin, or their toxic products, taking full
advantage of the ability to utilise more effective methods of dissemination and unusual portals of entry. BW has been aptly
described as public health in reverse.

[*Effects of Biological Warfare*, us Department of Health Education and Welfare, July 1959]

The above is perhaps the most comprehensive and accurate definition so far offered of biological warfare. General J. H. Rothschild, a
former head of the Research and Development Department of the
Army Chemical Corps, entitled his book on the subject *Tomorrow's
Weapons*. It is obvious from the documentation in Part 1 that these
are rapidly becoming the weapons of today. For this reason it is
essential that we understand them. Before a detailed consideration
is made, however, it may be useful to mention some of the more
general ideas surrounding the subject.

In the layman's eyes biological warfare is associated with invisible
and creeping death for a large proportion of the population. Biological weapons have other uses, however, and there is reason to
believe that perhaps among the most effective of the possible agents
are those which affect plants. Biological weapons can in fact be
utilised to produce a whole spectrum of different results. It may
perhaps be helpful at this point to delineate some of the more
specific reasons for the importance of biological weapons and indicate why the authors have given them special consideration.

It is frequently argued that one is just as dead from the effects of napalm or high explosives. On a personal level this is undoubtedly true. Nevertheless, it should be noted that with napalm or high explosives it is possible to be selective in one's target. The choice is in the hands of the disseminators. It is in the nature of BW systems that they are most useful against whole populations. In the event of a military target being in the centre of a town, for example, the whole town suffers. This fact is readily recognised by the apologists for BW and is in some cases even used as an argument in their favour. Rothschild has suggested that BW is a far more effective deterrent against China for the very reason that it would affect the whole population.

In terms of their effects on civilian populations, biological weapons may be comparable with nuclear weapons. In terms of world peace they may ultimately constitute an even greater threat.

Biological weapons potentially possess a very high effectiveness and thus, in spite of certain unknown factors which would be connected with their use, they receive serious consideration as a weapon. The only proper test of such weapons will come with their use on a real population just as the experience of Hiroshima and Nagasaki provided a reasonable basis from which to deduce the effects of nuclear warfare. Any estimates at present are liable to certain imprecision. This is increased by the unpredictable nature of the biological materials themselves.

One consequence of the use of biological weapons could be a permanent imbalance of some part of a natural system. Their use may, for instance, result in diseases becoming established where they were previously unknown. Uncertainty is inherent in biological warfare, and a good example of this is the test carried out on the island of Gruinard.

All these points are considered in detail later; they are listed here merely to indicate the importance of these weapons. The considerable advances in microbiology in the last twenty years are of tremendous importance. On the credit side is a deeper understanding of the basic processes of life. On the debit side is a possible new pathway to genocide.

1. THE BIOLOGICAL WEAPON

As in the discussion of the chemical agents, we are here first going to consider the possibilities for biological warfare. The US Army lists the following five groups of biological warfare agents.

1. Micro-organisms (bacteria, viruses, rickettsiae, fungi and protozoa).
2. Vectors, carriers of disease (usually insects).

3. Toxins (poisonous chemicals derived from living organisms).
4. Pests of domestic and commercial plants and animals.
5. Anticrop agents, herbicides, etc. These have been dealt with already.

We are mainly concerned with numbers 1 to 4.

It is important to consider in what situation biological warfare is to be used. From available data, several things become clear. Biological weapons are of military importance in that, like chemical and nuclear weapons, they affect large areas. This would mean that their use is most likely to be strategic. The US Army has currently standardised at least three agents for use. Their identity is not published in any unclassified sources. On account of delay in their effects it seems unlikely that these are contemplated for tactical use. They have several military advantages:

1. They are area weapons.
2. They attack the population. Installations, factories, etc., are all left intact.
3. Detection and identification are difficult. With current techniques it is also slow, but this is being speeded up.
4. There is a possibility that incapacitating agents may be used. (Whether this is likely to occur in practice is rather dubious and will be discussed in more detail later.)
5. They are effective in very small amounts. Comparisons drawn with nuclear weapons are not valid but there is reason to believe that their effectiveness may be of the same order.
6. They can be produced in a very short time.
7. They are very cheap to produce.
8. Protection is difficult.
9. They may be applied covertly. This is an important consideration with the current state of nuclear balance.
10. Dissemination systems and plant can be easily disguised. Biological agents could be produced in an antibiotics factory or a brewery. Dissemination systems need not be very sophisticated.

Military disadvantages, apart from their general lack of application to a tactical situation, are remarkably few. These are:

1. Dependence on meteorological conditions for spread by aerosol (the most favoured means). It should be noted that for certain situations, where food or water supplies may be contaminated, this does not apply.

2. The possibility that the weapon may become retroactive on its users or their allies must be considered.

Having considered both the advantages and the disadvantages, it is now necessary to see whether these advantages can be realised in practice. There is usually a great difference between possessing a potential weapon and having a usable effective device. There are several criteria by which potential agents must be measured.

Assessment of the biological weapon

1. There are two possible types of agents for use against man. These are incapacitating and lethal agents. Obviously, they must have a certain effectiveness. The limits applied depend on the situation in which they are to be used. There are a number of possible situations. These are summarised as:

  1. Overt: (a) tactical—for a limited military objective;
              (b) strategic—against populations in large-scale attack.
  2. Covert: (a) tactical;
              (b) strategic.

It is unlikely that in situation 1(a) biological weapons proper (viruses or bacteria) will be used, since symptoms develop too slowly. Toxins, on the other hand, could be used to great effect. No steps are taken to ensure secrecy in this case, as in case of war in Western Europe, where each side knows the other to possess these weapons. Military personnel involved will have adequate protection. Protective clothing, masks, etc., will prevent casualties but will obviously reduce military efficiency, which is the major tactical effect.

Situation 1(b) is that in which biological weapons would be used against populations in open war without attempts at secrecy. This case would occur if nuclear war broke out now. Both sides would use these in conjunction with nuclear and chemical weapons. The effects of all three types of weapon would be supportive of each other. Nuclear bombs would have the effect of forcing people into shelters and possibly damaging these. CB weapons would penetrate damaged shelters and after some time even the most carefully constructed undamaged shelters. Situation 2(a) might possibly arise if one belligerent in Western Europe, for instance, wished to gain an exploitable advantage over the other side. Operations could be mounted to coincide with the time when the effects would become manifest. Situation 2(b) probably represents the greatest danger.

In this case an aggressor could release agents in water supplies, etc., or more probably in aerosol. Britain is very prone to just such an attack. It would be possible for a submarine off the west coast of Ireland proceeding northwards to disseminate in less than 24 hours sufficient agent to affect most of England. Detection, the appearance of symptoms in this case, would probably not be possible until the whole area had become thoroughly affected.

It should be emphasised that the above are only crude examples of types of situations. For most of these cases described, in fact, such use is unlikely.

For military use the agent must be effective to within quite stringent limits.

(a) With lethal agents 25–50% deaths would be necessary in field operations.

(b) With incapacitating agents in use against enemy troops 20–30% 'takes' would be demanded (including some fatal cases). If the aim is strategic incapacitation for prolonged periods without death, then efficiency should be about 50% (among civilians). If illness of only a few days' duration is to be caused in a strategic situation, an efficiency as high as 90% would be necessary. In all cases there must be rigid adherence to the criteria, for example in the case of a fatal disease estimated at 25–30% fatality, at least 20% deaths must be assured. Many organisms could satisfy these criteria—*Pasteurella pestis* as a lethal agent, or Tularemia as an incapacitating agent.

These apply to anti-personnel weapons of the microbial type, viruses, bacteria, etc. The use of toxins in war is most likely in situations such as 1(a) or 1(b) and possibly 2(a). Practical difficulties would make 2 (b) less probable.

Agents affecting domestic plants and animals would be almost exclusively of the lethal or extremely damaging category. Some agents have the bonus effect of acting on both man and animals, for example anthrax. Plant diseases would be those affecting main crops. The stem rust of cereals would be most useful in North America if special forms could be bred. In south-east Asia rice blast fungus is the obvious choice. A Fort Detrick research worker got the us Army's highest award to civilians for her work on rice blast fungus. A highly virulent strain of this has now been developed; its main use would be in Asia.

2. The onset of effects must be predictable and for the largest proportion of the population must be manifested at the same time. Obviously, a disease with chronic effects such as syphilis is not likely to be used. The military requirement is that the effects should be

manifested in 75% of the 'takes' within the stated incubation period. This period should ideally be between 24 hours and three days.

3. Large-scale rapid production must be possible. Of the micro-organisms, the bacteria are most easily produced in large quantities by the method of continuous cultivation. Porton did some valuable pioneer work in this technique. In this the bacteria are grown in a fluid medium from which they are regularly harvested. An installation a fraction of the size of Porton would be sufficient, if devoted specifically to this technique, to produce an effective biological weapon. Large-scale production of micro-organisms must be possible for the production of vaccines. A machine is known that has a capacity of 50 cu m. This plant could equally be used for the production of weapons. A large-scale plant for this purpose was developed at Camp Detrick in World War II.

Two points deserve emphasis here. First, the clandestine production of micro-organisms is easy. The actual installation need be no bigger than, say, an average size church or small factory. Secondly, that, despite this, a really sizable effort, such as that of the United States—involving missile warheads and bombs—is almost impossible to conceal. However, for covert use of the type involving, say, a submarine off the coast of Ireland, concealment would be very easy, as little specialised plant for filling munitions, and no highly specialised design, would be required. This represents one of the greatest dangers after the large stockpiles which the US is known to have, and which the Russians may possess. This is also likely to give rise to major difficulties in disarmament talks.

In the case of viruses, it is difficult to perform large-scale production as they require living tissues in which to reproduce. This can be partially offset, however, by, for example, growing viruses on the chorio-allantoic membranes of hen eggs. It is also true that viruses are effective in much smaller doses. Theoretically, using a dozen chicken eggs in this fashion, enough psittacosis virus could be produced to infect everyone on the earth. This impressive figure indicates the potential but points to an aim which cannot be realised in practice.

It is also necessary to consider the plant pathogens. Plant diseases even today claim approximately one-third of all crops grown. Viruses probably do more damage to plants than any other group of pathogens. Two factors act in the favour of plant diseases, their effectiveness and their difficulty of detection until damage is apparent. (This may be partially offset by the use of modern techniques, for example by infra-red aerial photography, etc. In this fashion, foci may be easily identified by a succession of aerial surveys.) For some disease, for example the stem rusts of wheat, the effectiveness of fungi is impressive, and a single infected barberry bush could infect an area of many hundreds of square miles. Infection of suitable intermediate hosts is not difficult. Plant diseases are also attractive because therapy is impracticable on a large scale, and for some diseases, for example the stem rusts, rots and mildews which attack cereals, there is no practical fungicide. It should also be noted that rice blast, for example, is very dependent on meteorological conditions for its effect. A minimum temperature of $20°-26°$ c is required and 90% relative humidity. Thus in some cases climatic conditions can give some form of warning as to when the disease is most likely to be used.

Vectors for the various diseases have also been produced on a large scale. This was a method tried by the Japanese against the Chinese in World War II. Methods for the artificial breeding of large numbers of rats, fleas, flies and other vectors were developed at this time. According to the report of the Khabarovsk Trial, some 4500 incubators were used for the breeding of fleas at Harbin. These fleas were infected with plague. The output was 45 kg in the course of three to four months. This is approximately 145 million parasites. At Fort Detrick today there are large breeding facilities for various vectors, for example the mosquito for yellow fever.

The bacterial toxins are of interest in terms of their large-scale production. This needs additional plant for the separation of toxins from the bacteria, but the finished product is easier to handle. This is probably the reason why the British developed the w bomb—which contained ricin (a toxin derived from castor bean seeds). Botulinus toxin was also produced by the allies on some scale during the war. Toxins from a wide variety of sources have been considered, from paralytic shellfish-poisoning toxin to cobra venom neurotoxin.

There is little difficulty in the industrial production of the bacterial toxins such as botulinus and those from others of the less exotic sources, for example ricin. Cobra venom neurotoxin, though of BW interest, is not a possible weapon.

4. Stability of the agent in storage and dissemination is essential. This can be accomplished in several ways for bacteria. Bacteria may be freeze-dried and, in this form, embedded in a protein matrix; they can be stored for several weeks. Brucellosis bacteria may be stabilised by addition of dextrin, peptides and petones to the medium. Decomposition inevitably occurs with aging but a usefully active product could be maintained for some time. The military requirement for minimum storage period is two to three weeks without a significant drop in activity. Some bacteria, for example *Bacillus anthracis*, form spores which are highly resistant to en-

vironmental changes even over long periods. Viruses, as they have no metabolic requirements, need little in the way of specialised storage. It is essential to avoid damage as viruses have no metabolism and cannot repair themselves. Their fragility is also a problem in their dissemination. Toxins can be stored quite adequately for long periods in sealed metal airtight containers. Botulinus toxin is oxidised if it is in contact with air, and storage must therefore be airtight. Some toxins, for example ricin, are more stable in storage than others.

Plant pathogens of the viral type can be stored in the same way as other virus material. Fungi form resistant spores. These, like those of *Bacillus anthracis*, can be stored for considerable periods.

5. Easy and effective dissemination are essential characteristics. There are several techniques to ensure this.

(a) Contamination of food or water sources. The advantage of this technique is that there is less shock due to dissemination than with other methods. By this means a single saboteur or group of saboteurs can be effective. This was considered as a means of retaliation in World War II if the Germans used chemical and biological warfare against the British. About half a kilogram of salmonella may be sufficient to affect a whole city's water supply. It could prove most useful where there were no water purification plants or these were ineffective. This particular technique is restricted to covert use.

(b) Use of animal vectors. This is a possible means of spreading diseases such as yellow fever. Several things render effective use unlikely. Large amounts of the vector are needed to ensure that some of them reach their target. Introduction of such a vector into a foreign environment would probably cause it to be removed by predators. Animal vectors also tend to feed infrequently. A further difficulty may arise due to the creation of pools of infection in the territory attacked. The vector may attack its victim, who contracts the disease. The victim may then be attacked by a non-disease-carrying vector which may then carry the disease. In addition, animal vectors may be restricted in their range and habitat, for example, the yellow fever mosquito is restricted to marshy areas where the temperature does not fall to below 15°C. The target has no such limitations. Animal vectors may be used to spread plant diseases. This method should be distinguished from the use of insects like locusts which are directly effective against plants, which is unlikely to be tried. The vector technique is not likely to have much application owing to the numbers of vectors needed and the difficulty of dissemination.

(c) Use of aerosols. Dissemination in this situation would be in the form of aerosols from bombs, shells, sprays or mines. Spray dissemination would probably, for maximum efficiency, be carried out by low-flying aircraft. Aerosol dissemination is currently the most favoured form of dispersal.

Much research published both in Britain and the USA has concerned aerosol dissemination; papers have been published from the MRE at Porton on, for example, the survival of 'Escherischia coli in an aerosol' (*J. Gen. Microbiol.* 1966, 45, No. 2). Several results are apparent from published work. Particle size is critical for effective aerosol dissemination. They must be about 1–5 microns in diameter. Larger particles than this fall to the ground too rapidly and may not be inhaled by the target in sufficient numbers, or may be less effective being removed from the air in the upper respiratory tract. Particles of 1–5 microns diameter reach the alveolar bed and thus pass into the bloodstream. Particles smaller than 1 micron tend to be exhaled without succeeding in producing infection.

Experiments to infect guinea-pigs with *Brucella suis*, a bacterium which causes an undulant fever (a disease of BW interest), have shown that 600 times as many 12-micron particles as 1–5-micron particles are required for successful infection.

The inhalation toxicity of botulinus toxin is 1000 times greater than that by ingestion. The above can give an indication of the potential for use of these agents from laboratory experiments. Results from field trials are discussed below.

In one experiment a cloud of 2-micron zinc-cadmium sulphide particles (459 lb) discharged over 156 miles of coast was detected over about 34,000 square miles of land. In this area, a minimum dose of 15 and a maximum dose of 15,000 particles were inhaled. Had this been Q fever, of which a single particle can cause infection, the result could have been that practically everyone in the area would have been infected. Other experiments with aerosolised harmless bacteria support this. A ship running a 2-mile course 2 miles offshore at right angles to the onshore wind discharged 130 gal of a suspension of *Bacillus subtilis*. There was recognised a tendency to vertical dilution owing to meteorological factors. Nevertheless, in buildings and open spaces over an area of 100 square miles, the equivalent of infectious doses were found to be present. It is important to note that in a normal aerosol only a small proportion of the particles would be in the right size range. The experiment on the guinea-pig shows that a large part of the aerosol would not be effective in producing infection.

The restrictions of this method are twofold. Aerosols of effective particle size and high infectivity must be produced. Secondly, meteorological factors can have considerable effect. Most BW agents rapidly lose viability and virulence. This occurs on dissemination owing to physical, heat and other stresses, especially in the production of the aerosol. The problem with most biological agents is keeping them viable for long enough periods for them to be effective. The humidity and its effect on the metabolism of the organism are critical factors. On the whole spores and some rickettsia, for example Q fever, are more resistant to environmental changes when in aerosol. Survival may in some cases be increased by using a special fluid suspension.

Oxygen and irradiation affect organisms in the cloud, reducing viability. Thus dissemination is likely to be carried out at night in cool weather. In addition to this there are problems due to dilution, rainfall and the particles hitting surfaces. After a while the heavier particles fall to the ground. Dilution depends on the meteorological conditions and the terrain. An aircraft travelling at right angles to the wind direction is not subject to losses of material due to dilution along the wind direction. Lateral diffusion is also slight. This mean that if a cloud is generated it may be expected not to be dispersed too rapidly for its effectiveness to be completely removed by spreading before reaching the ground. Vertical mixing as opposed to drift can affect particle concentration drastically. For this reason attacks are most likely on clear nights when the earth's surface is cooled by radiation. In these conditions there is a lid of warm air to prevent upward movement. During the early morning or late evening convection currents occur close to the earth which mix the particles. Dissemination at a height of between 500 and 1500 m coupled with these currents could spread the aerosol over possibly hundreds of square kilometres. This is a description of the probable operational use. It is not ideal, but shows more how the agent would be applied in practice.

As seen by the US Army now, the ideal conditions for a large-scale biological attack include the following:

Attack at midnight, over an extended line at an altitude of about 300 ft. (This is very difficult to achieve operationally, hence the use mentioned above.) Wind direction steady at about 12 miles/h. The use of an infectious agent that can induce disease by the inhalation of fewer than 100 particles, and whose viability and virulence decline very slowly. Most of the material in the aerosol to be in particles less than 5 microns in diameter (larger particles would get trapped in the human nose and be inactivated by local defense mechanisms). Material to be disseminated for about 30 miles at a rate of approximately 1·6 gal/mile.

These conditions represent approximately 1000m. organisms per foot of flight line and, with limited vertical mixing, could result in a cloud some 600 ft in diameter that would deliver 1500 times an infectious dose to about 30,000 people.

In 1941 T. Rosebury, then at Fort Detrick, recommended that the aerosol method of dissemination was the most promising. Limited attacks could possibly be mounted using small aerosol generators. This could have special significance for such situations as attacks on military headquarters, parliament buildings, etc.—even a ship at sea.

It is necessary to examine more closely the possibility of sabotage mentioned above. Concentration of key personnel in certain places, command centres, etc., means that small-scale saboteurs can be effective. The increase in size of slaughter-houses, food processing plants, etc., the increase in population density and the extent of communications and mobility all combine to make the job of the saboteurs more easy. If a saboteur put half a kilo of salmonella into 5 million litres of water in a reservoir, drinking 100 ml could result in serious infection. To achieve the same effect, 10 tons of potassium cyanide would be required.

Of the three methods considered, vector transmission is the least probable.

6. Infectivity on the whole must be fairly high, but this is dependent on the type of agent used. Viruses, which are very small, may show a larger variation in infectivity than bacteria for BW use. A high infectivity is more critical for bacteria as they are generally bigger, and a greater amount of material has to be taken in to cause infection. It is the amount of agent which has to be absorbed which is of significance here. Some organisms are extremely potent; in the case of Q fever, for example, one organism may be sufficient to cause infection. Infective doses of smallpox and dengue fever are of the same order. For plague (*Pasteurella pestis*) only a few organisms (about 2000) may be necessary for infection to be effected. Tularemia (less than 50 organisms) is another organism of possible interest. More infectious strains of all the organisms mentioned can be produced by the techniques described in the section on the production of the biological weapon. Anthrax, another disease bacterium (causing infection with some 20,000 bacteria) is a very suitable agent. It possesses the added characteristic of being infective to both animals and to man. Infectivity, unless it is very low, is not necessarily a limiting factor to the use of an organism as a biological weapon. Consideration in relation to other criteria is necessary.

7. Epidemicity is the capacity of an organism, assuming its

initial infection to have been successful, to spread among a population and to infect a large proportion of it. This requirement depends on the situation in which the agent is to be used. For the lone saboteur to be at all effective he would use agents of high epidemicity in the hope of having the maximum effect. This would apply for any covert use as the incidence of the disease could be blamed on a naturally occurring epidemic.

For large- or small-scale use overtly non-epidemic agents are of most use. This avoids the dangers of causing the 'human conflagration' which could result. It is obvious that once a living organism has left its disseminators there is no further control over it. J. Lederberg has pointed out the dangers of this. It is quite possible that the agent could mutate to a lower or a higher virulence. The consequence of this could be an ineffective weapon or an uncontrollable epidemic which could affect friend or foe alike. Despite serious attempts to work out mathematically the possible growth of natural epidemics, so far there is limited success only when small groups are considered. For larger groups the theory breaks down because so many variables are introduced.

The property of epidemicity is not directly dependent on infectivity, which is only one factor involved. This may be seen from studies on plague. Plague has a high epidemicity which is due less to its high infectivity than to its methods of transmission. Plague is most efficient in causing epidemics in the pneumonic form. Airborne transmission is the factor which greatly contributes to the effectiveness of the pulmonary disease. The epidemic usually starts in the bubonic form and this later becomes pneumonic. Bubonic plague is transmitted through rat fleas. Good hygiene can prevent this, but it is less successful against the pneumonic form.

It is unlikely that a non-epidemic agent could initiate an epidemic even if it mutated, but it is impossible to be sure. An interesting example is that of cholera. A strain known as El Tor, which was widely known in Asia and thought to be static, has caused recent outbreaks, according to the World Health Organisation (1967). The reason for this sudden epidemic spread is unknown. Natural organisms vary in the course of their history. The influenza epidemics are a case in point. These show a rough periodicity. Once every fifty years or so, a severe epidemic breaks out. They seem to have their origin in southern Russia. Despite intensive studies of the 1957/58 pandemic, its severity and prevalence, although feared, could not be predicted. The information gained from this pandemic is unlikely to be of much predictive value.

In addition to the problem of the size of the epidemic there is also the possibility that it may be retroactive. This may arise for several reasons. The first of these is the epidemic spread to neighbouring countries. The second is that due to air travel and the speed of modern communications infected people could rapidly be dispersed all over the world. (Smallpox has been brought to England from India and Pakistan in this way.) A third possibility is that vectors could be spread even to the country of the attacker. It is easier to exclude people than it is to exclude insects.

There would appear to be some doubt concerning the possibility of disease vectors being spread in this way.

Dr. Stockard, chief of the U.S. Aid Missions (Preventive Medical Section) in Vietnam maintains that the odds that the plague will be carried to America are pretty small despite the growing traffic of ships and planes.

But a five-day rodent and parasite seminar held last week by the WHO in Geneva, had other ideas.

The dangers of plague recurring will increase with the growth in size and number of the world's cargo planes. They could convey, as ships now do, a clandestine passenger list of rats. . . .

Both rats and fleas set on the move in Vietnam's multiplying bomb-sites and uncollected refuse are enjoying a nauseous freedom.

The danger will grow acute as growing urbanisation brings the city rat closer to wild rodents.

[*Sunday Times*, 30 October 1966]

Vectors need not be the means of dissemination originally employed. If an aerosol is spread over a wide area, then in addition to people being affected, insects, rats and other vectors would be contaminated. In this fashion diseases could be spread by vectors other than the normal ones.

For plant diseases obviously the agent of highest effectiveness is used. If the main crop of a defender is different from that of the attacker, then epidemic agents may be used with relative impunity.

8. Virulence is the property of the strain of organism used which determines whether fatality or incapacitating effects predominate in the people affected. A virulent organism is one which would produce serious symptoms in a high proportion of the people infected. A disease which is variable in expression is very unlikely to be used, for example, Rocky Mountain Spotted Fever.

Biological weapons may be classified into two very loose groups on the basis of their effect: (*a*) fatal and (*b*) incapacitating.

(*a*) Fatal diseases cause death in the majority of the subjects infected usually with little residual incapacitation in survivors.

Pasteurella pestis (plague) is in this category. It is usually fatal for 65–85% or more of those affected. In this respect it is well above the criterion for military usefulness quoted in section (1). A virulent strain of anthrax is also known, producing more than 80% fatalities in the population infected.

(*b*) Incapacitating diseases, such as tularemia or Q fever, cause upwards of 65% incapacitation. For these, low fatality of about 5–10% may be expected.

The above statements must be qualified, however. For tularemia a fatality of 5–8% is generally only true where treatment is available. In other conditions, the death rate may be as high as 30%. An illustration of the variation due to specific conditions is Rocky Mountain Spotted Fever, which can show a fatality range of 20–80%.

To describe a disease as producing particular effects is impossible. Variations in the target population, its general health and other characteristics can cause unprecedented effects with respect to the percentage of fatalities incurred. The examples cited all refer to normally occurring strains; the effects of biologically altered strains are totally unknown (see section on the production of the biological weapon pp 275–82), and any definite statement about the virulence and effects of any disease must therefore be considered very carefully.

Of the classes of biological agent originally discussed, both the microbiological weapons and the toxins are equally useful. Toxins are more stable than organisms as they are not living. They are good lethal agents. Plant diseases used would be aimed at preventing crops from being utilised.

It seems extremely unlikely that incapacitating agents would be used in any situation in war. It has been shown in the past that application of less than lethal weapons against populations can stiffen rather than decrease resistance. An example of this was the German bombing of London, which had little effect on the war effort and, contrary to expectations, even boosted morale. It seems from the number of papers produced on the subject that there is a keener military interest in the more lethal agents. Of the agents the Americans have definitely standarised and have ready for use, there are two incapacitants and one highly lethal agent (greater than 90% mortality). The incapacitants may be brucellosis and tularemia. The lethal agent is most probably anthrax, of which a highly virulent strain is known. These are for use in normal military situations.

Epidemic agents if contemplated for use are unlikely to be standardised in this fashion.

9. Stability is the characteristic which allows an agent to be used and the duration of its effects to be predicted. We have previously mentioned stability in storage and in dissemination. What we are more concerned with here is the effects after the agent has reached its target. We have already discussed the property of epidemicity. It is instructive to consider anthrax, a spore forming agent. Anthrax spores, despite changes in temperature and humidity, etc., may remain effective for considerable lengths of time. The effects on the island of Gruinard mentioned previously, which will be infected 'for 100 years', should be remembered. Such persistency could be a considerable embarrassment militarily because after the attack when the attacker's own troops advanced they would be exposed to the danger of infection.

In this respect the bacterial toxins are of great significance. Botulinus toxin is inactivated within 12 hrs. For agents like this decontamination is possible. There is in addition no problem of epidemic spread. This is undoubtedly the reason for their popularity with the allies in the last war.

Examples of the lack of stability are illustrated by the following: In the case of the influenza virus each new appearance of the A-type is the advent of a new disease. Several variants have been distinguished: the initial, active from 1932–44; the A prime, 1947–57; and the Asian virus, 1957–58.

It is not yet clear how or where the virus remains dormant while undergoing change. Another instructive example of change in a natural epidemic is the case of myxomatosis in Australia. This was purposely released in 1950. The strain originally came from Brazil, where it had little effect on the local population of rabbits. In Australia it was 99·8% fatal. Within a few years, however, several strains had made their appearance. Some of these were 90% or more fatal, others about 30%. The 90% fatality strains were rapid acting, the less lethal strains slower in effect. This gave opportunities for mosquitoes to bite the victims and spread the disease to other animals. This meant that the less virulent strain became established by natural selection. An equilibrium of about 90% mortality was attained. Similarly in Europe in the Department of Eure et Loire, France, in May 1952 one or two rabbits were released with myxomatosis. By the end of 1953 this had spread through twenty-six Departments in France and through Holland, Belgium, Germany and Switzerland. Sometime later it arrived in England. This disease killed between 60 and 90 per cent of the rabbit population.

The above have been cited (see *Scientist and Citizen*, August/

September 1967) as examples of the terrible effectiveness of biological weapons. This is however, questionable. Rabbits do not have the
capability to immunise themselves or to practise elaborate hygiene
or sanitary precautions. These examples are more instructive as
illustrations of the dangers due to instability of epidemic agents.
Extrapolations to man are impossible and invalid. A further
example of topical interest is that of foot and mouth disease. This is
a viral disease which seems to have a high stability even in the soil.
Its effects in the 1968 outbreak in Britain were disastrous, even in
spite of the elaborate precautions taken to prevent its spread. Even
after the initial outbreak had been contained a second emergence
of the disease occurred in some cleared areas. It should be emphasised that to predict the course of a disease it is necessary to know
what changes can occur, whether it is in any way persistent and what
possible vectors could be infected. It may be seen from the above
that, on our present knowledge of any of these three things, this is
impossible.

The above is one of the strongest arguments against the use of
these weapons. Biological warfare is a danger to the attacker as well
as being possibly catastrophic for the attacked. It is unlikely in a
normal situation that biological warefare could wipe out humanity.
It is, however, impossible in any way to be sure about this. Use of
chemical, nuclear, radiological and biological warfare in combination could jeopardise man's survival. The final result is impossible
to predict but it would be unfortunate if this hypothesis was ever
tested.

In conclusion, it may be seen that there are several characteristics
which biological weapons must possess. The two most probable
types of agents for use are the toxins and the bacteriological
weapons. Plant diseases and defoliants are likely to be of limited
application. It is useful to consider which classes of microbiological
agents would be most likely. Current opinion seems to favour
bacteriological rather than viral or rickettsial agents. Viruses cannot
repair any damage incurred outside their hosts as they have no
metabolism. Many viruses are also rapidly inactivated outside their
hosts. Cultivation usually requires the cultivation of the specific
hosts and these are more difficult to produce than bacteria. Viruses
reside in the cells of the host, where they are protected from the
body's defences. Viruses hidden in this way can continue to multiply
even after the symptoms of the disease have disappeared. This means
that the host's body defences are continually stimulated, conferring
long-lasting immunity. Points in their favour militarily are firstly
that they are unaffected by antibiotics and secondly they are sus-

ceptible to manipulation (see the later section on the production of biological weapons); they are also effective in small quantities.

Of the viruses and rickettsiae (simple organisms morphologically similar to some viruses but possessing a rudimentary metabolism) several have been considered for BW use. Such a variety of viruses are known which are capable of radical change when they are manipulated genetically that it is impossible to predict which are likely to be of importance. At the Pugwash Conference on Biological and Chemical Warfare in 1959 the viruses which were thought to be of possible use were smallpox, and some of the arbor viruses. Respiratory viruses and enteritic viruses were thought to be unlikely as agents. One suspects that at this time too little information was available to make good assessment possible. The rickettsiæ such as Rocky Mountain Spotted Fever, Q fever, etc., were not thought to be of much use. These are susceptible to antibiotics and many are extremely labile outside their hosts. This type of agent causes interesting diseases of high mortality but transmission is usually by means of vectors. To use these efficiently it would be necessary to disseminate them in aerosol.[1]

Bacteria and toxins are at present the most useful weapons. There are, however, no organisms even among the bacteria which are ideal for biological warfare. If this were the whole story, then they would have practically no potential as weapons. It is because they are living material and can be manipulated and altered that they have any use at all. Here the description 'public health in reverse' takes on its greatest meaning.

To produce a biological weapon the aim is to breed into organisms all those characteristics most feared by doctors. Drug resistance, high virulence and so on are the aims of the BW researchers. The methods of achieving them are discussed in the next section.

2. PRODUCTION OF THE BIOLOGICAL WEAPON

The author apologises for the difficulty in this section to non-scientists. He has done what he could to alleviate it but it is impossible to do this completely. The author has assumed that the reader knows what bacteria and viruses are and what they do.

Many of the points discussed here refer to common microbiological problems. In our original document some critics said it was inessential. The author disagreed then and he still does now. The techniques described are quite standard but the approach to them of the BW practitioner is very different from the normal. The dis-

[1] Some success in producing aerosolised infective viruses and rickettsiæ has been recorded at Fort Detrick. To write these off as BW agents may be premature, especially in the case of Q Fever.

cussion might be of more use to people with little biological knowledge.

We have already shown that many characteristics of organisms are necessary for BW use. Genetic manipulation is the means by which the agents can be altered to fit the particular criteria in which they are unsuitable.

Perhaps the disease most suited for use in BW is melioidosis. This disease has no known treatment, no vaccine, does not respond to antibiotics therapy and is almost invariably fatal. It is, however, rare and insufficiently studied.

There are some 160 or so infectious diseases known to man. For one disease organism, *Pasteurella pestis*, in 1959 more than 140 different strains were known. There is thus a wide variety of possibilities for alteration should the ideal not be immediately apparent. The relevant techniques are discussed below. They are considered under three headings: (*a*) alterations in growth medium; (*b*) mutation; (*c*) gene transfer; (*d*) virus manipulation.

Alterations in growth medium

(*a*) Alteration of the growth medium can have several effects. It may be used in selection for certain types of bacteria. The medium may sometimes produce specific effects on the structure of the organism. More usually, tolerance to such environmental factors as temperature or humidity may be produced. In some cases virulent strains may be selected. A neurovirulent strain of poliomyelitis virus (which normally produces clinical effects in 0.5–5.0% of the population) has been developed by growth in tissue culture at 41°C.

In general, strains of bacteria are more susceptible to change when grown in artificial media. By altering the growth medium of *Clostridium botulinum* (adding trypsin) the potency of toxin type E is increased 40–400 times. This is not a general case. More usually, decreased virulence results from artificial growth. Mutagenesis in certain media may have the effect of apparently producing higher mutation rates, as a selective advantage may be given to some of the strains produced. The more usual effects on a growing culture of bacteria concern selection of strains altered with respect to their response to the environment. Growing *Brucella suis* on yeast extracts from different sources produces organisms which show a variability in survival at high and low humidity.

There are limitations at present in the use of alterations of the medium. Certain organisms cannot be grown in artificial media at all; syphilis for example must live inside a human host (though recently this obstacle has been overcome for this particular disease). It is also a characteristic of certain viruses that they do not grow well outside the host, for example, the agent causing infectious hepatititis.

Alteration of the growth medium has its greatest effect in selecting more virulent strains. By suspending bacteria in the correct medium their viability in aerosol may be enhanced; for instance, if chloride is excluded from the medium, tularemia organisms do not lose their infectivity for 20 hours.

Mutation

(b) Mutation means an alteration in the hereditary material of an organism (the process is called mutagenesis). There is a certain natural mutation rate for each individual gene of an organism. Naturally such rates are low, otherwise impermissible alterations in the genetic structure would occur and genetic continuity would not be maintained. Natural mutation rates may be increased by several means. These can be divided into two main classes: chemical mutagens and irradiation (by ultra-violet, X-ray and gamma radiation).

It is currently believed that we cannot induce gene specific mutagenesis (that is, mutations at a particular site causing a specific enhancement or depression of the activity or production of a particular gene product, leaving the rest of the genome untouched). Irradiation mutagenesis causes random breakages and cross-linkages of genetic structure. Chemical mutagens can, to some degree, cause a particular *type* of mutation, for example it is thought ICR 191 causes frame-shift mutations in bacteria. The usual effect of mutation on a mildly virulent strain seems to be to decrease virulence. Few mutations with increased virulence are found. This makes isolation of mutants more difficult than it may seem at first consideration. Even with irradiation to 95–98% death of the organisms treated, only perhaps 5% of those recovered, will be mutant. Even fewer of these, if any, will be mutant to increased virulence. Pathogenicity (the ability of an organism to harm its host) has been shown to be very complex. Two distinct types of pathogenic bacteria can be distinguished, those which produce toxins, which actually cause the disease, and those which do not. It has been suggested that pathogens which do not produce toxins act by a similar mechanism to auto-immune diseases, that is, they stimulate the body to damage itself. Thus it is impossible, on the basis of our current knowledge, to see any way of increasing the pathogenicity genetically, especially as several genetic factors are at work. In such cases it may be that mutation of several factors at once is necessary to increase virulence, and so most mutations will lead to reduced virulence.

Even if selection of mutants is effective through several generations of growth, what tends to occur is that other undesired effects creep into the strains used. For example a mutant with increased virulence is obtained, but this result is accompanied by lower stability (or increased temperature sensitivity, etc.) than the original. As one selects through several generations in which mutagenesis has been practised, one may expect to pick up mutations in other than the gene one wishes to mutate. This is a consequence of the random nature of the process. By means of subculturing a bovine strain of *Koch bacillus* (causing tuberculosis) on potatoes which had been boiled in beef bile, a strain of low virulence was obtained. This was the BCG vaccine.

The oldest way of selecting for virulent organisms used a similar technique in reverse. A strain, isolated from an animal with an acute disease, is passed through a succession of animals. In each case the animal developing most rapidly the severest symptoms is chosen to pass the strain on. The agents, virus or bacteria, are taken from this animal and used to infect several others, the most ill of these is taken and the process repeated to infect another group. By picking the bacteria or virus from a particular organ, for instance the lung, a particularly virulent strain for that organ can be selected. Other techniques can be used to select for particular strains.

Of particular importance are selection procedures by which the immunological characteristics of a bacterium could be altered. The body's antibody defences depend on recognition of the invading bacterium, especially its external coat. If the antigenic (antibody stimulating) characteristics of the bacterium are different from the vaccine injected previously, the vaccine will have had no effect in conferring protection. The antibodies stimulated by the vaccine will not be able to recognise the incoming bacteria. Thus vaccination may be rendered ineffective.

A second consequence of this is that the quickest detection method (the FAB technique) depends on a dye-labelled antibody recognising the bacterium. A few per cent of some bacterial cultures can cause a little reaction with the specific antibody—a cross-reaction. This can cause confusion in some cases. The removal of the antigenic properties of the bacterium may mean that a cross-reaction could be confused with recognition, and definite recognition could be prevented (this is discussed further in the section on defence).

(c) Gene transfer

Transfer of the hereditary material may be performed in several ways. All are possible in the laboratory and have been performed there.

1. Transformation

This technique involves the transfer of the DNA (*only*) of one bacterium into another. An event there occurs by which incorporation of some of the incoming DNA into the host cell DNA is effected. This treatment causes integration of a small part of the bacterial genetic material into another bacterium. This technique is used in the laboratory, but for genetic transfer other techniques are probably more useful for BW purposes.

2. Transduction

This is another transfer of genes, in this case mediated by a bacteriophage (a virus which attacks bacteria) from one bacterium to another. This is quite a rare event, but larger numbers of genes are transferred than in transformation. A bacteriophage may be present in association with its host's DNA. It may remain dormant for several generations. Then the period of lysogeny, as this association is called, terminates, and new virus particles are formed. Sometimes portions of the host's chromosome are incorporated into the virus DNA and may then, in the virus particle (DNA with a coat of protein), be passed to another bacterium. This process results in the transfer of genes close to where the phage is incorporated into the host DNA. Thus one has a possibility of transfer of a restricted set of genes. In transformation it is largely a matter of chance which genes are transferred; almost any information on the DNA can be passed.

3. Conjugation

This process involves exploiting the ability of certain bacteria to mate sexually. A tube is formed between one bacterium and another. This is followed by one cell (the male donor) passing its DNA down the tube to another cell (the female recipient). By a process not yet understood, some of the donor cell genes become part of the recipient's cell chromosome. This transfer is made possible by a factor usually present in the cytoplasm (the F factor) which initiates tube formation, followed by a sequential transfer of genes. Usually the cells break apart before the whole of the donor cell DNA has entered the recipient. This means that, as the circular DNA breaks in one spot, and one end always goes in first, some genes are very rarely transferred. However, in different strains of bacterium factors may attach at different places on the DNA, hence a variety of genes can be transferred between different bacterial strains if mating can be induced. By means such as this, virulence or drug resistance may be transferred between bacterial strains of the same species, for example streptomycin resistance in *Escherischia coli*. Attempts are being made to effect gene transfer between different species of closely related bacteria. This could have considerable BW significance.

4. Resistance transfer factors (RTFs)

These are particles present in the bacterial cytoplasm, related to the F factors mentioned above. They initiate tube formation between bacteria, rapidly replicate and are transferred among members of a bacterial colony very quickly. They confer antibiotic immunity to a bacterium in which they are present. An example of the effectiveness of their transfer can be cited from hospital data, in conditions where attempts were being made to remove organisms by the most effective methods known.

In 1957 *Shigella dysenteriae* bacteria (causing bacillary dysentery) were isolated from hospital cases by the Japanese and found to be resistant to conventional antibiotics. They were, moreover, concomitantly resistant to usually more than two antibiotics (in this case streptomycin, chloramphenicol, tetracycline and sulphonamide). In 1959 10% of the *Shigella* strains isolated were resistant to all four drugs. To date resistance has risen to above 50% of the strains of the bacterial population (a recent resistance to ampicillin has also been noted). In this case, occurring in natural conditions, it is believed that *Escherischia coli*, a normally harmless gut bacterium, transferred its resistance to antibiotics to *Shigella* strains (pathogenic organisms). Such an occurrence is potentially extremely dangerous and reduces the value of modern chemotherapeutic methods. This is now occurring in other species, and it has been shown to obtain for *Salmonella typhi* in a strain isolated in Britain.

The significance of this process lies in the *multiple* resistance and its transfer *between* different *species* of bacteria, a feature this process possesses in common with transformation (under such conditions not very effective). This makes it a most powerful, perhaps the most powerful, technique for producing resistant strains of bacteria. In America this technique has been tried in resistance transfer on, for example, *Pasteurella pestis*. It would seem that American research workers may also succeed in overcoming the decrease in virulence often associated with this process.

(d) Virus manipulation

There are essentially two types of virus manipulation likely to be considered suitable: alteration of the protein coat of a virus and alteration in the DNA of the virus.

(1) Protein coat alteration

Normally a virus infecting an animal is recognised by the particular structure of the coat protein around its hereditary material (DNA). Laboratory experiments have shown that it is possible to separate the protein coat from the DNA (or RNA). The technique considered here involves the separation for two different viruses, one pathogenic and one non-pathogenic. The pathogenic virus DNA is then reconstituted with the non-pathogenic protein coat. There is reason to believe that infectivity will remain at a useful level. There are two possible results to be obtained from this process: (a) disguising the virus as a non-pathogenic organism to by-pass the body's defences, and (b) providing the virus hereditary material (in this case determining the production of more pathogenic type virus particles) with a coat more likely to withstand the shocks involved in dissemination. The coat is, of course, not reproduced by the virus after infection, but by such a method the mode of infection can be tailored to suit a particular dissemination mechanism, for example tough coats for aerosol dispersal. This method is not yet well developed, and may in fact be more useful in plant infection where viruses are of the RNA type, and seem more amenable to this treatment.

(2) Production of virus hybrids

It was observed (Heubner et al.) that in tissue culture cross-infection with two different viruses may occur. As a result a virus which resembles one of the original viruses in its protein coat (due to alteration in its DNA) and also possesses characteristics of the other virus may be produced. If, by this process of hybridisation (not yet understood), a pathogenic strain gains the DNA of the protein coat of a non-pathogenic strain, it would be suitably disguised to the animal or plant it was infecting. Unlike the case of protein coat alteration, this virus would reproduce the hybrid form, as it involves the incorporation of a particular section of one virus DNA into the other virus genome. This may prove an extremely useful technique in the future development of BW virus agents.

This concludes the section on the production of the biological weapon. A wide variety of techniques are available. All these methods are probably the subject of research for BW purposes, and may be used to alter any unsuitable characteristics of a given organism to requirements described in the section dealing with the attributes of a useful weapon.

Of these techniques conjugation and resistance transfer by factors are probably of most interest to BW researchers at present. It is in the context of this section that the 'pure' research of the BW establishments should be examined. Anthrax (a highly virulent anti-biotic resistant strain has been produced), plague and tularemia have been successfully manipulated by techniques mentioned above. Recently workers from Porton in conjunction with those from Fort Detrick have been concerned in gene transfer between strains of harmless bacteria closely related to plague. This has been described as the way to a weapon 'of genocidal potential'. Amongst other things studied in addition to antibiotic resistance are survival in aerosol for long periods, production of increased virulence, stability, etc. In fact, the accentuation of all the problems that doctors have been trying to eliminate or counter for hundreds of years is the province of the BW researchers.

The present writer confesses himself quite baffled by the mentality of a doctor, whose duty is to preserve life, and who yet can deliberately try to do the opposite, to create mass destruction. He finds himself similarly baffled by the accounts of the physicians at Auschwitz, with whom he thinks there is a close parallel. In both cases their work is the antithesis of what it should be. This is not to say that the writer is against the people engaged in legitimate defensive work so much as the mentality of those concerned in weapon development. In the writer's opinion they may well be assiduously digging the grave of mankind. An indication of their attitude is in a story told by Lord Ritchie Calder, who once asked a scientist involved in 'defence biology' what he was working for. The answer was 'a cure for metabolism'. Recently, a Fort Detrick researcher was awarded the Army's highest award to civilians, the Distinguished Service Medal, for her work on the development of rice blast fungus. This regularly ravages Asian rice crops, causing famine and starvation. One trusts that she is happy in her work and the peak of achievement she has reached.

An American concerned with recruitment said that the problem was that BW people were competing for the same researchers who would be interested in cancer research. The above speaks volumes for the attitudes of those engaged in BW development. How far this is a betrayal and perversion of the aims of science and medicine, probably only scientists and doctors would properly understand. These people seem to have the same criminal negligence towards the consequences of their work as builders of human crematoria would have in concentration camps. Their moral awareness is comparable with that of the Nazi physicians who lacked the courage to disobey orders. The Detrick researchers are volunteers involved in work of similar moral purpose and value.

7

THE USE OF CHEMICAL AND BIOLOGICAL WARFARE

1. CHEMICAL WARFARE

World War 1, 1914–1918

Although Lord Dundonald had advocated gas warfare (by the burning of sulphur to produce sulphur dioxide) in 1811 and this technique was again suggested for Sebastapol in 1855, to render the works at Malakoff and Redan untenable, it was not effectively used until World War I. The argument against its use at Sebastopol was its inhumanity. A later Lord Dundonald, the twelfth earl, revealed to Lord Kitchener in 1914 his grandfather's plans for chemical warfare.

Chronologically, the first use of gas in this war may have been French use of tear gases. However, the first effective use of chemical warfare was against French and British colonial troops in trenches around Ypres on 22 and 24 April 1915. Some 168 tons of chlorine were released from cylinders on a 4-mile front. There resulted 20,000 casualties, of which 5000 were fatal. In the following four weeks the Germans discharged a total of 300 tons of chlorine, causing a further 9000 casualties and 2000 deaths. Little exploitation was made of this advantage. The German High Command had little faith in the new weapon. Fortunately, chlorine is one of the easiest war gases to protect against as it is readily absorbed by a solution of washing soda and photographer's hypo. The first gas masks, consisting of cotton pads soaked in these chemicals, were within a short time issued to the British troops.

Phosgene was later tried by the Germans mixed with chlorine. The attack was expected and gas masks had been previously prepared. The massed German troops suffered huge losses from artillery fire. The Germans rapidly abandoned the idea of using gas cloud attacks, partially because too often the wind was blowing from the British lines, which gave the latter the advantage in applying this technique. Because of this, and the methods they rapidly developed, the Allies retained the upper hand for the rest of the war. This was largely due to superiority in the production of gas masks and in techniques for setting up extremely large concentrations of gas in small areas, and good gas discipline. Allied retaliation was, to judge from German reports of the time, highly effective.

The first gas masks have already been described. One million of these are said to have been made in a single day. The next form of respirator was a flannelette bag worn over the head. This had a celluloid window and the flannelette was soaked in hypo solution and glycerine (which was added to keep it damp). At its highest state of development, this respirator had glass eye-pieces, an outlet valve, and sodium phenate and hexamine were added to protect against phosgene. This was known as the PH helmet. This was largely superseded by the box respirator, which started production early in 1916. The PH helmet finally went out of use in July 1917 after the Germans had started using mustard gas. The gas masks reduced casualties enormously for both sides. German masks were less efficient than the British; their casualties were reputed to have been much higher. It is probable that had the Allies realised its potential, more gas than high explosive munitions would have been produced. Nevertheless at this stage a form of stalemate had been reached.

This situation was somewhat relieved by the invention of the Livens projector. Several hundred or thousands of tubes were buried in the ground at an angle of $45°$. These steel tubes had one open end which faced the enemy. The projectile was a steel drum which carried about 3 gal of liquefied gas. These were fired simultaneously electrically. Thus, all the drums arrived together on a small target. This had two effects. Concentrations were built up too soon for the Germans to don masks, and these concentrations were so high that they saturated the gas absorbent in the masks. From preliminary results from the early attacks, Livens estimated that his technique of killing the enemy cost 16s. per head. As the war was then costing £3 million per day, this was remarkably cheap. The Germans were never quite able to master this method.

After gas clouds, the next method the Germans espoused was the gas shell. The first agent to be used in this way was mustard gas. However, by the time of its introduction, gas masks were very efficient. In the Ypres salient in July 1917 the Germans first used mustard gas shells. Some 50,000 of these were fired, filled with 125 tons of gas. The results from the German point of view were extremely disappointing. There were less than 2500 British casualties from this new weapon and eighty-seven deaths. In the next three weeks, the Germans fired one million rounds of shells containing 2500 tons against the British lines between Nieuport and Armentières. Total casualties were 15,000 with only 500 deaths. Mustard gas was a new departure in gas warfare; it affects through the skin as well as the lungs, and therefore by-passes gas masks. With efficient masks, however, serious casualties are few. The Germans had cause to regret the introduction of mustard as a weapon, because when the Allies retaliated, they used it to much greater effect. The German process for the production of this gas was that of Victor Meyer, which was very complex. The British and French used Guthrie's method, which was much simpler. This was so effective that the French were able to use the gas against the enemy in June 1918; the British in September.

The use of gas shells during the war was essentially a failure. Too much effort was wasted in filling these with lachrymatories. Obviously it is best to use the most effective agents available if shells are to be used at all. The shells at this time could carry 10% of their weight as gas, as opposed to 50% for the Livens projector and 90% for aeroplane bombs. One of the early failures of the gas shell technique was hydrogen cyanide (AC). This compound has a very high toxicity but is dispersed so rapidly that it is of little field use. It took a surprisingly long time for the British and Germans to realise the limitations to the use of the gas shell. It is only useful with highly effective agents.

The next breakthrough was in the development of the toxic smokes. These are the substances DA, DC and DM. Respirators at this time were adequate to deal with any toxic vapour, but they could not deal with smokes. (The distinction between a vapour and a smoke should be explained. The vapour is absorbed by a chemical reaction with the gas mask filling. The smoke by-passes this chemical barrier. A physical barrier is necessary to provide protection.) The effects of the agents dispersed as smokes were sternutatory, causing sneezing or vomiting. The compounds used were DA and DC. The British respirator was modified to give adequate protection. Although the Germans used fourteen million artillery shells containing these agents, their casualty record was slight and deaths were exceedingly rare. Towards the end of the war, in 1918, the French began to employ 'sternite', a mixture of a sternutant and a toxic arsenic compound.

There was, however, worse to come. Professor Roger Adams of the University of Illinois had prepared a new gas, DM—adamsite. This was easier to prepare and was more effective. A thermo-generator bomb was prepared, the M device. This was a great advance on previous techniques as it formed a true smoke. The war finished, however, before the gas, on which high hopes had been pinned, had become ready for effective use. It has had some subsequent application as a weapon of war. For the whole of World War I, the gas casualties totalled 1,296,853 men, of whom 91,198 were killed. The proportion of deaths is given as 7·3% (A. M. Prentiss, *Chemicals in War*).

It is significant that in the first attack some 25% of casualties were fatal.[1] The low final percentage is due to a large extent to the efficiency of protection methods developed during the conflict and the inefficiency of dissemination. At one stage the Germans were using 8 tons of gas to kill one British soldier. On the Russian front the percentage of Allied casualties was much higher—11·8%. This was largely a result of lack of protection and the fact that the wind was more often blowing towards the Russian lines. It is notable that the large figure of gas casualties represented only 5·7% of all the wounded. Only 1·4% of total deaths were due to gas.

Such figures as these—despite the inaccuracy of some of the estimates of casualties involved, for example, those of Austria-Hungary, 3·0%—have been used as an argument for the humaneness of gas warfare. It should be emphasised that in many cases use of gas was experimental, and often ineffective. Many of the protagonists were protected, and no weapons of great toxicity were employed effectively. In view of the reliance placed on the arsenical smokes and mustard gas and the inefficiency of munitions the results of this relatively new weapon were encouraging. The fact that these weapons were inefficiently used in World War 1 does not mean that their effective employment could not occur in a future conflict. Undoubtedly the first experiments with gunpowder were not very effective. To argue from the statistics about the humaneness of gases is meaningless.

The problems which arose in developing gas as a weapon in this period set the pattern for future advances in this field. Consideration of dissemination systems, meteorology, munitions, protection and the agents themselves and their integration into weapons systems and defences, dominate current thought on the subject.

Abyssinia, 1936

The accounts of the use of gas in Abyssinia are not of great interest technically. The Ethiopians attacked were not protected and no novel gases were used. Gas was not used extensively prior to the dispersal of the Ethiopian Army. The agent employed was mustard gas. This was ideal—so was the situation. The hot, dry climate of the Ethiopian table-land, the scanty costumes of the natives, their lack of gas masks, all contributed. The agent was disseminated by spraying from aircraft. It had been realised in World War 1 that aircraft were probably the most promising means by which these

[1] Though these figures may have been inflated for propaganda purposes.

agents could be disseminated. No one had, however, used them in this fashion.

Use of spray or bombs from the air means that maximum use can be made of munitions. The wasteful necessity for propellant charges could be dispensed with. Both the Russians (with hydrogen cyanide) and the Germans had preparations for the use of gas in this fashion should chemical warfare be used in World War II. The most effective height for spraying had been found to be 50–100 ft (A. M. Prentiss). The Italians used groups of 9, 15 and 18 low-flying planes following one another, so that the fog issuing from them formed a continuous cloud. In the words of James Kendall, former liaison officer with the allied services on chemical warfare, 'Against tribesmen with no effective means of defence, it was as easy as spraying fruit orchards in California.'

Yemen, 1963–67

(It is advisable here to refer to Part 1 (pp 6ff), the section dealing with use of gas in the Yemen.)

Having considered the documentary evidence at our disposal, we have come to the conclusion that it is almost certain that gas was used in the Yemen. A certain amount of doubt remains concerning the actual gases used.

The agents were disseminated in bombs. Significantly, it has been noted that in these reports craters due to these weapons were in general shallow. In addition they were largely downwind of the target. This is consistent with gas weapons having been used.

There are two incidents which have been considered in detail. The first of these is the attack on Kitaf on 5 January 1967. As a result of this incident a medical report was produced by a team of Saudi Arabian doctors. The symptoms described by these as seen in the survivors follow.

Body pains, difficulty in breathing, coughing, dizziness, burning sensation in the lungs, and spitting of blood. Tests showed additional findings; inflammation of the eye and throat, accumulation of fluid in the tissue of throat and lungs, low blood pressure and rapid pulse.

These symptoms and signs are consistent with the effects of nerve gas, but they are also consistent with the effects of other chemical agents.

[Cf. J. D. Salvia, *Scientist and Citizen*, August/September 1967]

It is impossible to let this extraordinary statement pass without comment. Symptoms will be dealt with in turn.

Dizziness, difficulty in breathing and coughing are possible results of nerve gas poisoning. Body pains, burning sensation in the lungs and spitting of blood are totally inconsistent with the effects of any known nerve agent. Inflammation of the eye and throat, accumulation of fluid in the tissues of the throat and lungs (pulmonary oedema) are utterly at variance with known effects of nerve gases. The other effects, low blood pressure and rapid pulse, in conjunction with the first rule out nerve gas application completely.

Nerve agents, unless this alleged one is quite novel, normally cause slowing of the heart rate and an increase in blood pressure. The fact that the Saudi Arabian doctors could draw the conclusion quoted above must cast serious doubts on their scientific ability.

One could conclude from the above symptoms that any one of a wide variety of agents may have been used. The symptoms are not inconsistent with the effects of vesicants or the acute lung irritants. From the high number of fatalities which reportedly occurred, a lethal agent of high effectiveness appears to have been used.

In addition to the victims, some carcasses, a blood sample and some allegedly contaminated cloth were examined. Autopsy of two of the animals revealed: 'The pectoral cavity was found to be filled with a bloody whey-like fluid.' This post-mortem finding is not consistent with nerve gas poisoning. It may have been that the carcass was in an advanced state of decay; partial decomposition of the other two animals had rendered these unfit for testing. The normal cause of death in nerve gas poisoning is asphyxia: in this case it would seem that extensive oedema had resulted.

The doctors claim to have conducted an analysis of the blood of the goat (the animal under examination) and to have demonstrated a significantly increased level of organic phosphate. In the normal case of nerve gas poisoning, as the agent is effective in such small quantities, no significant increase in the organic phosphate level in the blood may be expected. They describe the level found in this animal as 'an extremely high proportion in relation to the normal average for ruminants'.

Of the 200 survivors of this attack and twelve at Taif. only one blood sample was taken. The results of this are once again difficult to interpret. A comparison of the figures given for normal phosphorous levels in this case and those which would be expected according to current literature reveals no agreement. Possible difficulties may have arisen in translation.

It was also claimed that the fragments of cloth 'revealed traces of organic phosphoric compounds which laboratory examination showed to have the effect of reducing blood cholinesterase. This is one of the poisonous groups of organo-phosphorous compounds.' Concerning this report, without quantitative data and a description of the assay methods, it is impossible to give any credence to it. Sophisticated biochemical analysis is necessary, involving the use of facilities which one might not expect to find normally in hospitals such as those at Najran and Taif. Such small quantities are involved that identification is extremely difficult without the use of mass spectrometers and other sophisticated apparatus.

The presence of nerve gas poisoning is extremely difficult to demonstrate if a period of over a week is allowed to elapse. Perhaps the best test immediately applicable is the administration of atropine to the survivors, of whom there were many. This was a technique that was applied on the sheep accidentally poisoned at Dugway. This results in partial or complete alleviation of the symptoms.

To assay for nerve gas poisoning organic phosphate content is not measured. The nerve gas itself is present in so small a quantity that it cannot be easily detected. It is the fall in acetylcholinesterase activity which is examined. A sample for analysis might quite adequately be provided by a drop of blood allowed to evaporate and dry out on a filter paper. An analysis on this may be performed up to a week after the initial incident. It may be very difficult to demonstrate acetylcholinesterase depression. The enzyme is slowly reactivated. The difficulty may be gathered from the fact that, even in the case of the sheep affected at Dugway, there was for some time considerable difficulty in getting agreement that nerve gas had been involved. This was using the best facilities available and highly trained people. The fact that the Saudi Arabian claim to have successfully demonstrated the cholinesterase activity depression must be viewed with suspicion.

Examination of the survivors and use of atropine to relieve symptoms would have been more useful. Tests on the blood of survivors should have been performed as soon after the attack as possible or the samples should have been stored in a manner similar to the one suggested. An example of the difficulty comes from a consideration of the fact that sarin causes depression of acetylcholinesterase only for a day after the exposure. Reactivation occurs within a few days and the effects are undetectable. Reactivation may also occur in samples for testing. With tabun inhibition may be prolonged, and is therefore easier to detect. Autopsy usually shows no gross pathological changes especially of the kind referred to in the report.

In *Scientist and Citizen*, August/September 1967, Mr. J. D. Salvia, in an article which was prepared in collaboration with members of the committee for Environmental Information, Scientific Division, states in explanation of the high organic phosphorous concentration;

Absorption also takes place through the skin, and if a person or goat were standing directly adjacent to the exploding bomb, his body surface might be liberally sprayed by the compound. In such a case absorption might continue through the skin long enough to raise blood phosphorous levels to some degree.

The authors would point out that in the human case cited the victim was still alive. Had he absorbed sufficient nerve gas for his phosphate level to be significantly raised his demise would have been achieved with spectacular swiftness.

Some additional criticisms can be made. The casualty figures given of 150 killed and 200 hospitalised are not what one would expect from the use of nerve gas. Because the difference between incapacitation and lethality is so small one would expect a much greater proportion of fatalities relative to the total number affected.

It is also doubtful whether, if non-persistent nerve agents were used, they would remain on scraps of cloth in an active condition for any length of time. If a persistent agent were used and contaminated substances were handled without suitable protective clothing, precautions and decontamination together with experience with these substances (none of which was mentioned), then fatalities would most certainly result amongst those involved in collection.

It is a great pity that the Saudi Arabian doctors should have attempted so desperately to prove that nerve gas was used in this instance. It is also a pity that Mr J. D. Salvia was not more critical. It is quite obvious that a poison gas has been used at Kitaf. It is equally obvious that this could not have been a nerve agent. The question therefore is what agent has in fact been used.

It would seem on the evidence given that the gas used on Kitaf was not mustard. The spitting of blood is not a characteristic result of mustard gas poisoning. Possible candidates include lewisite, and the lung irritants. Lewisite and the lung irritants, trichlorethylchloroformate and chloropicrin, seem unlikely. Lewisite causes vesication, which was not noted. It seems probably that the gas concerned was phosgene or phosgene plus chlorine. It is impossible to say with certainty, without autopsy results.

It should be emphasised that our criticism of the Saudi Arabian report neither proves nor disproves the use of nerve gas in the Yemen. Our comment should only be viewed in the light of the evidence on this one incident.

The second incident concerns the attack on Gahar on 10 May 1967. The International Red Cross was present shortly after the attack. This is well documented and very little can be said in addition.

The report and autopsy findings of this incident were submitted

to the University of Berne Institute of Forensic Medicine. Their
conclusion was that nerve gas had not been used, but that a toxic
gas had been used. The pattern of effects is different from those
observed at Kitaf, where there was evidence of heavy pulmonary
oedema. This is a characteristic of the effects of phosgene. The
picture on autopsy of the lungs of cases from Gahar shows a less
marked oedematous response. For phosgene the oedema is massive
and fluid drips from the lungs on sectioning. In this case, despite
the lack of reports of vesication (which is a normal characteristic of
the effects of the mustard gases), this was probably the agent used.
The smell of garlic noted on opening one of the communal graves
supports this. In conclusion, it is quite clear that toxic gases, probably phosgene and mustard gas, have been used against the Yemen
Royalists.

It has been a disquieting feature of this conflict that both sides
have attempted to confuse and mislead the rest of the world. The
attractions of this method of warfare for the UAR are obvious. It is
admirably suited to this type of counter-insurgency operation in
addition to being cheap and highly effective. The decision to use
gas may have been influenced by the precedent which had been set
earlier by the Italians.

One factor leading to the use of CW in the Yemen may have been
the attitude of the USA. As early as 1962 the USSR had accused the
USA of setting a dangerous precedent with the use of defoliants which
Izvestia described as 'a poisonous gas'. The ambiguity of US policy on
the use of chemical weapons undoubtedly helped create the climate
in which the UAR felt it possible to use gas without fear of international censure. The fact that they had made use of gases as early as
1963, without there being any public outcry, illustrates this well.

Vietnam 1961

The discussion which follows will deal only with gases, since
herbicides and defoliants have already been considered at length
(pp 223–52).

We have already discussed the effects of the gases used in Vietnam
in some detail. Comment is therefore restricted to certain aspects of
the accounts of use itself. The sources of much of our information
from both sides may not be reliable. Bearing this in mind, we have
attempted to assess these reports in the light of known facts.

The gases admitted to have been used in Vietnam are DM, CS and
CN. We have quoted in full the description of these gases given by

Mr McNamara. These should be examined in the light of the official descriptions of their effects given earlier from various military sources.

In the initial publicitiy in March 1965 these were described variously as 'non-lethal', 'tear gases' or 'riot control agents'. These gases are not non-lethal but in an open situation one would expect very few casualties. The tear gas effect is the primary action but other results such as lung damage, eye damage and death can and do occur.

There are three major ways in which these gases have been used:

1. Riot control

This is the situation to which Mr Rusk was referring at his press conference on 24 March 1965, 'riot control or situations analogous to riot control'. He stated at the time that in the three incidents of its use to date, the gas was dissipated by the wind and had not achieved its purpose. The last known case of its use in this fashion was on the citadel at Hué during the Tet offensive. It is extremely unlikely in view of the above that this is how it is mainly used.

2. Use against people in confined spaces

It has been frequently reported that gas is used to flush the Vietcong out of bunkers. One report states that it is standard practice on entering a village. A device has been developed which can be used to blow gas at a very high rate into tunnels, etc. This device, called the 'Mighty Mite', when used in large tunnel systems with adequate ventilation may not cause serious effects. Its use on small shelters could cause lethal concentrations to be built up before the occupants could get out. Another important point concerning use in this situation is the effect of panic which can result in the jamming of exits, etc.

In addition to this, as the occupants of the shelters cannot be determined before gas is used, women, children, the old and the sick may be exposed to very high concentrations. The qualifications given in official military sources regarding the effects of these agents refer to 'standard' men. They can in no way predict the effects on, for example, children. Reports from Vietnam issued by the NLF and DRVN indicate that the majority of casualties due to gas occur among the classes mentioned above; for instance in the attack on Vinh Quang. (Out of 54 casualties 26 were women and 28 children —35 died as a result.) These casualties were distributed as one would expect. The figure of 35 dead, however, seems high for the agent used. This seems to be the pattern in all cases of this use. Despite the abnormally high casualty figures, which may have been inflated (as might have been predicted), these gases affect the adult Vietcong least. There seems no doubt that a number of fatalities have resulted from the use of gas in this fashion.

Dr Vennema's letter supports this. The gas which is most likely to have been responsible for the 10% mortality amongst adults and the 90% amongst children is DM or DM/CN. The use of the gas mixture may be expected to have graver consequences than either gas alone. It should be remembered that fatalities can occur amongst fit men if DM alone is used in riot control situations. Its effects in a mixture with CN would be expected to be severe. The same would be true of CS, though to lesser degree. These qualifications apply equally to the third situation in which gas has been used.

3. *Application of large concentrations over an extremely large area*
This is a technique which is admirably illustrated by the raid in Tayninh mentioned in the first part. Here 80-lb drums were dropped with explosive charges attached to cause a rapid build-up of a very high concentration over an area of a few square miles. It will be realised that a person caught in the middle of such a cloud will receive a large dose of the gas. In the case of Tayninh, it would not seem to have been very effective.

A further type of use is in conjunction with air attacks. The purpose here is to drive the Vietcong into the open where they will be easy targets for pattern bombing or the use of anti-personnel weapons. As the Americans have not yet developed a gas which will selectively force out the Vietcong, the whole population will be expected to suffer in the event of such an attack.

These are several allegations concerning the use of gases other than those mentioned above. Vietnamese, American and French sources are responsible for such reports. These are dealt with in turn. Dr. Nguyen, who was quoted in Part 1 (p. 29), alleged the use of both CN and CA. CA is available to US forces as a tear gas. Although more dangerous than CN, there would seem to be no barrier to its use. Without knowing the method of analysis by which this gas was identified, it is impossible to comment. Its use must be a distinct, possibility. Dr Nguyen also mentioned the use of a gas which had the characteristics of chloroform. This, one suspects, may easily have been CNS, which is a mixture of CN, chloropicrin and chloroform. Chloropicrin is an acute lung irritant, and a lethal agent.

It is possible that the description in *Le Monde*, 14 January and 13 January 1966 (Trung Lap) refers to a more acute irritant than CN. It is here described as a gas which when it catches bare arms or exposed areas of skin causes a pain as if burnt. This may be the effects of CN or CS in a tropical climate, but could be that of a stronger irritant. The effects of these gases, one might suspect, would be worse in high humidity.

A third more serious case was reported in March 1966 by Pierre Darcourt in *L'Express*. This referred to the use of the gas BZ. US officials have denied its use in Vietnam. Darcourt referred to 'grenades' of BZ. The agent is not available in hand-grenades, according to *Chemical Reference Handbook* of the Department of the Army (January 1967).[1] It is, however, possible that this use was experimental. This would not be the first time that the Pentagon had defied the State Department and initiated the testing of chemical weapons. Despite warnings to the contrary, testing of defoliants in Thailand was undertaken by the Army in direct opposition to the State Department's wishes. It may be possible that other agents are being tested in Vietnam. Candidates for this are the nerve gases and LSD 25. Such tests would be subject to the highest security classification. It is rumoured that tests have occurred on the Vietnamese border with Cambodia in Tayninh province. It should be emphasised that observers on the border from neutral countries have not notified cases of this.

We would point out that all these cases are based on a very small amount of evidence. Since the use of gas has been admitted, allegations which could previously have been dismissed as fantastic can no longer be dismissed quite so easily. The American equivocal position with respect to international law and the Pentagon's disinclination to be influenced by the State Department, in addition to the initiative allowed to field commanders, must give rise to grave fears.

It is possible that experimentation in the use of these agents could occur without the knowledge of the policy makers. Attempts by the Army Chemical Corps which in the past have been successful in influencing members of the Senate must also be taken into account. The initial use of gas in Vietnam was a major victory for the apologists of this form of warfare.

As an illustration of the extent of misinformation of the State Department, Mr Dean Rusk's statements in March 1965 are an excellent example. Misinformation is a more likely explanation than the fact that Mr Rusk was lying while in full position of the facts because, first, the State Department had not been consulted on the initial use of gas, and, secondly, these statements would be easily demonstrated to be true or, as it is shown below, manifestly untrue.

---

[1] This should, however, be qualified, as the *Wall Street Journal* in its article in praise of toxic warfare stated that BZ was available in grenades. BZ is standardised, and standardised munitions include a 'field dispenser', of which the present writer unfortunately has no details.

Mr Rusk said, 'We are not embarking on gas warfare in Vietnam.' This is an incredible statement in the light of subsequent events. It was no more than a pious hope.

'We are not talking about agents or weapons that are associated with gas warfare.'
The gas CN was used in World War I without much success. The gas DM was intended also for this use but the 1914/18 war finished before it could be employed. All of these gases are now associated with gas warfare.

'We are not talking about gas that is prohibited by the Geneva Convention of 1925 or any other understanding about the use of gas.'
The Geneva Protocol states: 'Whereas the use in war of asphyxiating poisonous or other gases and of all analogous liquids ... has been justly condemned by the civilised world ... this prohibition shall be universally accepted as part of international law binding alike the conscience ... and practice of nations.' There is no ambiguity in what is condemned. The gases used in Vietnam are thus forbidden for use in war, even the so-called tear gases.

'The decision was made to employ tear gas to deal with that situation as a riot control type of problem in order to avoid the problem of whether to use artillery or aerial bombs that would inflict great damage on innocent people.'
In subsequent use the problem of whether to use artillery or aerial bombs or gases was successfully resolved. The use of gas with one of the other two was found the most effective. It inflicts the greatest amount of damage on the Vietcong and incidentally the same on the innocent civilians.

'We do not expect that gas will be used in ordinary military situations.'
This was an expectation not shared by the military. The military, having been supplied with a new weapon, naturally used it to its maximum effect. They have not been noted for great concern over civilian casualties, which have been known to inflate the numbers of dead Vietcong.

'The anticipation is of course that these weapons be used only in those situations involving riot control or situations analogous to riot control.'
CS is used in Vietnam in three ways: as bulk powder, as CS1, a very fine powder, and as CS2, a silicone-treated moisture-resistant powder. 367,000 lb of CS were used in 1964 and 6,063,000 lb in 1967. The

total for the period 1964–1969 is 13,736,000,000 lb, or over 6,000 tons. The figures for CN and DM are not published. By no stretch of the imagination can this be called riot-control. The figures indicate that the gas is used on a large scale in the second and third forms. By any definition, this is chemical warfare.

2. BIOLOGICAL WARFARE

The remarkable fact about all alleged cases of use in war of BW is that never has one fully authenticated case been unambiguously proved to the satisfaction of all concerned.

World War I

Some allegations were made; for example in the Merck Report 1946 reference is made to 'incontrovertible evidence' that horses exported from America to Europe had been infected with disease. Several other allegations were also made, but it seems likely that BW had little effect because in 1924, as the League of Nations record states, ' "the bacterial Arm" has not been employed in war'. These allegations are of little interest today. Evidence was extremely sparse.

World War II

Both Germany and Japan prepared for BW, as is shown from the record of the Nuremberg trial. The Germans, however, do not seem to have got beyond the stage of experimentation (sometimes on prisoners). Allegations (of the use of typhus) were never officially made, although unofficially much was said about this; the Germans were charged with 'preparing'. The allies were at this time far in advance of the Germans.

The Japanese effort was a more coherent and effective one lasting from 1936–45. Field tests were performed at proving grounds. Sabotage was also examined as a possible means of use of BW. Preparations had reached the stage where a factory for the production of bacterial toxins, vectors and other means for prosecuting biological warfare had been built at Harbin in Manchuria. Use of biological warfare was alleged in the trial of twelve Japanese prisoners of the Kwantung Army, including the Commander, at Khaborovsk, USSR. The details of the trial were published in 1950. These charges were credited by Thomas Parran, then Surgeon-General of the US public health service, and by R. Pollitzer, a League of Nations epidemiologist. It was revealed that interest had started in 1931 and that two large installations had been built, one at Harbin in 1936. Agents researched included plague (most studied), anthrax, cholera, typhoid and paratyphoid fevers. Fleas and other vectors had been bred in large numbers. Later the ISC (see p 56)

revealed that 700 victims had died as a result of Japanese attempts
to use BW in 1940–44. Hiroshi Akiyama, who claimed to have been a
witness, alleged that 1500 to 2000 prisoners had died (*New York
Times*, 1955). The Harbin installation was destroyed by the Japanese
before the Russians could capture it. It had been disguised as a red
cross unit. This was in August 1945. The fate of the other establishment is not known, but it may be the source of Chinese gas weapons
captured in Vietnam, and reputedly exported to the United Arab
Republic.

A further allegation after the war was made by East German
authorities. This alleged the spread of colorado beetles by American
planes over Germany. According to the report submitted 15 June
1950 by Paul Merker, State Secretary of the Ministry of Agriculture
and Forestry of the German Democratic Republic, this had occurred
from May to June of that year. In commenting one must conclude
that this was very unlikely. No evidence was offered. This was
mainly a propaganda move. The reasons why America is such an
excellent target for such propaganda warfare will become apparent
later. Some other equally improbable allegations have been made.

Korea, 1952

Allegations that the Americans had used BW in Korea were made at
the United Nations on 8 May 1951. Detailed charges were made.
These referred to specific incidents involving insects. The US Army
Chemical Corps, Biological Warfare Section, was alleged to have
manufactured sixteen kinds of bacteriological weapons. In March
1951, according to Bak Hon Yong, Minister for Foreign Affairs of
the North Korean government, on 22 February 1952, US Landing
Ship 1091 sailed to Wonson. This ship was commanded by Crawford
F. Sams, chief of the public health and welfare section of the UN
forces general headquarters. This, it was alleged later, went to Koje
Island, where it was claimed they used Korean and Chinese prisoners
in experiments. A report that gas had been used in Korea is likely
to have arisen out of a use of riot-control agents on prisoners who
were causing disturbance. Allegations were also made of the use of
'germ' shells. In themselves, these allegations meant nothing, representing merely propaganda. It was the work of a scientific commission of Communist sympathisers from the scientific world that
later posed the question of BW seriously.

The report could, as T. Rosebury, an expert in the field, has
written, 'be read as an imaginative work of fiction or as a study in
abnormal epidemiology'. The full report consists of 665 pages of
text with many illustrations. It was published in 1952 in Peking.
Amongst the more interesting evidence is Appendix Q. This is an

abridged account of an article which appeared first in a Japanese newspaper written by Ryohei Sakaki, who claimed to have been a major in the Kwantung Army Epidemic Prevention Service. This was the division concerned with BW under General Shiro Ishii, named at the Khabarovsk trial as 'the ideologue of bacteriological warfare'. This paper describes 'spraying', 'dusting' and 'showering' as well as the efforts made to produce large numbers of vectors. It also describes earthenware bombs and self-destroying paper containers. Containers to transmit rats and other vectors, including insects, were prepared. In the words of Rosebury, 'If this be science fiction, it has a considerable verisimilitude.'

The commission examined whether the Americans had used methods which were essentially Japanese. It was unable to come to a conclusion on this point. Its findings were based on studies made in Korea and North China between 23 June and 31 August 1952. Some three weeks of this time was spent in the areas said to have been attacked.

The first point one would make about the reports is that the criteria they set down for the study of BW use, as diagnostic features, were excellent. With the state of knowledge and equipment available at that time, this approach could not be faulted. The same cannot be said for their conclusions from the data presented to them. For a coherent picture of BW use, they gave the following as the most conclusive evidence possible.

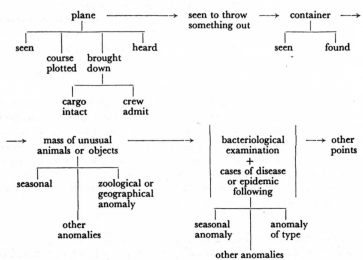

They state that the pattern above will rarely be encountered.

Prior to their own report the ISC received data presented in a group of documents by a commission of lawyers published in Prague. Almost all the evidence referred to here pertains to insects. Previously, some unrecorded Asian species were discovered in northeast China. It was not the exotic character of the insects that the commission considered significant, it was more the abnormality in their distribution, arrival and ecology. The commission excluded meteorological or other factors perfectly legitimately. The abnormality of large numbers of insects appearing at strange times of the year, often with snow on the ground, was hard to explain. Very high concentrations of, for example, springtails, would have to be present for these to be noticeable at all.

The evidence for the strangeness of the appearance of insects was as follows. The present writer's comments are in italics.

1. Connection with air raids. *In some cases not conclusive.* Wolf spiders, etc., found in 4-compartment bombs. *In several cases the link with air raids was a tenuous one; in one case the 'bomb' was found over a week after the raid.*

2. Eye-witnesses—*some of these reports are not very convincing and will be discussed later.*

3. Anomalies of locality—fleas were found on the ground, not with hosts. Springtails were found in large numbers in a concrete sports stadium. *We have already mentioned the probability or otherwise of using springtails as a weapon of war.*

4. Seasonal anomalies—*with these it is impossible to disagree or offer an alternative explanation, other than that some of the incidents mentioned were misinterpreted or did not in fact occur.*

5. Anomaly of numbers—swarms of field crickets were found— an insect which does not normally form swarms. *We have also discussed field crickets as weapons.*

6. Anomaly of association—for example, springtails were found with fleas in Ku'an Tien. *This phenomenon is also inexplicable.*

7. Anomaly of distribution—discovery was mainly along the travel routes of American planes. Other allied species of the insect population were not affected, for example, for helomyza several species are known for the affected area only one of which was active at the wrong period. *This too is inexplicable if the account was accurate.*

The author would point out that the commission saw none of these incidents personally. The validity of the phenomena concerned depends on the Chinese and Korean sources. If their eye-witness reports are disbelieved, or were mistaken, the above could be explained.

Some uniformly-acting factor causing early development of these insects was postulated. This could be excluded by examining the degree of agreement between orders of appearance of the odd insects and the order of their natural appearance. There is little similarity between the two. This would argue in favour of an artificial factor acting. The suggestion that napalm had heated the earth causing the abnormal appearance of these insects was discounted as many of the incidents occurred in north-east China, where napalm was not used.

One of the strongest arguments against bw use, it has been said, was the reliance placed on vector transmission. D. W. Jenkins, ex-head of the entomology division of the Army Biological Laboratory, said that such vectors were first considered as weapons after the Chinese allegations. To use insects as weapons, these have to be produced on a very large scale. The Chinese charges were that one of Ishii's former colleagues, Ojawa, supplied the insects.

The insects disseminated were a rather mixed bunch. For bw one uses insects living in close proximity to known hosts, which have a definite vector activity, for example mosquitoes, carrying yellow fever, which by biting transmit the disease used. The use of non-biting stable flies (*Muscina stabulans*), sun-flies (*Helomyza*), house-flies and even Isotoma (a primitive wingless insect) must be viewed with suspicion. These are not very likely weapons at all. Use of beetles, for example Ptinus fur, spiders, etc., is equally unlikely. In defence of what seemed to the commission strange, they added, 'not only the great latitude of the so-called specificity of vectors and also certain aspects of the vector-host relationship not yet classified' should be considered. If a vector is to be used, one uses one which is known to transmit disease. Use of some of these vectors is highly improbable; even the commission had to posit extremely complex chains of infection, none of their arguments is convincing. Although the points they make would be valid for public health, the commission seems to apply public health problems and the attitude to these to biological warfare. They hypothesise that even the most curious vectors may possibly be used for bw. bw to be effective must be fairly direct. For any bw developer to use these vectors with any hope of success would suggest a knowledge of the vector potentialities of a wide variety of Asian, mainly Chinese and Korean, localised insects. Biting insects would be used, in any case, not the wide variety of curious non-biting ones. If insects other than fleas were to be used, they would be flying. The use of Isotoma, which neither flies nor is associated with man, must be viewed with suspicion. The commission suggests that strange vectors were used in the hope that the Koreans would be unable to deal with them. Insecticides, such as DDT, kill insects whether they are vectors or not. In addition, it is very improbable that insect-mediated BW would be used in the extremely cold conditions referred to in the report. In many cases the insects were dead or dying when found. Most had reduced mobility. Abnormalities of their distribution are considered later.

Of more interest, and much more believable, were the allegations of plant pathogens having been used. This represents, in the writer's opinion, the best case the commission made. The diseases used were identified, almost certainly correctly, in view of the given credentials of the identifiers. The first of these was purple spot fungus, *Cercospora sojini* Hara. This is a plant pathogen reported from Korea and China to affect soya bean crops. The sample was said to be thoroughly infected.

A second fungus (anthracnose) (*Glomerella* sp.), was reportedly found. There are two types of this fungus; one attacks solely cotton, the other many other plants but not cotton. The case given was of a fungus which attacked both, of a wider host range than usual.

The third case referred to a fungus affecting peach leaves. This was found to be *Macrophora kuwatsukai* Hara, which causes apple and pear fruit-rot. It was not on its normal host and it was shown to be highly infectious. Of the plant material on which the fungus was found some was indigenous to South Korea but not North Korea.

Corn kernels infested with Thecaphora were also alleged to have been used over Liaotung province in Manchuria. Thecaphora was unknown in China on corn kernels. A European species is known to affect legumes.

The above allegations seem dubious to the present writer, in that had anyone intended to use BW covertly one would expect them not to present cast-iron proof that the material could not have been indigenous. It is incredible that the Americans would have used leaves of a tree whose distribution is limited to South Korea. A second point is that while the fungi with extended host ranges would be good, credible BW weapons, they would have taken some considerable time to develop, time which the Americans had not had.

In favour of the ISC's thesis are the disease agents which were used. Many of these, plague, respiratory (pulmonary) anthrax, encephalitis and cholera are still of BW interest today. With respect to the specific instances of use certain doubts arise.

In the report, the first disease discussed is plague. It had not been endemic in North Korea for 500 years. Its appearance was a recent phenomenon. Human fleas infected with plague were alleged to have been found. Usually in their natural state the rat fleas are the carriers. The human flea was the animal used by the Japanese against the Chinese in World War II. From the cases involving plague the commission (on second-hand evidence) determined that BW had been used with human fleas acting as vectors.

Another case that the commission considered was in Kan Nan. This referred to the use of voles (*Microtus* sp.) as carriers of plague-infected fleas. The species of vole was a completely foreign one. The animals were deceased or dying on arrival. Some 717 were found over a very large area. The report itself points to a difficulty in this case in reference to the means of dissemination; the voles had no containers around from which they could have been disseminated. If 717 were found, several containers would have to be used (unless they were sprayed!). Not a single trace was noted. The report cites self-destroying paper containers as a suggestion. If these had been used, then the sick animals would have had little chance to become distributed a great distance from the point of landing. They were almost dead on arrival. Had they been spread by container most would have been found near the remains of the container. That they could have been widely distributed in their condition must appear doubtful. The use of voles as a BW weapon cannot survive critical scrutiny. Of the more improbable agents for BW purposes, the writer considers voles to be the strangest. It is here that the 'imaginative fiction' question of Rosebury begins to take its toll of the student. Voles are not largely associated with man. Rats could be used, and this was considered by the Japanese. The use of voles as BW carriers strikes one as belonging more to the realms of fantasy than scientific fact.

The next case given in the report concerns anthrax. This was allegedly spread in Kuan Tien by anthomyiid fleas (*Hylemia*) and spiders (*Tarentula* sp.). There is little to be said other than general criticism of the unlikely vectors and the fact that there was a nine-day gap between the raid and the discovery. Spiders and fleas were found, even after this time, close to the bomb. (This was the calcareous type discussed later.) The explanation given for the location of the insects was that they landed in snow which immobilised them. Among other cases of anthrax in Liaotung and Liaohsi a Ptinid beetle was found to be a vector, allegedly found in large numbers. A red thermos-flask-shaped object was the 'bomb' used which exploded above the ground. Eye-witnesses were examined by the commission. Several people had contracted respiratory anthrax and were subject to post-mortem pathological investigation. One feature of the commission's report is that all the pathological work seems extremely thorough. The disease referred to, causing pulmonary infection, haemorrhagic fever and meningitis had a very rapid onset and very similar development in all the cases. Anthrax was practically unknown in China. The explanation of the respiratory anthrax given by the report was that spines on the elytra of the Ptinid beetle could be infected and inhaled. This writer would like here to record his considerable scepticism; no animal experiments were performed to examine the feasibility of this; the basis was microscopic examination solely.

Another incident referred to was the use of infected clams (the Dai Dong incident). These allegedly carried cholera. Marine clams (*Meretrix meretrix*) were found on a hillside by a peasant woman near a reservoir. They were wrapped in straw. She and her husband ate some and died subsequently of cholera. These clams are usually sold in Korea in straw packing as they were found. The commission set great store by the fact that they had not been sold in North Korea since the war and were one month out of season. It was alleged that American planes had previously attacked and damaged the purification plant of the nearby reservoir and that the clams were an attempt to spread the disease. In this they would have been eminently suited in the opinion of the commission. Cholera is a halophile (literally, 'likes halide-ions', of which there are high concentrations in sea water). The slow death of the mollusc in fresh water would cause gradual release of the cholera. It should be noted that there is, in fact, no particular reason to use a vector here at all. A few kilograms of bacterial paste would be expected to be quite effective in this form of contamination. The cases discussed by the commission seem to indicate an obsession with vectors, the least likely mode of transmission.

The commission also examined the techniques of dissemination. Spraying was quoted, and seems one of the most feasible suggestions. The problem of doing this with insects is that immense numbers are needed, and even with protective wadding many die. The commission relied to some extent on the evidence of the captured American airmen. This will be discussed more thoroughly later. This method would not be feasible for mosquitoes, but could be used for fleas, in the commission's opinion. Without having verified this experimentally the author is not in any position to criticise this: the lack of experimental evidence to corroborate this somewhat bizarre suggested means of infection indicates another of the weak points of the report.

The second type of dissemination considered was paper packets. These were in the opinion of the commission quite probably released from larger bombs by explosion. The commission states that hardy insects might be dropped from a height just packed in paper. Again, no experiments were conducted.

A third munition discussed by the commission was the 'air-bursting, variable-time fuse leaflet bombs'. These were allegedly used in many cases for insect dissemination, and were said to have provision for a parachute attachment for slow descent. Some controversy surrounds the use of this type of bomb for BW. Major-General E. T. Bullene said in congressional testimony that BW weapons could be made from the leaflet bombs. A Pentagon report said that leaflet bombs of the type shown could not be used in BW. This was due to the pressure changes on release of the agents in mid-air, from the bomb, killing them. In the author's view this is a reasonable criticism of the use of these bombs. They could, however, be used quite possibly to disseminate, for example, bacterial toxins. This is more likely to be what Bullene was referring to. Several variants of the leaflet bomb were also referred to from the US pilots' testimony but were never found in use. One opened on impact, a highly unlikely method of spreading biological agents over a wide area.

Paper or carton cylinders were also suggested and examples examined by the commission. These were suggested for use for delicate vectors, for example midges. In the writer's view these containers described were so small that unless used in very large numbers could not constitute a credible weapon. Yet they were only found on isolated occasions. This seems unlikely to be a BW attempt as the numbers involved must of necessity be too small to be of any consequence. In any attack using vectors many will be lost on impact or as a result of storage. Further, many will be lost by predation. Use of insects in the fashion described in the report is more likely to produce a meal for the local bird population than epidemic spread of disease.

A self-destroying paper container dropped by parachute was described by Sakaki in Appendix Q. These were suggested for the Kan Nan incident (voles). These would also have to be anaesthetised in flight to prevent them from gnawing their way out. This in addition to the extremely poor condition they were in at Kan Nan would preclude their dispersal over a large area. They were, needless to say, reported over a large area.

General Ishii had developed an earthenware bomb. The commission believed it had found a modern version of this in a calcareous 'egg shell' container. These were used in the Ku'an Tien incident. The significant point that strikes one concerning these is that their shell is so thin (0·8–0·9 mm) that fracture on release from the aircraft would seem certain. This did not escape the commission. 'Something is still lacking in our understanding of the facts since it is not yet clear how so fragile a container can stand the shock of departure from a plane.' The suggestion that the incident was faked, and so was the bomb, never appears to have occurred to the commission.

Amongst other novel containers shown to the commission were green plastic artillery shells.[1] The Koreans claimed that these, containing insects, had been fired at the Communist forces. The commission, in view of the complete incredibility of this idea, asked the Minister of Health of North Korea if he could amplify on this, giving details. The way in which the question was put speaks volumes for the attitude of the commission. 'Perhaps by some mistake it had been intended to say shells containing bacteria, which would be much more possible.' In Appendix 1, the stated answer was, 'No reply was given, except that the commission had been shown the fragments of a green plastic shell.'

In addition to the above, in one case lyophilised proteinaceous material was found, in company with Isotoma. This was identified as a freeze-dried culture of dysentery bacteria. In the words of the reply of the Minister, 'The relation of the material with the Collembola, *Isotoma negishina*, found with this material remained unclear.' The reason for using this material in this fashion is totally beyond the writer's imaginative powers to conceive.

We now come to the testimony of captured agents and military personnel. One captured agent was interrogated by the commission. There is nothing very improbable in attempting to gain intelligence of the efforts of biological warfare. Little can be made of the interrogation of a South Korean agent mentioned in the report.

Rather more can be gleaned from the testimony of the aviators and more especially their 'confessions'. All of these were revoked by the airmen who returned to America. This writer confesses himself not to be entirely convinced by a document allegedly written, unaided, by an American pilot (John Quinn) entitled, 'How I was forced to take part in the inhume [sic] bacteriological warfare launched by the US Wall Street.' It is redolent with such spontaneous gems as 'brought up as I was on the propaganda lies of the Wall Street imperialists'; also, 'It was a crime against all the peaceloving peoples of the world'. The testimony of F. B. O'Neal (second lieutenant) is also revealing, 'The use of germ warfare is against all humanitarian principles, and all the peace-loving peoples of the world are against it.' The testimony of the other pilot, Paul B. Kniss, bears the same stamp, 'This inhuman warfare must be

---

[1] How these escape melting or being blown to bits when fired must remain a mystery. An informed source consulted by the writer completely discounted the idea of plastic shells.

stopped'; also, 'All men of the world are brothers and until we all learn to live together and help each other, we cannot have the world peace we desire so much.' Much of the corroborative evidence of the commission comes from these sources. An open letter by F. B. O'Neal to his erstwhile comrades in the USAF is also of interest. 'Let us change the tune of the piper and dance to the tune of peace'; also, 'Speak! Act! and your efforts for peace will be blessed.'

Although we have been unable to go into the report in as much detail as we would have liked, the above illustrates the points of severest criticism. It is instructive to examine the commission's conclusions. The commission recognised that its reports differed from current American thoughts on BW. It stated that important technical advances had rendered these opinions obsolete. Rosebury was quoted as having expressed the view that plague could be used but only in situations remote from friendly territory to prevent the attack backfiring. To quote the commission, 'In Korea the commission's work has revealed repeated attempts to diffuse plague at places not far removed from the front lines, contrary to the opinion of so distinguished a bacteriologist as the former Director of Camp Detrick.' Dr Rosebury was head of the airborne infection project at Detrick; as far as the writer knows he at no time was promoted to the illustrious heights suggested by the commission. Needless to say, this writer disagrees that the commission's work was conclusive.

The commission does make one reference to the possibility of airborne infection having been used, but could not conclude definitely that this had in fact been the case.

The commission came to the following conclusions without reservation.

The peoples of Korea and China have indeed been the object of bacteriological weapons. These have been employed by units of the USA armed forces, using a great variety of different methods for the purpose, some of which seem to be developments of those applied by the Japanese army during the Second World War.

The present writer would like here to discuss the reaction to these charges. Trygve Lie, then head of the UN, suggested that all the UN medical services would be used to aid the Koreans and Chinese if BW had been used. Major Brock Chisholm was of the opinion that serious epidemics would have been rampant had the Americans used BW. This is a good point. In all the Korean incidents the use was not as effective as one would have expected. Serious large-scale epidemics seem not to have occurred. Many of the instances were bungling and ineffective and could not, even if the accounts were true, have been describable as serious attempts to prosecute BW. The curious munitions are another strange feature. The sheer inefficiency and waste of efforts are the first points which strike one concerning the Korean case. The use of Japanese methods by the Americans, who had been developing their own, almost certainly more effective, weapons for over ten years, would also tend to discredit the report's authenticity. The use of insect vectors is another improbability. The whole BW 'campaign' on Korea is totally at variance with most of the published data in America or elsewhere, except for Japan. There is no evidence that the Americans were prepared to use this weapon in this fashion. The dissemination systems and the vectors, if not the agents, were almost all quite bizarre. The use of the American pilots' testimony unreservedly, in view of its somewhat dubiously spontaneous nature, is also a weak point, as is the lack of experimental data. In conclusion, on the evidence, almost all of which was based on second-hand Korean or Chinese reports, one would think BW not likely. It is the author's opinion that the commission acted in good faith. It is equally his opinion that they failed to be anywhere near critical enough, especially in their conclusion. To be effective, any team must be totally unbiased and apply the standards of its severest critics; this the ISC did not accomplish.

The Chinese and Koreans rejected offers of help by the World Health Organisation, UN, etc. This in itself reflects doubts on the strength of the Chinese case as they waited until a sympathetic team had been built up. Even the sympathetic team could find inadequacies in the data—even if it could not accept the conclusions we have derived from these.

The fact remains, however, that the Chinese scored a major propaganda victory. Many people, in the Far East especially, are convinced on very little evidence of the truth of the Chinese allegations. Two major reasons for the success of this campaign were, first, the ineptitude of the people trying to counter the Communist allegations; secondly, the fact that America already possessed BW weapons. The same reasons hold for the case of Vietnam. This makes it very difficult to repudiate allegations. It would seem that the Korean case was a propaganda victory for the Communists on a very large scale.

As to whether BW was or was not used, it is impossible to say definitely. The present writer's opinion is that it was not. This is supported by a publication *Bacteriological Weapons and how to defend against them*, Arkhangelsky *et al.* (Military Publishing House 1967). This Russian publication in its historical review of BW makes no reference at all to Korea. Japanese use in World War II is followed directly by the use of American defoliants in Vietnam.

Vietnam

This section will consider only the use of biological weapons proper (i.e. not defoliants). It has been suggested that the United States would use BW. It is unlikely that it would be militarily feasible or useful for the NLF to use this weapon. It is possible that the North Vietnamese might fake a BW attack by the US for propaganda purposes, on the model of the successful Korean exercise discussed above (pp 297–308). An American attack on the Vietnamese is the only context in which BW makes sense.

It is obvious that secrecy would have to be maintained in any use of BW in Vietnam, and covert application would be necessary to avoid the world condemnation which the public use of such methods would arouse. A covert attack would require a very different agent and method of dissemination from normal. It would have to be possible to blame the incidence of disease on a naturally occurring epidemic, and thus, contrary to usual practice, epidemic agents would have to be used. None of the currently standardised agents is a possible candidate: it would, for example, be highly suspicious if pulmonary anthrax appeared in Vietnam. In addition to being non-epidemic, some standard BW agents are non-endemic, and it would be necessary to use a disease which is not exotic to the country concerned.

The only target of such an attack would be the population of Vietnam. In order to reduce the chances of detection, strategic application against the population would require the use of a highly epidemic agent which would not have to be spread over large areas. The fewer aircraft and the less time required, the less risk there would be of an aircraft's being shot down with its incriminating cargo on board. Research has been carried out recently in the United States into tanks for disseminating freeze-dried bacteria which can be jettisoned after use and fragment on reaching the ground, thus reducing the risk of an aircraft's being brought down with its BW equipment intact.

With a highly epidemic agent, two or three aircraft spraying over the area of Vietnam would probably be enough to cause a large epidemic. The problem in such circumstances would not be starting, but stopping, the outbreak.

The disease used should be endemic to the country, but localised, with very few cases a year. This avoids the possibility of a large proportion of the population's being resistant to it. It would, of course, be necessary to protect the troops of the US and its allies, and sympathetic members of the population, with vaccines.

The possibility of retroaction on the disseminator's own territory must also be considered. In this case, the large expanse of sea between the United States and Vietnam might be considered to make the problem negligible. This is the view taken by the US military authorities, although the World Health Organisation Conference takes a more serious view. It is, however, unlikely that this consideration would be a serious barrier to the use of BW.

A decision would have to be made as to whether a lethal or incapacitating agent should be used. Incapacitating agents have several disadvantages. In the first place, people who recover from one attack of the disease may be more resistant to a second. Secondly, the advantage gained by using an incapacitating agent must be exploited quickly, and this is not possible in the conditions of Vietnam. A population which survived a BW attack and realised what it had undergone might also be strengthened in its opposition to those who used such weapons. Lethal agents would eliminate all these problems. There is no need for early occupation of territory really hard hit by lethal disease, and the epidemic could be allowed to run its course.

A further argument in favour of using lethal agents is that as long as the operation was kept secret it would hardly matter which was used; on the other hand, if the operation became public, as well be hanged for a sheep as a lamb.

In Vietnam only one agent is likely to be of use, the pneumonic form of plague, *Pasteurella pestis*. This is a highly lethal, highly epidemic disease, restricted previously to a few river valleys and occasional cases in ports caused by the influx of foreigners. The cases in the river valleys were ascribed to downstream traffic from neighbouring countries. The population probably has very little resistance.

It is relevant to ask whether US troops and those of their allies would be affected if plague were used. All US troops receive two innoculations of plague vaccine before leaving for Vietnam, and boosters subsequently at four-monthly intervals. Careful spraying of NLF-controlled areas would ensure high casualties among enemy forces (and also among the civilian population, particularly the old, the sick and children). Casualties might be expected to be low among US and allied forces, but the effect on the enemy would be disastrous. *Time*'s remark quoted earlier (p 64) that vaccine was available could have been caused by bad techniques for handling BW materials, although in view of Gordon Goldstein's letter quoted below this is unlikely.

In connection with the possibility of retroaction, it is worth mentioning that at least one US soldier has brought plague back to the United States. The plague he contracted was pneumonic, which could have been caused by bites from infected fleas or from bad techniques for handling BW materials, although in view of Gordon Goldstein's letter quoted below this is unlikely.

It is difficult to say whether plague is available as a weapon. There has been long-standing opposition in the United States to the offensive use of BW. In the article in *Viet Report* quoted in Part 1 (p 64) reference was made to a memo from the State Department to the President in June 1965 in which the Department reversed its previous opposition to the use of such weapons. This confirms that there was 'a good chance' that BW would be used. Furthermore, it stated that the resultant disease would be blamed on a naturally occurring epidemic. Since then it has been stated that tularemia and not plague is being developed. Tularemia is not a good epidemic agent, while plague is. This implies that it was indeed plague which the statement just quoted referred to. It seems unlikely that an epidemic could be started with tularemia.

There is very little reliable information on whether plague is available for strategic use. There have been other reports (including one from Dr Jonathan Beckwith of Harvard) that workers in the United States were producing antibiotic-resistant strains of plague. After the article in *Viet Report* several denials were made that the Traveler's Research Company was involved in plague production. It was said both that tularemia was the organism in question and that no work at all was being done. The evidence on this case so far available is inconclusive.

Having discussed the means of using BW, one may now ask where the bases are. In the original version of this work it was postulated that special bases would be necessary. Confirmation of this hypothesis seems to be contained in an article in *Flight International* for 14 March 1968, which said:

> An unprecedented admission that the US has deployed weapons of biological warfare, by implication airborne weapons, in South East Asia has been made by the chairman of the US Office of Naval Research, Mr Gordon Goldstein. Mr Goldstein made the admission by implication in a letter to Indian newspaper editors refuting allegation (said to be spread by Chinese agents) that biological weapons have been handled incompetently and are responsible for the current bubonic plague epidemic in South Vietnam.
>
> Mr Goldstein's letter, according to the *Times* Calcutta correspondent, refutes the charge, saying that 'at every special base the delivery, storage and supervision of biological weapons is assured through the most up-to-date technical means'. He asks

editors to refute rumours spread by Communist agents to slander 'America's struggle for peace and freedom in South East Asia'.

Significantly, this reveals the presence of BW bases in Thailand. The refutation was not concerned with plague as a weapon. It was not denied that plague was used as a weapon, but simply that it was possible for it to have escaped from the bases. There is little doubt that a variety of US aircraft could operate from Thailand to spray the biological weapon over Vietnam.

A further point to be drawn from this is that US policy on the deployment of BW seems to have changed. Previously, it was policy not to store biological weapons on foreign soil. Their swift movement was allowed for if a situation calling for their use seemed likely to develop. This change seems to be part of the general policy change since the late 1950s towards a policy of 'first use' where this was deemed necessary. CBW is now part of the policy of 'massive retaliation'. Consequently, barriers to its playing a similar role to other weapons in logistics and planning are being broken down. In 1959 the Pugwash conference could say that the military seemed to have specified no particular requirement for CBW. Now its military application is clearer.

It is obvious that any use of BW must be reflected in the statistics for disease in Vietnam published by the World Health Organisation. These have already been quoted (p 63). It is evident, in spite of the unreliability of the statistics, which grossly underestimate the extent of plague, that plague has reached epidemic proportions. In October 1966 *The Times* reported that twenty-two of the twenty-nine provinces north of Saigon were affected. Normally plague kills 65–85% of those infected. The low casualty rate in reported cases indicates that many have received treatment. They must represent a small proportion of actual cases.

It is interesting to note the chronology of these events. State Department objections to BW were dropped in 1965, and the first cases of pneumonic plague were reported in June 1966. If BW was used, the spread of the pneumonic form could be argued to be the natural progress of the epidemic. Whether BW was used or not, the scale of the epidemic is horrifying. There was a twenty-fold increase in cases of plague between 1964 and 1966.

These are damaging pieces of evidence in support of the accusation that BW has been used already, but on balance the authors feel that the case is not proven. There are a number of indications to the contrary. It is probably significant that, with one exception, all the allegations of the NLF and North Vietnamese are unspecific.[1] There

1 And the exception, a claim about the ravages of 'killer insects', is hard to take seriously.

is no direct evidence of the use of BW from even the most anti-American visitors to Vietnam. If BW had been used, the propaganda services of the NLF, the North Vietnamese and the Chinese would have had a field-day. They would have a marvellous propaganda victory. Even the preparations for BW already mean a loss of face for the United States in the Far East. In the long run their presence there could only alienate friendly Asian countries. The fact that these preparations are being made—and it is clear that they are—is the most disturbing feature of the situation. The fact that they are stockpiled must mean that their use is contemplated.

3. CBW—CAPABILITIES AND POTENTIALS

It is extremely difficult to assess CBW capabilities since they are not publicised, and one is forced to talk in terms of probabilities. It is even more difficult to forecast future developments.

The greatest CBW force in the world is probably that of the United States. A list of some of the munitions available to the US forces is given below. In terms of quantity, shells are most important. Shells filled with GB and VX are available for: 105-mm howitzers, 5-in guns, 155-mm howitzers, 155-mm guns, 8-in howitzers. The highest calibre artillery shells for US equipment are much lighter than that of the Russians, who seem to have a greater interest in higher calibre equipment.

Nerve agents are available for 318-mm rockets (Little Johns) and for 5-in and 155-mm rockets (Bolt). Chemical warheads are available for Honest Johns. Chemical and biological warheads are available for the Sergeant missile and for the newer Lance. Details of warheads for larger missiles are not available, but warheads of five to six tons weight containing CBW agents are thought to have been prepared.

Aerial bombs of up to 1000 lb are available for use but are probably less important than the missile and artillery capability. Land-mines are also available.

The next largest CBW capability is that of the Russians. It should be emphasised that, as far as is known, Russian capabilities are exclusively in the chemical field. There are no reliable data on Russian BW preparations. The Russians may think that BW is not useful enough militarily to merit development. They have, however, a very high chemical capability. In 1959 the US Intelligence Service estimated that one-fifth of the total Soviet military capability was chemical. According to a recent estimate, one-third of the shells on the Warsaw Pact front are chemical. This may be offset by a comparable US capability. It is not known what warheads are available for Russian missiles, although the Scud and the Russian equivalent to the Little John certainly have chemical warheads.

Chemical warheads may have been developed. It would be very strange if the Russians did not have chemical warheads for long-range missiles. For a time, when the West had a notable lead over Russia in nuclear weapons, the Russians must have had a great incentive to develop CBW warheads. The spectrum of Soviet chemical munitions probably closely resembles that of the US, except that infantry weapons, such as flame-throwers adaptable for use with persistent agents, seem to have received more attention. The Russians have trained officers in CBW techniques, like the US Chemical Corps, which is active in advising on its use.

The CDEE has been assigned a patent for an aircraft spray device which could be used for chemical agents. The main British capability would, however, be in shells and missiles (of which we have few). The British capability would then be in one or more of the following classes which we have in common with the United States.

Designation		Calibre	Type	Description and Comments
US	UK			
L14	L5	105 mm	Geb. H.	Italian gun, NATO standardised. (The British self-propelled gun ammunition is not standardised)
M109	M109	155 mm	s.f.H.	self-propelled howitzer
M2AI	M2AI	203 mm	F.H.	field howitzer
M110	M2AIEI	203 mm	s.f.H.	self-propelled howitzer
M107	M113	175 mm	s.f.K.	self-propelled gun. No CW ammunition available

The M2AI and M110 rows are bracketed together with "8 inch".

The basis for the British attack capacity in this field could be in the M110 or M109. The M110 is an 8-inch barrel (as for the M2AI) on an M110 (175 mm gun) chassis. This will take a nuclear or chemical shell. These guns are deployed with missile regiments. The time needed for the British to move from defence to attack in this field might be just the time taken to load a chemical instead of a high explosive shell, a matter of seconds or minutes.

The question of the British capability is still shrouded in mystery. Although it is quite obvious that Britain could have little or no BW capacity (we have no suitable delivery systems), chemical munitions are a different matter. This probably forms the basis of the British capacity. British officers go to Dugway each year for training in the use of chemical munitions. There may be a second British capability in the Honest John missile deployed with missile regiments, for which chemical warheads are available. Such capabilities as these neatly avoid problems with production and storage of these weapons in Britain, since British troops can use US stocks.

It is also relevant that NATO forces possess gas weapons. Shells with different types of filling are colour-coded. Colour codes are in bands on the shells, varying for high explosive, gas and so on. The NATO troops are issued with instructions on the colour codes and what they mean. Harassing agents, probably mustard gas, are available. The present writer has no details of other agents, but they include persistent and non-persistent types.

It is through NATO that other powers could gain knowledge of and access to CBW equipment. Whether this does occur or not the present writer does not know, but it is a question which must be answered. It is possible that the West German Army could acquire chemical weapons in this way. Recently information has become available that West German interest in CBW is not entirely defensive (see above, pp 121–31, 136–37, 160–63). For West Germany to have access to CBW would require the collusion of the other NATO countries, particularly the United States. The West German artillery has a greater range of US weapons than the British. US supplies may therefore form the basis of a West German CBW capability. West Germany is committed not to manufacture CB weapons, but possession is a different matter.

Other countries which may have CBW capabilities include France and Egypt. Israel quite probably has chemical weapons in addition to napalm. Two allegations of the use of CBW by Israel have been made, but there is insufficient evidence to corroborate them. CBW is an attractive prospect for many countries. Any country adjacent to China has a good reason for starting a CBW programme. China has considerable interest in CBW, and has exported chemical munitions to various countries. It is quite likely that South Korea, Formosa and possibly Japan are thinking in terms of CBW. The first two have had considerable US assistance in other military matters.

Canadian and Australian efforts are closely related to the British and US joint projects. In April 1963, according to Seymour Hersh,[1] weapons with biological warfare capability were supplied to NATO allies. The Pentagon has acknowledged that CBW materials have been shipped to West Germany. However, after the recent gas escape at Okinawa they have denied storing biological weapons abroad. It is probable that bases are prepared to receive BW agents, but only receive supplies when their use is fairly likely. This is the situation implied in what few references there are to the storage and transport of biological weapons. Chemical and biological warheads go through the same channels as nuclear ones. There has to be provision for rapid mobilisation of such weapons because they cannot be stored abroad; they deteriorate rapidly, and would have to be periodically recalled to the United States.

[1] *Chemical and Biological Warfare*, London 1968.

It is thought that South Africa is developing a CBW capability, but as yet no details are available about what form this might take. There are obvious reasons why South Africa should be interested in chemical warfare. Her neighbours are hostile, and she runs the risk of serious internal disturbances. Bombing black areas might be part of the strategy in the event of a large-scale black revolt. The increasing separation of black and white areas makes this type of operation more and more feasible. Even fairly unsophisticated techniques could be used against black revolutionaries; they could be isolated, and white areas protected, by the use of persistent agents.

The future of CBW

Future employment of CBW systems in East–West confrontations probably means a large increase in strategic missile capability.

It has been suggested that chemical and biological weapons could be used selectively against populations to leave cities intact (in the USA), and nuclear weapons could be used on missile sites, which would be generally sited away from cities. This strategy would have no application to most of Western Europe, and it is here, especially in Germany, that most damage will be caused.

Even in the United States it is difficult to conceive of a situation in which cities would be spared in chemical, biological and nuclear war. Important cities are important centres of communication. Most important installations would presumably be protected against chemical and biological warfare. It is widely recognised by US chemical warfare experts that the advantage of CBN war lies in the supportive role of chemical and biological weapons. It is equally a fallacy to suppose that in tactical situations chemical or biological warheads are interchangeable with nuclear ones. The military assign targets to particular weapons. Chemical weapons are used to harass enemy troops, who have to use protective devices, and also if troop concentrations can be surprised. If a battery of self-propelled guns is to be attacked, nuclear weapons would be used, since in this case CB weapons would have no effect. Similarly, suggestions that CB weapons could be used tactically against command centres are not plausible. Command centres are nuclear targets. In nuclear and CB war it is important that command centres and critical units should be neutralised as quickly as possible, and weapons are therefore used to maximum effect. No commander would be afraid to use too much force.

If war broke out today in Europe, nuclear weapons would quickly be used; NATO's ability to contain Warsaw Pact forces depends on this. In no circumstances could chemical and biological weapons perform the same function. All three classes of weapon would be brought into action rapidly. The consequences of this would be extremely serious for the population of Germany. With such a high tonnage of chemical and nuclear munitions used in short-range equipment, German civilians would suffer appallingly. Without doubt, a high proportion of the population of East and West Germany would be affected.

The situation in Europe is not likely to change in the near future. Big increases are likely to be in strategic weapons, and as yet little is known of these.

In areas outside Europe much less sophisticated systems could be used. Israel and Egypt have certainly given much thought to CB weapons, and taken some steps in the field. Nerve gas is probably available to the Egyptians. The Israelis have kept quiet about what weapons they possess, although there have been unconfirmed reports of their using chemical weapons.

The most significant use of CB weapons are in counter-insurgency and counter-guerrilla operations. It is necessary to distinguish between the two situations. Guerrillas mix with the population when not militarily active. Insurgents are separate from the population and bear arms continually. Gas has been used against guerrillas in Vietnam, though without much effect. This is due to two factors: first, the most effective agents were not used, and secondly, the application was too indiscriminate and affected too many innocent parties. In general, it would seem that except when a victory involving huge civilian casualties can be envisaged, the potential of gas and BW in guerrilla war is low. Ultimately, the only effective weapon in guerrilla fighting is a well-trained soldier, who can be used as a truly discriminating weapon of war.

In counter-insurgency operations the situation is very different. Here, if particular groups can be isolated, chemical weapons can be used effectively. This was tried in the Yemen, though not with maximum effect. CB weapons can also be used in the later stages of guerrilla warfare.

This is the present situation. The future will no doubt see more toxic agents than those available at present. With their introduction strategic chemical and biological weapons should partially supplant nuclear ones. No country can afford to protect its entire population, and chemical weapons will provide a cheaper and possibly more effective adjunct to nuclear ones. In a few years, if nothing is done to halt their development, chemical and biological weapons may constitute a threat to humanity beside which current weapons would pale into insignificance.

8

DEFENCE AGAINST CHEMICAL AND BIOLOGICAL WARFARE

The impression may have been gained as a result of the previous discussions that chemical and more especially, biological weapons are impossible to protect against. 'Doomsday bugs' and other horrors of the day are as yet products of the imagination rather than weapons of war. Against existing weapons a variety of protective measures are available. Whether it is feasible to use these measures or not is doubtful. In very few countries is there any defence plan. The general consensus seems to be that no protection of the population, in terms of cost or effectiveness, would be of any use. For most nations, even the USA, defence is more of a token with respect to these weapons. Some 20 million Russians are said to have had training in what to do after a CBW attack. The extent of Soviet preparedness in shelters, gas masks, etc., is not known. They do, however, seem to have made a more serious attempt at civil defence than the western powers. How far any defence system may be effective may be judged from the discussion below.

There are three major lines of defence: psychological defence, physiological defence and physical and chemical defence.

Psychological Defence

The target of BW is people (more so than CW).

It is the duty of those responsible for defence therefore to make sure that in the event of war the people are psychologically prepared to meet the emergency. With the current irrational fears surrounding CBW, panic could present a serious problem if CW or BW was ever used. Apathy was once defined as the fear of being afraid and in this may lie a clue to the attitudes of many governments. CBW problems do not disappear if they are ignored. It is essential that the reality of CBW, which is bad enough, be faced, rather than that irrational feelings should prevent serious discussion.

In discussions it is very easy for the scientist to fall into a jargon which can obscure the real importance of what is said. 'Overkill' and 'megadeath' refer to people not abstractions. Any discussion must bear in mind the very real consequences of CBW.

Mass communications media if prepared could have considerable significance in the event of BW attack. For this they would have to be prepared and instructed. By rationalising the organisation of survivors and broadcasting warnings and information the mass media would have considerable usefulness. Equally if every time an epidemic occurred some newspaper highlighted it as a biological attack, it would not contribute much to the calm of the population. The knowledge of CBW potentialities in case of attack is most important. If, as Rosebury has suggested, BW attack was not as effective as the aggressor hoped, its effects might be considerably enhanced by panic in the population. An informed public is necessary for any civil defence.

Physiological Defence

This section also applies only to biological warfare.

The body itself possesses potent defence systems against invasion by micro-organisms. It is to circumvent these that the biological warfare planners have prepared novel means of dissemination. It now seems probable that the major method of application considered is by aerosol.

The body's lines of defence are as follows. The first defence against an aerosol is provided by the nose and naso-pharynx. These trap particles larger than 10 microns and even as much as 50% in the effective 1–5 micron range. Deposition in the upper respiratory tract, except where the organism concerned is capable of infecting through this region, is very useful in filtering out these agents. The particle size for successful infection through the nose is quite critical. The LD_{50} can be affected by a factor of several thousands if the particle size is too large. This depends on the amount of mouth breathing which the animal performs and is one of the reasons for the great difference between the LD_{50}s of the monkey and the guinea-pig. The geometry of the nasal passages and the amount of mouth breathing both alter the LD_{50}. This makes the LD_{50} for man hard to determine by animal experiment.

A second defence is provided by the muco-ciliary lining of the respiratory tract. The cilia are small hair-like processes which sweep trapped particles out of the lungs. The 1–5 micron particles penetrate to the finest branches of the respiratory bronchioles. These tubes have no ciliary lining and thus the effective particles remain there for long periods. This is why they are so efficient in causing infection.

In addition to these factors there are also cells in the lungs which ingest micro-organisms. In some cases this may be a factor in penetration, as opposed to their more usual role of protection, and could render infection even more easy.

Immunity

Non-specific immunity and specific antibodies are defences which act throughout the whole body. Non-specific immunity is the defence of the body to any invasion by foreign substances; some blood cells, for example, ingest incoming bacteria. The specific antibody response is due to the body's defences recognising a foreign substance (antigen) they have 'seen' previously, which may be a foreign protein or some characteristics of a bacterial cell. This is a very powerful response and is the basis of vaccine and toxoid effect. These substances are so similar to the pathogenic bacteria, or toxin, that the specific defences are activated if the pathogen infects. It is however, possible to remove the antigenic 'fingerprint' of an organism by genetic manipulation, thus making vaccines ineffective. The non-specific defences though less effective are immediately mobilised in case of infection. The antibodies take some time to form if the foreign substance has not entered the body previously. Vaccination is effective solely in allowing the body's defences to be mobilised very rapidly, reducing the chances of an infection gaining a serious hold.

It is obvious that if one wishes to use biological warfare an effective vaccine must be available to one's own troops and preferably unavailable to the enemy. A problem with BW defence is to know what agents to protect against as it is impossible to protect against all of them. Intelligence information would have to provide data for this. It is impossible to arrange protection against more than a small number of potential BW agents. There are some 160 or so infectious diseases known to man, and for some of these, hundreds of distinct strains are known. To immunise against even a small number of these would be difficult. There is a limit to the amount of foreign substance which the body will accept.

For such potential BW agents as Q Fever, *Pasteurella pestis*, *Bacillus anthracis*, etc., attenuated living strains for use as vaccine are known. The problem with these is stability on storage. Non-living vaccines, toxoids against tetanus, diphtheria and botulism and certain vaccines of dead bacteria and viruses generally confer protection for about six months to a year. The attenuated vaccines give protection usually for longer periods. Military interest in vaccination problems has had great significance for the peaceful uses of microbiology. Porton has done extremely valuable work on continuous cultivation and the biochemical basis of pathogenicity in brucellosis. The Porton injector also has considerable importance as a means for injecting large numbers of people, for instance, diabetics who must have many injections.

The Russians are known to be interested in aerosol vaccination from the air. Difficulties arise with doses. Systemic reactions can occur and thus cause complications. The current aim of the BW researchers is to produce effective multiple vaccines. Soviet volunteers have been immunised against four diseases at once by exposure to an aerosol containing attenuated strains of anthrax, tularemia, brucellosis and plague. The problem with this is that there is no guarantee that the other side will play cricket and not use a strain against which the vaccine is ineffective. It is possible to produce resistant strains more easily than new vaccines. In addition to this if a large dose of a micro-organism is given then the body's protection mechanism may be saturated and over-ridden. In the words of an American giving evidence before a House Committee '... the doses we use are massive.' There is also the possibility that when an organism is accepted through an unfamiliar pathway its normal vaccine may not be effective against it. All of the cases of accidents at Fort Detrick have involved people who have been protected immunologically against the disease. All seventeen Detrick personnel who contracted brucellosis during World War II had been vaccinated.

Physical and Chemical Protection

These are the only protections available against both chemical and biological weapons. The first obvious consideration, currently an area of much research interest, is early detection methods.

Detection

This may be subdivided into: warning, sampling and identification.

Early warning is a more critical requirement for chemical weapons than for biological ones. Most biological agents with the exception of the toxins are effective after a lag of several hours. Chemical agents such as the nerve agents can have their effects before a mask can even be put on. With a nerve gas, once the symptoms have begun to appear it is almost too late to help. The nerve agents, which are the only weapons at present worthy of consideration in terms of strategic use, can be combated by chemical means discussed earlier. This assumes, however, a population relatively well prepared and protected in the form of masks.

Chemical weapons require some form of dissemination system, aircraft, missiles, etc., which is detectable. Their effect is due to contact and cannot be remote. Detection of nerve gases is possible by means of a chemical pad which changes colour. In America a sampling device which draws air through crystals in a tube is available. Colour changes indicate the presence of nerve or mustard gas. It is doubtful whether this warning system would be of much use because even if readings were taken every few minutes, lethal doses could have been effective in the meantime. Continuous sampling and monitoring by an apparatus kept on top of high buildings has been suggested. Another suggestion is that warning should be issued when the meteorological conditions would favour a biological or chemical attack, rather like fire warnings in forest areas of the us. Porton has been instrumental in producing nerve-gas detectors; two were on show at a recent open day. They are electrochemical devices, probably similar to the one recently announced by Edgewood Arsenal. After years of study it has been reported that an automatic portable field alarm has been developed. It weighs 15 lb and continuously monitors the air. An electrochemical cell in the alarm is activated by the presence of nerve gas and causes electricity to flow, setting off the alarm. It is said to be capable of detecting nerve gas at below hazardous levels.

Systems to implement and operate early warning systems especially against biological weapons would require complex organisation. A central organisation would be responsible for warnings to mask, working out populations affected, population densities, target importance, terrain parameters, meteorological conditions and the types of dispersal (whether a moving or stationary point source or sources were used, whether one or more clouds were generated simultaneously or in succession, etc.).

Simple devices issued to small groups to detect biological agents are so far in the future that they do not need serious consideration here. To be truly effective, warning systems would have to be international, probably along similar lines to those against nuclear weapons. In America the firm of Goddard has been attempting to detect bw agents by using the property of living organism to synthesise ATP (adenosine triphosphate). This is the universal energy source of both animals and plants. This substance can make certain chemicals luminesce. It is obviously non-specific, but could provide warning of abnormally high levels of biological materials in the atmosphere. A similar device for measuring water pollution, again using ATP as a diagnostic feature, has been developed and could have some use if sabotage of water supplies had been suspected. Technical difficulties in producing an automatic warning device for air sampling are many. One problem is that large variations in the amount of biological material in the atmosphere occur quite naturally and seasonally. It is therefore difficult to set a level of biological materials which could form a base line to detect increases. More specific automatic warning devices would have to measure small amounts for protein and nucleic acids. This in itself is a considerable problem. More sophisticated warning systems are also being prepared using long path light scattering, and infra-red absorption for example. The utility of these is dubious.

In the event of a biological attack it is unlikely that any system at present available or in development could assist in preventing extremely high numbers of casualties. It is probable that in such a case, in addition to aerosol attack, sabotage of food and water supplies could also be expected. The use of biological and nuclear weapons together would confuse the situation still further.

Sampling: several devices are now available; membrane filters can be used for water, milk food stuffs, etc. A similar situation exists for aerosols where several devices are known which can select for the 1–5-micron size particles. These could be activated by early warning devices. A device recently developed mimics the size discrimination of the respiratory tract but still samples at a high rate. The agent is collected in fluid. Another very promising device can collect 10 cu m air/min into a small amount of liquid. This opens whole new vistas because it makes possible detection of airborne agents with 1000 times the sensitivity of previous means. Once successful sampling has occurred the sample must be removed to a special laboratory. The number of laboratories equipped to identify BW agents is small. Highly trained personnel would have to be used on the sampling teams so that not too many samples need be taken and the facilities of the analytical laboratory swamped. Difficulties could be greatly increased with covert use.

Rapid identification is necessary to minimise the number of casualties and to render possible the correct treatment. This requires an understanding of what weapons could conceivably be used and what features of these are useful in diagnosis. The actual list of organisms currently usable is probably only between ten and thirty types, allowing for manipulative possibilities to change diseases to a more suitable BW form. It is very unlikely that the more exotic diseases would be used. A considerable amount of knowledge is necessary for the aggressor. It is also preferable that the persons attacked have no vaccine.

The question of whether new diseases could be used is of considerable interest. Vervet monkey disease may well be an example of a whole new class of disease-causing organisms. Handling of blood and tissues without precautions causes infection. It is unaffected by any antibiotic substance so far tried and is unrelated to any other organism. It causes fatality in some cases and can be venereally transmitted in man. In the words of Dr C. E. Gordon Smith, 'It has possible potential as an infectious disease of man.' It presumably is also of BW interest. New virus diseases are continually appearing (chikungunya and o'nyong-nyong fever for example). In addition to these there are the possibilities of virus and bacteria being genetically manipulated to produce 'new' organisms.

All the above factors can complicate identification. The importance of rapid identification can be judged from studying the case of pneumonic plague. For this disease the mortality rate approaches 100% for cases not treated until after twenty-four hours of illness. Therapy at an earlier stage reduces this rate considerably. *Escherischia coli*, harmless in the intestine, its normal location, can cause a fatal pneumonia if it travels to the lungs. Fatal results are usually due to the time it takes to identify it in this rare occurrence. The variation in mortality due to tularemia is also a result of when and how the disease is identified. Several techniques have been researched for possible use. Most of the current methods are time consuming. The characteristics of an organism in culture and the media in which it is most successful, and the metabolic products as well as the slide agglutination characteristics, can be used to diagnose organisms such as salmonella, shigella, anthrax, plague, tularemia, etc. Recent successes in America have been recorded using gas chromatography to identify metabolic products. The first difficulty in this method is the time required to get the sample to the laboratory, the time factor being one of the greatest problems in any method. Organisms must be grown to a sufficient number if cultural and biochemical characteristics are to be determined and the agglutination test to be applied. The main drawback in this test is the number of organisms required, and time necessary for growth. This method has the two disadvantages of slowness and the fact that living organisms are required. This latter limitation applies to all techniques such as the use of bacteriophage and the examination of the metabolic products of bacteria by gas chromatography.

It was hoped by a study of these methods to cut down the time needed for analysis of a specific type of bacterium to a matter of minutes, rather than days. Specific phages gave encouraging results for typhoid, cholera, anthrax, malleomyces and plague. Specificity was good, method rapid, techniques simple and cost low. However, phage-resistant strains may be used in war (which would make this method useless), and in highly contaminated cultures or in the presence of small amounts of certain contaminants, the technique would not work. Even with improvements, this technique is not rapid enough. Characteristic patterns for particular bacteria have

been obtained by use of the infra-red spectrophotometer and unknowns have been identified by comparison. This technique possesses some of the disadvantages of the phage technique and requires
very specialised equipment. It is not the most useful technique as
the analysis of mixtures can be very difficult.

Studies by the US Public Health Department in conjunction with
Fort Detrick workers resulted in the development of FAB techniques.
This involves labelling with dye (fluorescein) an antibody specific
for a particular pathogen. The organism is fixed to a slide. FAB is
added and washed off after some time. Tests are made for residual
fluorescence. This will indicate the presence of that particular
pathogen. The advantages of this technique are:

1. Very small amounts of substance can be used.
2. It works well with living or dead organisms (other techniques
   require living organisms at some stage).
3. Time needed is one hour.
4. Specificity for the pathogen even among contaminants.
5. No tissue sections are required.
6. It is a simple method.
7. It is potentially applicable to all micro-organisms.
8. It does not require too much specialised equipment.
9. FAB solution if stored properly will last for two years.

This represents the best means at present available for the rapid
determination of a specific agent once an attack is known to have
occurred.

FAB techniques can now be brought to a fantastic sensitivity.
Several agents, such as Venezuelan equine encephalomyelitis virus
and Rift Valley fever, have been identified by this technique. Of all
the types of techniques which could be used, ones which involve
specific recognition by antibodies or are connected with this recognition seem the most useful.

In conclusion, it should be remembered that conventional techniques, such as direct staining of the sputum which might disclose
for example pneumonic plague, are still of use. Relatively large
numbers of bacteria are however necessary. Microscopical techniques
of this type are likely to form the backbone of diagnosis for a long
time to come.

The identification of chemical agents is a much simpler operation
than with biologicals. The nerve gases all belong to one type of
compound and in all cases their symptoms are relieved by atropine
and therapy. Other gases are quite clear in their effects. The
potentiality for covert use is much less than for BW so the problems

of detection are simplified. Difficulty with chemical agents would arise if a totally new class of agent were used strategically, especially if like the v nerve agents they were effective through the skin. To prevent this occurring one would need intelligence reports on whatever the enemy was planning. Intelligence assumes a tremendous importance with respect to the development of defences against these agents. It is essential not to be presented with a novel agent. The limit of effectiveness of chemical agents is probably still a long way in the future.

For chemical agents which are not effective through the skin, identification is not of the greatest importance. Current protective devices, suits and gas masks, would probably be effective.

Protective equipment
The technology of this has reached a very high level. The modern operating theatre and special care units for patients who have had, for example, transplant operations, are instances of the creation of germ-free environments. Even under the best of conditions some invasion of micro-organisms still occurs. There are two forms of protection which can be used, personal protection and shelter protection.

Personal protection
This is in the form of suits and gas masks. The latter are available to the armed forces and civilians in America and to the armed forces in Britain (e.g., the s6 mask). These masks, both the military and the non-military type, remove nearly all particles in the 1–5 micron range. Some 99·9% are removed. It should be emphasised that even an efficiency of 99·97% would not be acceptable against biological agents. Even the standard attained is no long-term protection at all. It is essential that people in affected areas should leave these as soon as possible. The situation with respect to gases is similar. In addition if v nerve agents are used it is necessary to have protective clothing. Porton has been instrumental in producing a very effective suit of chromium-complex impregnated microporous polyurethane. This protects against nerve agents quite adequately. According to *Sanity* (July 1968) it is subject to certain limitations. The suit is described as of a rough, loose fabric, green on the outside, black within. The suits are made in three sizes and pressure-packed into 10 × 8 in packages for carrying in a battle-dress pocket. Large numbers have been ordered for NATO forces.

Sanity admirably illustrated and pointed out its limitations.

The material is inflammable [*Sanity* set fire to a piece without difficulty], surprisingly porous, easily torn, and with a reported battlefield life of only six hours. The shelf life may be less than a year and if this is so, constant renewals will obviously be necessary.

This information is no doubt cheering to the Russians. One wonders if the British soldier is as happy about it. The military significance of these suits is that the efficiency of a soldier forced to wear one is halved.

Shelter protection

As far as we have been able to ascertain the only country which provides any more than token form of civilian shelter against CBW is Sweden. Undoubtedly in both Britain and America selected underground installations have elaborate air filtration systems. In England in the event of an attack the regional seats of government would provide some form of protection for such useful members of society as civil servants, the military and selected government officials. To talk of information from Porton prejudicing defence programmes is laughable. There are no defence programmes. One assumes this statement to mean prejudicial to the safety of those members of the establishment that have been considered worthy survivors of our society in event of war.

An ordinary house or establishment could not be in any way adapted for protection against CBW. In Sweden special basements are constructed. Air filtration systems are fitted in most cases by law. The positive pressure principle which has been applied in operating theatres is used in shelter construction. This means that the pressure inside the shelter is greater than that outside, so that if a leak occurs, no agent can get in due to the air escape out. This is the principle of an inflatable field casualty installation for use in CBW situations.

In Britain, the average citizen's chance of surviving CBW attack at present is about as great as his chance of returning nuclear missiles with a tennis racquet. The present lack of knowledge on this subject does not enhance his chances in the slightest. In Sweden, instruction leaflets are issued to every household and further information is available on request. Civil defence is concerned with the assistance and protection of the population in the event of an attack—nuclear or CBW. The British civil defence was disbanded in January 1968.

It should be emphasised that no system currently available is proof against CBW for any extended period of time. Despite the most stringent precautions and the finest filtration systems available, Fort Detrick has had many accidental infections. This is where extensive vaccination and immunisation procedures are practised. Decay and decontamination have particular significance for the effectiveness of any defence procedure.

Decontamination and decay

The us position on decontamination is quite clear. The American manual on the subject, *Emergency Manual Guide on Biological Warfare 1959*, states:

Decontamination of extensive areas is not considered practical. Rather, natural decay, assisted by sunlight, temperature and air movement must be relied on.

[us Department of Health Education and Welfare]

Some agents such as anthrax exhibit a great persistence on reaching the ground and also in aerosol form. Anthrax itself may persist for years; cholera may persist for long periods in the soil and has been known to reinitiate an outbreak eighteen months after it had seemingly died down; foot and mouth disease may well persist in the soil. A further problem concerns the production of vectors. The sterilants ethylene oxide and beta propriolactone have been suggested as decontaminants. The former is less practicable in open field situations. It would be most useful for small objects which had been contaminated. Beta propriolactone is effective on exposed surfaces and especially useful for decontamination of large interior spaces. Insecticides would be used against infected insect vectors.

Decontamination of chemicals is a more feasible proposition. Many of the nerve gases are quickly hydrolysed and therefore rendered inactive. The persistent agents may easily be removed by decontaminating solutions of, for example, calcium hypochlorite. For some of the nerve gases use of this solution may generate the highly poisonous cyanogen chloride. Persistent mustards may also be removed by bleaching powder. Decontamination of mustard-gassed air is possible using solutions of iodine monochloride adducts of the polyvinyl pyrrolidones. These substances are all that is necessary for decontamination.

Medical Defence

America has made special provision, such as packaged disaster hospitals, for a national emergency. Out of the entire population of the us these can cater for 400,000 patients for thirty days. If stand-by facilities are to be used in case of an attack, they would have to be extensive. In the event of biological attack the American facilities would be of little use. Britain, as far as we have been able to ascertain, has not even a token disaster service.

The first obvious necessity in case of attack is early diagnosis. We have already discussed the difficulties involved in this. A further complication might be the use of several agents together, even synergistically. The best approach to this is to have central laboratories, experienced and capable of rapid diagnosis. Clinicians specially instructed in BW and the sort of clinical pictures which might be presented would be particularly useful.

Biochemical defences against biological agents in a future war may not be as effective as one might hope. A strain of anthrax has been developed in America which is resistant to most antibiotics. Chemotherapy in such a case would be difficult. As a prophylactic measure, large-scale application of antibiotics is unlikely to be useful. Extensive stockpiling would be necessary for treatment if a BW attack was feared. Antibiotics with vaccine can together produce a useful protection against some diseases.

In the event of BW attack, much of the subsequent work after initial diagnosis need not necessitate medically qualified personnel. Thus public health measures may not necessarily put too great a strain on available medical personnel. For really effective use, the attack may be launched after military action, such as bombing, had disrupted the public health system. An alternative to this is to saturate the system with refugees. What would happen in the event of a nuclear war is a matter for conjecture. It would be essential in such a situation to attempt to mobilise the fit and the less injured to look after those more seriously affected if possible. With the current state of public knowledge this seems unlikely. For any medical service to be effective in such a situation, plans must be laid in advance. It is useless to talk of 'civil' defence if the civilian population has no idea of what to do. A more realistic approach than some of the literature produced in Britain some years ago advising courses of action in the event of a nuclear attack would be required. One suspects that the shock caused by an attack under present conditions would make any organisation break down. Panic could be a major factor if attack occurred. Mass communications media could play a very important role if they were able and instructed in doing so. Isolation of infected cases is not likely to be effected. If nuclear weapons are not used, then the US thinks that available public health systems could cope. In the current situation it would seem that in an attack on the US all available weapons would be used. To imagine that one side would feel restricted to the use of one type of weapon is an unrealistic optimism, prompted perhaps by the fear of contemplating the combined effects of all these systems.

In conclusion, then, it may be seen that the best defence against CBW at present is to prevent its development. The US Department of Public Health Education and Welfare produces a pamphlet on CBW attack, which is not very convincing of the effectiveness of CBW defence. Defence is possible but not very effective, and, as these weapons are effective against populations, it is almost certainly prohibitively expensive.

Disarmament of these weapons must be a priority.

Of the two classes of weapon, chemical and biological, the biological is currently the greatest threat to civil populations. In the event of extensive war in Europe, however, one may expect that much of Western Europe would be affected by both chemical and biological weapons. Some BW or CW warheads are available for ICBM's, but the number of these is not known. Chemical defence and biological defence we have seen to be of little use at present. We conclude with the words of Dr T. Rosebury, who held a position at Fort Detrick during World War II:

> Defense against BW as a whole is pitiably weak. so weak that none of us, civilian or military, can find much comfort in its prospect. To the military, for BW, as for all other modern weapons defense must be pushed for all its worth, but it isn't worth much. For BW as for others, from the military point of view the best defense will be offense . . . retaliation in kind, if possible doubled or redoubled. I hope you can find some comfort in the thought; it leaves me very cold.

As the trend with respect to the development of these weapons has continued without concomitant development of defensive aspects, then Dr Rosebury's fears (expressed in 1949) have been justified. The years since this original statement have seen much development. The offensive side has blossomed and brought forth the new weapons; defensively, the position is effectively the same as it was then. Cyrus Vance has admitted to a House Committee of the US Congress that there is, in effect, no civilian defence.

The above must represent a very powerful, urgent argument in favour of disarmament.

DEFENSIVE RESEARCH

It may be seen from the previous discussion what defensive research is concerned with. Some research is easily demonstrable as defensive. With other research it is difficult to discern the narrow line between what is necessary for defence and what is necessary basically to form an offensive weapon.

Several suggestions have been made as to methods of distinguishing offensive and defensive interests, none of which is really very useful. It is notable that defensive measures in this field are less dependent on knowledge of offensive techniques than others. The number of micro-organisms and mutant strains which are potential biological weapons is so great that it is not feasible to develop and administer a specific preventative or therapy for the effects of each. Broadly, the classes of research interests which could be described as defensive are those concerned with early detection, identification, protection such as masks and air filters. Future research may be aimed at discovering multiple vaccines and super broad spectrum anti-microbial therapies. As these are of public health and medical interest, they need not be kept secret.

Unfortunately, there is a large body of research which cannot be so easily classified as either offensive or defensive. Much of the British effort falls into this class. The question of whether weapons are being developed is in these cases difficult to assess. Obviously, if some of the research is suspect and some of the other research is secret, any country in this position must lay itself open to charges of development of weapons systems. The only way round this is to have an effort which is demonstrably defensive, where nothing is classified or so very little that the country could have no offensive ability. This cannot prejudice the purely defensive work we have mentioned.

It is interesting to survey the positions of the various powers. America and Russia have made substantial offensive preparations. A large proportion of information (more than 80% in America, probably more in Russia) is not published. It may be possible that the Russians have no offensive BW preparations (though interest in CW is great). Many nations have little interest in this field at all, although how much longer they are going to continue in this fashion is doubtful. Some nations have a purely defensive effort which is demonstrably defensive.

Sweden has such a policy. Almost all of the research work is published. Because CBW affects populations the Swedes have a very active civil defence. They believe that a logical approach to CBW is to have an informed, protected population. Such efforts boost morale considerably. This is a national policy followed by very few other countries. The Swedes do not seem to think that publication of their results is prejudicial to their safety. This is what one would expect in the case of a purely defensive effort. It seems likely that an aggressor would be more deterred by the fact that an attack would not be effective than by the uncertain prospect of retaliation. Evacuation plans and other measures have also been proposed in the event of an attack on Sweden.

Another nation whose effort is 'defensive' is Britain. Britain, unlike Sweden, does have a substantial amount of secret research. The reasons for secrecy are not clear but are probably political rather than due to fears of prejudicing the defensive systems. The alleged defensive brief of Porton is difficult to understand. Sweden, which is concerned with defence, has an active defensive programme. The same cannot be said for Britain. Study of BW without any defensive systems being applied seems a strange form of intellectual masochism in the circumstances.

Current expenditure in Britain must be approach £3 million per annum. The result of this in terms of defence of the targets of biological warfare, the population, is nothing. The people who would, in fact, be affected in case of attack have remained in a state of complete ignorance as to what to do in the event of attack. If an extensive war was waged in Europe, it is possible that chemical, and possibly biological weapons would be used against Britain itself. Chemical weapons would be effective more in the immediate areas of conflict. Chemical, biological and nuclear attack would be practised on populations to judge from statements by, for example, Marshal Zhukov and Admiral Goshikov.

It is interesting to note that H. A. Sisson wrote in 1938:

> First-aid outfits for the treatment of gas casualties will no doubt shortly be offered to the public, but it is hoped they will not need to be as complete as a recent set said to contain, in addition to the usual odds and ends, the burial service in three languages.

Such is our state of preparedness, some thirty years later, that we do not even have the benefit of the burial service in three languages, to say nothing of the odds and ends.

It may have been gathered by now that the defensive effort of Porton is restricted almost entirely to the military. As the civilian population would be most affected in a BW attack, this would at the least be described as short-sighted. The reason for this lack of interest is quite obvious. The provision of gas masks and shelters for the British population would be prohibitively expensive. It seems likely that this is also the reason for the current lack of information on CBW. The facts would be difficult for the public to accept; if revealed they would politically embarrass whatever party was in power at the time. If the British effort is defensive it probably entails the defence of the military in the field and the politicians in the shelters. The regional seats of government (RSGs) and other emergency installations undoubtedly have the finest CBW protection which Porton and the taxpayers' money can provide. It is rumoured that there are underground installations at Nancekuke, even possibly an RSG. If this is so, then one may expect it to be provided with the best possible air filtration unit Porton can produce. No such facilities are available to the general public. Suitable provision has no doubt also been made for the Minister of Defence and other politicians. Despite the fact of its having been in existence for many years, Porton has contributed nothing to the defence of the general population. It could be even argued that its existence in its present form is more of a danger than an aid to our security. This is discussed further in the section on disarmament.

The 'defensive' British research effort into CBW merits closer examination. The first obvious fact is the difficulty of doing this. Some 80–90% of the work of the MRE is published, and a lesser proportion, probably about 50%, of the CDEE's work. The nature of some of the published work may give rise to some disquiet, for example the gene transfer between *Pasteurella pseudotuberculosis* strains mentioned above. Whilst it may be argued that this is fundamental research such transfer could result, if properly developed, in a weapon of genocidal potential. The research in itself is innocent. If any university microbiological laboratory had done this, it would have excited no comment. The fact that Porton workers did this in association with workers from an establishment whose interests are mainly offensive (in this sense as opposed to defensive) must give rise to grave concern. The virginal innocence with which Porton workers assert their non-offensive capabilities must be sullied by this revelation. One is prompted to ask if, in view of the close co-operation which exists between England and the US, the defensive argument is at all justified.

If one examines the major functions of the American, Canadian and British establishments, one may conclude that their respective roles dovetail together quite well. For an aggressor to use these weapons he must possess defences. Porton, it has been said, maintains contact with America so as to prevent duplication of effort. This may be interpreted as meaning that the British concentrate on fundamental research and defence and the Americans on developing weapons. This contention may be reinforced by some of the developments in which Porton has had a hand. The V nerve agents were discovered and early research on them was performed in England and the information passed from Porton to America. These are perhaps the major chemical weapons in terms of size of stockpiles and lethal capabilities in the US armoury. Mr Healey has claimed that the policy of sharing with the Americans has not resulted in any increase in US offensive capabilities. This statement implies one of several things. Either he is unaware of the extent and precise nature of US capabilities or he has not read the minutes of evidence given to the Select Committee on Science and Technology (para 1072, p 254), and he does not know the British contribution which was made. We assume that he had access to pp 1–244, and five of the questions which were deleted from the final form of the 257-page report. On the basis of this, one would expect his knowledge to be more extensive than appears. A final possibility, of course, remains that this statement by Mr Healey was made with the intention of misleading the public. It is a matter of the reader's own choice which of these explanations he thinks most probable.

Mr Healey has said that the work done at Porton is concerned with how an enemy in possession of CBW might use them to attack this country and which targets would be vulnerable. He has said, 'For us to publish this information would be absolutely absurd and very dangerous to the country's security.' We have already shown how, and on what targets, biological warfare could act. As we have no protection for the populace, which is the BW target, the security of the country could not be affected. What would occur is that the public would learn how totally unprepared Britain is against CBW attack. BW is a strategic weapon. To discuss specific 'targets' is ridiculous; it is akin to the situation of attacking a military installation in a town with a nuclear bomb: the town would be destroyed. For BW also it is towns, cities and even countries that are the objects of attack. For a long time the US military have recognised this fact. One can only assume that this information has not reached Mr Healey.

A second argument of Mr Healey's concerns the fact that by telling an aggressor what we are working on, he may gain information about our intelligence sources. This assumes that the enemy has not got intelligence sources just as capable as ours of determining what was happening, for example, at Porton. Even if secret research is conducted, no doubt the Russians know as well as the British government what their interest in CBW is.

Mr Healey also mentions that in CBW research you discover how weapons could be made and to publish this would be dangerous to the British and the world's security. We have shown the difficulty in development, the necessity for field testing and the difficulty of concealment of any large-scale effort. World security is more likely to be endangered by people starting programmes to combat the 'threat' from Porton, Suffield, etc. The point that this knowledge would prejudice Britain's security is ludicrous when the Swedes, who have a larger effort than ours, publish almost all their results. This renders our secrecy singularly pointless.

Mr Healey has also said that Britain's knowledge of what other people were working on might, if revealed, cause them to search for more deadly agents. This is a curious statement as the whole aim of the biological arms race anyway is to produce increasingly more toxic products than the enemy. Thus development is not likely to be hindered by lack of information about the British effort. Lack of detailed knowledge of the Russian BW effort did not prevent an extensive offensive development in the US.

Mr Healey has said that he is satisfied why the British effort must remain secret, and that it will continue in this fashion. All one can say is, if the above is Mr Healey's argument, he is easily satisfied, or has failed to understand what CBW is about. Naturally, it is unlikely that Mr Healey's words were just a smoke screen, and he was attempting to deceive the public and the reasons for secrecy were entirely different! Such considerations would hardly have entered the mind of a member of the British Cabinet.

Of perhaps more serious consequence than the above is the suggestion that while our own effort is defensive, we may posssess an offensive capability through agreements with our allies. The possibility that NATO stockpiles may exist has been suggested. This, one suspects, is not unlikely. Of the NATO countries, West Germany has said (2 June 1968) that she possesses no offensive weapons nor has access to them. This was following allegations in a book written by a former first press secretary to Mr E. McCarthy, Mr Seymour Hersh.

Two of the questions in the minutes of evidence given to the Select Committe for Science and Technology give support to this.

Question 1069: (Off the record)
Answer: (Off the record)

Question 1070: Following that point further we would certainly not have *the* stockpile. [Our emphasis. This obviously refers to a stockpile previously mentioned.]

This would seem to indicate the presence of a particular, previously specified stockpile. It does not, it should be emphasised, say that there is no stockpile, but only that this stockpile was not in British hands. One suspects that this is in the possession of the Americans, because they are the major developers of these weapons in the West. It is most likely that chemical weapons are of British interest. The British have no means of delivering long-range strategic BW weapons effectively.

It may be asked in what form would the British use these weapons. We have already hazarded a few guesses concerning the British effort. The systems we have discussed would probably be the basis for a British offensive capability in this field. In support of this is another question from the Select Committee Report:

Question 1083: Does it represent a breach in the Geneva Convention to have *the* attack capacity in this field? [Our emphasis.]

Answer: No, because the Geneva Convention permits retaliation in kind, not only retaliation against aggressors, but also retaliation against the allies of aggressors.

Again, there is reference to a specific capacity to retaliate. This reference cannot be referring to America as she did not ratify the Convention. Britain did, but preserved the right of retaliation.

Speculation on another aspect of Porton's work concerns our own potentiality for a home-grown CBW weapon. The fact has tended to become obscured over recent years that in the early period of its history its purpose was far from defensive. Exactly when the character changed is not known. It is rumoured, however, that in the early 1950s the CDEE was concerned in producing a special bomb for the dissemination of nerve gas. In principle, it was concerned with the spreading of the agent over the widest possible area before it hit the ground. Support for the belief in Britain's involvement in offensive chemical warfare research is gained from the *Canadian Almanac and Directory*.

Throughout 1952 the chief emphasis at Suffield was on the testing of CW munitions for both the United Kingdom and the US equipments.

In 1952 also a significant development took place. This was the establishment of the pilot plant at Nancekuke. The function of this plant is the investigation of the possibilities for large-scale production. Similar facilities for the examination of the growth of bacteria in continuous culture are available at the MRE. This gives rise to another important point. At what stage does one stop a feasibility study of a weapon if one is only interested in feasibility? To give an example, knowing the principle of the wheel, knowing about engines, guns and tracked vehicles, it would be possible to construct a tank. It is not necessary to construct the tank to study its feasibility. This is the problem with CBW. It would seem possible that feasibility stops at the point at which the Americans could develop British work into a weapons system.

It is possible that there might be perfectly reasonable explanations for the points we have raised, other than the most obvious ones. Whether this is so or not—and many British governments, all of which consisted, no doubt, of honest men, have asserted our strictly defensive interests—the point is that the policy of secrecy has raised these questions. It may be seen then that Britain's CBW involvement is highly suspect. Should this position be maintained, then any British attempts at initiating disarmament talks must seem very suspicious to other nations. No one is going to pay a great deal of attention to a nation whose public protestations are of innocence, and which privately seems to be preparing to use chemical or biological warfare. In the same way, had British initiatives at Geneva been accompanied by some form of gesture to reduce tension, e.g. declassification of Porton, even for a short period, they would have had much more force. In view of the above, British proposals have been viewed with the cynicism they richly deserve.

In conclusion, then, it may well be argued that despite governmental assurances, Britain's defensive work is suspect. In view of the earlier discussion the existence of Porton in its present form, with its secret research, can do little to strengthen Britain's preparedness if no civil defence effort is contemplated. The secret research, we have shown, give rise to the possibility that Britain assists in the production of offensive weapons; this is admirably illustrated by the case of the v agents. It may even be possible that Britain could in fact possess chemical or (less probably) biological weapons for use.

None of the above can help British initiatives on disarmament.

Until these questions are resolved satisfactorily, little progress towards disarmament may be expected. It is also interesting to reflect on the evasions practised by the many governments which have been in office since Porton began its extended operations. If any access to offensive weapons is available, then the attitudes of the various governments to CBW over the years must represent a record of duplicity, attempts to mislead and almost direct lying practically unequalled in British political history.

DISARMAMENT

Regrettably, despite the great dangers of CBW weapons, some countries, notably America and Russia, have made considerable efforts in their production. This has resulted in the deployment of chemical and biological weapons in Europe. There are essentially two approaches to the problem which have occurred to the present writers. The first of these concerns the position of Britain with respect to CBW and the second an approach to international disarmament.

We should like to emphasise that our argument in favour of disarmament is not concerned with the mode of action of these weapons. If one is going to die, then the means has less significance than the end. War in itself is a terrible thing. It has been said that what is attempted in CBW disarmament is the same as, for example, attempts to ban napalm. This is not so. Chemical and, more especially, biological weapons cannot be aimed; napalm or high explosive can. The important point here is the element of choice. C and B weapons are impossible to aim and their effects are even less predictable than those of nuclear weapons. Their effects, in terms of the number of people affected, are quite possibly of the same order as for nuclear weapons. A short examination of some of the arguments of the more passionate apologists for these weapons is given below. The military logic of the apologists for cbw is bizarre. General J. H. Rothschild has given the following reasons for development of these weapons.

1. They are humane.
2. They are effective.
3. The Russians are working on them.
4. Retaliation in the event of nuclear attack is simply punitive. General Rothschild believes that we should include the use of lethal biological agents along with the nuclear to ensure that our deterrent is as strong as possible.
5. In the event of China initiating nuclear war, the General has said: 'I don't believe we would wait for much investigation, but would immediately launch a retaliatory attack on the USSR, and of course receive all its might in return.'

He believes biological weapons would be a more effective deterrent to China than nuclear weapons.

6. It would be extremely valuable in equalising the Communist numerical superiority on the battle field.
7. These weapons would seek out a hidden enemy.
8. He believes that they could be used against a friendly country which was occupied 'since it would be desirable to keep killing damage to a minimum'.
9. The biological problem, as these things can be so easily hidden, is comparable to the clandestine weapons problem in the nuclear area.

By way of conclusion the general has said:

From a military standpoint, we must establish the fact that chemical and biological weapons are a normal usable means of war. Our military must be prepared to use these weapons and to defend themselves against them, something which is not true now. In the total context CB warfare, and particularly the biological in conjunction with nuclear war, adds up to the fact that war in the future is a completely unacceptable method of solving world problems.

Other gems of military thought are also instructive. The hearings of the us House Committee on Science and Astronautics (June 1960) are informative. Some selections from the evidence given previously are quoted below:

The best immediate guarantee the US can possess to ensure that
CBR is not used anywhere against the free world is to have a
strong capability in this field too . . . I would hate to see us enter
into any agreement with anybody regarding CBR so that if we
are going to fight we are going to do it with our hands tied behind
our back.

General Stubbs (on 'The Chemical Corps' Role in National Defense';
speech printed by the Department of the US Army Chemical Corps).

The greatest deterrent to war is to have such an offensive capability that an enemy would refrain from attacking for fear of our
retaliatory measures. We in the Chemical Corps are not neglecting
this area.

1. The first point made by General Rothschild is not of great
interest. War by definition is inhumane. One may, however, attack
his argument, which was based on World War I statistics. In summary this was that the proportion of fatal casualties for chemical
weapons was less than for high explosives, etc. The only thing that
this proves is that the weapons were not very effective at that time.
This is hardly relevant now.

In *Callinicus: a Defence of Chemical Warfare*, by J. B. S. Haldane,
the following interesting passage occurs.

In 1915 a British chemist proposed to a general who was concerned in such questions that the British should use dichlorethyl
sulphide. 'Does it kill?' asked the General. 'No,' he was told, 'but
it will disable enormous numbers of the enemy temporarily.'
'That is no good to us,' said the man of blood. 'We want something that will kill.' It is interesting to find how completely the
ideas of this worthy soldier, as to the object of war, coincided
with those of the average intelligent child of five years old.

To judge from the brighter military suggestions for solution of the
Vietnam problem, nuclear weapons, etc., generals are little changed.
'War', as General Groves has said in his book, *Behind the Smoke
Screen*, 'is not conducted in accordance with the laws of logic, or
even in accordance with common sense.' This is admirably illustrated by the case of Vietnam. Logic, law, common sense and
humanity have all been forgotten in a long drawn out bloody
scramble. Even in the use of the gas weapon 'humanely', the
rationale for its original use has gone by the board. It is the difference in the attitude of minds of the user and the attitude of the
person developing it which is likely to make the humane use of
these weapons very unlikely.

2. That they are effective is very true. The problem is that their effects could be radically different from those predicted. We have already discussed this and do not intend to go into it further here. 3. Point three is that the Russians are working on CBW. This is an interesting illustration of a form of double-think characteristic of the apologists of this kind of warfare. The way this works is that our side, by definition the 'goodies', has to prepare these weapons in order to combat the other side, by definition the 'baddies'. The first essential is to get money for the programme. This is done by assuring the government that there is a threat which must be combated.

MR SIKES: 'Does intelligence tell us what the Russians are really doing in this field?'

VANCE: 'Our intelligence indicates that they are devoting considerable attention to it.'

To support this, assessment may be made of the size of effort required. Hence the inauguration of a vigorous five year plan on the part of the US to 'equalise' the situation. US intelligence sources have revealed Russian interest in chemicals but not in biological weapons, in fact most probably before the 1950s they had little interest in biological warfare at all. One need have no doubt that they have considerable interest now. The Russian arguments for an increase in budget, one supposes, were along the same lines.

One thing to emerge from this is the dependence upon intelligence. What Secretary Vance has said is in fact nothing; it gives no indication of where Russian effort is directed. Even if the Russians had a genuinely defensive effort this could just as easily have been used as a lever for the procurement of funds. What has happened here is that rather than institute research to lessen the effect of this threat, a strong counter-threat is developed. What follows is an inevitable round of escalation which we have all seen before in nuclear weapons. In effect, whatever the threat, the Army Chemical Corps was given *carte blanche* to develop anything it wished. This may have been totally out of proportion to the original Russian effort.

From the Russian side, undoubtedly the existence of Fort Detrick, Dugway, Suffield and Porton is more than ample reason for the development of weapons of their own if they apply the same logic. One can imagine a similar appropriations committee in Russia being told that all the above establishments that are involved in secret research are working on offensive weapons. Porton, which is at least partially engaged in secret research, is effective in contributing towards this escalation. Most probably somewhere in Russia Dr Ivan Ivanovich is engaged in defensive research, many of the results of which are published. One need only look at the bulletin of the Academy of Sciences of the USSR to see their active interest in the organophosphate compounds which gave rise to the nerve gases. The point is that any secret research can be misconstrued, possibly even wilfully, to be offensive.

4. Perhaps one of the most illogical arguments. General Rothschild believes that biological weapons should be used in conjunction with nuclear weapons. This seems bound to occur in the event of large-scale war, if things are allowed to remain the way they are at present. To increase the strength of the deterrent in this way is not a logical response. It is like cutting off a man's head and then castrating him. The latter is not really necessary. Use of biological weapons in the fashion suggested by the general could possibly lead to a situation in which man himself would be in danger of extinction. It is difficult to be sure, but one would prefer not to find oneself in a position to evaluate first hand the data.

5. The fifth point is directly related to the fourth. The general believes that biological weapons would be the best deterrent against China. The people against whom the use of these weapons is suggested varies as to whether the 'red menace' or 'the yellow peril' is currently the most favoured. If the aim of future war is to kill whole populations, then General Rothschild is right. If, however, the aim is to remove the potentiality for effective aggression, then there is no reason to choose CBW rather than nuclear weapons. The latter used on centres of population, administrative headquarters, etc., would quite effectively render the Chinese powerless. Should the general be contemplating genocide of the whole Chinese race, together with at least parts of Russia and probably the whole of south-east Asia, it is impossible to refute his argument. This would, of course, provide an adequate solution to the problem of Vietnam.

6. This concerns the value of these weapons in reducing Communist numerical superiority in the field. This assumes that the Communists are not protected against the agents developed. It also assumes that they are going to be sporting about it and refrain from using these weapons themselves. Should this not be so, then little change in the relative strengths of the two sides would result; just a dramatic decrease in total numbers.

7. The next point deals with the ability of CB weapons to seek out hidden enemies. This is a property that these weapons share with radioactive fallout. The only consolation in this is that there are no effective systems capable of excluding CBW agents for any length of time. Even the shelters which governments have probably provided for themselves are at best only of short-term usefulness. We trust that this consoles the reader as much as it consoles the authors.

8. This point gives us admirable means of examining a policy and its execution. The general says that these could be used against friendly occupied countries to avoid killing and damaging civilians. This altruistic policy is perhaps best illustrated by its present application in Vietnam. Great ingenuity has been practised in some cases by the US Army in making sure that civilians are not 'damaged' or killed by the use of gas. Large numbers have not been killed by gas in Vietnam; probably, at the most, only a few hundreds or thousands have been. The use of gas in combination with other techniques is, however, different. Effectiveness, rather than humanity, has been the major consideration of the military.

The problem is that whatever the political considerations the Army seeks to wage war as efficiently as it can. The policy-makers define the ends, and in Vietnam the US Army is the means. One of the priorities of a commander is to avoid casualties amongst his own men; he therefore uses the weapons at his disposal to the greatest effect. This is definitely the case in Vietnam. The problem about this conflict is that the policy-makers cannot control the military, and in addition are totally at the mercy of military 'experts'.

The degree to which General Rothschild's thesis is being considered by the military may be readily determined from the size and content of CBW stockpiles. Of the chemical munitions the nerve agents are the most abundant. In view of their effects it seems unlikely that these are contemplated for use as incapacitants. A quick survey of research contracts reveals that lethal agents are of much more interest than incapacitants. It does not seem that this emphasis will change in the near future.

9. Finally, the general points out the fact that these weapons, especially the biologicals, can be easily hidden. On other occasions he has indicated that an offensive capability is a way of maintaining America's security. We have already referred to his statement of what he thinks would happen if the Chinese made a covert nuclear strike. If in such an instance CBW had been initiated from, say a submarine off the coast, the problem would be where to retaliate. Any one of a hundred nations could develop the technology necessary for CBW. To retaliate massively against China and Russia could be a serious error. The idea of a deterrent strategy of this type is disconcerting. The military obsession with deterrence against any weapon produced is horrifying: it has no logic at all. This strategy is inapplicable to these weapons. Deterrence only has meaning when the potential aggressor knows that retaliation is inevitable. It will be realised from the above that in the current situation, any nation opposed to the major powers or even a sizeable group of individuals could attack with practically no fear of being detected. Should these

weapons be developed to a high state of efficiency then the whole uneasy basis of the peace between the two armed camps of the world could be undermined. Such development could make all the progress towards nuclear disarmament completely meaningless.

General Rothschild's concluding statements are indeed strange. The reasoning behind them seems to be that, as war becomes more terrible, sooner or later it will be realised that it is inconceivable as a means of settling disputes. Whilst appreciating his pacifist aims, one must conclude that his way of trying to realise them is fraught with danger. We are at present treading a very narrow tight-rope and the consequences of a slip is destruction. The general's basic premise seems to be that we will manage this trick long enough to realise the stupidity of our position. There do not seem to be many signs of this realisation at present and one fears that the general may be making a tragic mistake in his ardent advocacy of these weapons. Such remarks seem to us to show even more clearly the urgency of a concerted and meaningful effort towards disarmament. Whether recent efforts have been meaningful may be doubted.

The long history of war has rarely seen the placing of restraint on a weapon before its development was far advanced, yet this happened in the case of CBW. It is instructive to see the succession of events which have led, despite this, to the deployment and use of these prohibited weapons.

Despite the widespread use of gas in the first world war, it never became accepted as a weapon, either by the military or by the public. This revulsion was largely due to the exploitation by British propaganda of the Germans' initiation of gas warfare. It was this climate of opinion which led to the signing of the Geneva Protocol on chemical weapons in 1925. It seems likely that the attitude of the United States at that conference was to favour the licensing of the use of gas rather than its complete prohibition. This would explain the decision of the US not to ratify the protocol after signing it. As a result of this general prohibition little development of gas warfare was carried on in the West until the thirties.

In the 1930s Japan, which had not signed the protocol, employed gas, as did Italy, which had signed it. This made the weaknesses of the protocol apparent. Firstly, there was no restriction on the possession of weapons; secondly, there was no effective international machinery for dealing with infringements. A third factor is that a number of countries did not sign or, as in the case of the United States, did not ratify the protocol. This largely accounts for the present situation.

In the second world war neither side used gas, although both had large stockpiles. The reasons for this were more fear of retaliation than respect for international law, at least in Europe. Churchill had threatened to saturate Germany with gas if the Germans began gas warfare, and a knowledge of the ruthlessness of the reprisals which would follow was a more important inhibiting factor than the Geneva Protocol.

Although the nerve gases were discovered before the end of the war, their use was not contemplated until too late, by Hitler when he was facing defeat. Churchill would have used CBW if the Germans invaded Britain. It was thus regarded by both sides as a last resort, a last chance of saving the situation. Apart from this, the only situation in which such weapons might have been used was by the United States against the Japanese, whose population was largely unprepared for such an attack. The Japanese accepted Roosevelt's declaration of 'no first use', and progressively decreased their work on CBW from that time until the end of the war. They (foolishly) relied on the public declaration of policy rather than the military capability of the United States. Had there not been something better (the atom bomb), it is probable that gas would have been used.

The post-war expansion of work on CBW was due mainly to the USA and the USSR. The Russians' CBW preparations were probably seen initially as an answer to the US possession of nuclear weapons, and largely as a stop-gap response. The Russian development of CBW expanded considerably in the late 1940s and early 1950s as an extension of the CW work which had been part of the war effort. (The Germans credited the Russians with a high CW capability, and in view of the previous cooperation between the two countries they were in a good position to judge.)

United States work on CBW during the war (especially in BW), and her failure to ratify the Geneva Protocol, resulted in her vulnerability to charges of the sort the Chinese made over Korea. Russian work was carried out so secretly that little knowledge of her CBW capabilities was available; significantly, she was also a signatory of the protocol. In terms of its propaganda effects, CBW has been a running sore in the side of the Americans ever since Korea.

Of particular interest in this connection is the work of the International Scientific Commission which investigated the allegations of BW in Korea (see above, pp 57–63). The ISC was not successful in proving its case. Its members had no training in, or experience of, biological warfare: access was too long after the events, and—not least—its members showed significant bias. There is much that can be learnt from this episode about the setting up of similar machinery today. A further factor in this case was the ineffectiveness of the United Nations, which set an unfortunate precedent. The absence of machinery for dealing rapidly and effectively with allegations such as those of the Chinese contributed greatly to their propaganda success.

The use of gas in the Yemen provides another illustration of these defects. The lack of publicity for the allegations contributed to the failure to arouse effective international criticism. Public opinion could have exerted pressure on governments, but the public was given almost no information. All the western countries, and Britain in particular, showed little interest, almost certainly for fear of compromising the United States in Vietnam if cw became a subject of public discussion.

From the late 1950s onwards, thanks largely to the efforts of the Chemical Corps to influence the government, the us budget for cbw increased. This was paralleled by an increased Russian effort, and by similar significant efforts in at least eleven countries, including France, the Netherlands, Belgium, Italy, Sweden, Norway, Poland, Czechoslovakia, Hungary, East Germany and Egypt. In addition to these, South Africa, Canada and Australia have done varying amounts of work.

The main success of the apologists for cbw has been Vietnam. And here again, for the same reasons as in Korea, the United States has sacrificed even more of its prestige for a doubtful military advantage. To attack rice crops in Asia is, quite apart from any other considerations, a politically insensitive action. One of the most important results of the us action in Vietnam is that it has further weakened the moral and psychological barriers to the use of cbw, as no doubt the supporters of cbw intended. This has not affected merely the United States, but the us action in Vietnam made it easier for the United Arab Republic to use in the Yemen. International reaction had a temporary effect in Vietnam, but the use of gas has now been resumed on a horrifying scale. Throughout, the un has been able to do little.

From this account, the priorities for disarmament would seem to be, first, getting general accession to the Geneva Protocol, secondly, the banning of stockpiling and the preparation for the use of cbw, together with provisions for efficient inspection, and thirdly, enabling the un to take a more positive role in examining allegations. The un would need the power to mount investigations and to operate disciplinary machinery.

It would also be possible to take action within Britain and other countries in a similar position. Such action at national level in Britain would involve the declassification of cbw research and the gradual loosening of ties with establishments in the United States. For best effect these could be combined with meaningful disarmament proposals. (The current British disarmament initiative is discussed at the end of this chapter.)

According to Dr J. Humphrey at the CBW conference in London, February 1968, the best means of working a declassification programme would be to start on a temporary basis with the MRE. More of the MRE's work is published and so this might be easier than for the CDEE. The chemical defence establishment could follow later. This would be greatly facilitated if a favourable international reaction to the declassification of the MRE occurred. A possible period of time for experimental purposes would be of the order of five to seven years.

By virtue of its close collaboration with the United States in the field of CBW, Britain is in a unique position to put forward effective proposals for disarmament. A gesture such as the phased declassification of the MRE over a period of, say, three years (to allow disengagement from US efforts) coupled with a genuine effort to draw up an effective international treaty would be a major step forward.

The arguments against declassification have been dealt with in the section on defensive research. It is obvious that the British position on CW is ambiguous, even if that on BW is clear. British cooperation with the United States and other countries makes the 'defensive' posture at best suspect. It has already been shown that the claim that British defence against BW would be jeopardised by declassification is nonsense. There is little doubt that US political pressure has been the biggest obstacle to declassification. The work of US and British establishments is so closely linked that the disclosure of British work might also reveal US offensive interests. Similarly, advice and other assistance from the US, for example, visits by British officers to US establishments, keeps Britain informed of developments in weapons and training. On the whole, in view of the possible gains, and of the lack of British interest in offensive BW, the MRE could clearly be declassified. The recent apparent decline of interest in CBW in the US may ease the pressure on the British government to keep this work classified. It would be a bigger problem to declassify the CDEE. As it stands, the MRE is an invitation to any country to start BW preparations.

We have considered the means and the end but what are the possible gains? Porton is undoubtedly potentially one of the finest establishments for the study of toxicology, microbiology and industrial hygiene in the world. Even now protective clothing against the V nerve gases developed at Porton is manufactured in Britain and exported to NATO countries. The CDEE could become a centre for toxicological study and the development of protection. Such enterprises would even contribute towards the cost of running the establishment. The centre could be administered by the Ministry of Health or Medical Research Council but the military would still have the advisory facility which Porton claims as one of its major functions today. Collaboration with the World Health Organisation and the Food and Agriculture Organisation on problems of mutual interest, even in the trial period, would be desirable.

The actual teams built up to study CBW would not then be split up but would be maintained and, should the experiment prove a failure, could return to their original work. One would emphasise though that should Porton gain a high reputation it would certainly attract the finest scientists in the land, many of whom would not go there under its present secrecy. Thus the declassification could result in the formation of stronger teams of experts than are at present there and many finer brains could be applied to problems. The usefulness of the establishment in an advisory capacity to the military may even be enhanced. Secrecy is quite often a cloak for bad science. The scientific standards of the establishment could be made higher by free exchange of information and scientists with outside establishments.

The above benefits would seem to us to outweigh any dubious advantage to be gained from secret research. One thinks that while Porton is not a particularly useful sword (or a shield for defence), in the words of Dr Humphrey, it could make a 'magnificent' ploughshare. Public opinion one feels sure would support this initiative.

We have now discussed the significance of defensive and offensive research and the need for declassification. The next steps seems to be now to stop CBW internationally. As we have said previously, the best way to stop CBW is not to allow it to start. There is still room for optimism at present. Concerted efforts on this problem could yield significant diplomatic and political results. The Nixon administration may well (if it has not done so before this book appears) ratify the Geneva Protocol and reduce the emphasis on CBW capability in the army. This would be a logical sequel to President Nixon's recent pledge to support genuine initiatives for disarmament in CBW, and the heavy cuts in the CBW budget for offensive lethal weapons.

The first step in any serious initiative in this direction would be an attempt to get all countries to sign and ratify the Geneva Protocol.

The first international initiative one would like to see is a general agreement made by which all nations affirmed their opposition to BW. Unanimity on such an agreement would be essential. This first step would provide a lever towards implementing disarmament plans. This would be important as the pressure of world opinion would be against any nation trying to back out of further disarmament preparations. Austria has already taken the step of abjuring the use of these weapons.

Following this it would be necessary to form a study group to examine in detail the particular problems. Unlike the group which recently produced the report for the secretary general, this would produce data on inspection and the feasibility of arms control, and make specific recommendations for disarmament plans.

Various members of the Pugwash organisation could usefully employ their knowledge on the subject of CBW disarmament here. This group of scientists has been studying CBW disarmament problems for the last twenty years.

The problems of the study group would be many. These would include, from the start, the difficulties in the detection of CBW research and development. A major aspect would involve the setting up of inspection teams. The experiences of the Western European Union, who have been examining disarmament problems of all types, would be of interest here. WEU teams usually consist of three men, one of whom is usually, but not always, a native of the country inspected. Obviously, such teams must have immediate right of access to be at all effective. At the present time it would not seem practicable to have a permanent team, though this must be the long-term aim. Problems of the team in operation could be discussed at regular times. Meetings and rehearsals would have to be regular to test the teams and to keep up morale. Specialised field groups would have to be briefed so that meaningful data would be collected. One suspects that inspection teams would be operative at three levels: first, the examination of installations for clandestine production; secondly, field teams to collect the data when use was alleged; thirdly, a scientific advisory team who would be of very high scientific standing to perform tests, examine evidence and keep problems under review. The first teams would be permanent and would perform routine inspections. The second teams could be permanent, or possibly a 'pool' of younger scientists, with training in the relevant fields, prepared for emergency use. If the scientific standard was high enough then one could reasonably expect good, valid conclusions, and very few unproven results. If there was a general ban on BW, then inspection, especially with respect to field trials, would be facilitated. Countries engaging in 'defensive' experiments would then invite observers from the teams to preclude any suggestion of possible 'offensive' preparation.

The brief of each of these teams would present special difficulties. Initially the inspection team's difficulties would be largely on account of the relatively large number of establishments which could possibly be involved in cbw production and research. Their work could be made easier by every possible cbw establishment in a country, industrial and research, submitting lists of its capacity and its personnel. As experience was gained, the questionnaires, etc., would improve. Dossiers would be kept, giving accounts of published work and work in progress of all the members. Thus if a suspicious concentration of microbiologists occurred at one place and too little information was available, an inspection team would be sent. This would mean a very large effort in collating the broad spectrum of information which would have to be surveyed. Probably inventories of equipment would have to be kept, for this the cooperation of instrument manufacturers would be useful. Detailed information on establishments, periodicals and publications, and general information, would be necessary. Storage and retrieval of data would have to be computer controlled. In addition to the bw concern, a centre for the collection of information on biological services could have considerable use as a means of providing a valuable service to scientists. In this fashion, reports of papers in their own fields of interest from a wider variety of sources than usual would be available. It would prevent the current waste of time involved in searches of the literature, which can result in information being missed. Again, in this case, secret intelligence would have a considerable significance in reinforcing the documentation effort.

Until such time as the system described or a similar one becomes operative, and it is obviously more of a long-term than short-term objective, encouragement of 'open' cooperation in non-sensitive fields should be practised. A further factor which would ease the problems of this team would be if the growing internationalism of biologists was exploited. Anyone who heard of suspect research could then communicate this to the relevant authority at regular gatherings of biologists, symposia, meetings, etc. Heden has suggested a dual passport system for microbiologists with international recognition in addition to national. This in Heden's view would ease the interchange of scientists. Such organisations as the international unions for the respective sciences would be important.

The significance of the 'open' system cannot be over-emphasised; it is a necessary first step towards effective information sharing. The peace-time desirability of this is that such a system would help the who with studies on epidemiology, assist development of protective techniques, provide evaluation of defensive measures and form a basis for cooperation in more sensitive, and at the moment secretly conducted, research.

The team involved in field use inspection would also face difficulties, some of which we have already discussed. Problems arising apart from these include complications over the appearance of new strains of disease, for example the new virulent strain of dengue virus causing haemorrhagic fever in south-east Asian countries, and other new virus diseases or even classes of organisms, for example vervet monkey disease. Examination after the event with current techniques is not very effective in determining BW application. Inspection in, for example, Vietnam at the present time would present a variety of difficulties not easy to surmount. Serious gaps in current identification techniques exist for certain possible BW agents, especially viruses. This applies particularly to many of the arborviruses, myxoviruses and enteroviruses.

A further problem at present is the lack of knowledge of the epidemiology of certain diseases in locations such as south-east Asia, the Middle East and other possible trouble spots. There is still too incomplete an understanding of epidemic spread of disease. Major efforts in the fields of immunological surveys, epidemiological surveillance programmes, with competent and repeated investigations, and the ecology of infectious diseases in particular areas, are required. These are necessary to provide base-line data and information to exclude the possible natural origin of what was suspected to be biological warfare. The existing facilities of WHO are at present rather limited. Their activities, if extended, could provide the basis for this programme.

The Food and Agriculture Organisation could have a considerable importance in the examination of plant disease—one estimate has given a likely increase in food available in the developing countries of 25–50% on existing amounts simply by applying known methods of controlling food-crop pests. This work is related to BW prevention and protection. Again, the research effort of this organisation could be profitably expanded.

The author would like to present his personal view that a central research organisation like CERN (for nuclear energy research) could be set up in the biological sciences. The presence of a single, large, centralised institute in some place, preferably in Europe, say, Switzerland or Italy, could have profound effects on biological research progress. One feels that such a place, if placed on an adequate financial footing, could fulfil an invaluable function. Special provision could be made so that a large proportion of the staff was on a short-term basis thus permitting scientists from many countries to study and return home again. This might form some sort of bridge between developing and developed countries. Such a project might also stem the current drain of manpower from the less developed nations and Europe to America. This interchange would also lessen the problems of surveillance considerably as mobility of scientists would be increased.

Such centralisation would carry the benefit that even while working on their own research interests the three types of team we have mentioned would be instantly available for use. This would also facilitate the examination and research into problems arising from BW application. It would permit all three suggested types of team to meet regularly and discuss problems of mutual interest, and it would prevent all the problems of extracting people from their own countries, where they could be subject to political pressures.

One further question remaining is who would coordinate this activity? The obvious candidate at present is the United Nations. So far no group of the UN family of organisations has developed a major interest in BW although much thought has been given to the problems. Extension of the WHO is proceeding apace, but would need to be on a much larger scale than suggested at present to make a meaningful contribution. The dovetailing of the activities of these organisations would be critical to the development of an international programme. The problem of how BW research could be fitted into the UN system is too complex to discuss in detail here. The difficulty, one suspects, would not be as great as it at first would seem. There is much inter-relationship between UN organisations and biological groups, for example UNESCO gives funds to the International Council of Scientific Unions which distributes these amongst various sciences, of which biology is one.

It is not suggested that this organisation should be controlled or financed by the UN, but rather that the UN could have an advisory function which, as the problem of CBW became more tractable, could be extended to cover conservation, environmental pollution and similar neglected problems. Any agreement which did not support political initiatives with large-scale scientific examination of the problems involved would be worthlesss.

Special guarantees, one feels, would have to be made to small countries. These if tempted by BW would soon find themselves involved in considerable research effort. Even a separate defensive effort by each of the smaller countries could put a strain on resources. The international centre we have described would allow for the interchange of scientists, especially from the smaller countries. (This would have to be done carefully, as it is possible that in some circumstances it could decrease world security.) This, one feels, would produce an increase of mutual trust. Any participating country must be subject to intensive study in its own epidemiology, etc., and the diseases prevalent. It should also have access to the information on public health, epidemics, immunology, biology in general to assist its own peaceful efforts. The function of the international research institute would be to aid with information and assist in preventing a spread of any disease (caused by BW or not). The assurance would be given that in the event of attack, or any other epidemic contingency, plans laid down by the organisation would be implemented, and all aid and support from the UN would be given. If the effects of the attack, if it was such, were minimised and the attacker identified, retaliation with conventional forces would be possible, even perhaps with the assistance of a UN force. For the aligned nations sufficient help of a military nature would be forthcoming from the Americans or Russians. For the non-aligned nation a UN peace-keeping force, or a force from an allied non-aligned country, might be preferable. This would provide a means of guaranteeing the safety of the smaller countries. It would also produce tangible benefits for those countries who suffer considerably from endemic disease.

For an international centre to be effective in the manner stated, its size would have to be in the region of one of the largest American universities. The budget one would like to see is about £100 million to allow the complete centre to be built and the workers installed. This is less than either the current American or Russian budget for CBW in one year. Spread over many countries this would not be a great deal individually. Should this sum seem excessive, it should be remembered that the installations at Fort Detrick, Dugway and Edgewood would cost more to build today, and this is one country's effort. Money should be available on an annual basis dependent on the magnitude of the effort or expenditure on installation equipment and number of staff. Some expansion would also be envisaged.

To a greater or lesser extent the same developments could be used for chemical warfare. The necessity for a centre is less. The necessity for inspection teams would be the same, however. Teams qualified in inspection could be set up by the control authority as before. The surveillance facilities would not need to be as great. Covert preparation of chemical weapons is more difficult than BW and they do not present as great a threat. Here difficulties would arise with the protection of the interests of commercial firms. It is essential to respect the secrecy of commercial firms to prevent the loss of patent rights, etc. If this is in any way breached, then the difficulties of inspection would increase. Centres for CW research could become centres of public health, toxicology and protective clothing research. Whilst undergoing the transformation they would still maintain their advisory capacity to the military. There is a much lesser need for a centralised toxicology facility on a supranational scale. In Britain inspection could be adequately supervised by the CDEE cooperating

with observers from foreign countries. It is in this respect that the
CDEE would still have considerable value. As before, treaty guarantees
would be necessary. At the present state of development, then the
problems and difficulties of disarmament are less than for BW, the
military commitment to chemical weapons is, however, greater. More
difficulty is going to arise with, for example, the US Army Chemical
Corps, which would deal with any threat to its existence with its
considerable lobbying power, and public relations facilities. It is in
this respect that the American government is vulnerable in that it
relies on advice from the military 'experts', who have a vested
interest in keeping these weapons in existence. Fortunately, the
same cannot be said of Britain, where there is no counterpart to the
Chemical Corps.

A problem is also likely to arise over the destruction of the stockpiles of agents. These are considerable. Possibly a greater number of
permanent CW inspection teams of the first type (for examining production and stockpiling) would be required initially than for BW.
The two functions could be combined.

It is hoped that the above rough discussion of one or two ideas for
disarmament may be of some use. These represent more a framework for discussion than concrete suggestions, and it is obvious that
many problems remain to be solved. The intention of this section is
to illustrate the possibilities for starting disarmament discussions. It
strikes the present writers as singularly short-sighted to campaign
for disarmament without offering any practical proposals for
enabling this to come about. The above represent what in our
opinion is a good starting point for examination of this problem.
One would point out that any campaign for CBW disarmament, unless it offers realistic suggestions, is not likely to be successful.

We may now examine the usefulness of the British proposals pre-
sented by Mr Mulley to the 1969 Geneva disarmament conference.
Significant points emerge from both the British draft treaty and
Mr Mulley's speech presenting it:

At the time of Mr Mulley's speech the UN Secretary General's
report on chemical and biological warfare had just been published.
The secretary general made three recommendations on the basis of
his study of the report. They may be summarised as follows:

1. All states should accede to the 1925 Geneva Protocol.
2. United Nations members should affirm that the protocol covers
tear gas and harassing agents in addition to all others.
3. All states should work 'to halt the development, production
and stockpiling of all chemical and bacteriological (biological)
agents for purposes of war and to achieve their elimination from
the arsenal of weapons'.

Mr Mulley agreed with the first recommendation wholeheartedly. With regard to the second he had some reservations. He pointed out that half the members of the United Nations are parties to the protocol, and added: 'It is for the parties to the Protocol, and them alone, to say what the Protocol means.' If it is intended that all states should accede to the protocol, it would seem right that other members of the UN wishing to follow the secretary general's recommendation should affirm what they are to be bound by.

Mr Mulley went on: 'Moreover, the Secretary General interprets the Protocol as covering both lethal and non-lethal chemical agents.' So did the British, before the second world war. The whole tenor of Mr Mulley's comments on the secretary general's second recommendation is to suggest that the protocol is ambiguous. In fact, its wording is quite clear. It prohibits 'poisonous, asphyxiating *or other gases*' (our italics). It is only the Americans who have clouded the issue in their efforts to justify their actions in Vietnam. Mr Mulley's remarks on this point are dangerous, in that they help to create the impression that there are gaps in the protocol where none in fact exists. It looks as though the British government, true to form, is trying not to offend the United States, and it is even likely that US pressure has been brought to bear in the matter. The second recommendation is clearly aimed at the situation in Vietnam, and the acceptance of this by the conference would clearly label US action as prohibited by the protocol. Mr Mulley is trying to avoid such an explicit statement by the UN members, which would considerably embarrass the United States; the US would find it very difficult to go unilaterally against the majority of its allies. British policy at the Geneva conference thus amounts to another contribution to the US war effort.

Mr Mulley's speech goes on to argue that lack of agreement on this point might cast doubt on the validity of the protocol. Even if there was dissent, however, there would certainly be a clear majority in favour of the secretary general's three recommendations which would leave the US position exposed.

It was to take account of the second and third recommendations that Mr Mulley presented his new treaty. This circumvented the difficulty of the second recommendation by ignoring it for the foreseeable future, and it is only the third which has relevance to Mr Mulley's proposals.

Mr Mulley quotes from the secretary general's report some interesting but rather dubious data, such as the comparison of the effects of chemical, biological and nuclear weapons. This ignores the most important danger of BW, which is not the area covered, but the dangers which arise from the unpredictability of biological warfare. In the view of the present writer comparisons of CBN effects are invalid, since the effects of CB weapons are considerably more uncertain than those of nuclear ones.

A point in favour of the treaty outlined by Mr Mulley is its recognition of the importance of BW disarmament as a first aim, and its attempt at relating this by an article in the treaty committing states to early attempts to prohibit chemical weapons. In the present draft, however, chemical and biological warfare are nowhere defined unambiguously. The bacterial toxins, for example, are not classified by the draft, which would be a very serious loophole. Some of Mr Mulley's examples in this section make one wonder if he has really grasped some of the fundamentals of BW. One example is the following:

> However, it is possible to envisage the use in war of biological agents which are not microbes; hookworm, for instance, or the worm causing bilharzia, or even crop-destroying insects such as locusts or Colorado beetles.

The real value of the agents mentioned as weapons of war should now be clear. Such a statement gives one little confidence in Mr. Mulley's advisers.

Hookworms are 8–11 mm long, too long for spreading by conventional means; they would have to be introduced into water supplies, and so on. They are also effective only where rainfall is higher than 50 in. per year, where hygiene is very poor and sanitation practically non-existent. Lavatories are a highly effective protection. Effective treatment is possible, and it takes a long time for infection to cause any noticeable effects; infection also has to be heavy. Treading with bare feet on faeces would make one liable to infection, but it is difficult to imagine widespread uses for such an agent. The bilharzia worm too is an extremely unlikely agent, for similar reasons, and also because of its dependence on the snail as an intermediate host. As for locusts, their last recorded use as a weapon, was by Moses (Exodus 10). They are large insects, and would have to be used in such enormous numbers that to keep them in a state of mobilisation and to deliver them so that they survived transit and dissemination would create an insuperable logistical problem. If small numbers were used, they would simply be eaten by local birds. Even if one could get large numbers of locusts on the ground, they only form swarms during part of their life, and the factors which influence them are unknown. As yet breeding locusts in captivity has not been successful, and would be impossible on the scale necessary for BW. If it did prove possible to raise a large swarm in approxi-

mately the right area, its direction and behaviour would be totally
outside the disseminator's control.

Colorado beetles come a little nearer to reality, but the group of
examples as a whole is largely science fiction.

Some of Mr Mulley's later statements give further, and more
serious grounds for concern:

> Verification, in the sense in which that term is normally used in
> disarmament negotiations, is simply not possible in the field of
> biological warfare.

Fourteen trial inspections for BW weapons production were carried
out in the eighteen months preceding April 1968 by the Stockholm
International Peace Research Institute in several participating countries. Seventy experts were asked to assess the results and estimate
the chances of detecting a secret attempt to infringe an international
BW treaty. Without the assistance of intelligence data (of crucial
importance in real situations like this), the estimate was 55%. The
chances of detecting a clandestine underground nuclear explosion of
less than five kilotons are 30%. The risk is thus acceptable. If the
Soviet and US intelligence services were involved in the investigation,
the chances of detection might be even higher. It should be remembered, however, that this estimate is based mainly on European
data and conditions; difficulties of detection may be much greater
in Asia.

Mr Mulley's speech goes on:

> The agents which might be used for hostile purposes are generally
> indistinguishable from those which are needed for peaceful
> medical purposes.

One might get the impression from this that the organisms used in
vaccine production must be the same strains as those used to prepare
biological weapons. In the preparation of a biological weapon
manipulative procedures are used to alter the agent's characteristics,
to increase virulence, resistance to antibiotics, and stability (see the
section on the production of the biological weapon). There are two
types of vaccine, live and dead. The live vaccines are strains cultured
and manipulated for lower virulence; the dead ones are killed
lethal organisms. The live vaccines are by definition different from
biological warfare agents (low virulence, etc.). The dead vaccines
are of killed lethal organisms. In order to achieve the highest possible degree of protection, the vaccine producers would normally
be provided with samples of the organism used as a weapon. Since
this is not normally possible in the case of biological weapons, any
virulent strain of the organism may be used (even without the exact

characteristics of the weapon) with an equal chance of conferring immunity.

Mr Mulley's speech also contained the statement:

> Militarily significant quantities of a biological warfare agent could be produced clandestinely in a building the size of a small house or large garage.

Several points should be made here. First, the statement presupposes an agent fully suitable as a weapon, which in its turn presupposes that some research and development has already been done before production, which would require laboratory facilities for the handling of dangerous pathogens. Secondly, to produce agents safely, without contaminating the workers, needs protective equipment, and special plant is needed for the preparation. If bought commercially this could be traced, and preparing one's own would require manufacturing facilities. Attempts to prepare agents without such precautions would run the risk of loosing the agents on the local population or the research workers themselves. Even a modest effort is more difficult to conceal than might appear at first sight. The loading of agents into munitions (even if these were primitive) and the dissemination systems would be liable to detection, even in the case of a fairly small capability. A large effort like that of the United States is impossible to conceal. The problems envisaged by Mr Mulley are thus not as insuperable as he thinks.

We are now in a position to review the draft treaty. We have mentioned points in its favour previously; the chief of these is the priority it gives to a ban on the production and stockpiling of biological weapons for offensive or defensive purposes. Its failings are too numerous to list; some have been discussed above. A glaring omission is the lack of any provision for the inspection of laboratory and production facilities or the detection of BW attacks. These are the two principal difficulties in the opinion of Dr Gunnar Persson, head of research into protection against CBW at the Swedish Defence Research Institute. As it stands, the treaty relies on intelligence sources rather than formal inspection to detect CBW activities.

There are two factors which could deter a BW aggressor, first, the realisation that BW would not be effective, and, second, the high probability of detection, leading to international action against him. The British proposals contribute nothing to solving either of these problems, and on the whole they are worthless, if not dangerous. They would still leave any nation open to false accusations which could not be publicly disproved. Such proof requires some form of inspection.

Unless complaints made to the UN secretary general can be quickly investigated by a trained and experienced team, and access to stricken areas granted immediately, no treaty will be effective. Similarly, although Mr Mulley dismisses the prospect of verification, it is only by large-scale work on the problems of inspection and detection that any advance will be made. Any nation which accedes to the treaty as it stands will not be decreasing the likelihood of the preparation and use of BW weapons, and may be even increasing it. The problems, both technical and political, in the way of BW disarmament are considerable, but to avoid them or to try to put them on one side is no solution. The technical problems are large, but by no means insoluble, especially if the sort of effort envisaged here is made.

The political problems are another matter. The Russians, the Poles and the Americans have received the British proposals very coolly. The last Soviet initiative was the general and comprehensive disarmament plan of 1962, which proposed that CB weapons should be abolished in the second three-year stage of a nine-year plan. The Western alternative advocated study of the difficulties in stage 1, halving of stockpiles in stage 2, and removal of the remaining stockpiles and the end of production in stage 3. Significantly, the Russian plan does not mention the problems of inspection and detection. Field teams of the first type mentioned here would probably be limited to overseeing the destruction of stockpiles.

Since then, however, the Canadians and the Poles proposed the secretary general's study on CBW, and one presumes that they support his recommendations. There seems recently to have been a slight thaw in positions with regard to peace and disarmament, of which the Strategic Arms Limitation Talks may be an example. There are some indications that the Russians are as sick of the arms race as anyone else. The main bar to realistic talks is the opposing stands of the United States and the USSR with regard to the Geneva Protocol. If the Americans do sign the protocol in the near future, there should be the possibility of an immediate improvement in prospects for disarmament. This may be the last chance for a major international agreement to ban this class of weapons of vast destructive potential. It would be tragic if we failed.

CONCLUSION

In the end only the absolute prevention of war will preserve human life and civilisation. This is the goal for which all sane people must aim. At present, however, achievement of this goal seems very distant. Some definite progress must be made, for reasons which should by now have become apparent. For several reasons we have purposely limited our brief to chemical and biological warfare, although there is nothing inherently more terrible in this than in any other kind of warfare. Our reasons for this emphasis are several. The effects and consequences of other means of waging war, with nuclear or conventional weapons, are well known; the methods and effects of cbw are not generally familiar. This lack of knowledge we have attempted to remedy. It is only by rational discussion and examination of cbw that the urgency of the disarmament problem can be appreciated. Appeals for disarmament, to have any prospect of success, must be based on logic rather than emotion. For this, accurate information is essential, and we have here tried to supply it. The practical reasons why cbw merits special consideration we have given previously.

We shall now summarise and re-examine some of the points of significance we have tried to illustrate in the text. Much that is relevant to any consideration of cw in general can be seen by reference to Vietnam. This represents a high point in the development of toxic warfare; the war has seen considerable technical innovations. Despite the fact that the effectiveness of aerial application was realised in World War I, Vietnam saw the first large-scale use of this technique. The course of refinement of both types of weapons, and their use, has already been traced. One may assume, because gases are still being used, that they are effective.

This is of considerable importance for the future.

If, as seems likely, the Vietnam conflict is to provide the pattern for future wars, for example in Thailand and South America, and these weapons are effective against guerillas, then their future use is almost certain. Similarly the use of gases in counter-insurgency operations, as in the Yemen, is now more likely. Two instances have already been reported of the use of gas against Arab guerillas. Further minor cases of the employment of these weapons on a small scale, and especially their field evaluation in Vietnam, are likely to remove unknown quantities in their use, and hence decrease any reluctance of the military in future application. It is in this context that use of so-called riot control agents in Vietnam should be examined. The fallacy in their description as non-lethal we have already exposed.

It seems unlikely, once use on a large scale has been seen to be successful, that even the more sane members of the military establishment will resist the further application of gases. It is significant that no military field commander has seen fit to ardently advocate the use of these weapons. Their most passionate apologists in America are the military concerned in their development, who, of course, have a vested interest. However, the deployment in Europe on any scale of chemical and (by America) biological weapons must mean that field commanders have a use for them. It has been suggested that they would be used in preference to tactical nuclear weapons in an attempt to contain a war in Europe, as a form of flexible response. CBW would be used in preference to nuclear weapons in the hope of not provoking strategic nuclear attack. Whether this would be effective is doubtful, as the application of chemical and biological weapons would not be on a large enough scale, with present stocks, to contain offensives on the scale the Russians are likely to mount them. It is very unlikely that the use of tactical nuclear weapons could be avoided.

CBW has been described as the poor-man's H-bomb. The cheapness of these weapons and, especially for chemical weapons, the ease of their manufacture and dissemination must make them very attractive to the less developed or smaller nations. The problem for these nations is not the development of these weapons but the turning over of manufacturing processes to their production. Development work is conducted by the advanced nations, Russia, Britain and America. Eventually the knowledge of these weapons will become common currency, through the efforts of those nations whose 'dependence' on them is least. An intensive espionage effort could well substitute in quite a large measure for lack of development facilities if development is proceeding elsewhere. In the same way espionage could be a safeguard if CBW is prohibited, to ensure that illegal development and deployment was not occurring.

Thus, rather than increasing the security of the world the development of CBW may be seen to jeopardise it. The 'nth power' problem of nuclear weapons is a future, if rather remote, threat to humanity. The possibility that weapons as effective as nuclear ones, capable of being produced by a small nation in a very short time, or even by a suitably equipped group of individuals, is indeed a chilling one, a biological nth power problem.

The Russians and the Americans seem to have adopted similar positions on CBW. The current state of affairs is such that little positive agreement is possible. It is in the context of this and the previous discussion that disarmament attempts should be examined. The realities of the current military and political situation are inescapable. This is not to decry disarmament attempts, but rather to point out the difficulties, due to present conditions. There is no simple or, at this time, complete answer to the problems of disarmament and prevention of the spread of these weapons. There are, however, signs that the political climate is becoming more favourable to CBW disarmament.

Many of the current disarmament problems could have been minimised had chemicals not been recently used in war. Large-scale procurement of CW and BW munitions in America did not start until the early sixties. The use of CW in Vietnam has set a dangerous precedent, as is obvious from the subsequent use of lethal gas in the Yemen.

In terms of effects this use pales into insignificance in comparison with the second US transgression. This was the use of defoliants. We have already discussed their significance in the context of their effects on the population of Vietnam and their possible ecological consequences. The use of defoliants in Vietnam has been described by one US ecologist as a 'valuable experiment' in ecology. Vietnam would then be being used as a testing ground. This is a charge frequently made against the United States, and it is certainly true in part.

The testing of weapons on the Vietnamese shows a quite staggering lack of humanity. The use of defoliants must surely rank as one of the most irresponsible and criminal acts of the century. It is ironic that some politicians in the US have said the US is fighting for 'principles'. It is hard to fight for principles while making it clear that one possesses none. Deliberately to court a catastrophe which could affect the lives of a foreign people for decades is a rare and chilling achievement in immorality.

It is interesting to note that defoliants are included in the US Army's definition of biological weapons. Thus it seems that, to the Americans, BW is already being employed in Vietnam. This must make escalation to BW agents proper much easier. It is a characteristic of CBW that the distinction between chemical and biological weapons is blurred. There is a continuous spectrum of agents of varying effects within both classes; the two classes also overlap. In any meaningful steps towards general disarmament, development of even the chemicals should not be permitted. The current state of the art is such that even chemical weapons are in prospect with possible casualty-causing effects many times greater than nuclear weapons. If one is to argue about these weapons, it is the quantitative rather than the qualitative effect which is of significance. Thus the removal of both types of weapons must be the aim.

Most relevant to the discussion of biological weapons are allegations concerning Korea and Vietnam. In both cases the allegations were against the US. In neither case, however, does BW seem likely to have occurred. The reasons for the allegations are not hard to see. The United States' development of CBW, her ambiguous position with respect to international law, and more recently the use of CW in Vietnam have weakened her position. The use of defoliants (which the US itself lists as BW) is also quotable. The communists have, by virtue of not using these weapons, and possibly not developing BW systems, gained a considerable propaganda advantage. In return the US has a weapon of dubious capabilities and incredible danger. In terms of propaganda losses and loss of prestige the debit side of biological warfare is considerable. To offset this, the advantages of the weapon are not so clear.

The case for BW use in Vietnam is still an entirely circumstantial one. The stance of the US on the subject of BW does not make it easy to refute the allegations. It is now probably only a matter of time before the US is the object of more substantial allegations which will result in another resounding propaganda defeat.

CBW is instructive in showing the commitment of governments to objectivity, truth and democratic principles. We have discussed Mr Dean Rusk's statements; Mr McNamara has made several statements of equal veracity. The British government, despite acquaintance with the facts concerning CBW, has not been notable for any condemnation of the American use, or even use in the Yemen. Reluctance in the latter case arose, one suspects, not from any particular feelings for the sensibilities of the UAR government but mainly to avoid any embarrassment for the US from counter-charges.

The British position on Vietnam is quite clear: 'Britain wholly supports American action in Vietnam', Michael Stewart, British Foreign Secretary. One would wish that the British position with respect to CBW was as clear.

Lack of information and misinformation seem to be particular problems with respect to CBW. This difficulty can be seen as operating at two levels: the level of use and the level of research and development. We have already dealt with these in detail.

Concerning the use of CBW in Vietnam, the position is not at all clear. The reason for this is the rigid censorship by the US of data allowed out of Vietnam. The head of the US Information Service considered this censorship justified: he referred to the public's right not to know in a period of undeclared war'.

The general manager of Associated Press, Wes Gallagher, has actually stated that 'news restrictions imposed by the Pentagon raise serious questions as to whether the American people will be able to get a true picture of the war in Vietnam' (New York Journal American, April 1965).

Lack of full information about use of BW in the Yemen is also important. Here the International Red Cross could have played a decisive role. Their attempts to influence the interested governments diplomatically was a total failure. The ICRC failed to make effective use of the information in their possession. For similar reasons little publicity was given to this matter. Use of gas continued for some years without any public medium having any knowledge of it, or at any rate featuring it at all prominently.

Misinformation on the use of gas in Vietnam starts with Dean Rusk and McNamara and proceeds through much of the information that comes out at present. This has been amply illustrated previously. A recent piece of misinformation concerns US use of defoliants. The US Department of Defense produced a 'summary' of a report prepared by the Midwestern Research Institute. It is a matter of the reader's own choice how this be read. It is quite possible to read it as a piece of imaginative fiction or as a biased presentation of a number of selected 'conclusions' the validity of which is, to say the least, doubtful. The world will be treated to further exercises in falsification as the Vietnam war continues.

In the case of the Yemen there is a further important side issue. The problem here is, in addition to the lack of information and unintentional misinformation, the lack of critical examination of the South Arabian doctors' report. It serves the interests of neither the South Arabians nor the anti-CBW campaigners to neglect to apply the most rigorous procedures in the search for the truth. In this respect Mr J. D. Salvia, as we have noted earlier, has failed. It is only by preserving our objectivity and critical faculties that a good case can be made against CBW.

A further example of misinformation is the propaganda war waged by the Communist powers against the United States. In no case has any allegation been shown to be founded on fact, and in some instances accusations are quite fantastic. In any analysis of what is actually happening, for instance in Vietnam or Korea, any statement from either side must be seen as coloured, if not completely distorted, by propaganda. The only means of really determining the truth is to examine the situation at first hand or to ensure completely reliable reports. In the case of Korea (pp 57–63 above), if there was a kernel of truth in the allegations, the ISC report did not make it any clearer.

Obviously the mass media have a considerable responsibility to inform the public of the truth. Comment must be at least cognisant of the basic facts, but unfortunately this is not always the case. For example, the *Guardian* editorial of 18 July 1968 states, with reference to Mr Mulley's British BW proposals at Geneva: 'This is a useful initiative which the government deserves all credit for starting.' This is open to question. This initiative, like so many activities of the British government, was too little, too late. It is unlikely that it ever stood a great chance of significant success. Its main function may have been to allay the stirrings of public opinion in Britain. The British proposals were received with the cynicism they deserved.

The editorial continues to quote the Geneva Protocol which forbids 'asphyxiating, poisonous or other gases'. It then proceeds to say that this is 'unclear' on the subject of 'lethal' and 'non-lethal' gases. This lack of clarity, however, is in the mind of the editor, not in the protocol. Similarly an article in the *Sun* for 17 June 1968 says, 'it is not clear whether the convention covers highly potent nerve gases developed in recent years'. Rubbish! The article later says: 'only the use, not the possession of poison gases would be barred'. As this is currently the major gap in the Geneva Protocol, proposals which do not attempt to seal it are hardly likely to be of much use. Elsewhere in the *Guardian* editorial we read that the protocol is 'inadequate on the subject of weedkillers and defoliants and unsatisfactory on the newer forms of microbiological agents'. This is also incorrect. If we accept the definition of the users and preparers of the weapons, they are forbidden within the terms of the protocol. One suspects that the people we have mentioned here have not read the protocol carefully enough.

The curious confusion in the minds of these people, and many others, about the lethal, non-lethal distinction may be due to the fact that some gases used in Vietnam are used in riot control situations, and have thus been erroneously described as non-lethal. The protocol specifies 'in war'. Therefore in normal riot control operations no contravention of the protocol occurs. All gases are forbidden in war.

This must represent a severe dereliction of duty. The newspapers are, through their own inefficiency, failing to provide accurate comment. In certain cases the reportage is also inaccurate, for example, the *Observer* at one stage referred to ricin, a vegetable protein, as a 'mould' product. Television and radio, however, have produced some useful information.

The importance of the mass media is that for people to be able to judge CBW they must be informed about its development and consequences. This has so far not occurred because of the restriction of information at the levels previously mentioned. Public opinion must be the weapon of the anti-CBW campaigners. An informed body of public opinion is unlikely to support the proponents of CBW on the evidence available. Thus the failure of the mass media may be seen to be disastrous. They are being, consciously or unconsciously, the tools of the policy makers, who have a vested interest in keeping the public in the dark. Revelation of CBW involvement would be a serious political embarrassment. Hence the politicians control the information available tightly, as we have seen with respect to Vietnam, and even the dissemination of it, with 'D' notices, etc. Public opinion has had some slight effect in the case of Porton. This has caused at least some explanation of the establishment's function and position. Here again the mass media have failed to criticise adequately the governmental statements, which well merit such criticism. 'Open days' are more a gesture of public relations than a clarification of the work in hand at Porton, especially if there are only one or two a year. The only thing open days would tell the observer was that bombs are not stockpiled in the corridors of the establishment. Little could be deduced as to the nature of the research. The responsibility for preventing or dispelling the current cloud of ignorance around these weapons rests in many hands.

Over the last year there seems to have been a gradual loss of interest in the CBW problem. Many people originally interested in it have carried on similar work in related fields. In view of the above this may be a mistake. A concerted effort by all those groups originally concerned with CBW is still necessary to keep up the impetus of public debate. In the United States the effort has been tremendous and is still increasing. It would be tragic if the British anti-CBW lobbyists lost interest through a mistaken impression that the fight was over. Public opinion and pressure is still necessary, perhaps more necessary than before. There is still a long way to go.

Politicians are elected to carry out the wishes of the people; for what they do in the name of the state they are ultimately answerable. This is, of course, an idealisation of the situation. Politicians bear a responsibility to the people for managing the state in an acceptable fashion. To permit a rational examination of policies, and of how the government implements them, the politicians must explain these to the people. While the British public is treated regularly to the prognosis and diagnosis of the financial position of the nation, little that is meaningful is said about defence and nothing about CBW.

In America the State Department is the official policy arm of the US government. The inaccuracy of Secretary of State Dean Rusk's statements we have discussed earlier, though, as we conjectured, it is unlikely that he was deliberately lying. However, between the policy and the execution there is a huge disparity. This brings us to the second important responsibility of the politicians, to ensure that their executive (in the case of Vietnam, the Army) follows the lines laid down. In Vietnam it is quite obvious that the Army is dictating policy to which the State Department is an unwilling accomplice.

In its 'operation blue skies' the US Army was also using available facilities to influence the policy-makers in producing an increase in procuring and developing CBW weapons. There is evidence also of a considerable military lobby in the US Congress. This has produced the intolerable situation in which the instruments of policy are dictating policy instead of being dictated to, obviously a highly dangerous situation.

Whenever a weapon is used there are several levels of responsibility. Immediate responsibility must be with the disseminators. The usual argument of the military is that when a weapon is available it should be used in the event of a suitable situation arising for its use. One would not expect the wider implications to be debated by people who are, in effect, the instruments of policy. However, neglect of the policy directives, such as has occurred in Vietnam, must place considerable responsibility on the heads of the military commanders. The military cannot be absolved from the blame of gross misuse of gas in conjunction with bombing, etc.

A favourite military argument is that anything is permissible in the cause of reducing one's own casualty lists. This is the sort of thinking that leads to suggestions like the possibility of achieving defoliation with nuclear bombs, or dropping tactical nuclear weapons on Hanoi, suggestions which equally would be justified by this argument, if one accepts it as valid. It is unacceptable because it places no limit to the action in which the military may indulge. It is licence rather than control. In the case of the United States, however, this policy does seem to be applied by the military, and with respect to CBW there is at least one good reason for this. A very important point was made by Brigadier General J. H. Rothschild in an article in *War/Peace* report in January 1962.

To sweep the problems of toxic warfare under the rug, which has been the policy of the US government in recent years, serves neither the military defense of our country nor the cause of peace.

Since then there has been no clear policy statement. The reader can draw his own conclusions on the effectiveness of the control and direction of the US forces in Vietnam. Equally there is the criminal incompetence and stupidity with which the US Army casually dumps gas in the Atlantic (paralleled by the almost equally casual British dumping of gas in the Baltic). Fortunately the US government has now awakened to the dangers of the appalling things the military can do if they are allowed. A much needed increase of control over military activities seems likely to result from the debate in Congress on gas dumping and the Congressional enquiry into it. Now that politicians have been given a lever to work with, it seems probable that the chances of a situation arising like that of Mr Rusk's disastrous press conference on CW will be greatly diminished. Closer control should certainly eliminate some of the more bizarre contradictions between policy directives and their execution.

In relation to CBW, scientists have a particular responsibility. They are in a position of special knowledge. There are three ways in which their responsibilities may be manifested.

Biologists, biochemists, toxicologists, environmental scientists, even botanists, and many others have by virtue of their particular fields of study an ability to appreciate the effects of CBW. They could to a large extent counter the misinformation and information gaps which at present hinder public debate on the topic.

An important illustration of this is the attempt by Dr B. Commoner, a highly eminent US biologist, to clear up some of the confusion about the herbicides being used in Vietnam. He was the first to mention the use of cacodylic acid, and elicited some response from the establishment. Certain magazines, for instance *Scientist and Citizen*, have also done this. The Physicians for Social Responsibility group of Boston have been concerned in the CBW debate from the early days.

It is interesting that a certain Dr Minarik attempted to refute Dr Commoner's allegations. We have discussed this in the section on defoliants.[1] It is sufficient to say at this point that this is a case of a scientist contributing deliberately to the misinformation. From the phrasing of Dr Minarik's reported speech it is quite obviously an attempt to whitewash the defoliation programme. It was widely reported as an answer to Dr Commoner; this it quite definitely fails to be. Dr Minarik's action seems highly irresponsible. The reader will be able to judge for himself how such statements reflect the

1 See pp 30–31 and 247–48 above.

integrity and honour of the scientists making them: Dr Minarik is the head of the plant science laboratory at Fort Detrick.

If the predictable dangers of CB weapons are disregarded because of insufficient concern on the part of the scientific community, or through some misguided patriotism, not considered at all, then the scientists, too, must bear much of the responsibility for the use which is made of them. The lesson of Hiroshima and Nagasaki for the physicists was that governments cannot be trusted. Many of the physicists concerned did not believe that the Allies would use atomic weapons unless themselves threatened. It is interesting in retrospect that one argument in favour of this use was the same as the one put forward for the use of CBW. That is to say, that the use would shorten the war and reduce casualties. This argument was about as valid then as it is now. The naivety of scientists then can never be regained; they can never again abdicate responsibility. They know the consequences, they have a useful precedent to consult.

It is unfortunate that many of those involved in the discussion of CBW seem to regard the question of the use of such weapons as almost an academic one. By attempting not to be alarmist, they have minimised the danger of the present situation. Some authorities have argued that chemical and biological weapons are unlikely to be used in view of the imprecision inherent in their dependence on environmental factors. When both the NATO and Warsaw Pact forces maintain large stocks of these munitions in Europe, such a view is shortsighted. There is obviously a well-defined military role for these weapons, and they will be used, imprecision or no. In any case, modern equipment and techniques minimise variations due to environmental factors, so that it is misleading to argue from earlier data.[1]

In this context the attitude of certain scientists is hard to understand. For some their purposive myopia about the consequences of their actions is considerable. As an illustration of this, a letter from Professor Ernst B. Chain to the *Observer* may be quoted:

> It is, of course, not the scientist and inventor who carries the responsibility for how the results of his research or his inventions are used.

This attitude makes possible a biological Hiroshima. It could as well form a justification for crematorium research in Nazi Germany as for CBW today. Scientists are no more able to shut themselves off from society than any one else. The doctors and scientists in

[1] This is a criticism which could perhaps be made of Julian Perry Robinson's otherwise excellent contribution to the London conference on CBW, 'Chemical Weapons', S. Rose (ed) *CBW*, London 1968, 19–34.

concentration camps, despite the fact that they were under orders, were held accountable for their actions at Nuremberg in 1948. Scientists have a particular responsibility because of the greater knowledge and appreciation of the possible effects of CBW. The Russians tried the scientists involved in CBW research on the Axis side in the last war. They were held accountable then, and there seems no reason to change this judgment now.

The second important point of action is the mobilisation of scientific opinion. This is what happened when 5000 scientists petitioned President Johnson to stop CBW. It is regrettable that this form of action is limited largely to America. International scientific opinion has hardly been active at all. It has rarely shown any signs of life in Britain. With the exception of a handful of scientists there seems to be complete apathy throughout the British scientific community. The concerted action of a large group of scientists would have considerable effect. The US President draws many of his advisers from the ranks of university academic staffs. A sustained protest from this sector of the community has some chance of success.[1] This is one effective way in which scientists can partially discharge their responsibilities.

The third means by which scientists can act is by restricting themselves to unclassified research. The supply of scientific manpower is limited. This form of action is possibly the one with greatest potential. One of the least valid justifications used by CBW researchers is that if they do not do it, someone else will. The major brake on CBW is not lack of money but lack of availability of research staff. In 1964 a US defence official described the main difficulty in developing incapacitating chemical agents in this way: 'We are competing for the same people who are working, for example, on cancer research.' This particular perversion of the aims of science poses the problem of CBW research well. With so many unsolved problems of disease, how can a scientist dedicate himself, or herself, to a conscientious attempt to undermine the work of other doctors and scientists? Is it right that he should fail to use his talent in a more constructive fashion? Any scientist contemplating such research would be well advised to consider where his own best interests and those of humanity lie. Professor Dean Fraser, a microbiologist from Indiana University, who refused an invitation to a symposium marking the twenty-fifth anniversary of Fort Detrick, wrote: 'At best it seems a little like celebrating the creation of the electric chair, and at worst like celebrating the establishment of Dachau.'

---

[1] This has recently happened with the anti-ballistic missile programme.

Perhaps the most horrifying aspect of the CBW question is the way in which the public has come to accept it. Information has only slowly filtered through to the public. By an insidious and gradual build up of reports of increasing savagery on both sides, the events of the Vietnam war, for instance, seem to have become accepted. Collected together, the evidence is horrifying, but by a slow and accumulating presentation, the public is conditioned to its acceptance.

A partial analogy can be drawn here between the people of America and the Germans after 1933. In Germany the persecution of the Jews began in a small way, smashing shop windows, daubing signs. When Hitler's final solution was implemented in mass deportation and murder, many Germans must have realised what was going on. Their progressive pathway towards acceptance of the final solution closely resembles the steady progression of the American public towards accepting what ten years ago would have been unacceptable. A defence against Communist charges in Korea was that use of BW was 'unthinkable' to the US. What was unthinkable then is policy now.

Much of the damaging information with respect to CBW comes from the USA and Britain. The authors regret this. They are not biased against the USA or Britain. This is in no way an attack on these particular countries but rather the particular insanity in which they are currently engaged.

Unfortunately the whole issue of CBW is concerned with more fundamental problems. In 1928 Haldane was writing about the problems of what could be described as 'pre-scientific thinking'. The people in power seem to have an inability to understand the facts of scientific life. In view of the impeccable scientific qualifications of Her Majesty's government, if this is reflected in other governments it is hardly surprising.

Fundamentally what the author believes is wrong is that science, whilst it affects our lives more and more, has little purchase upon government. Scientists are seemingly inarticulate when it comes to explaining to politicians. Attlee said after the A bomb was used on Japan that had he known about its terrible effects he would never have supported its use. But politicians may accept scientific data which support their preconceptions, and ignore uncomfortable data. It is similar to the British government's formation of commissions. If it likes the conclusions of the commissions and committee, they are possibly implemented. If not, then they are totally ignored. This is an exercise one cannot afford in science. We are now at a cross-roads. At this stage, if human society fails to come to terms with science, then it will eventually become extinct. One cannot possess the power that scientific progress has given us without controlling its direction and purpose, otherwise catastrophe is bound to result.

It was said in *Unless Peace Comes* that man can have war or science but not both. This is incorrect: one can have both but only if they are restricted, in the case of war, and directed, in the case of science. Without direction now, we may look forward to a future on the model of *Brave New World*, new and more fearsome weapons with hundreds of times the capacity of the present ones for removing human life.

AFTERWORD

Since the publication of the first edition of this book in Britain in November 1969, there have been a number of important developments in the field of CBW. Many of these are of considerable importance and a large part of this Afterword is devoted to them. In making these additions a certain amount of cross-referencing with the text has been necessary and we hope this will not cause too much confusion.

In the book we attempted to present as fully as possible much of the data currently available on this subject. It would be impossible for us to deny that we hold certain opinions on CBW and we freely admit that we stand firmly opposed to it. These opinions were expressed in the book but we tried throughout to indicate to the reader where fact ends and opinion begins. We tried as far as possible to present a balanced view but were hampered by the shortage of the evidence supporting the case for CBW, and by the quality of that available.

It was not until March 1968 that CBW became subject to public scrutiny in the United States. Early in that month at the Dugway Proving Ground in Utah, some 6000 sheep accidentally died as a result of an open-air nerve gas test (p 77). This initiated a sequence of events which gradually brought to public attention the extent and significance of the US CBW programme. A critical factor in the exposure of US activities in this field was the part played by the press and television in providing a platform from which well-informed and responsible scientists, politicians and others could discuss the matter.

On 5 July 1968, in the wake of the furor created by the sheep deaths, Secretary of the Army Stanley R. Resor announced the formation of a safety committee to review procedures at Dugway. The committee, headed by the US Surgeon-General, William H. Stewart, submitted its report the following November and its recommendations were immediately accepted. These laid down conditions concerning the manner of testing, and imposed restrictions on the amount of the agent which could be used. More stringent checks on local weather conditions and on the possibility of gas escaping from the test area were called for. The report nowhere implied that the Army had been guilty of negligence in applying existing regulations, but suggested instead that the regulations themselves were at fault. Following the implementation of these recommendations open-air testing was resumed.

CBW was not to remain out of the public eye for long. In February 1969, during a television programme, the Smithsonian Institute was accused of being involved in BW research (p 80). It transpired that the Army had requested information on the migration of birds in the Pacific and had asked that samples be tested (by the Army) for pathogens. The Institute had undertaken to conduct a survey on their behalf. Several possible reasons have been advanced for Army interest in this topic. One of these, which is certainly pure science fiction, is that the birds were to be used as disease vectors. Two more credible possibilities were presented. Firstly, the Army may have needed the knowledge in order to choose a BW testing site where there would be a low risk of the accidental spreading of disease by birds in the area. Secondly, it may have been that the tests had already been carried out and the Army was suffering serious misgivings after the event. The former seems more likely. The whole issue was something of a storm in a teacup as the involvement of the Smithsonian was far from sinister, but the ensuing publicity and criticisms, not all of which were well founded, were a portent of things to come.

Later in the year a milestone in the history of US CBW policy was reached: CBW became a national issue. Most of the political action can be more or less directly attributed to the untiring efforts of one sincere and dedicated politician, Richard D. McCarthy, Democratic Representative for New York.

Mr McCarthy's interest began when he saw a NBC TV programme in early February, which he later described as 'rather gripping and shocking'. At his wife's insistence he sought further data. As a first step he managed to arrange a Pentagon briefing for fourteen concerned Congressmen and Senators. This only succeeded in confirming his belief that yet more data were required and he wrote to the Secretary of Defense and to the Defense Department requesting information. Although very little solid information was forthcoming, McCarthy's probing did have some results. John S. Foster, Jr, Director of Defense Research and Engineering, revealed the figures for the CBW defence budget for 1969. (Figures for preceding years had been classified.) The 1969 total expenditure was given as

$350 million, $240 million for procurement, $20 million for main-
tenance and operation of facilities, and $90 million for research,
development and testing. The Congressman found it 'difficult to accept' this estimate and later revelations confirmed his scepticism.
In mid-November the Stockholm International Peace Research Institute published its estimate of the total us cbw expenditure, calculated by summing the cost of individually announced items of the
programme. The Institute concluded that the budget was in fact
in excess of $550 million for fiscal year 1969.

McCarthy became increasingly critical of the whole cbw programme and on 21 April 1969 gave his views at a news conference.
He pointed out that us cbw stocks constitute a danger to the whole
world. There were then enough chemicals in Colorado to kill millions but no contingency plans for the protection of civilians or
troops. He alleged carelessness on the part of the Army in its handling of weapons and its transportation of them around the country.
He insisted that us action in Vietnam was classifiable as cw and thus
contravened the Geneva Protocol. He recommended that the protocol be re-submitted to the Senate for ratification and that the
President support British attempts at the Geneva Disarmament
Conference to ban bw.

Seeking a forum for discussion, McCarthy approached Senator
J. William Fulbright, Chairman of the Senate Foreign Relations
Committee, and as a result the cbw issue was added to an already
crowded agenda. The initial hearing was on 30 April.

The general subject of cbw, although of great importance, raised
little interest among McCarthy's fellow politicians until he began to
stress the safety aspects of the weapons and to relate them to the
problem of pollution. The incident which really opened the flood-
gates of criticism was McCarthy's revelation of an Army plan to
dump obsolete poison gas stocks in the Atlantic.

This was not a novel procedure. At the end of World War I and
World War II hundreds of thousands of tons of gas had been
dumped off the southwest coast of Ireland, in the Bay of Biscay,
off Rockall, in the Atlantic and in the Baltic. Late in 1969, fishermen from Bornholm suffered mustard gas burns caused by munitions sunk in the Baltic area after World War II. They were lucky:
had they been affected by the nerve gas (Tabun) which had been
dumped in the same spot they would almost certainly have died.
As it happened, a number of corroded gas bombs drifted ashore
and were examined by Danish military authorities. It is thought
that much more of the material lies in shallow water fairly near
the shore. The us Army showed considerable interest in the Born-

holm incident, probably because of their intentions and past policy in this respect.

The hazards of gas dumping are well recognised. In March 1960 German divers salvaged the last of 28,000 corroded Tabun shells which had been dumped in the Baltic after the second world war. They contained enough tabun to poison the entire Baltic area. The shells were defused and packed in concrete, then re-dumped in the South Atlantic.

McCarthy revealed details of the US Army's dumping plan (obtained from an undisclosed source) in a letter to Defense Secretary Melvin Laird and to Secretary of Transportation John Volpe. He protested a waiver of normal procedure and precautions the Army had received for the planned transportation of the gas across the country to the coast. He urged the dumping be suspended until there would be 'a thorough review of the proposed safety measures, a review of the consequences of dumping large quantities of toxic material in the sea, and a consideration of alternative methods of disposal of these highly dangerous materials'. He referred, in passing, to a 'poison gas spillage' in Kansas City which had occurred twice in 1968-69, and to another incident in St. Louis. The gas in question was phosgene. In addition to the pollution hazard, McCarthy was particularly worried by the possible consequences of accidents to trains carrying the gas.

After the Army plan was disclosed, the Congressmen representing states to be traversed by this lethal cavalcade protested so strongly that the plan was sent to three congressional sub-committees for examination. These were sub-committees of the Senate Commerce Committee, the House Foreign Affairs Committee and the House Merchant Marine Committee; all three were highly critical of the Army.

The most significant revelations were made before the House Foreign Affairs Sub-Committee. Following McCarthy's disclosures the Army had requested a postponement of the hearings to allow time to assemble experts and data. The hearings were finally held on 13 May. It soon became obvious that McCarthy's fears had been well founded. The munitions were not merely World War II stocks, but were more modern weapons. When the nature and size of the proposed shipment was revealed it became obvious why the Army had rejected a suggestion made by a group of scientists from Washington University that the weapons be disassembled and the agents rendered harmless.

Some 27,000 tons of material (agents and munitions) were to be moved. This consisted of 2125 tons of nerve gas (GB) in rockets and bombs, 4786 tons of liquid mustard in steel containers, and 3.4 tons of CS gas in steel drums. The largest part of the shipment, according to Charles L. Poor, Assistant Secretary to the Army, was to have been a set of 1000-lb bombs each containing 76 dispersal bomblets of GB. Each bomblet contained about .5 lb explosive tetrytol and 2.6 lbs GB. Poor said that these weapons were in too advanced a state of decay to be disassembled on site without risk of major disaster. The problem was that the explosive had deteriorated with time and become unstable and hence was sensitive to both heat and pressure. Some 440 carloads of gas bombs at the Rocky Mountain Arsenal were in this condition. This was the cargo which was to be quietly transported through major population centres. In addition, there were about 12,000 'Bolt' rockets containing GB for the 55-mm rocket launcher. These were encased in steel and concrete coffins and so less dangerous.

From the information available it would seem that the plan was as follows:

Beginning 16 May, 20 trains (809 cars) were to be run from these CW depots: Rocky Mountain Arsenal, Colorado; Anniston Army Depot, Alabama; Blue Grass Ordnance Depot, Kentucky; and Edgewood Arsenal, Maryland. The destination was the Naval Ammunition Depot at Earle, New Jersey. This phase of the operation was to take three months. In the past, federal agencies had generally allowed the Army to transport what it liked where it liked and how it liked. The responsibility for safety had rested with the carrier.

Allowing the Army to be responsible for safety would appear to have been a major error. The route of the trains took them through major population centres including Indianapolis, Dayton, Philadelphia and Elizabeth, New Jersey. There were no stringent speed regulations and no provision for pilot trains to pace the trains actually carrying the munitions. Even those precautions stipulated were of a doubtful utility. These were to include buffer cars to separate the lethal cargo from the rest of the train, the use of specially trained Army guards and the forewarning of the relevant civilian authorities. The first of these proposals was to diminish the effects of minor leakages, reducing the hazard to the rest of the train if not to those close to the railway line. The specially trained guards would be capable of dealing with minor incidents. The Army was in fact admirably equipped to deal with small-scale problems, but would have been totally useless in the event of a large-scale disaster like a derailment or a massive leakage or explosion. As to the provision for informing civilian authorities, it seems unlikely that this would have been properly carried out because it had not been on previous occasions.

As might be expected, the Congressional sub-committees were not enthusiastic about the Army's plan. The chairman of the Sub-Committee on Surface Transportation described the Army's attitude as 'cavalier'. Senator Williams of New Jersey called the plan 'a poisonous parade' across America, and a 'bizarre scheme' representing 'the ultimate in railroading risk'.

It is interesting to speculate how easy it would have been to sabotage one of the trains had the original plan been followed. So many trains travelling over such an extended period must increase the security risk because secrecy cannot be easily maintained. It would be necessary only to derail a train, causing an explosion in a city like Indianapolis, to produce a catastrophe. Dr Gordon Kilgour (chairman of People Against Nerve Gas and also of Portland State University's chemistry department) was quoted in April 1970 as saying with reference to a gas shipment we will discuss later: 'The derailment of a trainload of bombs in Wisconsin a while ago isn't exactly comforting.' As originally envisaged, the rail transport plan would have presented a golden opportunity to that 'isolated madman' we have all come to know so well and so often since Dallas in 1963.

The Army plan got a rough ride on its surface transportation aspects but it had an easier passage in the examination of the ocean phase of the operation. This involved the sinking of four gutted Liberty ships full of munitions in 7200 feet of water about 150 miles east of Atlantic City.

The Army testimony included an assurance that a thorough examination of safety factors had been made well in advance. The Army admitted to previous CHASE (an acronym for 'Cut Holes and Sink 'Em') operations involving CBW materials, and also admitted that no follow-up studies had been made of either the ecological effects or the state of the munitions so far disposed. Even so, an impressive body of data was marshalled in support of CHASE No 13.

Several interesting points were made at the hearings. Firstly, it was revealed that mustard gas 'freezes' at the temperature of the depths of the ocean. Secondly, should leakage occur hydrolysis by sea water would inactivate the gas; even if the whole cargo exploded, provided it was more than 1000 feet down, no appreciable surface contamination would result. Thirdly, the area of contamination would be restricted to the immediate surroundings of the dump due to the stillness of the ocean at such depths. The rate of decay of the gas was claimed to be so fast relative to its rate of diffusion through water that no active agent would reach the surface or travel far in its toxic form.

There are obvious faults in this analysis. No mention is made of the danger of accidental sinking in shallow water close to the shore, making salvage hazardous and even impossible. In this case the cargo would present a long-term hazard. Further, no account is taken of possible ecological effects. But in spite of these objections, this phase of the operation appears to show considerably more foresight and care than the plans for the surface transportation phase. We will come back to this.

During the hearing Mr Poor (for the Army) on occasion showed surprising lack of tact. For example, he said that the ocean floor had always been considered a kind of 'Davy Jones locker' where 'things could be put away and forgotten'. Needless to say, in view of the growing concern over pollution this did not go down well with the committee. The chairman acidly reminded Mr Poor that the sea was the food locker of the future. The Secretary retorted that explorers of the sea bed should consult the charts which mapped the sites of the dumps before embarking on their researches.

In short, the Army case was that ocean burial was the cheapest and safest method for disposing of surplus cw munitions. Mr Poor described the type of unacceptable situation which led to gas dumping on this scale. He detailed the hazards at Rocky Mountain Arsenal where the stockpile is in fact visible to passengers flying in and out of Denver airport. The Arsenal has about 100 steel tanks of GB and vx stored above ground. One estimate gives a figure of 100,000 million lethal doses for the amount of gas stored there. The population of the world currently stands at about 3000 million —an interesting example of overkill.*

---

* This is a field in which drawing the line between guesses, estimates, and facts in assessing cbw capabilities is difficult. Our assertion that the us cbw capability is the largest in the world (p 312) is based on the known expansion of us efforts in the cbw field in the 1960s, as well as on reports occasionally appearing publicly in the West from defectors. An estimate, made by General Hebbeler, that the us has seven to eight times less capacity than the Russians is a surprise, but as it stands it is not very informative since it gives no indication of the fields in which the ussr is superior. Usually data such as Hebbeler's is only given when there is a political reason for it and the basis for the estimate is not revealed. In keeping with the differences in their military philosophies, it is likely that the us lags behind in gross tonnage of munitions; the difference probably lies in shells, smaller weapons such as mortars, etc., and personal weapons. This disparity is probably compensated by a higher efficiency and more modern munitions on the us side. Field studies from Vietnam have undoubtedly aided cbw development in the United States. If General Hebbeler's

In the meantime, the Army agreed to suspend its dumping plan until it had heard the views of a panel of experts from the National Academy of Sciences which had been asked to examine the problem.

Even before the panel reported, more holes began to appear in the Army's case. In an excellent article in *Science News*, the true background of the Army's careful preparations came to light. Several scientists whose work had formed the basis of the Army's case were interviewed. It was revealed that much if not all of the data quoted by Army representatives had not even been in their possession at the time of Mr McCarthy's disclosures. The data were sought only after the plan had been made public—in fact on 9 May, only one week before the transport was due to start and four days before the postponed sub-committee hearings. Yet on 13 May the Army testified that safety calculations had been made long before. Not only had the Army failed to do this, but it had also presented a distorted version of the evidence so hurriedly obtained.

Dr Bostwick Ketchum of the National Science Foundation, one of those consulted on 9 May, confessed amazement that so little was known about the effects of pressure, the rates of sinking, diffusion rates, rates of inactivation of the chemicals and water movements. In fact, the Army had collected practically none of the data necessary for making any real assessment of the plan. Dr Ketchum was quoted as saying that there were gaps 'even in the most obvious areas such as the terminal velocity of the ships on hitting the bottom, let alone what the effect would be on the gas containers and explosive charges'. The Army had obtained much of this data by the time of the hearing.

Dr Akiro Akubo of Johns Hopkins University was the scientist who related the rate of inactivation of the agents to the speed with which they would diffuse through the water. This is obviously critical for it determines whether or not active nerve or mustard gas can contaminate large areas of ocean and affect fish, fishermen or the inhabitants of the coast. Dr Akubo stressed the theoretical nature of his calculations which, while generally valid, may not be applicable in particular situations. He cautioned that a 10% error in the computation could mean 'appreciable surface contamination'. He also mentioned the unpredictability of water movements in the ocean depths which could invalidate his calculations. To quote *Science News*, 'among other scientists opinions range from firm

---

figures are correct, the chief justification for the us cbw programme—equalising Communist superiority in this field—is not valid. In addition, this figure suggets considerable expansion in the cw capability of the ussr.

reservations about CHASE 13 to very thorough opposition'.

A comment worth noting was made by US Navy Captain T. K. Treadwell, commanding officer of the Naval Oceanographic Office. He said that 'the results could be truly catastrophic'. He also warned that currents in the area of the dump could cause concentration rather than dispersal of the contaminants. Furthermore, the Navy had data on deep sea currents and water movements suggesting that in the area of the dump the gas may move much more quickly than the Army had allowed for in its estimation.* It is this sort of fundamental information that the Army had failed to collect, an amazing oversight in view of the magnitude of the operation and the potentially disastrous consequences of miscalculation.

It soon became obvious that even in the very unlikely event of a favourable report from the NAS panel, time would be too short for the plan to be implemented that year. Yet it was essential that the transportation phase be completed before the first winter storms rendered the ocean phase even more hazardous than it already was. Dr George B. Kistiakowsky of Harvard, head of the panel, hoped the report would be ready in June. For the moment the gas dumping controversy fell from public view.

Later in May, just as things were beginning to quiet down a little, there were further revelations. This time a House sub-committee on conservation chaired by Representative Henry S. Reuss (Wisconsin—Democrat) held hearings on the open-air testing of CBW materials. The atmosphere from the beginning was hostile and the unusual step was taken of swearing in Army witnesses. The Army's record of lies and evasions following the 6000 sheep deaths at Utah was exposed. Representative Van Der Jagt (Michigan—Republican) detected 'a pattern of deception' behind the Army's prevarications. The adequacy of safety procedures was criticised by Dr V. W. Sidel, who pointed out that if sheep could be killed thirty-five miles away from a test in one direction, then there was no reason why Salt Lake City, eighty miles in another direction, could not be similarly affected if a test went wrong. The public impact of these hearings was not very great. The Army gained support from the fact that its revised safety precautions could answer the severest critics and, moreover, were backed by the Surgeon-General. Even so, the hearings were unprecedented in the severity of their criticism (p 79).

---

* This is a probable reason for the change of venue to a deeper area of ocean for the 1970 dumping of nerve gas rockets. This suggests that the original potential for serious pollution was greater than may have appeared at first sight. The safety of other CHASE dumps may be questioned.

This hostility was a complete reversal of previous attitudes of Congressional committees discussing military matters. In the past these committees had seemed to exist merely to be informed of the Army's requirements or its activities and to meet such requirements with the necessary funds. None of the committees, whatever their function, were usually critical of the Army. There were several reasons for this temerity. Firstly, it was generally felt that the military best knew its own needs. Secondly, dissenting non-Army witnesses were rarely if ever called. Thirdly, the committees directly concerned with military matters on the whole had a hawkish and military orientation and some of their members represented states to a considerable extent economically dependent on the armaments industry or military installations.

The reasons for the change in attitude are many. In the first place, the large cost of Vietnam in men and money and the spiralling budget for the war had had an effect. Secondly, the military desire for new weapons systems like MIRV and ABM have cost astronomical amounts and there is a limit to which any committee can continue to vote money, especially in a period of financial difficulty. There is also a feeling that a halt must be called to the way in which the Army can begin a programme described as essential and exhaust funds before the project is complete, making necessary the voting of even more money to avoid a total loss. In extreme cases vast amounts of money have been invested in systems so unworkable they never see the light of day (e.g. the Cheyenne helicopter), or so complex, heavy or unuseable that they are less effective than the systems they were developed to replace (the new F14 aircraft).

Another factor is that even though committees concerned with strictly military matters rarely if ever called witnesses hostile to the Army's intentions, others peripherally interested (like the Senate Foreign Relations Committee) do so. As a result, the more indirectly involved committees very often have a better all-round appreciation of the situation, sometimes with embarrassing results for military-orientated committees. This, together with the growth of articulate and informed non-military pressure groups—for example, among scientists—has resulted in the military committees' agreeing to call hostile witnesses in the future if necessary.

Finally, the Army in recent years made many crucial mistakes like the sheep deaths. The myth of an all-knowing, powerful and efficient Army establishment has disappeared. In the long run these developments will benefit all concerned with a return to a firmer control of the activities of the Army by the politicians.

During June, further data on CBW appeared from a variety of

sources. At the end of the month President Nixon ordered that a policy review of this question be conducted by the National Security Council. At about this time McCarthy and twenty-five other members of the House again urged ratification of the Geneva Protocol, one of the specific questions to be considered in the policy review. McCarthy also revealed that the Defense Department had conducted tests on the island of Eniwetok in the South Pacific. These had been BW tests and although the island was uninhabited there was thought to be a danger from dissemination by migrating birds. (This may partially explain the Smithsonian contract mentioned earlier.) McCarthy asked for a moratorium on all open-air BW tests.

In late June the NAS report on the gas dumping plan appeared. Noting the possibility of a 'catastrophic' accident, the panel recommended that the plan be altered. In spite of previous Army objections, the method recommended in the report was disassembly of the weapons wherever this was possible; dumping in the sea was to be used only as a last resort. Most of the criticisms previously made of the plan were upheld. Thus, in spite of the argument originally advanced by the Army that de-activation was time consuming, costly and dangerous, the panel considered that risks to human life and to the environment should be minimised 'even though this may complicate and make more costly . . . operations'.

The recommendation was that the 1000-lb bombs be disassembled and the nerve gas inside inactivated by hydrolysis. The panel's report concluded that under the original plan, especially with respect to this class of munitions, there would have been the 'remote possibility' of a catastrophic explosion being caused by a railway accident, a sniper's bullet or a ship collision. As a result, on 27 June the Pentagon decided to accept this recommendation.

The panel felt that disposal of the liquid mustard agent should be effected by means of burning, which was to be carried out in areas where air pollution would not be a problem. Mustard gas is a mutagen and therefore the panel was anxious that it should not contaminate living things, leading to unforeseeable deleterious ecological consequences. The Pentagon accepted this recommendation also.

The other materials—GB rockets in steel and concrete coffins, steel containers contaminated with unknown chemicals, and CS drums embedded in concrete—could be dumped at sea if no other means of disposal could be found. It was suggested that the 12,000 rockets be de-militarised if this was possible and the Army subsequently set up a panel of its own to look into this. The NAS panel noted that 'various chemical warfare agents have been repeatedly disposed of in the ocean by the United States and other nations. . . . we have no information regarding possible deleterious effects of these operations on the ecosphere of the seas'. For the future the panel recommended that the Army consider disposal when it designed weapons and disposal methods should avoid dumping at sea.

It is worth remembering that this was the fourth CHASE gas dumping operation. Presumably the potential for disaster was present in the other three cases, a comforting thought for the inhabitants of those towns through which the lethal cargoes must have passed en route to the sea.

More embarrassing incidents were to be revealed. On 8 July a leakage of GB nerve gas from a stockpile in Okinawa affected twenty-three servicemen and one civilian. The Army reported that all those affected recovered. Public and political pressure subsequently led to the removal of the stockpile. The incident led to the revelation that there were 'limited amounts' of CW weapons abroad, notably in West Germany. Another possible store may exist in South Korea. (What constitutes a 'limited amount' will become apparent later.)

Also in July, allegedly top-secret CBW plans were leaked to the European press, mostly probably through the KGB. Other leakages followed. One document contained a list of US targets in *West* Germany to be hit with nuclear weapons should this ever become tactically necessary. Some of these were quite large German towns and the Germans were understandably displeased by these disclosures. The suggested source of this information was a US sergeant who had been spying for Russia; he had, however, been apprehended five years previously and therefore the plans were not new and had probably been superseded by others. Early denials of the authenticity of these papers were changed in September to an admission that they were genuine but 'very old', according to *Sanity* (September 1969). Basically, the CBW papers dealt with conventional-force support for guerilla operations in areas overrun by enemy troops. The United States was to train personnel in the use of CB weapons and to supervise their employment where possible. The prospect of CB weapons in the hands of irregular and hastily trained forces leaves the authors of this book very, very cold. It seems likely that these plans have been discarded, to be replaced by others equally secret and irresponsible.

Meanwhile, the way in which CBW was continuing to lose favour at home was reflected in the Senate's acceptance of an amendment to the military procurement authorisation bill. This amendment was put forward by Senator Thomas J. McIntyre, a member of the

Armed Services Committee, together with eight other Senators on 12 August. It was accepted by a vote of 91-0, mainly because no objection was raised by the Secretary of Defense and it was backed by the chairman of the Armed Services Committee.

As a result, $45 million was taken from the defence research budget, $16 million from research and development into offensive CBW systems. The following controls were incorporated:

1. No money is to be spent for delivery systems specifically designed to disseminate lethal chemical agents, disease-producing biological micro-organisms or biological toxins.
2. Lethal C and B agents cannot be stored in a foreign country without a notice to that country and to Congressional committees having jurisdiction.
3. Before CBW agents can be transported outside military installations the Surgeon-General must determine that there is no hazard and notice must be given.
4. No money can be spent for storage or testing of agents outside the United States unless the Secretary of State determines that there will be no violation of International Law.
5. No money will be spent for open-air testing of lethal CBW agents unless the Secretary of Defense under guidelines approved by the President determines that such tests are necessary for national security and the Surgeon-General determines that there are no health hazards.

No such amendment was made by the House of Representatives, which required only that there should be periodic reports of CBW spending. As a result, two different versions of the bill had to be reconciled in conference and further changes were made. The most significant of these was that the power of the Surgeon-General to veto transportation and open-air testing was removed. In spite of this watering down, the importance of the amendment is not lessened: it marked an important advance in the growing attempts to regain Congressional control over the military.

It is ironic that only two days later the rail shipment of gas once more became the focus of attention. On 14 August there was a secret movement of phosgene from Denver, Colorado. These were the last stocks of phosgene in the US stockpile. In all there were seven trainloads of fifteen carriages each. All were destined to pass through Iowa. Three years previously the Department of Transportation had issued blanket permits for rail shipment of phosgene. The railroads were obliged only to inform the Department before each shipment was made. No further checks were required and safety precautions were minimal.

Objection was raised by Mr Robert Ray, Governor of Iowa, after the shipment on 14th had been made. As a result of this protest the Federal Railroad Administrator, Mr Reginald Whitman, decided to rescind all permits for phosgene transportation. This was an interesting decision since after the 14 August shipment no phosgene remained for disposal by the US forces.

In early September hints of a new US initiative on CBW were leaking out. On the 20th the Pentagon admitted that tests had been performed with GB (nerve gas) and BZ (incapacitant) during 1966-67 at a site on the side of Mt Mauna Loa in Hawaii. In a letter from a Pentagon spokesman to Representative Patsy Mink it was disclosed that tests had been made seven miles away from inhabited areas to determine the effectiveness of the gases in tropical conditions. The lease for the site, due to expire in 1971, specifies that the land be used solely 'as a site to conduct classified meteorological and related tests'. Comment on the wisdom of the Army's using nerve gas so near to population centres and the honesty of its interpretation of the terms of the lease would be superfluous.

Meanwhile, the policy review continued. A meeting of the National Security Council on 5 November was delayed. The official reason was that the CIA and the State Department wanted more time to prepare themselves. The policy review had only been finished about a week before this meeting was scheduled. When it finally convened in mid-November the stage had been set for battle between the Joint Chiefs of Staff and Mr Spiers of the State Department who had presided over the policy review committee. He was supported by Dr Lee Dubridge, Presidential Science Advisor, and Henry M. Kissinger, National Security Advisor. The man who tipped the balance seems to have been Secretary of Defense Melvin Laird, who refused to back the Chiefs of Staff. Laird was not previously known for advanced thinking in this field. He had stated earlier that year that 'if we want to make sure this weapon is never used we must have the capacity to use it'. What may have happened is that the Pentagon dropped its insistence on an offensive BW capability. This interpretation is supported by the distinct lack of enthusiasm for BW on the part of Pentagon experts in recent committee hearings. For instance, the testimony of Dr D. M. McArthur before a House appropriations committee emphasised the shortcomings of BW as a weapon. McArthur is Deputy Director of Research for the Defense Department.

On 12 November McCarthy reiterated his plan to the President, asking him once again to submit the Geneva Protocol to the Senate and also accusing the Army of using tear gas as a lethal weapon in Vietnam. The next day the House Governmental Operations Committee called for a halt to open-air large-scale tests of CW agents. The Army was accused of lack of candour, deception and disregard of the public interest in its handling of such tests. The Army was once more blamed for the 6000 sheep deaths in Utah and accused of dishonesty in the subsequent inquiry.

Finally, only two weeks after the National Security Council meeting had been concluded on 25 November, President Nixon made his long awaited speech on the US position on CBW. The text is as follows:

> As to our Chemical Warfare program, the United States reaffirms its oft repeated renunciation of the first use of lethal chemical weapons, extends the renunciation to the first use of incapacitating chemicals. . . .
> Consonant with these decisions the Administration will submit to the Senate for its advice and consent to ratification, the Geneva Protocol of 1925 which prohibits the first use in war of "asphyxiating poisonous or other gases and of bacteriological methods of warfare." The United States has long supported the principles and objectives of this Protocol. We take this step toward formal ratification to reinforce our continuing advocacy of international constraints on the use of these weapons. . . .
> Biological weapons have massive unpredictable and potentially uncontrollable consequences. They may produce global epidemics and impair the health of future generations. I have therefore decided that the U.S. shall renounce the use of lethal biological agents and weapons and all other methods of biological warfare.
> The U.S. will confine its biological research to defensive measures such as immunization and safety measures.
> The Department of Defense has been asked to make recommendations as to the disposal of existing stocks of bacteriological weapons.

The significance of the President's statement cannot be fully realised unless understood in the context of other events. For example, it is notable that on 25 November a White House spokesman made it quite clear that the United States does not consider that either tear gas or defoliants are covered by the Geneva Protocol; thus the President's statement could in no way effect US practice in Vietnam.

A large part of the President's speech was subject to some 're-interpretation'. Pentagon officials claimed that toxins were classifiable not as biological but as chemical agents because they were not 'alive'. State Department officials argued that to include toxins as chemicals would in effect invalidate the sense of the ban. These differences were finally resolved in February 1970 with an official confirmation that toxins did come within the terms of the biological ban. This issue was one of a number of ambiguities brought to the fore by Nixon's statement.*

Earlier in this book we discussed cs tear gas, which is extensively used in Vietnam and which has been shown to cause severe burns and vesication comparable with the effects of mustard gas under certain circumstances. This leads us to a discussion of us policy on tear gas in general. The whole history of us policy in this area is tangled and confused. The current attitude is best summarised in a statement made by Mr Nabrit before the UN General Assembly on 5 December 1966:

The Geneva Protocol of 1925 prohibits the use in war of asphyx-iating and poisonous gas and other similar gases and liquids with equally deadly effects. It is framed to meet the horrors of poison gas warfare in the First World War and was intended to reduce the suffering by prohibiting the use of poisonous gases such as mustard gas and phosgene. It does not apply to all gases. It would be unreasonable to contend that any rule of international law prohibits the use in combat against an enemy for humanitarian purposes of agents that governments around the world commonly use to control riots by their own people.

One serious error in this statement is that the Protocol was in fact framed with tear gas in mind. During World War 1 lachrymatories were extensively used and their banning was obviously a point at issue.

In 1930 the British government presented a memorandum (Cmd 3747) to the preparatory commission for the Geneva Disarmament Conference of 18 November 1930. Acknowledging the fact that problems would arise as to whether lachrymatory gases were covered, the memorandum states: 'From every point of view it is highly desirable that a uniform construction should prevail as to whether or not the use of lachrymatory gases in war is considered to be contrary to the Geneva Protocol of 1925.'

The British government's own position was given as: 'Basing itself on the English text, the British government has taken the view that

---

* It should be emphasised that the classificatory distinction between different types of gases is not a clear one. The gas DM, for instance, is partly incapacitant and partly lachrymatory, as is cs. The latter in certain situations can be effective as a harassing agent. like mustard. It can even kill if used in confined spaces.

the use in war of "other" gases including lachrymatory gases was prohibited.' This view was supported by Britain, France Rumania, Yugoslavia, Czechoslovakia, Japan, Spain, the USSR, China, Italy, Canada and Turkey at Geneva on 15 January 1931. The US representative, Ambassador Hugh Gibson, said that the question of tear gases was complicated and he hoped it would receive further consideration.

The Disarmament Convention subsequently examined this question. An advisory committee including a representative of the United States was set up. It accepted that tear gas should be prohibited but put no restriction on domestic manufacture and use. This was explicitly accepted by the US representative, Hugh K. Wilson. Thus the generally agreed view was that tear gas was forbidden in war but domestic use was permissible and this was expressed in a resolution adopted on 23 July 1932; however, it never gained the status of a formal treaty.

From the 1930s US policy as revealed through League of Nations records remained consistent on this point. With the massive expansion of the CBW programme in the 1950s a changing attitude could be detected. The United States occasionally reaffirmed its allegiance to the Geneva Protocol although it was still not a signatory. At the same time the Pentagon manuals on CBW expressly denied that the United States was bound under international law in this field (p 145). The statement made by Cyrus Vance, then Secretary of Defense, before the disarmament sub-committee of the Senate Committee on Foreign Relations on 7 February 1967 is an example of official government thinking:

> We have consistently continued our *de facto* limitations on the use of chemical and biological weapons. We have never used biological weapons. We have not used lethal gases since World War I and it is against our policy to initiate their use.

In this statement there is a notable omission with respect to any mention of either tear gases or defoliants, for by this time the United States was using both in vast quantities in Vietnam.

Be that as it may, the history and interpretation of the Protocol make the present US position untenable. The Protocol was always intended to form part of the body of international law to which all nations should subscribe, signatory or not. The original wording of the Protocol itself illustrates this: 'This prohibition shall be universally accepted as part of International Law . . .' (p 141). This much is accepted by the US. For example, a letter of 22 December 1967 from William B. Macomber, Jr., Assistant Secretary of

State for Congressional Relations, addressed to Congressman Rosenthal of New York, reads in part:

> We consider that the basic rule set forth in this document [the Geneva Protocol] has been so widely accepted over a long period of time that it is now considered to form a part of customary International Law.

This then would seem to be general US policy in spite of the odd statement to the contrary produced from time to time by the Pentagon. But acceptance of the Protocol is virtually meaningless unless interpretation of terms is agreed upon. The revised US interpretation is not endorsed by any of the signatories to the Protocol, with the very recent exception of Britain (see below).

Thus President Nixon's pledge to submit the Protocol for ratification has caused problems. There are two possibilities: either the Protocol must be re-interpreted by all the signatories or the United States must admit that its current policy in Vietnam is a contravention of international law.

The latter course is obviously preferable in every way. The United States would naturally suffer considerable loss of face at first, but in the long run the contribution thus made towards real understanding and disarmament would be immeasurable. However, all the evidence seems to indicate that it is the former course which will be pursued. The British government has already been persuaded to alter its interpretation of the Protocol to conform to the Americans'. This being so, it may be useful to consider the reasons why President Nixon made a speech at all, as it raises more problems than it solves.

In the National Security Council review of CBW the State Department Legal Office indicated the difficulties resulting from US tear gas policy. The question of herbicides and their position vis à vis the Protocol is also in dispute but it does seem that most nations will consider that the use of these in war is banned by the Protocol. Further to this, the report of the UN Secretary-General on CBW was published in July 1969 and explicitly called for a ban on the use of tear gases in war. All these things caused problems for US policymakers.

The reason why President Nixon made such a contentious statement was that he was under pressure. A quarter of the membership of Congress had given their support to various resolutions tabled by Mr McCarthy and Senator Hartke (Indiana—Democrat) calling on the administration to submit the Protocol for ratification. More pressure was forthcoming from committee hearings relating to CBW

to be held by the House Foreign Affairs Sub-Committee on National
Security Policy and Scientific Developments and the Senate Foreign
Relations Committee.

The first session of the Congressional hearings opened on 18
November and was chaired by Representative Clement J. Zablocki.
The witnesses included a number of Congressmen; George Bunn,
former general counsel of the Arms Control and Disarmament
Agency (ACDA); and Ivan L. Bennett, director of the New York
Medical Center. All the witnesses agreed that the Protocol must be
considered in relation to the Vietnam War. Bennett, one of the
advisors on the UN Secretary-General's report on CBW, stated on 20
November that due to American actions in Vietnam:

> American credibility in discussions on the control of CBW has
> been compromised and we are being subjected to increasingly
> vigorous and bitter criticism by the representatives of many
> nations, by no means only those of the Eastern Bloc.

By this time the Senate Foreign Relations Committee hearings
were in preparation. The combination of CW in Vietnam, increasing
knowledge about long-term effects of herbicides and defoliants and
increasing concern over pollution is newsworthy. Add television
cameras and journalists and it could become political dynamite.

President Nixon had been steadily attempting to remove Vietnam
from the focus of public attention, but the combination of events
described above could easily have awakened the sort of feeling which
led to the Moratorium. After Nixon's statement those who sought
ratification of the Protocol had to choose between delaying this
while concentrating on the problem of CW in Vietnam, or keeping
quiet until ratification had taken place. In the end there was less
noise generated then expected, indicating perhaps that the latter
choice had been made. Even so, the Zablocki hearings gave a good
platform to critics of America's policy.

We turn now to President Nixon's proposals for a complete ban
on BW and his endorsement of the British BW proposals at the disarmament conference (p 352). The provision for destruction of BW
stockpiles can hardly be said to have stemmed from altruistic
motives. The Pentagon's final rejection of BW is based on good
military sense. The National Security Council considered that BW
was only really viable 'primarily . . . for first use'. Previous hearings,
especially those before the House Appropriations Committee, had
already sealed the fate of BW. It was realised that this would most
probably be a relatively inefficient and ineffective weapon.

The most significant feature about the British proposals is that there is very little chance of their being accepted. What little chance they may have originally had disappeared with the government's *volte face* on tear gas.

Thus Nixon's speech can be seen in its true perspective. This leaves, however, the problem it has raised about US policy on tear gas relative to the Geneva Protocol. The United States cannot easily present its case on CBW in Geneva while facing a united opposition from the signatories of the Protocol. The difficulty is that the Protocol itself can be considered as a contract between parties. Therefore if any one signatory refuses to accept any of the terms, the whole agreement can be rejected by the other parties. As an outsider the United States has little chance of directly gaining the support of other nations. It is here that the British government shows its true value to its American ally.

All British governments from the 1930s until recently have insisted that lachrymatories are covered by the Protocol. Yet on 2 February 1970 Mr Stewart, British Foreign Secretary, stated in a reply to a House of Commons question that the government considered CS and other such gases as outside the scope of the Geneva Protocol. He quoted, by way of explanation, an answer to a Parliamentary question given by Dr Dalton in 1930:

> Smoke screens are not considered as poisonous and do not therefore come within the terms of the Geneva Protocol. Tear gases and shells producing poisonous fumes are, however, prohibited by the Protocol.

Mr Stewart expanded his argument by insisting that the 'CS smoke' produced by modern technology was less 'harmful to man' than the tear gases of the 1930s and was thus beyond the scope of the Protocol. These same views appeared in a letter from Mr Wilson, the Prime Minister, to Mr John Pardoe, MP, of which the following is part:

> Modern technology has developed CS smoke which unlike gases available in 1930 is considered to be not significantly harmful to men in other than exceptional circumstances.

This dubious assertion is analysed in more detail later. The argument was reiterated by Lord Chalfont in the House of Lords on 26 February:

> The reason why we are taking what Lord Brockway calls unilateral action is because in any international instruments it is

up to the individual signatories to interpret the treaty they have signed.

This statement is remarkable and yet typical. The principle of international agreements is that nations agree between themselves on a common interpretation of an agreement. If one party expresses a view contrary to the consensus, especially if this runs counter to previous statements by the party concerned, then the party is clearly in conflict with the agreement. Lord Chalfont's statement shows cynical and flagrant disregard for all well-established and accepted conventions on international law and practice.

The key question prompted by the British action was dealt with in oral answers in the House of Commons on 4 May 1970. Mr Stewart expressed the opinion that Britain's exclusion of cs gas from the Geneva Protocol would not encourage other nations to remove their pet weapons from the ban. This is a most eloquent comment on British diplomacy: Britain may be setting a very dangerous precedent for wholly obscure purposes.

It must be made clear at this point that Mr Stewart's distinctions between gases and smokes are merely an exercise in semantics. cs and cn, commonly described as tear gases, are in fact solids which may be disseminated from smoke grenades. Very few of the so-called 'tear gases' are true gases; most are particulate as dust, smokes or even sometimes liquids. It is entirely dishonest to cite smoke screens as being equivalent to cs or similar agents. Smoke screens are generated in order to hide the activities of troops. Generally, any toxic consequences are merely unwelcome side effects, as is recognised in Dr Dalton's statement. cs and similar gases are toxic and are produced specifically to affect the physiology of those exposed to them. By taking Mr Stewart's argument to its logical conclusion, water, aspirin or any other substance which can accidentally produce death or incapacitation is a chemical weapon.

The real test of cs is to ask whether its military use resembles that of standard cw agents; in short, is its action mainly physiological? The answer is manifestly yes.

The reasons behind recent British actions are not immediately obvious. The Geneva Protocol does not affect the domestic use of cs. Even Sweden, renowned for her opposition to cbw, has used cs to control riots. It is interesting to reflect upon the significance of the British decision, especially as the issue caused several senior British government members to consider resignation. It seems unlikely that Britain is considering using cs in war herself and that the change in position is therefore due to us pressure. One can only conclude that Britain is far more dependent on and subservient to the United States than is generally realised. It does not seem likely that a highly unpopular decision such as this would have been taken except under the most extreme pressure.

The impact in international circles has been more or less predictable. In December 1969 the General Assembly of the UN voted by 80 to 3 in favour of a resolution demanding the extensive interpretation of the Protocol—that is, to include tear gas. The three opposing votes came from the United States, Australia (both involved with CW in Vietnam) and Portugal (involved in Angola). Britain abstained. The subsequent defection of Britain to the American camp must have pleased Washington for now, as a member of the Geneva disarmament conference, Britain can virtually act as spokesman for the United States and propagate the American view to the signatories of the Geneva Protocol. American thus has gained the support at Geneva she lacked for so long.

Needless to say, the British initiative was coolly received at Geneva. On 12 March 1970, Mrs Alva Myrdal, the Swedish delegate, described the British attitude as 'purporting to establish a unilateral re-interpretation' of the Geneva Protocol. Mrs Myrdal said that CS, 'which is a tear gas whatever other names you may attach to it', was banned in war 'under the generally recognised rules of international law as embodied in the Geneva Protocol'. On 19 February, the British delegate, Lord Chalfont, had offered the conference the same justifications used earlier by Mr Stewart. Following the attacks of Mrs Myrdal and others, including Mr Hussein from India, Lord Chalfont refrained from offering these same justifications again. Mrs Myrdal stated that it was disquieting to see the lethal/non-lethal distinction being reintroduced into the discussion. The Protocol had made no such distinction for reasons which had been thoroughly discussed in the 1920s and which were, more to the point, solidly based.

The British delegation was reported to be extremely annoyed with the bitter attack delivered by Sweden on what it considered to be the British government's legitimate right to interpret the Protocol as it wished.

In 1969 several governments including the British submitted, or announced their intention to submit, draft conventions restricting CBW. Britain and the USSR proposed draft treaties; Japan intimated that she would do likewise. Several nations contributed papers and reports. The British proposals (p 352) concentrated exclusively on BW, leaving CW to be dealt with at a later date. There was understandable scepticism about the British treaty proposals, especially from the USSR which feared that the British treaty would in effect prolong CW. The British delegation was reported to be disappointed with the diplomatic cold shoulder the draft treaty received, but, assuming it had been studying the problem with reasonable seriousness, it must have expected this. There are two ways to explain Britain's failure with the BW treaty. The first is incompetence and lack of understanding of the problems involved. The standard of official statements from various British statesmen throughout this period would lend a certain credence to this interpretation of the situation. They are confused, vague, mutually contradictory and sometimes an insult to the intelligence of those to whom they are addressed. Lord Chalfont, in an article in the *New Scientist* of 25 December 1969, referred to the draft Soviet treaty which planned to take CBW as a whole and stated 'it does have certain weaknesses, one being that it makes no provision for verification'. This makes an interesting contrast to the statement of Mr Mulley, a delegate to the conference in 1969, who explicitly said that 'verification, in the sense in which that term is normally used . . . is simply not possible in the field of biological warfare' (p 355).

The other possibility, and by far the most likely one, is that the British government's BW treaty was essentially a political gambit. It can be seen as the beginning of the process which led to Britain's defection from the Protocol as originally interpreted. If accepted it would most certainly have slowed any agreement on CW and consequently to some extent removed some of the hostility which was beginning to build up against American use of CW. Its acceptance, however, was never considered crucial. It effectively blocked the USSR draft treaty and for a time at least it took some of the steam out of the domestic criticism of Britain's role in CBW. Ultimately, however, in the light of more recent developments, the move has been recognised for what it was. Britain can take credit for deliberately endangering a uniquely effective piece of international law of more than forty years' standing.

By the end of March, the other allies were falling into line on the subject of biological warfare. In a statement issued to the disarmament conference, Canada stated that she does not possess biological weapons and does not intend to develop, produce, acquire, stockpile or use such weapons at any time. The Canadian government stated that it would produce and use chemical weapons only in the event of a CW attack on Canada and her allies. In view of the close co-operation between the various CBW establishments in allied countries, and the near monopoly on cbw weapons held by the us, it is hardly surprising that another member state of the quadri-partite agreement should follow the initiative of the us.

In May 1970 the British were again vigorously attacked, this time by Mr J. Winiewicz, the Polish delegate, for treating chemical and biological warfare separately. The Polish delegate suggested tighter complaint and verification procedures than those in the Soviet draft treaty. These did not meet the approval of the us and Britain.

Until the "redefinition" of the Geneva Protocol there was a re-mote chance of agreement on cbw. This redefinition stands as a vast single obstacle to such agreement. Any advances of the past year have been nullified and the suggestion could be made that this was done with calculation, deliberately, in full knowledge of the conse-quences. The conference may have been sabotaged by the British and the Americans, to whom too rapid progress in the field of cbw disarmament may have seemed politically undesirable.

The situation outlined above is serious enough in itself, but, in addition, the long-term effects of cbw agents are now beginning to be understood. Lack of data concerning these effects is, in our opinion, one of the most disquieting features of the cbw story. In various places throughout the book we expressed our fears on this subject, especially with respect to cs, nerve gases and defoliants. Now that more information has become available the reality seems to have surpassed the worst suspicions.

The gas cs, widely used in Vietnam and elsewhere for riot control, is not as innocuous as was at first supposed. A British Ministry of Defence study of this gas was completed a year ago; but it has not been published, nor are there any signs that it will be in the near future. One of the reasons for this may be a us Army report, 'Evaluation of the effects of thermally generated cs aerosols on the human skin', which effectively explodes the myth of the harmlessness of cs. It is based on a study conducted at the Edgewood Arsenal laboratories in 1967 and de-classified the following June.

Four groups of four volunteers were used in the study. The report states that 'the human subjects in the tests conducted by this in-stallation are enlisted volunteers. There is no coercion or enticement to volunteer'. Grenades of cs were placed in one chamber and the gas was blown along to a second which was kept at a temperature of 97° F and with 100% humidity. Under these conditions the right arms of the volunteers were exposed to the gas. Group I were ex-posed for 15 minutes, Group II for 30 minutes, Group III for 45 minutes and Group IV for an hour. According to the report: 'Be-

cause of the marked delayed reaction that occurred unexpectedly
in Groups III and IV the study was immediately discontinued to
preclude serious injury to volunteer subjects.' The report went
on to say:

> All volunteers uniformly noticed stinging of exposed forearm
> beginning five to ten minutes after exposure was begun. Im-
> mediately after being withdrawn from the chamber their arms
> were rinsed with cold running water for one minute to remove
> most of the white CS powder that visibly clung to the hairs. The
> stinging increased with washing but subsided within the next
> five minutes.

With the sole exception of a Negro volunteer, the eight subjects of
Groups I and II suffered an immediate skin reddening which persisted for about 30 minutes. No discernible after-effects were noted.
For Groups III and IV the red reaction persisted for three hours.
Between 12 and 24 hours later first and second degree burns
appeared on all the members of the two groups. Blistering occurred
in four of the eight volunteers.

In one of the volunteers a very severe reaction occurred. The
results were strikingly similar to those achieved by exposure to
mustard gas, namely, huge blisters three to four inches across.
This volunteer and several others were treated in hospital. In all
cases the blistering cleared after ten days following treatment to
minimise the possibility of infection. The report concludes:

> It should be emphasized that without adequate treatment,
> especially under field conditions, severe local infections could
> be expected in a large proportion of second degree burns pro-
> ducing concomitant complications and further incapacitation.

One of the reasons why the study was initiated is revealed in an
appendix to the report which describes an incident involving members of the US forces engaged in a field exercise at Fort McClellan,
Arkansas, on 4 August 1966.

> As they approached the roadblock [their mission was to capture
> it] micropulverised CS 1 was directed toward them from a por-
> table disperser—a modified flamethrower. Because of the rain the
> CS hung in the air as a heavy cloud. It completely enveloped
> twelve men and contacted some others at the periphery. All the
> twelve men caught in the cloud eventually developed various de-
> grees of vesticulation [blisters] that corresponded clinically to
> the second degree burns produced experimentally. About half of
> the men who were at the periphery of the CS cloud developed
> first and second degree burns.

The second degree burns were treated with tetanus toxoid, ointment and dressings. The large blisters were opened surgically. The data from the field corroborates that obtained experimentally. Other 'field data' from action in Vietnam may also now be viewed with a little more credibility (see report from *Le Monde*, p 20).

There are a number of points which should be taken into consideration in any assessment of these data. The experiments were conducted on the tough and healthy skin of soldiers' arms. What would the effects have been on highly sensitive lung tissue? The vesicant effects closely resemble those of agents like mustard gas. Mustard gas—and, it is alleged, cs—falls into the class of compounds called alkylating agents. Some of these are among the most carcinogenic compounds known. Although cs does not chemically resemble these particular carcinogens, in the absence of relevant data there must remain a suspicion that cs may be a carcinogen. As mentioned before, the British studies on both the toxicity and carcinogenicity of cs have still not been published.

The point is not so much whether cs is carcinogenic but rather whether this attribute would bar its use. Is the carcinogenesis hazard of cs, when used in riot control, balanced by the dangers which would result from not using it? One could always argue that a slight risk of cancer is preferable to a bullet. The question cannot be properly discussed, however, until more information is forthcoming. The apparent suppression of data on the effects of cs can only continue to arouse the worst suspicions as to what that data is. In any case, while there may be some cause for argument where relatively small doses of cs are involved—for instance, in riot control—the same cannot be said of its use in war. A consideration of cs as used in Vietnam makes this clear. The quantity of the agent used in Vietnam is so great that even a slight carcinogenic or teratogenic effect could be significant. Since 1964 over 6000 tons of cs have been used (pp 295-96). us manuals state that 50 lbs of the agent can effectively cover 0.4 square miles. The quantity used in Vietnam is therefore sufficient to cover 100,000 square miles, while the area of the country is only 66,000 square miles. Unlike defoliants, cs is used primarily on inhabited areas, thus maximising any adverse affects. *Army Training Circular TC 3-16* states:

> In addition to use against unmasked hostile forces, CS munitions may be used as a most effective weapon choice against a target area containing mixed friendly-hostile or neutral-hostile populations where casualities are to be minimized . . .

The instructions for use against hostile forces given in this same manual, however, illustrate that cs will be used specifically in ways which make prolonged exposure inescapable. In the high temperature and humidity of the country this effectively simulates the experimental conditions described above. The manual states:

1. The concentration of agent must be dense enough over the desired target to be intolerable to unmasked personnel.
2. The concentration must be extended around the target periphery in sufficient quantities so that escape (by closing eyes and/or holding breath) is difficult.
3. The concentration must be capable of being established within a short time (1 minute or less).

This manual is dated April 1969; ignorance as to the effects of these chemicals cannot be offered as an excuse.

In considering the nerve gases we see the difficulties involved in assessing the long-term effects of cw agents. The more subtle long-term effects may be impossible to demonstrate after the event, a point which also applies to both cs and defoliants.

A brief history of the nerve gas cases may be useful here. Most of the recent evidence is from Britain. In the last two years several men working at one of the British cw centres, Nancekuke, have complained of disability due to past occupational exposures to nerve gas. In many cases there has been a long and ultimately unsuccessful fight to obtain disability pension rights, or at least recognition of the nature of the incapacity. These men display a variety of nervous and psycho-pathological disorders. Persistent attempts, notably by the British anti-cbw group led by Mrs Elizabeth Compton, gained little response from the Ministries concerned. Ministry of Defence officials repeatedly asserted that there could be no long-term effects due to nerve gas exposure, although this was in direct contradiction to the little evidence available.

One example of the evidence which the Ministry ignores is a paper delivered by U. Spiegelberg before the 14th International Congress on Occupational Health held in 1963. This paper discusses 'whether delayed and permanent neurological and psychopathological damage occurs after many years of exposure to phosphoric acid esters'. The study is based on a number of workers employed from 1934-45 in the German gas warfare centres in Berlin, Spandau and Münster. From 1956-63, 150 of these workers were investigated. Of these, six were found to have been exposed solely to alkyl phosphates (nerve gases and their derivatives). All of these men suffered slight poisoning over a period of between two and eight years. A typical example was that of a thirty-eight-year-old technical chemist who had been exposed to these compounds for six years. He showed

> a deep-seated physical alteration with lowering of the vitality, a change in temperament to depression, slightly dementive states and general coarsening and lowering of the personality.

Another case was that of an electrical installation technician, aged 48, who had been exposed to nerve gas for a number of years:

> He became ill directly after industrial employment with central nervous attacks with outbreaks of sweating, trembling and nausea. . . . After 2 years a gradual alteration of the personality set in with change of temperament towards depressive loss of energy and mental power.

The third subject had a history of depression and suicide attempts. All these cases paralleled closely those of the British cases mentioned above. Other work on this subject is quoted by Spiegelberg:

> Reinl has published one case which shows neurological and psycho-pathological deviations one year after acute industrial poisoning. A report by Sturm likewise justifies the assumption of residual clinical damage with chronically persisting central nervous and psychiatric disturbance.

As Spiegelberg himself admits, these studies are open to criticism. Because of the small number of people available for examination after occupational or acute nerve gas exposure, there can be little statistical data to support his thesis. Decisive proof will be difficult to obtain. In spite of this, there is no justification whatever for the Ministry of Defence to blandly assert that there is no evidence that a sub-lethal dose of nerve gas can cause long-term damage when all the evidence would seem to indicate the reverse. One may well ask in the light of this whether experiments on servicemen or other volunteers are permissible (p 108). These questions are as relevant in America as they are in Britain. In the United States many more people have been exposed to nerve gas, in factories, laboratories and tests, than in most other countries. Mortality and illness statistics of these people should be carefully studied for both their own sakes and that of their colleagues elsewhere.

The outcome of Parliamentary pressure in Britain resulted in the action of the Ministry of Defence in 1969 in setting up an enquiry into the health of workers involved in nerve gas production. It is doubtful whether this enquiry will prove conclusive because of the very nature of the subject. There is almost certain to be a lack of relevant data, for even at Nancekuke only a small number of men are actually exposed to the agents. In any event, the health data from Nancekuke would be most useful for comparison with similar data from other laboratories. Reports from the US suggest that chemists as a whole tend to have a reduced life expectancy, probably due to a number of factors not all easily discernible. It is to be hoped that this British enquiry will be effective. A considerable and prolonged effort is necessary if reasonably definite conclusions are to be reached, since this is a notoriously difficult field of medicine.

It is now apparent that the defoliants in use in Vietnam also have long-term effects. This story is perhaps the greatest indicator of what CBW can do to those affected and what it makes of those who use it.

Since US defoliation operations became public knowledge, the scientific community has been increasingly concerned. For the last three years the American Association for the Advancement of Science and its council have tried to encourage debate and study on the long-term effects of the chemicals involved. The original fears of the scientists were mainly about the ecological consequences and a committee under Professor M. Mendron of MIT is expected to have a report on the subject by the end of 1970. In the latter half of 1969 the question of mutagenic and teratogenic effects of the herbicides was raised. It is important to note that the question of teratogenic effects is not a new one.

The first suspicions of teratogenic effects due to the chemicals were raised in several Saigon newspapers in the summer of 1969. On 26 June the Saigon newspaper *Tin Sang* alleged that catastrophic teratogenic effects had resulted from herbicide spraying in one province. This was followed by a report from a doctor from the Huong Vuong hospital who also reported malformations. One prominent US molecular biologist has been quoted as saying that he has letters from anguished Vietnamese alleging that women have 'given birth to monsters'. Professor E.W. Pfeiffer of the University of Montana has said that the number of abnormal births in Saigon has risen so alarmingly that the relevant files of the Saigon Health Ministry are classified as secret. For some time the reports from Vietnam were strongly criticised as being alarmist.

On 29 October a statement was issued by Dr Lee A. Dubridge, President Nixon's chief science advisor. Dr Dubridge stated that offspring of mice and rats given large doses of herbicide in the early stages of pregnancy showed 'a higher than expected number of deformities'. The government therefore undertook to restrict the applications of 2,4,5T both domestically and in Vietnam. Domestically the Department of Agriculture and the Department of the Interior were to restrict the use of 2,4,5T to unpopulated areas or places where residues would not reach man. Registrations of 2,4,5T for use on food crops were to be cancelled by the Department of Agriculture. The Food and Drug Administration was required to obtain data in order to establish safe legal tolerance levels for food contamination. The Department of Health, Education and Welfare was to define these tolerance levels. Failing the establishment of these limits the restrictions were to become effective from 1 January.

The Defense Department was ordered to restrict the use of 2,4,5T to 'areas remote from population'. The value of this directive is at best limited. Following the White House statement the Defense Department said that no change would be made in the policy governing use of 2,4,5T in Vietnam, because it was felt that the current policy conformed with the directive. This has not been the experience of the Vietnamese or visitors to Vietnam. An example has been given by Professor Pfeiffer who was observing a defoliation mission in March 1969 when 1000 gallons of chemicals were evacuated at one spot over the Mekong Delta. On another occasion he claimed that an aeroplane in difficulties had evacuated its whole cargo over the town of Ho Nai. Professor Pfeiffer was quoted as saying (*Sunday Times*, 30 November 1969): 'The Pentagon has said that the chemical would be limited to uninhabited areas. From my own information I know this to be a lie.' Even if it intended to follow the directive, the Army would find it difficult, if not impossible, due to the high population density in much of Vietnam.

An article by *Washington Post* reporter Richard Homan supports Professor Pfeiffer's allegations. An early statement on 2,4,5T had said it was used against 'training and regroupment centers'. The statement was quickly expunged after it was asked how this was compatible with the directive.

In December 1969 Rear-Admiral William E. Lemos, Director of Policy Planning and National Security Council Affairs, said: 'We believe this usage [of herbicide] has been wise and has been accomplished with restraint.' This is a statement worth considering in the light of the above and what follows (see also text pp 26-52 and 223-252).

Dr Dubridge asserted that 2,4,5T had saved lives in Vietnam but did not specify how it did this or whose lives had been saved. He also claimed that almost no 2,4,5T was used by home gardeners. This directly contradicts a statement by a spokesman for Monsanto,

one of the big producers of 2,4,5T, who said such use was widespread.

Dr Dubridge (a physicist) made the observation that

> it seems improbable that any person could receive harmful
> amounts of this chemical from any of the existing uses of 2,4,5T
> and, while the relationship of these effects in laboratory animals
> to the effects in man are not entirely clear at this time, the actions
> taken will assure the safety of the public while further evidence
> is sought.

How accurate this statement is will be clear later. It is notable that
restrictions on 2,4,5T use in the US are fairly stringent, in contrast
with the loose control of use in Vietnam. The American public is
better protected than the Vietnamese, who have been bombarded
with far greater amounts of these compounds for years and thus
face a many times greater risk.

Beyond revealing that the work on which the ban was based
was performed by the Bionetics Research Company of Bethesda,
Maryland, the US government was exceedingly reluctant to divulge
the full content of the report, much to the chagrin of interested
scientists. In April 1970 the report had still not been published. The
study was started in 1965 under contract to the National Cancer
Institute and the results were known to the government more than
twelve months before the Dubridge announcement. The reason
for the unprecedented statement is not hard to see. Dr Dubridge
had been warned that the content of the report was leaking through
the scientific community and it was only a matter of time before it
appeared in the popular press. Undoubtedly the statement was
made to forestall critics of the defoliation programme who would
clamour for action. Dr Dubridge wished to appear to be acting
of his own volition rather than being forced under the pressure
of criticism.

In the opinion of some of those who have studied the report, the
statement was politically sound if less than candid in its treatment
of the data. In this Dr Dubridge seems to be following the precedent
of the Department of Defense in its 'summary' of the MRI report
on herbicides (pp 47-49, 249-252).

What the authors have been able to gather of the actual content
of the report is summarised below. Its title is *Evaluation of the
teratogenic activity of selected pesticides and industrial chemicals
in mice and rats*. The report is quoted as saying that for mice, with
the exception of very small subcutaneous single doses, 'all dosages,
routes and strains resulted in increased incidence of abnormal

foetuses'. Abnormalities described included lack of eyes, faulty eye development, cystic kidneys, cleft palates and enlarged livers. In these experiments 2,4,5T was given to two strains of mice at different dose levels. In one series of experiments with AK mice, oral administration of 113 mg/kg on days 6 to 15 of pregnancy produced 49% deformed foetuses, notably cleft palates. At the lowest oral dose used on mice enlarged livers were noted. At the highest dose 100% of foetuses had at least one noticeable deformity and 70% were grossly abnormal.

The results on rats were even more striking. It proved impossible to demonstrate teratogenic effects in this species using thalidomide. This was not so with 2,4,5T. The usual proportion of abnormal foetuses is 7 to 13%. In each case the compound was administered daily on the 10th and 15th days of pregnancy. A dosage of 4.6 mg/kg induced 39% abnormal feotuses; at 10 mg/kg 78% were abnormal; 21.5 mg/kg gave 90% abnormal foetuses; 46.5 mg/kg gave 100% abnormal foetuses.

Two considerations are important in discussing the above; firstly, the data are scant and preliminary and their statistical significance is not clear; secondly, such limitations notwithstanding, the results are very striking but cannot be easily extrapolated to man. There are several reasons for this: species differences in response to teratogenic agents may be great and man may be more or (less probably) less sensitive than experimental animals; and any extrapolations to real situations involve too many unknowns to be even rough guides to effects. It can be said, however, that in Vietnam humans could be exposed to doses within an order of magnitude of those which caused malformation in rats and mice.

In addition to the data on 2,4,5T, listed as 'probably dangerous', there is data on 2,4D, 'potentially dangerous'. This is the more widely used of the chemicals both at home in the US and in Vietnam (pp 246-247). In the US more than $25 million worth of 2,4D is sold per year. This is not being restricted and the reasons are not hard to see. In the US 2,4D is used on food crops and its restriction would cause considerable economic disruption in home agriculture and in the pesticide industry. The Joint Chiefs of Staff oppose restriction very strongly and military and economic considerations have prevailed over humanitarian ones.

Following the Dubridge announcement more information on the effects of 2,4,5T has gradually filtered through to the public. An article by Thomas Whiteside in the *New Yorker* stimulated interest which culminated in a Congressional enquiry. This article gave details of the teratogenic effects of 2,4,5T which were to be revealed in full later at hearings of the Sub-Committee on Energy, Natural Resources and the Environment of the Senate Committee on Commerce.

Ironically, information on the adverse effects of these compounds on man did not come from far-off Vietnam but from Globe, Arizona, eighty miles from Phoenix, where from 1965 to 1970 extensive local herbicide spraying was being conducted. This was alleged to have caused a variety of ailments.

Mrs Willard Shoecraft was sprayed in the garden of the twenty-acre estate owned by her husband and herself. She suffered vaginal bleeding, numbness of the limbs and difficulty in breathing. Women neighbours from adolescents to those in old age suffered in the same way. (It is interesting to compare this with reports on pp 32-34 and p 234.) Forestry officials asserted repeatedly that 2,4D and 2,4,5T were completely harmless.

Other complainants soon came forward. The McCusick family—Robert, Charmion and their three young children—were doused by a chemical spray. According to Mrs McCusick, 'We breathed it in, droplets formed on our skins. We drove home to wash with strong soap but we all had breathing difficulties, chest pains and muscle spasms. Our two dogs went down with a sort of pneumonia. Although I had a hysterectomy after the birth of my last child twelve years ago I experienced a painful breast discharge of milk'.

Mrs Shoecraft claimed that one of her dogs had an unusually large litter, one of which was deformed. Her youngest son's pet guinea pigs, hamsters and white mice died; some had deformed offspring. Mr McCusick kept a herd of goats on his mountain farm. Since spraying began in 1965, 60% of the kids had been born deformed or dead. They were found to have cystic kidneys or enlarged livers.

Mrs McCusick, an ornithologist working for the National Parks Service, had kept records:

Between 15th and 28th May 1966, eleven brown towhee finches were found in our yard unable to fly, eat, drink or stand upright. They had eyes discharging or swollen shut. All died within three days . . .

In 1967 a change in bird populations was quite noticeable. No towhees, no resident cardinals, jays, tanagers . . .

In 1968 [after spraying] the leaves fell from the trees in our garden and were eaten by geese and chickens, which became sick immediately . . . A peacock was found paralyzed, with feet clenched like fists . . . The inside of a fig, fed to a mocking bird we were raising, caused paralysis and death . . .

'Viewed as a whole', commented University of Arizona ornithologist Dr Stephen Russell, 'they point to something pretty alarming'.

Until April this year forest officials were still claiming the defoliants were harmless. Tests on samples of plants from private lands in the area were found to contain the herbicides. 2,4D was found in Mrs Shoecraft's skin tissue.

Prior to last October two official task forces had visited Globe but their findings were inconclusive. They did imply, however, that the effects were not due to the defoliants.

The restriction on 2,4,5T seems not to have been enforced by the relevant authorities. In any event, Dr Dubridge's statement failed to affect the practise of those agencies it was aimed at. Following this and the Bionetics report the independent National Health Federation demanded a Congressional enquiry into the herbicide matter and especially into how it had affected Globe.

Professor E.W. Pfeiffer, who had been to South Vietnam as a representative of the Society for Social Responsibility in Science, was quoted (in the *Sunday Times,* 19 April 1970) as saying:

All of our interviews with the local inhabitants consistently disclosed that village livestock became ill for a period of several days soon after spraying. Whereas the larger animals (water buffalos, cattle and mature pigs and sheep) became only mildly ill and all recovered, some of the smaller ones (chickens and ducks and young pigs) suffered more severely and in some cases were reported to have died. [See also pp 32-34.]

Apparently many wild birds became partially paralysed and could be captured easily. There are also a number of small dead birds found at the time in the woods and fields.

The above and other reports forced the Pentagon into making an enquiry into the military uses of herbicides. A comparison of Professor Pfeiffer's observations with those of the people from Globe and others from Vietnam reveals common features not easily ascribed to coincidence.

Other data are available from workers who have been exposed to these chemicals. In Britain workers have complained of skin rashes and boils and acne. Men without respirators have been overcome by headaches, nausea and unsteadiness. It has also been suggested that temporary impotence is another consequence of exposure. Whether these effects are due to the herbicides or due to contaminants is not yet clear. According to Gensuikyo, the Japanese Council against Atomic and Hydrogen Bombs, on 23 July 1969 it was stated in the

Foreign Affairs Committee of the House of Representatives of Japan:

Ohmuta factory of Mitsui Koatsu has been manufacturing poison gas powder [sic] of the type 2,4,5T/2,4,5TPC. Thirty workers have been suffering from skin diseases, abnormal leucocyte count, cirrhosis of the liver and there are still some patients coming for treatment.

In April 1970 scientific data appeared which seems to support some of the reports we have discussed above. These were given at the hearings of the Sub-Committee on Energy, Natural Resources and the Environment of the Senate Committee on Commerce. The Departments of Agriculture, the Interior, and Health, Education and Welfare finally undertook to restrict the herbicide as Dr Dubridge had recommended the previous October and to ban its use in Vietnam until the situation became clearer.

Much of the scientific work was concerned not only with 2,4D and 2,4,5T, but with tetrachlorodibenzo-p-dioxin (often referred to as dioxin) a contaminant of 2,4,5T. The credit for this work goes to Dow Chemical, Dr Jacqueline M. Verrett of the Food and Drug Administration, and the National Institute of Environmental Health Sciences.

According to Dr Julius Johnson of Dow Chemical, a 2,4,5T manufacturer, his company responded to Dr Dubridge's announcement by searching for impurities in their formulation. 2,4,5T is manufactured from 1,2,4,5 tetrachlorobenzene by hydrolysis to form the sodium salt of 2,4,5 trichlorophenol. This is then treated with the sodium salt of monochloracetic acid. According to Dr Johnson, 'since 1950 we have been keenly aware' that highly toxic compounds are formed from 2,4,5 trichlorophenol at high temperatures (and alkalinity). In 1965 the most significant of these compounds was identified as 2,3,7,8 tetrachlorodibenzo-p-dioxin. Since 1965 Dow altered its plant to remove dioxin formed to levels of less than 0.5 parts per million. The material used in the Bionetics study described earlier (made by the Diamond Alkali Company) was shown by gas-liquid chromatography to contain 27 ± 8 parts per million of dioxin.

The reason for the ban on 2,4,5T was given by the Surgeon-General of the United States, Dr Jesse L. Steinfield. The National Institute of Environmental Health Sciences had shown that 'nearly pure 2,4,5T was reported to cause birth defects when injected at high doses into experimental pregnant mice but not in rats'. Dr Samuel S. Epstein, chairman of the Mrak Commission's panel on teratogenesis, said that in these studies cleft palates were produced 'at dose levels of 150 mg/kg with scattered abnormalities at 100 mg/kg; the cleft palate incidence in control mice was essentially zero'.

Dr Verrett's study for the FDA had involved re-crystallized 2,4,5T and dioxin samples. In studies of chicken embryos Dr Verrett showed that 50 micrograms of the Dow 2,4,5T was equivalent in effect to 6.25 micrograms of the sample used in the Bionetics study. Re-crystallized herbicide also produced abnormal embryos but only at five times the dose. One-millionth of a gram of dioxin has been shown to produce a noticeable toxic effect on chicken embryos, although it was argued at the hearings that studies on chicken embryos were not good indicators of what would happen in other species.

Other work by Dr Verrett on pregnant hamsters is more directly relevant. For manufactured 2,4,5T (containing 0.5 ppm dioxin) 100 mg/kg caused death of 80% of foetuses. A three times re-crystallized sample produced 55% deaths under the same conditions and with the same dose. Three of 38 pups were detectably malformed. Further purification gave samples which caused early foetal deaths of 70% of embryos but no 'gross terata' at 100 mg/kg. Dioxin is roughly 1000 times more effective than 2,4,5T—9.1 micrograms per kilogram caused 98% foetal deaths.

Dr Verrett's conclusion was similar to that of the National Institute of Environmental Sciences, that production-line samples of 2,4D and 2,4,5T are teratogenic and even purified samples of 2,4,5T may be. The National Institute of Environmental Health Sciences report states: 'But since pure 2,4,5T is not marketed and could not be produced in commercial quantities, this is not a practical issue for consideration.'

One problem with comparing the results of the different studies is that different people used different test animals. The figures for different strains of the same species should not vary greatly; between species the variations may be considerable.

Dow Chemical used Sprague-Dawley rats by agreement with the FDA. In these animals a Dow production line sample of 2,4,5T produced no embryo losses at doses up to 24 mg/kg. At this dose 29 out of 103 foetuses were deficient in sternebral ossification (as opposed to 4 in a control group of equal size). Another Dow study showed that dioxin stimulated the resorption of foetuses when fed to rats between the 6th and 15th days of pregnancy at 2 micrograms per day or more, also that gastrointestinal haemorrhage is found at doses between 0.125 micrograms and 8.0 micrograms a day and there is a reduction of foetal weight within this range.

These studies raise new problems. As Dr Epstein pointed out, cystic kidneys were common (probably due to dioxin) in the Bionetics study but were rare in recent studies of dioxin and almost pure 2,4,5T. In Dr Epstein's words, 'this discrepancy may reflect synergistic action between dioxin and 2,4,5T'. Recent Dow experiments support this, but more results are needed.

There are a number of conflicting problems which need to be considered in any appreciation of the above data on herbicides. On the basis of the residues of 2,4,5T retained in foods, Dr Johnson claimed that banning the use of this compound was not justifiable on the scientific evidence. This is probably true for America where there is some selectivity of use and generally low concentrations of material are used on crops. But in Vietnam heavy applications are used and there is often little selectivity. Of the 50,000 tons of herbicide used in Vietnam, 20,000 tons have been dioxin-contaminated. There is also the question of whether dioxin is persistent in the environment and how it may be produced under natural conditions. Dr Verrett pointed out that it may be produced by burning any of a variety of chlorophenol derivatives. These are widely used in industry and there is always the fear that large amounts of dioxin could thus be introduced into the environment. It is even possible that small amounts could be produced by the action of sunlight.

There are further problems, as Fred Tschirley noted after visiting Vietnam in the dry season. At this time fires are easily started accidentally or deliberately (to clear the ground) and such fires are very common. The burning of defoliated areas which are very sensitive to fire is another possible way in which significant amounts of dioxin could be produced. Orians and Pfeiffer have reported that over 40% of the pine plantations in South Vietnam have been burned recently. When the wet season comes, dioxin could be washed away and contaminate drinking sources. Similarly, wood from defoliated areas may be used for firewood (see p 35) with similar results.

In addition to the large quantities of chemicals and the heavy applications used, there is the question of other impurities. Dioxin is only one of a large number of impurities in these herbicides. The toxicological effects and the identity of the others are still unknown. Synergism between dioxin and 2,4,5T seems to be indicated. It is equally possible that further instances of synergistic action with other impurities or herbicide mixtures may occur. It has long been known that cacodylic acid may be teratogenic. The United States is in the position of now knowing that for eight years she has been showering a foreign people with a lethal cocktail of toxic and teratogenic agents. Data show that all the herbicides used in Vietnam can cause congenital malformations.

Much has been said to date of teratogenic effects but little is known about the mutagenic or carcinogenic dangers of the herbicides and their constituents. These are still areas of study in which ignorance is almost complete. It should not be forgotten, as we pointed out earlier, that even the toxicity data is woefully inadequate, especially relating to inhalation toxicity.

Despite the above it should be remembered that the teratogenic or carcinogenic hazards are not the most important aspects of defoliant use in South Vietnam. These hazards are likely to affect at most two or three generations of Vietnamese. The real disaster of Vietnam is the effect of the war, especially the defoliation programme, on the ecology. The problem here is altogether greater and more serious, yet in this field the relevant information is even more sparse. Such information as there is comes almost entirely from Drs Orians, Pfeiffer and Tschirley, some of whose reports we quote in the book (p 246). Detailed comment on the situation in Vietnam is not possible as yet because despite tremendous efforts, notably by Professor Pfeiffer, the picture is still fragmentary and inadequate. The AAAS is looking into the problem of setting up a field study group but this will probably only be active after the war is over. To make a real job of surveying the damage will require a considerable amount of scientific manpower. Thanks to the work so far produced we do know that great changes in the environment of Vietnam are occurring. The significance of these changes for the future of that country is completely unknown.

We have discussed long-term effects of certain CBW agents both here and in the text. It should not be assumed that this is the end of the story. Other CBW agents have not been discussed because no one has tested them for the effects we have discussed. A scrutiny of other agents in the same detail would probably reveal similar horrific effects.

The history of the use of defoliants is interesting. An essentially military decision to use defoliants has now become a considerable political embarrassment to the United States. The Army started a programme with no knowledge or apparently serious consideration of long-term effects. The result, even considered solely in terms of the loss of prestige for the US in Asia, has been absolutely disastrous.

The question may be asked where on earth were the scientists of Fort Detrick, Edgewood Arsenal, etc., and what were they doing when these chemicals were unleashed on people? Why did the relevant military authorities not look at long-term effects or, more to the point, did they look at the long-term effects and ignore them? The matter of gas dumping was equally casual. In these cases the Army is unilaterally making decisions which should be decided politically. The honesty of the Army's responses to questions asked by Congressional and Senate committees is also questionable. How is the Army to be controlled if it lies when asked about its activities and how can it be made accountable? In practically all cases we have mentioned no matter what the rights and wrongs of the situation the Army tried to cover things up, heedless of the damage being caused.

An admirable illustration of the above was provided in August 1970 when the Army implemented a plan to dispose of the 12,500 nerve gas rockets which formed a part of the aborted 1969 CHASE 13. Without warning friendly governments, the US Army announced a plan to dump the rockets 280 miles east of Cape Kennedy, 165 miles north-east of the Bahamas. Both the Bahaman and Bermudan governments requested the British Government to make a formal protest. The British Government sent advisers to examine the question.

Congress was told that the rockets were liable to blow up on site in Kentucky and Alabama if they were not removed. (This is an interesting contrast to the military expert who, when asked of the possibility of disaster answered, 'virtually nil'. The rockets were dangerous where they were. They are certainly more dangerous when suffering the shocks of being moved.) The House Subcommittee on Oceanography reluctantly approved the plan, describing the Army as showing 'inexcusable conduct' and 'unbelievable negligence'. There was little else they could do once presented with a fait accompli. Naturally there was a welter of protest. U Thant, the Bermuda government, which asked for a delay to allow an international group of scientists to review the situation, mayors of towns along the route of the gas train, and the Governor of Florida, Claude Kirk, all added to the barrage of criticism. Mr Kirk tried to get a court injunction to delay the plan.

In 1969 it was realised that the rockets were unstable and it was thought necessary to dump them as they were sensitive to heat, shock and pressure. One year later, having admitted that they were likely to explode at any time, the Army sent them through population centres to the sea and then prepared to dump them near the territory of a friendly government. The statements of Drs Akubo and Ketchum should clarify the incredible dangers of this move.

While the control of the military at home leaves much to be desired, political control of it abroad seems to be non-existent. The case of the initiation of gas warfare in Vietnam and the use of gas with bombs (see p 20) springs to mind. There is also a plan (if this does not turn out to be false) to give guerilla forces CB weapons. Most impressive is the matter of the gas stored at Okinawa. In April 1970 the US was making plans for the removal of the stock. The size of the dump was 'a limited amount' of some 10,000 tons. Naturally, when it came to bringing it home there was a wave of protest, even a note from the Canadian government because the shipment would pass through the Straits of Juan de Fuca, twenty miles from the city of Victoria, on its way to off-loading at Bangor, Washington. It was then to be taken by rail to Umatilla Ordnance Depot, Hermiston, Oregon. Extensive precautions alarmed people on the route and the protest at the time of writing is still growing. The governors of Washington and Oregon have prepared a lawsuit to serve on the authorities to prevent the shipment. An important question is how the gas was transported to Japan, through which ports? What were the safety precautions and did the shipment pass close to friendly countries like Canada? Were these countries informed of the shipment? In addition, how big are the 'limited amounts' of cw materials stored in West Germany and South Korea? How did they get there?

These questions are of considerable political significance. It is also significant that few if any American politicians seem to have the answers. Like the Palomares incident with nuclear bombs, any of these shipments could have caused a political storm for the US with friendly governments. The decision to move CBW and nuclear materials abroad should not be left in military hands. Providing friendly powers, or even irregular forces, with CB weapons needs to be examined. The US Army's record in its handling of delicate, politically sensitive issues is not impressive.

It is necessary to return to the disarmament question. President Nixon's statement may be seen to have been hasty, poor in conception and even poorer in execution. Despite the way it was hailed as a leap forward, this it definitely was not. No material change has occurred in the policy for use of chemical weapons, just an affirmation of a previously held position. The Geneva Protocol has not been signed by the US and there are no immediate signs of this happening. The US continues to use gas and defoliants in war. The only material advance is the phasing out of superfluous weapon systems.

Most significantly the US and Britain have cast doubt on the first major international step towards limiting and eventually banning war, the Geneva Protocol. As if being the first nation to use nuclear weapons in war were not distinction enough, the US has added the first use of defoliants and the first major use of gas since World War II. Internationally the US has been assisted by a British government. The effects on international prestige of all concerned are such that their standing in disarmament conferences is now very low. International prospects for agreement on CBW have rarely been bleaker.

Recently the authors have seen points advanced on the disarmament question which need answering. The first of these is the view that if every nation decides that BW is not worthwhile (as the US recently has done) then verification and inspection plans and international treaties are superfluous. There are a variety of objections to this thesis. The first is that it is assumed that everyone will agree that BW is not worthwhile. Such unanimity is unlikely. The military situation of other countries may be such that what is useless to the US may seem to be vital to someone else's survival. A nuclear power can afford to discard a dubious 'deterrent' when it possesses a more powerful one. A non-nuclear power may look for any deterrent it can afford. Probably the major consideration in President Nixon's mind was the unpredictability of BW, not the contentious matter of its effects. There remains the possibility, as yet unprovable one way or another, that BW could be effective. To assume that predictability is a criterion in the consideration of possible deterrents when a country is threatened by superior hostile forces is to misunderstand the deterrent arguments. Deterrence is a psychological concept and is not related to the acceptability of use of a weapon. Weapons for 'deterrent' purposes are not intended for use but to deter other nations. The paradox of deterrence is that no weapon is unacceptable so long as it deters and the 'deterrent' is effective, but if deterrence fails and war starts then there is the problem of whether or not to use unacceptable weapons. (By unacceptable weapons is meant those whose use would make any military advantage completely irrelevant against a background of disaster on a vast scale.) Far smaller nonnuclear countries may consider the deterrent argument valid, hoping never to face the breakdown of deterrence.

A second argument is that BW may not be very effective. This is not a consideration which affects the US very much. The Strategic

Bomber force contributes to the 'deterrent', although to all intents and purposes it would be useless against the USSR. In the case of deterrence it is the threat that is important; the weapon is secondary.

Mr Han Swyter, at a National Academy of Sciences symposium on CBW, gave related arguments for the retention of CBW on the grounds that this may deter Russian CBW use. The premise here is that to deter an enemy one must be able to retaliate in kind and at the same level. At present the US can retaliate in kind but not in similar quantity. Russian forces are alleged to have considerable superiority in weight of chemical warfare munitions.

In the text we have largely eschewed arguments about particular conditions or situations and have not quoted large numbers of meaningless simulations and war games. Arguments of percentages of fatalities in cities attacked by BW are not of any real value for reasons which we described earlier (p 272). When we have used illustrative examples we have indicated possibilities not necessarily related very closely to the real military situation. Mr Swyter's argument is not related to the real military situation either. The real situation is incredibly complex.

To understand the reason for this it is necessary to return to a greatly simplified military argument. Let us analyse situations. If CBW is used by an Army which is advancing on a retreating enemy, then when the Army advances it has to prepare by masking, using protective clothing, and operating equipment 'closed down'. This greatly reduces military efficiency and thus loses its advantage as both sides have to fight under the same conditions and both sides would necessarily sustain heavy casualties. In addition, the attacking force would have the logistical burden of vast quantities of unusable CW munitions. For many years the Soviet military has prepared CW materials, which are probably intended mainly for use in halting or slowing an advancing army, to cover a retreat. At the tactical level this makes very good sense since the advancing army has to operate with reduced efficiency and the retreating army can operate and re-group under optimum conditions. This is the reason why control of the use of CW is in the hands of field commanders rather than politicians. BW is probably not considered particularly useful by the Soviet military.

NATO strategy is more obscure on both nuclear and chemical weapons. Current NATO strategy is a 'first use' policy of nuclear weapons employment in certain situations as was outlined in Brussels last year. It is probably that NATO use of chemical weapons would follow a similar line to that of nuclear weapons. In both cases the situation envisaged is such that at the time of use the NATO forces would already be in deep trouble, and use would be a last-ditch measure. By the time nuclear or CW was used on the battle-field the initiative would already be with the enemy and unless strategic weapons were used (instant escalation) no real military advantage would be gained. If strategic weapons were used any military gain would be illusory. Even if tactical use of nuclear or chemical weapons were contemplated, the problem of restricting hostilities to the battlefield would be insurmountable. Mr Swyter also suggests that CW provides a choice besides conventional or nuclear weapons. At present this option is unlikely to be exercised by NATO and we have already shown that this suggestion is not valid (p 315).

The above gives comfort to no one. It is not reassuring to feel that NATO policy is a little confusing and confused. The problems raised for disarmament are considerable and the above gives an idea of the type of arguments which must be dealt with.

It may be gathered from our discussion that the problems are not small. In addition, there has been a diffusion of the efforts of those working on CBW into fields such as conservation, environmental pollution, etc. This could be a mistake because the problems of disarmament are as vast as they were and the need for progress is great.

August 1970

GENERAL INDEX

WEST GERMANY,
and Geneva Protocol, 160
and Hague Convention, 160
international cooperation, 135ff
manufacture of CBW, 161
NATO stockpiles in, 135
policy on CBW, 160–3
research on CBW in, 121–31
WHO (World Health Organisation),
and epidemics, 270

and international disarmament, 349
report on plague in Vietnam, 64ff,
311

Yemen,
CW in, 6–14, 287–91
dissemination, 288
ICRC report, 8, 12, 13, 29
type of gas used, 290
UN investigation, 7, 11

INDEX OF CHEMICAL AND BIOLOGICAL
AGENTS

MONTHLY REVIEW

an independent socialist magazine
edited by Paul M. Sweezy and Harry Magdoff

Business Week: ". . . a brand of socialism that is thorough-going and tough-minded, drastic enough to provide the sharp break with the past that many left-wingers in the underdeveloped countries see as essential. At the same time they maintain a sturdy independence of both Moscow and Peking that appeals to neutralists. And their skill in manipulating the abstruse concepts of modern economics impresses would-be intellectuals. . . . Their analysis of the troubles of capitalism is just plausible enough to be disturbing."

Bertrand Russell: "Your journal has been of the greatest interest to me over a period of time. I am not a Marxist by any means as I have sought to show in critiques published in several books, but I recognize the power of much of your own analysis and where I disagree I find your journal valuable and of stimulating importance. I want to thank you for your work and to tell you of my appreciation of it."

The Wellesley Department of Economics: " . . . the leading Marxist intellectual (not Communist) economic journal published anywhere in the world, and is on our subscription list at the College library for good reasons."

Albert Einstein: "Clarity about the aims and problems of socialism is of greatest significance in our age of transition. . . . I consider the founding of this magazine to be an important public service." (In his article, "Why Socialism" in Vol. I, No. 1.)

DOMESTIC: $7 for one year, $12 for two years, $5 for one-year student subscription.

FOREIGN: $8 for one year, $14 for two years, $6 for one-year student subscription. (Subscription rates subject to change.)

116 West 14th Street, New York, New York 10011

Modern Reader Paperbacks

ained at www.ICGtesting.com

/P